Trading on Sentiment

The Wiley Finance series contains books written specifically for finance and investment professionals as well as sophisticated individual investors and their financial advisors. Book topics range from portfolio management to e-commerce, risk management, financial engineering, valuation and financial instrument analysis, as well as much more. For a list of available titles, visit our website at www.WileyFinance.com.

Founded in 1807, John Wiley & Sons is the oldest independent publishing company in the United States. With offices in North America, Europe, Australia, and Asia, Wiley is globally committed to developing and marketing print and electronic products and services for our customers' professional and personal knowledge and understanding.

Trading on Sentiment

The Power of Minds Over Markets

RICHARD L. PETERSON

WILEY

Published by John Wiley & Sons, Inc., Hoboken, New Jersey.

Published simultaneously in Canada.

For general information on our other products and services or for technical support, please contact our Customer Care Department within the United States at (800) 762-2974, outside the United States at (317) 572-3993 or fax (317) 572-4002.

Wiley publishes in a variety of print and electronic formats and by print-on-demand. Some material included with standard print versions of this book may not be included in e-books or in print-on-demand. If this book refers to media such as a CD or DVD that is not included in the version you purchased, you may download this material at http://booksupport.wiley.com. For more information about Wiley products, visit www.wiley.com.

Library of Congress Cataloging-in-Publication Data is available:

ISBN 9781119122760 (Hardcover)
ISBN 9781119163749 (ePDF)
ISBN 9781119163756 (ePub)

Cover Design: Wiley
Cover Images: brain social media © VLADGRIN/istockphoto.com; summer background
　　　　　　© Magnilion/istockphoto.com

Printed in the United States of America

10 9 8 7 6 5 4 3 2 1

To the MarketPsych team. Your inspiration and persistence created something entirely new in the world.

Contents

About the Author

From investor neuroimaging to developing sentiment-based market models, Dr. Peterson spends his time exploring the intersection of mind and markets. Dr. Peterson is CEO of MarketPsych, where he is a creative force behind the Thomson Reuters MarketPsych Indices (TRMI). The TRMI is a data feed of emotions and macroeconomic topics in social and news media covering 8,000 equities, 130 countries, 30 currencies, and 35 commodities. Dr. Peterson has published in academic journals, including *Games and Economic Behavior* and the *Journal of Neuroscience,* written textbook chapters, and is an associate editor of the *Journal of Behavioral Finance.* His book *Inside the Investor's Brain* (Hoboken, NJ: John Wiley & Sons, 2007) is in six languages, and it and *MarketPsych* (Hoboken, NJ: Wiley 2010) were named top financial books of the year by *Kiplinger.* Dr. Peterson received cum laude Electrical Engineering (B.S.), Arts (B.A.), and Doctor of Medicine degrees (M.D.) from the University of Texas. Called "Wall Street's Top Psychiatrist" by the Associated Press, he performed postdoctoral neuroeconomics research at Stanford University and is board-certified in psychiatry. He lives in California with his family.

Preface

As a 12-year-old boy I was befuddled when my father—a finance professor—gave me trading authority over a small brokerage account. At the time I didn't understand what the stock market was, and I had no idea how to proceed. He educated me on how to read stock tables in the daily newspaper (this was 1985), call a broker, and place an order. I was set free with my limited knowledge and zero experience with the goal of growing the balance.

To select investments, I first turned to the local newspaper. I reviewed the micro-text of the stock tables. The numbers didn't make sense to me—my first dead-end. For Plan B I visited the library, and the librarian referred me to dusty books from the 1960s that extolled the virtues of 'tronics stocks and Dow Theory. "Nothing for me here," I thought. I wanted to know what to buy *right now*, not to learn ancient theory.

Next I went to a bookstore. A young attendant directed me to the magazine section, and the first magazine I picked up listed the Top 10 Growth Stocks of 1985. "Perfect!" I thought. I went home, called up the broker, and dictated the top 10 names to him, buying shares in each.

Over the next few months, I didn't pay attention to the stocks' performance. About a year later I figured it would be a good time to check in. I expected to hear that I had made big gains. In fact, I fantasized that the broker would soon be calling me for investment advice. When I opened an account statement I saw—to my disbelief—that the account was down 20 percent.

Confused, I went back to the bookstore. I related my tale to another attendant, and he condescendingly informed me, "Clearly you bought the wrong magazine." "He's right!" I realized. This new, wiser guide helped me find a magazine extolling the Top 10 Most Innovative stocks of 1986. I went home, invested in a few of the top 10, and waited. I paid more attention this time, and I noticed that the first three monthly account statements were positive. I felt good, back on track, and I imagined I would be redeemed as a genius stock investor.

A year later, after a nine-month hiatus, I opened the latest account statement. The damage was worse—my account was now down nearly 50 percent from where it had started. "This can't be right," I thought. I sheepishly called the broker. He confirmed the loss.

I wanted to understand what the experts knew that I did not, so I started reading books by investing by gurus such as Benjamin Graham and Peter Lynch. I noticed that these books were teaching me not only about fundamentals, but also about psychology. It seemed that many of history's most successful investors used an understanding of investor behavior. Baron Nathan von Rothschild, an early scion of the Rothschild banking dynasty, in 1812 guided investors to, "Buy to the sound of cannons, sell to the sound of trumpets." Benjamin Graham wrote, "We buy from pessimists, and we sell to optimists." Warren Buffett modernized the saying as, "Be fearful when others are greedy and greedy when others are fearful." This advice seemed like useful guidance, but it wasn't specific or easily actionable.

Psychology-based investing advice seemed too *vague*. I wanted more concrete guidance, and as I embarked on engineering coursework in college, I found what I believed was a true advantage in investing—a deeper understanding of mathematics and models.

MATHEMATICAL MAYHEM

While the markets had beaten me as a 12-year-old investor, in college I vowed to learn their tricks and recover my losses. Working through a university degree in electrical engineering, the solidity of mathematics—of software development and machine learning algorithms—seemed like the best path to resurrecting the now-dormant brokerage account. I obtained long price and volume data histories, reserved CPU time on the engineering department's fast RISC machines, and wrote code to identify patterns in the prices.

The predictive systems I built seemed promising at first. The algorithms found basic patterns in prices, and they had decent accuracy in their out-of-sample predictions. As a result I decided to use the systems in live trading. Over the following three years, I traded S&P 500 futures contracts based on these systems' directional signals.

While they were initially successful, two problems emerged as I used these predictive systems. First, I saw what quantitative analysts call alpha decay, the phenomenon in which good mathematical trading systems gradually fade in their profitability. The models worked well on their "training set" in the 1980s and early 1990s, but every year through the late 1990s the profitability declined. Perhaps other traders were finding the same patterns and arbitraging them out of the markets, or perhaps markets were changing.

The second problem with these trading systems was more personal. Sometimes they indicated I should buy stocks as the prices were plummeting and the news was exceptionally negative. Other times, they told me to sell stocks as the market was charging higher. Such signals *felt* wrong to me. They required trading against the herd, and they were emotionally difficult to execute. Even though I intellectually knew that cherry-picking trading signals is a bad habit, too often I made excuses and deviated from the plan. After retrospectively analyzing my behavior, it seemed that the best trading signals were the most emotionally difficult to follow. I would have to battle my own human nature in order to trade well.

Considering these two problems together, it occurred to me that the most enduring edge in markets—the one least likely to suffer alpha decay—might lie in identifying the information and feelings (sentiments) that compel traders to move as a herd, too often at their own peril. Sentiment has a way of pulling traders in, of fooling them again and again. I wanted a way to quantify sentiment so I could use it without simultaneously being its victim. I became a scholar of sentiment to gain perspective on it.

Through four years of medical school and then four more years as a psychiatry resident, I researched the biology of decision making. During residency training I began coaching investors, and it was through coaching that I gained a deep appreciation of the very human, and very diverse, natures of successful traders.

Near the end of psychiatry residency I started neuroeconomics post-doctoral studies at Stanford University with Brian Knutson. Knutson's lab studies subjects undertaking financial risks, using tools such as brain fMRI and psychometric testing. I wrote extensively about this research in the book *Inside the Investor's Brain*.[1] Researchers such as Knutson have demonstrated, even when the expected value of a risk is fixed, differences in the presentation and description of the potential gain or loss predictably alter behavior. I wondered how to quantify such "soft" factors in the information stream. Financial social media and news seemed like a good place to start.

FRAMING THE ISSUE

The field of text analytics—quantifying sentiment, topics, and tones in investment-related language—is the quantitative basis for this book. While it's self-evident that the release of information such as corporate earnings leads to gyrations in stock prices, the impact is sometimes counterintuitive. For example, a company might beat consensus earnings estimates but the stock price immediately loses value. Given the preponderance of online stock conversations where earnings estimates and other opinions are shared, it seemed that if one could measure and quantify the important content in those messages, then perhaps a predictive edge could be identified in markets.

In pursuit of such a predictive edge, in 2004 the MarketPsych team built financial text analytics software. First, we built search engine technology to gather news and social media as quickly as articles were published. Then we built text analyzers to quantify influential characteristics in text. We created time series of each high-impact factor—factors such as fear or excitement—for each stock over time. Finally, we tested the data statistically to determine its correlation with future price action. We found promising results, and we resolved to start trading.

TRADING ON SENTIMENT

Using our early text analysis engines on social media, we set up simple investment strategies. These strategies ran automatically and posted their results online. Over 18 months through 2007 the strategies earned a 34 percent absolute return on paper. The strategies were written up in *Popular Science* in February 2008,[2] and that article stoked interest from investors. We raised a small fund to trade a market-neutral hedge fund strategy. As far as we know, the fund was the first social media–based hedge fund.

On September 2, 2008, we launched the fund with $1 million under management and dreams of big growth. Three days after we started trading, Fannie Mae and Freddie Mac failed. Lehman Brothers and AIG went under the following weekend. Fortunately, we had prepared for the increased chaos by creating primarily fear-based strategies. Despite the onset of the financial crisis, the fund's returns held up through mid-2009.[3,4] Over its first 12 months, the fund was up 40 percent net, putting it in the top 1 percent of hedge funds through the financial crisis.

We had built trading models that made money in volatile, emotional markets. As the dust cleared from the crisis, we needed to adapt. Managing $1 million was not enough to pay our expenses, regardless of the stellar performance. We economized as best we could, and we went offline every few months to tune the software and develop strategies for the new bull market. But these efforts weren't enough to save the fund.

By the time we closed it, we had traded the fund over a period of 2 years and 4 months and made a 28 percent return net of fees, beating the S&P 500 (including dividends) by more than 24 percent. The fund's returns were sharply positive for its first 12 months, then declined, as seen in the equity curve depicted in Figure P.1.

At the end of 2010, we received inquiries from hedge funds looking to buy the sentiment data we had created. To pursue this new opportunity we set a goal to produce and sell the global standard in media sentiment data. To that end, in 2011 we joined forces with Thomson Reuters, and

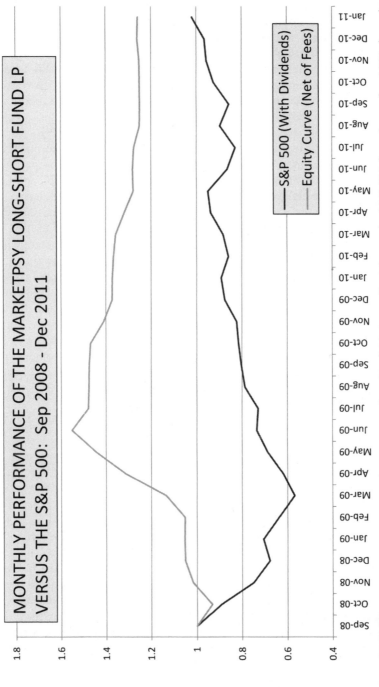

FIGURE P.1 Equity curve of the MarketPsy Long-Short Fund LP (upper line) versus the S&P 500 from September 2008 through December 2011.

with its assistance we expanded our asset coverage to include currencies, commodities, countries, and global stocks.

The data feed we produce is now called the Thomson Reuters MarketPsych Indices (TRMI), and Thompson Reuters distributes the feed to funds, banks, brokers, governments, and researchers who use the data to predict global economic activity and asset prices. Insights derived from the TRMI are woven throughout this book. Research cited in this book was produced by Aleksander Fafula and CJ Liu of MarketPsych, Elijah DePalma of Thomson Reuters, and various university academic researchers.

Aleksander Fafula joined the MarketPsych team as a data scientist after earning a PhD in finance (he already had a master's degree in computer science). Aleksander completed his innovative PhD thesis by developing trading models that tapped into collective misperceptions of stock price charts.

I heard rumors about CJ before I met him. A professor at the University of California at Berkeley—Terry Odean—had heard of a sentiment aficionado developing models in the financial engineering department, where CJ was completing his Master's degree. As a child CJ was an expert in the card game Big Two. Big Two is similar to the English card game Liar. The goal of Big Two is to dispose of all of one's cards without being caught in a deception. The best players can detect what cards others are holding through behavioral cues. CJ's interest in behavioral analysis is similarly evident in his poker talents. CJ once took a trip to Las Vegas with other members of our team. While everyone else slept, CJ played Texas Hold'em all night long, winning a significant amount of money. He later described how he had made unpredictable bets in order to throw the professionals off his scent (similar to the strategy of Jesus Ferguson described in Chapter 15).

THE BOOK

This book is based on a simple claim: There are patterns in market prices. While that assertion is controversial among academics, belief in that notion is a prerequisite to work in the investment industry. Investors who propose to beat the market attempt to harvest some mispricing, somewhere, often systematically.

This book covers broad scientific and experimental ground as it makes the case that not only do price patterns exist, but the most predictable patterns are rooted in the anatomy of the human brain and the biology of its information processing networks.

Some information provokes emotional reactions—as we describe in subsequent chapters—and these reactions predictably alter trading behavior. In this book the term *sentiment* refers to emotions, feelings, outlooks, attitudes, and beliefs. Sometimes investors reveal their sentiment through their statements in news and social media, and those statements become the predictive information of interest. Sentiments alter collective behavior, leading to patterns in prices.

This book is organized into five parts. Part One explores the foundations of investor behavior. Investor sentiment has been found predictive of market price action based on humans' innate information processing networks and specific characteristics of information. Part Two examines short-term price patterns that result from both news and social media. Part Three lays out the longer-term price patterns associated with sentiment, including momentum and value enhancements with sentiment. Part Four describes complex price patterns such as speculative bubbles and patterns in commodities and currencies. Part Five turns its attention to individual investor psychology, sharing tools to help investors avoid the biases whose effects on collective trading behavior cause the price patterns examined in this book.

Usually media sentiment is a reaction to already-past events. But in some cases sentiment itself appears to predict price action. In other cases—such as when examining traditional investment factors—sentiment improves an already-existing predictive advantage. The book examines market price patterns based on the independent power of sentiment and the conditioning of sentiment with fundamental and price variables.

Some readers may be disoriented by the numerous proofs—such as equity curves and charts—provided. This voluminous evidence is offered because the field of sentiment analysis is controversial to some, and we hope to convincingly demonstrate its intrinsic value.

This book is not designed to give a one-size-fits-all investing strategy or trading system, and it does not intend to promote a specific product (however, it indirectly promotes the Thomson Reuters MarketPsych Indices because that is the primary data source utilized). This book is based on more than a decade of research into the nature and role of sentiment in driving trading behavior and market prices. It reviews relevant academic research on the topics of interest in each chapter. When appropriate, some writings are recycled from past MarketPsych newsletters and books. While others have not yet produced data with the level of detail available to our internal research, we believe that due to the universality of our process, the studies in this book are replicable. The particulars of markets may evolve, but the general principles of human behavior change slowly, if at all.

There are major potential weaknesses in this book's approach. First of all, it is based on the quantification of meaning in an enormous amount of textual data—literally billions of financial news and social media articles published since 1998. Given this large volume of information, there is a risk of making spurious correlations. This pitfall is addressed in Chapter 5.

Over the years we have found many preliminary results that could not be replicated due to statistical errors or bugs in the analytics code. The findings presented in this book were repeated on various data versions, using pricing data from different providers, after much debugging, and typically following forward-testing. As a result, we hope that the results presented here will prove robust, but only additional external replication and the passage of time will confirm them. Second, explaining a phenomenon from the brain level to the market level requires deductive leaps that may never be supported by scientific research. While such connections are suggested in this book, they are not definitively established. Third, because the book is building on established academic findings but is written for practitioners, it intersperses both academic and trading jargon, findings, and examples. It tries to make the text flow smoothly and the linkages clear, but despite our best efforts, fluidity is not guaranteed. In many cases, research results are quite complex and nuanced—for example, academic findings about the predictability of Twitter sentiment deviate from those derived from Facebook—and as a result, readers may be confused by the breadth of findings. Fourth, this book simplifies sentiment-based investing. This approach may be the most difficult and dangerous investment discipline, as it contravenes our human nature. Only seasoned professionals with excellent risk management should attempt the strategies described herein. Given its unusual format—part textbook, part investment guide—the book is modular in its approach, and readers should feel free to skip ahead to sections of interest.

There is a clear conflict of interest in this book. This book is written by a data vendor, and it contains research by ourselves and competing vendors who have a financial interest in data sales. To lessen this bias, the book reviews existing academic literature. We distributed the TRMI sentiment data to qualified global academics for research, and their results are included in the relevant chapter sections. Additionally, we have endeavored to be as statistically honest in our own research, and all of the equity curves in this text have been replicated under various conditions and limitations to ensure robustness. Nonetheless our conflict of interest is inescapable. Evidence from the field of medicine indicates that such conflicts are unconscious, pervasive, and too often denied. We acknowledge that we are susceptible to significant bias, and we hope this bias does not diminish the overall quality or long-term impact of this work.

Financial markets are a creation of humans: humans who respond with fear and uncertainty, humans with damaged egos, humans who curse others for their mistakes, humans who make predictions, and humans who follow the crowd. Market prices, like humans, are sometimes—but not always—driven by sentiment. This book is about the systematic and collective investor sentiments that leave telltale patterns in prices. Readers can learn both to take advantage of these patterns and to manage sentiment in themselves. We hope you gain new insights into financial markets and become a superior investor (and human being) as you journey through this book.

NOTES

1. Richard L. Peterson, *Inside the Investor's Brain: The Power of Mind over Money* (Hoboken, NJ: John Wiley & Sons, 2007).
2. Robert Armstrong and Jacob Ward, "Money Minded: How to Psychoanalyze The Stock Market," *Popular Science* (February 19, 2008). Posted online at: http://www.popsci.com/scitech/article/2008-02/money-minded-how-psychoanalyze-stock-market.
3. "The Interview—Richard Peterson, MarketPsy Capital: Understanding the Workings of the Brain Unlocks a Trove of Novel Investment Strategies," *Hedge-Week* (June 30, 2009). Downloaded May 20, 2105, from http://www.hedgeweek.com/2009/06/30/interview-richard-peterson-marketpsy-capital-understanding-workings-brain-unlocks-trove-n.
4. Rachael King, "Trading on a World of Sentiment," *BloombergBusiness* (March 01, 2011). Downloaded from: http://www.businessweek.com/stories/2011-03-01/trading-on-a-world-of-sentimentbusinessweek-business-news-stock-market-and-financial-advice.

Acknowledgments

In 2004 the MarketPsych team set out to decipher how information and sentiment impact global markets. The team was deeply inspired on this journey by Dr. Tom Samuels. He is dearly missed following his passing in 2013. Dr. Samuels hoped that through sentiment analysis the business community would more fully understand the importance of the unconscious in driving business and market activity. He provided exceptional resources and encouragement to the company from its inception.

This book was written as a team effort over several years. So many people influenced its production that we cannot do justice to their individual contributions. The ground-breaking work of data scientists including Changjie Liu, Aleksander Fafula, and Elijah DePalma is featured throughout this book. Without their insights and statistical studies this book would not have been possible.

Without a world-class sentiment data product, the statistical evidence would have been impossible to gather. As CTO and sysadmin extraordinaire, Diego Gutierrez dedicated enormous time and countless sleepless nights to developing a flawless data product. Thomson Reuters product manager Eric Fischkin devoted his unparalleled expertise and sharp mind to creating the data architecture. Eugene Smolanka's work on information aggregation, Alexey Karakulov's project management and QA, Tayyab bin Tariq's data analytics, Zulma Cao's crawlers, and Alexey Verenikin's determined detective work were also essential to the production of the data that underlies this book. Additionally, we feel much gratitude to the ongoing development assistance of Vesna Gvozdenovic, Dmytro Ivanysh, Kostyantyn Leschenko, Konstantin Nikolayev, Ramiro Rela, and Ante Kegalj. Past team members including Thomas Hartman, Yury Shatz, Jacob Sisk, Ali Arik, and Richard Brown (Thomson Reuters) contributed invaluable insights and efforts that are bearing fruit in the publication of this book. Contributions from interns Robin Tu, Davis Matthews, Eric Bet, Alan Liu, and Alan Morningstar are apparent in the book, while dozens of others were instrumental in the data's production and QA—too many to list all of their names. We have been incredibly lucky to assemble a global team of A-players.

Over the years we've also benefited from the support and guidance of Steve Goodall, Paul Zak, Richard Friesen, Mark Harbour, Frank

Murtha, Gene Dongieux, Dennis Thomas, Doug Samuels, Tom Samuels Jr., Victor Lacy, Jeff Ehrlich, and Scott Martin. The team at Panoptic Fund Administration—Georgia Goodman, Matt Pringle, and Jeff Lambert—are delightful people and were a constant source of encouragement during our trading days.

On the Thomson Reuters' side, James Cantarella and Dennis Goett kept our partnership progressing. The infectious enthusiasm of Thomson Reuters' Sunny Qu, Christopher Kleparek, Steve Dean, Nathan Attrell, Adam Garrett, Love Srivastava, Kazuhisa Matsuda, Joy Thaler as well as dozens of others has been deeply gratifying. Many others have provided insightful guidance and real-world feedback including the Amareos team members Jerome Favresse, Philippe El-Asmar, Ryan Shea, and EOTpro's Bill Dennis.

We also extend our appreciation to the loved ones who didn't see us for many days, evenings, and weekends. For the children who wondered what their preoccupied parents were up to, we hope they will one day feel as inspired and driven by their work as we do by ours. And on a personal note, much love to Sarah, Dr. Peterson's amazing wife, for her unflagging optimism and patience during the writing of this book.

We are extremely indebted to the hundreds of academics and researchers—such as Brian Knutson, Camelia Kuhnen, Jiancheng Shen, Feng Li, Paul Tetlock, and Joseph Engelberg—whose studies provide support and context to our findings. Without their dedication and passion, human knowledge would not advance.

And appreciation goes out to this book's readers. Your willingness to question, challenge, and understand the world from a new perspective is fundamental to progress. We hope you find this book as fascinating and enjoyable to read as it was for our team to produce.

Foundations

CHAPTER 1

Perception and the Brain

What we are betting on is that the perceived risk exceeds the actual risk. That's fundamental to the theory of everything we do.

—Wilbur Ross

Hurricane Katrina struck the U.S. Gulf Coast in 2005, and it was followed by another category 5 hurricane—Hurricane Rita—several weeks later. Following Katrina's impact, the media were saturated with tragic images of submerged residential neighborhoods. Videos cycled on major news networks of flooding victims stranded on their rooftops. They waved to news helicopters for help against a backdrop of dead bodies floating in the murky brown floodwaters. Katrina was the most expensive natural disaster in U.S. history with total property damage estimated at $108 billion (in 2005 USD). At least 1,833 people died in Hurricane Katrina and the subsequent floods. Insurers were liable for billions of dollars in damage claims, and they raised their premiums over 50 percent in each of the following two years.

There was an increasing perception that category 5 hurricanes would devastate the Gulf Coast more frequently. An influential scientific study published in 2005 identified an acceleration in the rate of powerful hurricanes in the Atlantic Ocean. Al Gore's movie, *An Inconvenient Truth,* about the catastrophic environmental risks of global warming, was released shortly after the hurricanes struck. The devastating 2005 Atlantic hurricane season appeared to imply that worst-case scenarios were coming to fruition even faster than predicted.

Savvy investors, especially reinsurers, smelled opportunity in the heightened risk perceptions. Both Warren Buffett's Berkshire Hathaway and billionaire investor Wilbur Ross poured money into Gulf Coast reinsurance enterprises. In a *Wall Street Journal* interview, Ross explained such investments by stating, "What we are betting on is that the perceived risk exceeds the actual risk. That's fundamental to the theory of everything we do."[1]

Fear, by definition, is an emotional response to the perception of danger. Fear arises when humans anticipate threat, and the unpleasant feelings associated with fear motivate action to avoid those threats and eliminate the uncomfortable feelings (e.g., urgently buying insurance against the next storm). Savvy investors locate such fear-driven opportunities and exploit them.

It's worth considering what investors fear. They fear zombie investments that never live up to their potential. They fear fat fingers, hackers, and ghosts in the machinery of Wall Street that can bankrupt them in milliseconds. They fear debt, incompetent governance, and terrorist attacks. There are too many risks to track on Wall Street (and in life). And while investors cannot understand or anticipate every risk, they can strive to understand when others are going astray in their assessments of such risks.

This book examines the market price patterns created by investor psychology. Prices typically don't respond in an obvious way. Sometimes they respond to events within milliseconds, other times over days, and sometimes not at all. Sometimes prices fluctuate and sometimes a trend is born.

Price patterns are a result of collective investor buying and selling in response to new information. That dry description doesn't adequately embody the euphoria, anguish, and boredom behind the real-world market events that drive manias, panics, and price trends. This book's goal is to demonstrate how information flow in the media-through effects on investor psychology such as the increased risk perceptions following a hurricane-creates opportunities for investors.

A LONG ESTRANGEMENT

> *When I went to financial economist training school, I was taught the "Prime Directive":*
> Explain asset prices by rational models. Only if all attempts fail, resort to irrational investor behavior.
> —Mark Rubinstein, from "Rational Markets: Yes or No? The Affirmative Case" (2001)[2]

The academic disciplines of psychology and economics were largely estranged from the Second World War through the early 21st century, but it was not always thus. Josef De La Vega's book *Confusion De Confusiones* was the first to describe the market microstructure of a stock market—the Amsterdam exchange—and it is also the first historical commentary on the emotions of market speculators. De La Vega notes that the Amsterdam bourse was dominated by the perpetual conflict between the *liefhebbers* ("lifters-up") who were "scared of nothing" and the *contremines* ("underminers") who were "completely ruled by fear, trepidation, and nervousness."[3] In ensuing centuries, such influential economists as David Hume (1780) analyzed the "motivating passions" that drive human economic behavior.[4] In 1939, John Maynard Keynes famously speculated that "animal spirits" drive economic growth.[5]

Despite these early references to psychological forces driving stock traders and economic activity, another field—physics—served as the inspiration for most post–World War II academic economists. Physicists were successfully applying complex mathematics to model natural phenomena, with the atomic bomb being the most dramatic example of the advances in that field. Emulating physicists, economists crafted overarching theories and employed complex mathematics to model economic processes. In order to streamline assumptions, economists adopted a view of human judgment and behavior as being purely rational. As Mark Rubinstein noted in the epigraph, many (if not most) academic economists consider this assumption the default position in theoretical models.

The assumption of the rational investor is generally quite useful in modeling, but it misses many important exceptions. As Peter L. Bernstein, a money manager and the first editor of *The Journal of Portfolio Management*, put it, "Indeed, as civilization has pushed forward, nature's vagaries have mattered less and the decisions of people have mattered more."[6] Overlooking the complexities and irrational nuances of human behavior has become a significant impediment to the advancement of academic economics.

Like economics, psychology was similarly beholden to theoretical orthodoxies in the latter half of the 20th century. Many psychologists worked based on the assumptions of Freudian theory and other unempirical dogmas. Behaviorists were an exception to this empirical drought, and research by experimental psychologists such as B. F. Skinner and Ivan Pavlov captured the public imagination. Their work demonstrated that human behavior could be systematically and predictably irrational, and it could be shaped with incentives such as rewards and punishments.

Rather than working on a grand unified theory of behavior, psychologists took a piecemeal approach to understanding human nature. They crafted independent theories—often based on experimental results—to explain individual idiosyncrasies or to solve specific clinical problems (such as how to relieve paralyzing anxiety). Meanwhile in medicine, research on pharmaceuticals identified chemical compounds—both recreational and therapeutic—that uniquely altered mood, judgment, and even financial risk taking. Based on work by empirical psychologists and psychopharmacologists, evidence-based treatments are currently deployed in the treatment of specific mood (e.g., anxiety, depression, impulsivity) and cognitive disorders (e.g., psychosis).

Over the past three decades, with new investigational tools and interventions, experimental psychologists and economists have begun collaborating. The fields of behavioral finance and behavioral economics represent these interdisciplinary, data-driven efforts. Researchers have now catalogued numerous predictable patterns in human judgment and decision making. These patterns include systematic cognitive and behavioral biases in risk-related judgment and behavior. A few of these biases occur collectively, across large groups, and they appear to impact economic trends and market price patterns, as described in this book. Rather than seeking a grand unified theory of market price behavior, this book takes a psychological approach, examining the unique information and crowd responses that independently fuel recognized price patterns, resulting in actionable opportunities.

The English economist John Maynard Keynes was one of the first economists to explore the relationship between mental processes and economic activity. He approached the problem from the cognitive perspective, attempting to understand market behavior from the perspective of a rational investor. In his allegory of the Beauty Contest, Keynes described how the best investors use cognitive skills (superior thinking) to outsmart their competition.

THE BEAUTY CONTEST

Therefore it is not important that the basic value of the shares be practically nothing as long as there are other people willing to close their eyes and support those contradictions.
—Joseph De La Vega, 1688.[7]

Keynes used an allegory to demonstrate how the collective behavior of investors moves stock prices. In the 1930s, newspaper beauty contests were occasionally held. In these contests one hundred photographs of faces were displayed in the newspaper. Participants were asked to identify the six faces that they believed would be chosen as the prettiest by all players. Those who guessed the consensus six faces won a prize. In this contest, one's own opinion of attractiveness was not as important as the collective preference. The key to selecting the winner lay in anticipating the faces others would select.

There are several ways to approach this game. The simplest strategy is to select the six prettiest faces in one's own opinion, without considering the preferences of others. According to game theory models, such a strategy is a Level 0 strategy. A more sophisticated player ought to understand and consider others' perceptions of beauty. Using that information, this strategy should be more likely to succeed—a Level 1 strategy according to game theory.

There is another, even more sophisticated level of play. A Level 2 player would consider the preferences of the Level 0 and the Level 1 players, asking, "What will the Level 1's think the others will like?" As you can probably guess, this strategy can be extended to Level 3 and higher. Each level is attempting to predict the consensus based on the reasoning of the level below. According to Keynes:

> *It is not a case of choosing those [faces] that, to the best of one's judgment, are really the prettiest, nor even those that average opinion genuinely thinks the prettiest. We have reached the third degree where we devote our intelligences to anticipating what average opinion expects the average opinion to be. And there are some, I believe, who practice the fourth, fifth and higher degrees.*

Keynes believed that investors use similar layers of thinking-about-thinking. Sometimes investors estimate the fair value of stocks based on fundamental value or where the price is heading. Other times they consider what the other investors think.

Rosemarie Nagel developed an experimental version of Keynes's Beauty Contest.[8] In Nagel's version, she asked participants to guess a number between 1 and 100 that is two-thirds of the average guess. A Level 0 player would select a number randomly. A Level 1 player will choose a number consistent with the belief that all other players are Level 0. Since Level 0 players guess randomly, the average of those guesses would be 50. Therefore, a Level 1 player would choose two-thirds of 50, or 33.

A Level 2 player would choose a number consistent with the belief that all other players are Level 1. Since a level-one player will choose 33, a level-two player should choose 22. This process repeats for higher-level players. The Nash equilibrium of this game, for a player with Level Infinity, is to choose the number 0.

Several magazines and research labs have performed variations of this game. On average, when asked to choose two-thirds of the average guess, the correct answer of a single-shot (onetime play) game is around 23, implying that the ideal strategy is between Level 1 and Level 2.[9,10] Several variations of the game have been tested, including pitting groups in competition against individuals. Interestingly, groups give worse guesses initially, but over several trials they learn faster than individuals. In another variation, experienced players were closer to the correct answer than inexperienced ones.

Beauty Contest games are static and learnable, and thus they are very different from the dynamism of asset markets whose prices surge with rumors and information, buffeted by traders' hopes, fears, and prejudices. But there are key similarities, as well. To win the Beauty Contest, investors ought to identify what features the other players are paying attention to. Do they value large doe eyes, bobbed hair, or prominent chins?

From the experimental Beauty Contest evidence, an approach to investing somewhere between Level 1 and Level 2, but probably closer to Level 2, appears optimal given the experience and learning that investors can accrue (versus the Beauty Contest games, which are one-shot). To think optimally in the financial markets investors benefit from understanding the rumors and information Level 0 investors are attuned to. Secondarily, investors should consider how the Level 1 players believe the Level 0 players will respond to information. To get the balance right, an estimate of the proportion of Level 0 and Level 1 players in the market is useful. During a speculative bubble, markets will have more Level 0 players. When there is little new information, price action may be dominated by Level 1 traders.

One of the oldest behavioral strategies in markets is called alpha capture. In a classic alpha capture system, researchers and analysts submit trading ideas to a central location, typically owned by a portfolio manager. The idea generators may be compensated depending upon the overall value of their ideas to the owner. Alpha capture was first deployed by Marshall Wace in 2001. TIM Group currently operates the largest alpha capture system globally.[11] Use of alpha capture is now common across the financial industry.

Alpha capture was originally a Level 0 methodology, but recent advances have elevated it to Level 1 and above. In its Level 0 manifestation, an automated portfolio manager acted quickly on the ideas from the top-performing researchers, typically those with the best historical risk/reward track records. In the Level 1 advancements, algorithms consider factors such as trade crowding, whether a particular researcher performs better in certain industries than others, and the optimal time period to hold recommendations from that researcher. Sometimes, if a researcher has particularly poor accuracy, the system trades against their recommendations. In fact, researchers who provide consistently wrong ideas may be financially compensated in order to encourage their continued delivery of (bad) trading advice. Trading against an inaccurate research provider can be as lucrative as trading alongside a good one—consistency is key.

Keynes theorized that thinking-about-thinking (the Beauty Contest) drives investor decision making. Long after Keynes' death, in 2012 researchers found that a trader's accuracy in predicting price changes in an experimental market correlates with an empathic understanding of others' intentions (called "Theory of Mind"). Empathy was dominant, and there was no correlation between accuracy in price prediction and mathematical problem-solving ability.[12] This result suggests that Level 1 (and above) thinkers have an advantage over math geniuses. The skill of thinking-about-thinking was the key differentiator of trading performance.

Keynes noted that there are two ways of looking at markets, investment and speculation: "Investing is an activity of forecasting the yield over the life of the asset; speculation is the activity of forecasting the psychology of the market." The dualism in Keynes' statement is false. Market psychology itself affects asset prices, and in the process yields change, as is described in this book. Every investor—even those who believe in the supremacy of rational markets—will benefit from an understanding of the psychological forces that drive investors. This book is written for all those who are now, or who aspire to be, higher level investors.

WHAT MOVES TRADERS?

By deploying the skill of thinking-about-thinking, investors could be successful using a variety of real-world tools and insights. Through my experience as a coach, I've seen that most successful traders access information derived from three types of market analysis to generate buy and sell decisions:

- Fundamental analysis
- Technical analysis
- Sentiment analysis
- Institutional activity

These four types of information are the foundation of most traders' toolkits. Traders look at fundamentals to understand the economic reality underlying prices. There are a variety of fundamentals to keep track of for each asset, including macroeconomic data, earnings, and interest rates. Traders examine technicals to understand price trends, price pressure, and resistance levels. Technical analysis may involve transformed price and volume data such as moving averages, stochastics, relative strength indicators, and market internals such as the order flow and bid–ask dynamics. Traders examine market consensus, positions of traders, and news reactions to ascertain market sentiment. The market behavior and impact of institutions on liquidity and volatility such as central banks, large funds, and high-frequency traders also change market price dynamics, so these are tracked as well.

When leading seminars, I occasionally ask the question, "What moves asset prices?" I then ask the audience to vote on which of the four options listed above is the primary driver of prices; the audience consensus varies. Accountant and analyst audiences typically choose fundamentals. Chartist audiences, predictably, often prefer technical factors or sentiment. College student audiences choose fundamentals (perhaps to appease their finance professor) or sentiment (if they suspect I am grading them). A sizable minority in most audiences believes (and blames) institutions for influencing prices. Wise (or confused) audiences don't vote at all.

Why would a wise audience abstain? The academic evidence on what moves asset prices is a smorgasbord, a compendium of stylized facts showing evidence for earnings, price patterns, sentiment, and institutional policies impacting prices over various time periods and in various situations. There is no single answer to the question, "What moves asset prices?" In fact, it's a useless question if one doesn't understand what drives traders to buy and sell in markets.

At its core, it is the behavior of traders—their buying and selling and order flow—that moves prices. A more useful question than "What moves asset prices?" is "What causes traders to buy or sell?" And the answer is much more complex than it may seem. Trader behavior is driven by influences from external news (e.g., an earnings surprise), to the molecular level (e.g., neurochemistry), to the societal level (e.g., what will others think?). Both neurochemistry and social perceptions are altered through observation of information flowing through the world around. Those observations are filtered in and processed through in the trader's brain. The simplest answer to what makes traders buy and sell is then: *Traders respond to information.* They respond on a brain level, and sometimes their resulting buy-and-sell behavior is synchronized.

Yet information itself does not move traders to take action. A positive earnings surprise doesn't press the buy button in a trader's account. What fundamentally moves traders to buy or sell is the motivation they get after receiving that earnings news—the "*Ah ha*!" or the "*Uh-oh*!" The emotion that the information evokes is the key motivator of trader behavior.

The English word *emotion* is derived from the Latin words *ex* (out) and *movere* (move).[13] Information provokes emotion when it is relevant to a mental model, beliefs, or expectation. For example, if one's mental model of expected earnings agrees with the consensus estimate, and the company reports earnings below the consensus (the reference point), then that positive earnings announcement is in fact a disappointment.

Crucially, the brain generates good or bad feelings, depending on how new information compares to its expectations. When traders compare new information to their expectations, neurochemistry shifts, and a feeling arises. If the information is better than expected, they feel good; if it is worse than expected, they feel disappointment. Going forward in time, a series of such events and their associated feelings accumulate and subtly pressure the trader to take action.

Intense, short-term emotions arouse an inclination to take action because "doing something" is how one discharges that emotion and restores balance to one's neurochemistry. When traders fail to take action, that emotion will linger—even if they're no longer conscious of it—and it will subtly affect judgment and decision making. Think of a short-term emotion as a pebble in one's shoe: It will irritate, and it will eventually alter one's gait if it is not dealt with.

It is human nature to react emotionally when events do (or do not) go one's way. Furthermore, nothing has to *happen* for someone to experience emotional reactions. The simple act of imagining possible outcomes, such as great successes or terrible losses, stimulates emotion. Every investor has emotional reactions to market price action, although this diminishes with experience. Most investors have felt elation, pride, and the fear of missing out during bull markets and intense doubt, anger, or panic during sharp market downturns. Each emotion uniquely alters how investors think and what they subsequently do with their capital.

In order to comprehend patterns in markets, first this book explores how information evokes both emotional reactions and behavioral responses. Then it examines how other factors—the mental models, expectations, beliefs, time horizons, attention placement, and reactivity of the mass of traders—predictably affect prices.

CHAINED TO THE MAST

First she said we were to keep clear of the Sirens, who sit and sing most beautifully in a field of flowers; but she said I might hear them myself so long as no one else did. Therefore, take me and bind me to the crosspiece half way up the mast; bind me as I stand upright, with a bond so fast that I cannot possibly break away, and lash the rope's ends to the mast itself. If I beg and pray you to set me free, then bind me more tightly still.

—Homer, *The Odyssey*

Odysseus is a legendary Greek king of Ithaca renowned for his cunning and resourcefulness. In Homer's epic poem *The Odyssey*, he spends 10 eventful years returning home after the Trojan War. During that long journey, he passed by the Sirens. The Sirens were beautiful female humanlike creatures who lured nearby sailors with their enchanting music and voices. If sailors were drawn too near, as they usually were, they shipwrecked on the rocky coast of the Sirens' island and remained there, frozen in enchantment.

Odysseus wanted to hear the Sirens' song, but he knew that doing so would render him incapable of rational thought. He made a pact with his men as they approached the Sirens, putting wax in their ears so that they could not hear the Siren song. He asked his men to tie him to the mast of his ship so that he could not jump into the sea as they rowed past. He ordered his men not to change course under any circumstances, to keep their swords pointed at him, and to attack him if he broke free of his bindings. Upon hearing the Sirens' song, Odysseus was driven temporarily insane and struggled with all of his might to break free. Figure 1.1 depicts Odysseus fighting to join the Sirens.

Odysseus passed the Sirens safely. He did so because he understood his emotional weaknesses, and he planned ahead for his moments of vulnerability. Trusting his leadership, his crew refused to untie him, and they kept their ears plugged with wax. In *The Odyssey*, Homer commented on the weaknesses of human nature: "Men are so quick to blame the gods: They say that we devise their misery. But they themselves—in their depravity—design grief greater than the griefs that fate assigns." The human struggle to do what is right, while resisting temptation, is a pervasive theme in classical Greek literature.

In Plato's *Phaedrus*, the human intellect is likened to a charioteer that commands two horses: one that is irrational and crazed while the other is

FIGURE 1.1 "Ulysses and the Sirens." Herbert James Draper, 1909.

noble and of good stock. The job of the charioteer is to control the horses as they proceed toward enlightenment and truth. Plato's characterization of the mind contained one key flaw. Humans *think* they are the charioteer, in control, but in fact the thinker is itself one of the horses. Controlling emotion is easy to consider intellectually, but reality is not so simple.

THE BRAIN: STRUCTURE AND FUNCTION

> *Of all creatures that breathe and move upon the earth, nothing is bred that is weaker than man.*
>
> —Homer, *The Odyssey*

The human brain is the product of millions of years of evolution, and it is designed to efficiently and effectively interpret information, compete in a social hierarchy, and direct activity toward achieving goals while avoiding danger. However, the human brain evolved in a stone-age world where dangers and opportunities were largely immediate, and social interactions were limited to other members of a clan. As the modern world grows ever more interconnected and fast paced, it is apparent that some features of the stone-age brain are not optimized for managing the complexities of modern life.

The brain can be conceptualized as having three anatomical divisions. Each division is like the layer of an onion, with complex processes such as analytical decision making in the outer layer-the cortex; motivations and drives arisie from the middle layer-the limbic system; life-sustaining physiological processes originate in the innermost core.

The cortex is the brain's logistical center. It is the director of executive function and motor control. The part of the cortex called the prefrontal cortex involved in abstract thinking, planning, calculation, learning, and strategic decision making.[14] The brain's limbic system is the emotional driver of the brain. The limbic system is the source of primitive motivations and emotions including fear and excitement. Both the cortex and the limbic system are displayed in Figure 1.2. The third division of the brain is called the midbrain (a.k.a. "the reptilian brain"). The midbrain manages the body's basic physiological processes, including respiration and heart rate, and it will not be discussed further in this book.

Running across the three brain divisions are neural circuits that operate two types of goal-directed behavior: (1) reward pursuit and (2) loss avoidance.[15] The existence of reward approach and loss avoidance systems has been hypothesized since the time of Aristotle.[16] Prior to the late twentieth century, both the reward and the loss systems were thought to drive

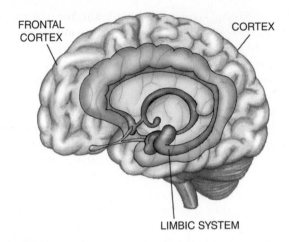

FIGURE 1.2 A depiction of the brain. The limbic
system is seen situated underneath the cortex.
The prefrontal cortex lies behind the forehead.

organisms toward pleasure and away from pain. Currently, scientists believe
that these systems encompass complex brain processes involving emotions,
cognitions (thoughts), and actions.

The evolution of the frontal cortex was an excellent thing—it's essen-
tially what makes someone human, allowing one to reflect on the future and
past, think strategically and abstractly, and plan ahead. The problem is that
the prefrontal cortex evolved after the limbic system, and thus while it sits
on top of the limbic system and manages and directs impulses, at times the
frontal cortex is knocked offline by emotional surges. When it is placed back
online, it tries to clean up the consequences as best it can.

The brain's prefrontal cortex helps humans to regulate emotions. In
children and adults of advanced age, the prefrontal cortex is thinner, and
emotions are more likely to influence financial judgment in unfortunate
ways (which is why children aren't allowed to have credit cards and
older adults are more susceptible to financial scams). For normal adults,
emotional self-regulation is intact when markets are trading as expected.
When price volatility arises, even normal adults lose their cognitive tether
as emotions come to dominate investment decision making.

Lying within the limbic structures is a motivational circuit called the
reward system. The reward system is comprised of neurons that predominantly communicate via the neurotransmitter dopamine. Dopamine has

been called the "pleasure" chemical of the brain, because people who are electrically stimulated in the reward system report intense feelings of well-being. The reward system coordinates the search for, evaluation of, and motivated pursuit of potential rewards.

A second motivational complex governs loss avoidance. The anatomy of the brain's loss system is less well defined than that of the reward system. The loss system is thought to consist of the anterior insula (pain and disgust), the amygdala (emotional processing), the hippocampus (memory center), and the hypothalamus (hormone secreting center). Loss system activation affects the entire body through bloodstream hormone and neuro-transmitter release. The perception of a threat activates the hypothalamus-pituitary-adrenal axis (HPA axis), which results in stress hormone and epinephrine ("adrenaline") secretion into the bloodstream. The body's sympathetic nervous system (SNS) prepares the whole body for the "fight-or-flight" response to danger with nerve signals transmitted to every major organ system. When under threat and experiencing fear, signs of SNS activation include trembling, perspiration, rapid heart rate, shallow breath-ing, and pupillary dilation. The SNS is also responsible for the physical signs and symptoms of panic.

Because the reward and loss systems influence thought and lie beneath awareness, they often direct behavior automatically through subtle emo-tional influences on judgment, thinking, and behavior. Based on the structure of the brain itself, humans don't *think* emotion is as influential over their behavior as it actually is. When thinking about emotion, one is thinking *as* the frontal cortex, a region that evolved in humans 70,000 years ago and is architecturally superimposed on top of the limbic system. Emotions are gen-erally unconscious—humans usually don't feel them or think about them, and as a result, humans consciously—on reflection—underappreciate their significance in driving behavior.

While the reward and loss systems are largely independent, when one system is highly activated, it may trigger a reciprocal deactivation of the other. In some (unpublished) neuroimaging research, evidence indicates that anticipating large financial rewards deactivates the anterior insula. Loss-avoidance is turned off by positive excitement. That is, excitement about potential wins deactivates the threat detection areas of the brain. This brain activity may be the source of the market aphorism: "Pigs get fat, hogs get slaughtered." Wanting to profit in markets is good (being a pig), but being so greedy as to ignore all risks (being a hog) leads to long-run ruin. Yet while the emotional explanation for trader behavior is simple and elegant, it is also incomplete.

EMOTION VERSUS REASON

There is nothing either good or bad, but thinking makes it so.
—William Shakespeare, *Hamlet*

So far, this chapter has vetted the idea that out-thinking others is the key to success in trading. It also explored how emotional inputs—arising from fundamental neural circuits and structures—influence decision making. In order to find gaps between perceived and actual risk, as Wilbur Ross suggested in the opening quote, then traders ought to understand how emotions alter perceptions, leading to such opportunities in market prices. Another question then follows: Is it more important to work on cognitive or emotional factors in decision making?

The information that traders receive is much more complex than that used in neuroimaging experiments, and it cannot be easily identified as "cognitive," as opposed to "emotional." Some high-impact cognitive information, such as a corporate bankruptcy, induces emotional response. On the flipside, information about others' emotions—such as hearing of a market panic—can drive a rational decision to buy shares from those who are over-reacting. Following Hurricane Katrina, it was likely the emotional state of fear drove homeowners to purchase insurance at premiums far above those justified by the actual flooding risk. While media might report high degrees of emotion among investors, savvy traders make cognitive assessments of such collective emotions. Wilbur Ross's was a cognitive decision to take advantage of that mispricing.

Using neuroimaging, researchers exploring the Beauty Contest game found that the level of activity in the brain's prefrontal cortex during decision making correlates with improved contest performance. Higher performance results from having a superior strategic IQ,[17] which is the ability to think analytically about others' thinking (and feeling). The prefrontal cortex receives useful information from, and also sometimes inhibits, the emotional circuits. Like Odysseus, the best traders use their cognitive powers to plan ahead for moments of emotional weakness. To take advantage of the gap between perceived risk and actual risk, investors can use cognitive strategies that consider the importance of emotion in driving market behavior.

IN SUMMARY

- Savvy investors identify when risk perceptions diverge from actual investment risk.
- The academic fields of behavioral finance and behavioral economics investigate the role of human psychology in economic decision making using statistical analysis and experimental technique.

- The Beauty Contest theorized by Keynes describes the importance of game theory and metacognition in markets.
- Traders are moved by information and their reactions to information. Such reactions are influenced by preexisting expectations, beliefs, and moods.
- The story of Odysseus and the Sirens illustrates how intellect is often subsumed by emotion. As Odysseus demonstrates, cognition may be used to plan ahead in order to avoid emotional and behavioral traps.
- The brain's structure, with the prefrontal cortex evolving 100,000 years ago on top of the limbic system, explains why humans think they have more control over their reactions and behavior than they actually do.
- The brain's major motivational pathways—the reward and loss avoidance systems—play a significant role in every risk-related human behavior. Their activity is reciprocal at times, amplifying vulnerabilities.
- To take advantage of the gap between perceived risk and actual risk, investors use cognitive strategies that consider the importance of emotion in driving market behavior.

NOTES

1. Wilbur Ross describing reinsurance investments after Hurricane Katrina in Liam Pleven, "Where Others Flee Storms, Ross Rushes In," *Wall Street Journal* (Jan. 20, 2007).
2. Mark Rubinstein, "Rational Markets: Yes or No? The Affirmative Case," *Financial Analysts Journal* 57 (3) (May/June 2001), 15–29.
3. Joseph De La Vega, 1688. *Confusion De Confusiones*. Paragraph 81, translated and excerpted in Teresa Corzo, Margarita Prat, and Esther Vaquero, "Behavioral Finance in Joseph de la Vega's Confusion de Confusiones," *Journal of Behavioral Finance* 15 (4) (2014), 341–350.
4. David Hume, *An Enquiry Concerning Human Understanding* (London: Oxford University Press, 1748).
5. John M. Keynes, *The General Theory of Employment, Interest, and Money* (London: MacMillan, 1936), p. 156.
6. Peter L. Bernstein, *Against the Gods: The Remarkable Story of Risk* (New York: John Wiley & Sons, 1996).
7. De La Vega, p. 341–350.
8. Rosemarie Nagel, "Unraveling in Guessing Games: An Experimental Study," *American Economic Review* 85 (5), (1995), pp 1313–1326.
9. A. Bosch-Domenech, J. G. Montalvo, R. Nagel, and A. Satorra, "One, Two, (Three), Infinity … : Newspaper and Lab Beauty-Contest Experiments," *American Economic Review* 92 (5), (December 2002), pp. 1687–1701.
10. Muriel Niederle, "A Variety of 'Beauty Contest' Games." Adapted from slides originally prepared by Rosemarie Nagel at UPF-ICREA 2009. Retrieved May 20, 2015, from http://web.stanford.edu/~niederle/GuessingGames.pdf.

11. http://www.timgroup.com/.
12. Bruguier, A. J., Quartz, S. R., & Bossaerts, P., "Exploring the Nature of 'Trader Intuition.'" *The Journal of Finance*, 65(5) 2010, 1703–1723.
13. Online Etymology Dictionary, "emotion," http://www.etymonline.com/index.php?term=emotion.
14. V. Prabhakaran, B. Rypma, and J. D. Gabrieli, "Neural Substrates of Mathematical Reasoning: A Functional Magnetic Resonance Imaging Study of Neocortical Activation During Performance of the Necessary Arithmetic Operations Test," *Neuropsychology* 15 (1) (January 2001), 115–127.
15. R. J. Davidson, D. C. Jackson, and N. H. Kalin, "Emotion, Plasticity, Context, and Regulation: Perspectives from Affective Neuroscience," *Psychological Bulletin* 126 (2000), p. 890.
16. H. Spencer, *Principles of Psychology* (New York: Appleton Press, 1880).
17. Alan Hampton, Peter Bossaerts, and John O'Doherty, "Neural Correlates of Mentalizing-Related Computations During Strategic Interactions in Humans," *Proceedings of the National Academy of Sciences of the United States of America*, Ed. by Edward E. Smith, Columbia University, New York, and approved February 20, 2008 (received for review November 22, 2007).

CHAPTER 2

Mind and Emotion

[O]ur decisions to do something positive ... can only be taken as the result of animal spirits—a spontaneous urge to action rather than inaction, and not as the outcome of a weighted average of quantitative benefits multiplied by quantitative probabilities.
—John Maynard Keynes[1]

As a young economist and statesman, Keynes vocally opposed the restrictive and punitive terms of the Treaty of Versailles, believing it would doom Germany and precipitate further conflict. He believed in the power of government spending—used judiciously—to stimulate economic activity. Following the 2007–2009 financial crisis, debate raged over whether governments should borrow and spend to stop the debt-laden economies of the developed world from spiraling into depression. Those who supported borrowing and spending held the *Keynesian* view, that fiscal stimulus could drive the recovery and stop a downward spiral of contraction and austerity.

Less well-known are Keynes's stock-picking skills. His Cambridge college—King's college—appointed him bursar in 1924, and he channeled its resources into the Chest fund. Between 1924 and his death in 1946, the Chest fund grew from £30,000 to £380,000. Given the stock market volatility over those years—boom, depression, and war—this return represents significant outperformance. An academic paper estimates that Keynes returned 15 percent annually between 1924 and 1946 versus 8 percent annually for the U.K. stock market over that period.[2]

Keynes understood that human psychology played a crucial role in driving economic activity. He introduced to economics a colorful term for one of the vital ingredients of economic prosperity—the naive optimism that drives human economic activity—*animal spirits*.

CROWDS MOVING MARKETS

Animal spirits animate crowds. Such crowds are made up of individuals—individuals who invest, trade, or manage portfolios. The decisions of these individuals are affected by the ebb and flow of news and rumor.[3,4] They are moved not only by what they read and hear but often more so by their emotional reactions to such information. Such emotional reactions represent Keynes's notion of animal spirits, and they fuel economic and investment activity.

Behavioral economics researchers have tested the impact of a variety of animal spirits on risk-taking behavior. According to such research, when new information provokes emotional responses such as joy, fear, anger, and gloom, individual trading behaviors are systematically biased.[5,6] As the intensity of emotions increases, they progressively exert greater influence on decision making.[7] And since individuals combine to form a market, their collective emotions manifest in observable market behavior. Indeed, news-derived sentiment metrics can be used to predict price movements.[8] That is, by altering investors' emotional states, information predictably alters the way they transact in markets. It follows that by better understanding the perceptions, preoccupations and concerns of market participants—their sentiments—traders can develop superior predictive models of market prices.

A basic depiction of a relationship between media sentiment and asset prices is evident in charts of stock sentiment moving averages. The details of the construction of such sentiment indexes are described in Appendix A and in subsequent chapters. The overall feeling tone—positive versus negative—expressed in the media about the S&P 500 and its constituent stocks is called sentiment. When simple moving averages of the net sentiment of the combined news and social media commentary about the S&P 500 are plotted against the value of the S&P 500 itself, a simple relationship is evident, as depicted in Figure 2.1.

When short-term sentiment drops below longer-term sentiment, prices tend to follow it lower. When short-term sentiment rises above the long-term average, S&P 500 prices often subsequently rise. This relationship isn't perfect, yet investors who remained out of stocks during declining sentiment periods (shaded dark gray) and who were invested during rising sentiment periods (shaded light gray) would have significantly outperformed a stock market buy-and-hold strategy.

In order to better understand the predictive power of sentiment, this chapter explores how emotions (themselves specific types of sentiments) impact trading behavior.

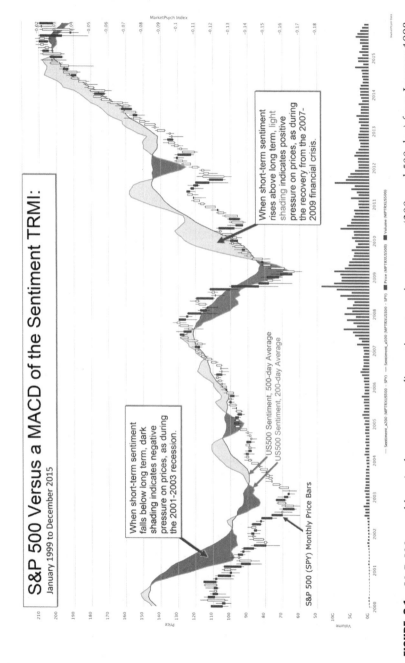

FIGURE 2.1 S&P 500 monthly price bars versus media sentiment moving averages (200- and 500-day) from January 1998 through January 2015.

EMOTIONAL PRIMING

At their most basic, emotions represent a singular response to complex information. What is an immediate reaction to hearing a company's name? Some companies inspire "*Meh*...." Some cause one to spontaneously think, "Nice!" Others cause traders to feel, "*Wow!*" Investors do not reference all of their memories about a company, its products, or its balance sheet each time it comes to mind. Rather they summon an impression. That impression—a feeling—underlies mental shortcuts that facilitate quick and efficient decisions. Such shortcuts form unconsciously, and they profoundly affect financial behavior.

Researchers have found that when emotions are provoked through words, video clips, photographs, or other means, they alter financial behavior—even in completely unrelated situations. The 2002 Nobel Prize in Economics was shared by the psychologist Daniel Kahneman for his work on Prospect Theory with Amos Tversky. Kahneman and Tversky found that the language used to describe monetary (and other) risks alters how people choose. If the words describing a financial risk differed in controlled experimental conditions—the odds of the outcome remained the same—those word differences might lead to significant differences in how subjects chose. They called this cognitive bias the framing effect. The framing effect occurs via the emotional reactions humans experience when digesting risk-related information. These emotional reactions, which underlie cognition, are a result of an effect called *emotional priming*.

In one experiment on emotional priming, researchers offered experimental subjects a choice between a guaranteed $10 profit or a gamble on the flip of a coin. If the coin landed on heads, they would win $30. If the coin landed on tails, they won nothing. The expected value of the coin flip was $15. The purely rational person should choose the coin flip each time. On average subjects chose the coin flip on approximately 50 percent of the trials, making non-optimal decisions at a high rate.[9] Next, before the choice between the $10 and the coin flip was offered, subjects were asked to label a photograph of a face as depicting either a man or a woman. Some of the faces were expressing emotions: fear, anger, happiness. It turned out that participants were most likely to select the riskiest option after viewing happy faces. However, after seeing an angry or fearful face, subjects were more likely to choose the safe option. Overall, subjects who saw a happy face were 30 percent more likely to choose the coin flip than those who saw a fearful or angry face. Something about the emotional expression on the face was altering the financial choices of the subjects.

At the end of the experiment, without being aware of the overall results, the subjects were asked if they thought the face had affected their decision making. They all denied it. They collectively replied along the lines of, "No, why would it?"

To explore whether their awareness of their emotional state had changed, subjects were asked to rate how they felt on a scale of 1 to 7 both before and after the experiment. Subjects showed no significant difference in self-assessed feelings regardless of which face they had seen.

Emotional priming by the emotionally expressive face had—on average—affected their choices substantially. Yet the subjects did not believe it had affected them, and they stated that they felt no different. A more recent study found that deciding whom to give money to in a microlending scheme is powerfully influenced by the emotional expression on a face.[10] It is possible that transient subconscious activations of the brain's fear, anger, and happiness processing centers biased the brain's evaluation of financial risk.

FEELINGS AND FINANCE

It is not only expressive faces that serve as emotional primes. Stock price changes—gains and losses—themselves alter investor feelings and subsequent risk-taking. Malmendier and Nagel (2011) found that individuals who more recently experienced low stock-market returns were reluctant to invest in equities and had pessimistic beliefs about future stock returns.[11] This finding was confirmed by professor Camelia Kuhnen, who found that "when faced with a sequence of mildly negative news (i.e., when the stock is bad, but likely not the worst possible), people are overly pessimistic."[12] Stock price movements change how investors feel. It's probable that such changes in outlook could then be quantified in investors' social media communications. Based on the research cited thus far, it appears that news headlines and stock price movements emotionally prime investors, subtly influencing their investment decisions. Additionally, social media comments by investors may reflect feeling states that are a result of emotional priming, such as pessimism.

The research cited in this chapter bridges information flow, collective feelings, and behavior. As one span in that bridge, expressions in social media correlate with financial behavior. For example, research on expressions of Twitter sentiment have found sentiment predictive of purchasing behavior. For consumer products, it's a logical assumption that consumers' feelings about a product influence whether they will buy it. One study classified Twitter sentiment (positive versus negative) in over 2.8 million tweets making references to 24 different movies released in a three-month period.[13] The researchers found that a model built from the average tweet-rate and tweet-sentiment ratio outperformed traditional measures in forecasting the box-office revenues of these movies. Individual sentiment expressed in tweets predicted movie ticket purchases.

The tone of business news broadcasts, the content of the morning newspaper, recent stock price changes, and one's work and home environments all contain emotional primes. Such primes may be reinforced in news headlines and discussed in social media, and they unconsciously bias how investors approach risky decisions. The collective impact of these primes is to alter financial behavior, creating patterns in market prices. Even if the influence of such primes were small, a 1 percent alteration in investment choices at crucial times can lead to large cumulative gains or losses over years.

HOW EMOTIONS MOVE TRADERS

Research demonstrates that information flow generates unconscious feelings (sentiments) that alter financial behavior. To quantify the sentiment of the information flow, commercial entities have developed proprietary sentiment analysis engines that score and quantify the sentiment of news articles including Thomson Reuters, RavenPack, Bloomberg, and IBM. Noncommercial sentiment dictionaries have also been created, including those developed by Tim Loughran and Bill McDonald at Notre Dame University and the Harvard General Inquirer. Furthermore, free code libraries are available for text sentiment analysis in R, python, and other software languages. The vast majority of commercial sentiment analysis offerings focus only on positive, negative, and neutral valence scoring, with additional considerations for the novelty and relevance of news articles. These approaches miss an important consideration: All negative sentiment (bad news) is not alike.

This book would be very short if its fundamental lesson were only "Buy on bad news." The reality it describes is much more complex. Bad news may come from a variety of sources, each more or less credible and with a larger or smaller overall audience. Bad news also differs in character, including such diverse topics as accounting fraud and negative earnings forecasts. Bad news also takes a different length of time to sink into prices, depending on its source, nature, and the emotional reactions investors experience to it.

Humans experience a broad range of emotions, and psychological research has demonstrated that more than just positive–negative valence has predictable effects on investor behavior. Researchers exploring dimensions of sentiment beyond positive and negative, such as Huina Mao and Johan Bollen, have investigated emotional classifications and have identified predictive value in narrowly defined sentiment indexes such as

Bullish and Bearish.[14] In order to study such narrow subsets of sentiment, it helps to proceed within a theoretical framework.

One common classification system of sentiments plots emotions on dimensions (axes) called valence and arousal. Humans can experience high or low levels of both valence and arousal. Pleasantness and exuberance are positive in valence, while boredom and fury are of negative valence. As for arousal, pleasantness and boredom are low arousal states, while exuberance and fury are high arousal states. Researchers represent the valence and arousal dimensions in the affective circumplex model of sentiment.[15] In Figure 2.2, sentiments common in financial news and social media are depicted on the affective circumplex.

Each dot corresponds to the emotion's location on the circumplex. Some of the sentiments on the circumplex are produced as sentiment data in the Thomson Reuters MarketPsych Indices (TRMI). The TRMI underlie the

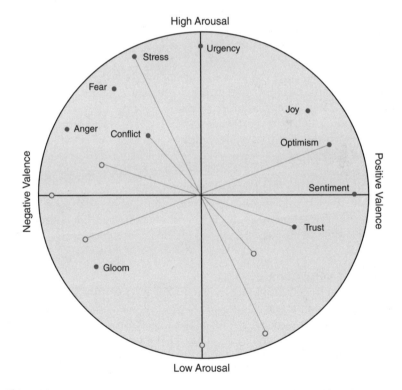

FIGURE 2.2   The sentiment-derived Thomson Reuters MarketPsych Indices (TRMI) plotted on the affective circumplex.

majority of the research in this book. In Figure 2.2, sentiments representing an emotion and its opposite are connected with a thin gray line between their positive and negative poles. The remainder of the chapter describes the theoretical value of such specific sentiments. A more detailed explanation of the text analytics underlying the TRMI is available in Appendix A.

AROUSAL, STRESS, AND URGENCY

People make significantly different decisions when deliriously sleepy versus when buzzing with caffeine. One's arousal level significantly impacts one's decision making. In a classic representation of the effects of arousal on judgment, stress levels map to cognitive performance in an inverse-U curve called the Yerkes-Dodson law.[16,17] When stress levels are very high, complex problem-solving performance drops and reliance on preexisting habits increases.[18] On the other hand, low stress levels lead to subpar performance in complex decision-making environments due to inattention and slow reaction times. Decision makers perform optimally when arousal is in the middle of its typical range.

In text, arousal can be captured in specific references to stress (negative valence, with high arousal) and urgency (neutral valence, high arousal). Both high and low stress and urgency scores are expected to correlate with decreased trader cognitive performance. One effect among traders of such cognitive distortions could be incomplete arbitrage of short-term price anomalies. Both high and low levels of arousal may predispose markets to exhibit price patterns such as momentum during low-arousal regimes and mean reversion during high-arousal regimes.[19]

Valence and arousal are only two dimensions out of many possible sentiment subsets. The following sections describe research on how other important emotions drive buying and selling decisions among traders.

ANGER, FEAR, AND GLOOM

Research has shown that strongly negative emotions such as anger, fear, and gloom have a unique and consistent effect in biasing how individuals set bid and ask prices in an experimental market.[20,21] Much of the research on this subject has been led by Professor Jennifer Lerner, now at Harvard University.

In a series of experiments, Professor Lerner induced emotional states of sadness, fear, and disgust in subjects using short movie clips. [22,23] She then studied how the subjects placed bids and offers in a simulated marketplace. Lerner found that participants in a disgusted emotional state were emotionally driven to "expel" or "get rid" of items they owned. Disgusted subjects had no desire to accumulate new possessions. As a result, they reduced both their bid and offer prices for consumer items.

The Anger TRMI encompasses angry sentiments ranging in intensity from disgust (low-level anger) to rage (intense anger). Based on Lerner's results, high anger readings are expected to increase selling and reduce buying in affected assets. Strategies based on this idea are explored in Chapter 13.

Professor Lerner also studied the effects of fear. Compared to anger, in Lerner's experimental markets fear provokes lower bid prices, higher ask prices, and pessimism about the future.[24,25] Fearful investors avoid transacting, paralyzed as prices slide until fear reaches an extreme level characteristic of panic. Panic drives a purge of assets, an event that is termed *capitulation* colloquially and *overreaction* in the behavioral finance literature.[26]

As for gloom, Lerner found that behavioral responses to sadness (a synonym of gloom) are characterized by higher bid prices, lower ask prices, and overtrading. Lerner noted that, "Sadness triggers the goal of changing one's circumstances, increasing buying prices [bids] but reducing selling prices [asks]." Compared to people in neutral emotional states, people who had viewed sad movie clips subsequently valued items they owned *less*, and they valued items they did not possess *more*.[27] This valuation disparity leads to an increase in economic transactions and may be one cause of both "shopping therapy" and "overtrading." As a result of the increased willingness of sad investors to transact, an equity sector with a high level of gloom might be expected to experience higher relative trading volumes.

INFORMATION IMPACT

In news and social media, authors describing an asset may reference an event (topic), its positive or negative impact (sentiment), ambiguity around it (uncertainty), the importance of the event (magnitude), its immediacy (urgency), surprise, and specific emotions relating to it (emotive sentiments). Thus far, this chapter has addressed the research rationale for studying sentiments such as stress, urgency, anger, gloom, fear, and uncertainty. The TRMI, the sentiment data which this book is largely based on, also measures complex sentiments such as governmentAnger and marketRisk, which encapsulate the relationship between sentiments and specific topics. In general, the TRMI quantify references to dozens of sentiments, topics, and macroeconomic influences across assets. Appendix A contains a table with the definition of each available index.

Keynes's animal spirits are much wider than positive feeling alone. A variety of emotional and cognitive states and information characteristics affect trading behavior, leading to patterns in prices. As seen in the next chapter, one of the most unusual price events of recent years—the flash crash—reveals how information flow impacts trader emotions and may fuel dramatic price action.

IN SUMMARY

- John Maynard Keynes used the term *animal spirits* to describe how positive sentiments drive economic behavior.
- Simple charts of media sentiment depict rising sentiment leading rising stock market prices, and several studies show that sentiment has explanatory power over market price movements.
- Emotional priming experiments show that many sentiments affect financial behavior through unconscious mechanisms.
- The Affective Circumplex is a model of emotion that demonstrates how each emotion varies by both valence (positive versus negative) and arousal dimensions.
- Behavioral economics researchers have demonstrated that when new information provokes sentiments such as joy, fear, anger, and gloom, individual trading behaviors are systematically biased.

NOTES

1. John M. Keynes, *The General Theory of Employment, Interest and Money* (London: Macmillan, 1936), pp. 161–162.
2. David Chambers, Elroy Dimson, and Justin Foo, "Keynes the Stock Market Investor: A Quantitative Analysis," forthcoming, *Journal of Financial and Quantitative Analysis* (JFQA) (2013).
3. J. Engelberg and C. Parsons. 2011."The Causal Impact of Media in Financial Markets," *Journal of Finance.* 66(1), 67–97. Available at SSRN: http://ssrn.com/abstract=1462416 or http://dx.doi.org/10.2139/ssrn.1462416.
4. J. Engelberg, C. Sasseville, and J. Williams, "Market Madness? The Case of Mad Money." Available at *SSRN* (2010): http://ssrn.com/abstract=870498 or http://dx.doi.org/10.2139/ssrn.870498.
5. J. S. Lerner and D. Keltner, "Beyond Valence: Toward a Model of Emotion-Specific Influences on Judgment and Choice," *Cognition and Emotion* 14 (2000), 473–493.
6. G. Loewenstein and J. S. Lerner, "The Role of Affect in Decision Making." In R. Davidson, H. Goldsmith, and K. Scherer (eds.), *Handbook of Affective Science* (Oxford: Oxford University Press, 2003), 619–642.
7. Ibid., p. 636.
8. P. Tetlock, "Giving Content to Investor Sentiment: The Role of Media in the Stock Market," *The Journal of Finance* 62(3) (2007).

9. J. T. Trujillo, B. Knutson, M. P. Paulus, and P. Winkielman, *Taking Gambles at Face Value: Effects of Emotional Expressions on Risky Decisions.* Manuscript under review.

10. Alexander Genevsky and Brian Knutson, "Neural Affective Mechanisms Predict Market-Level Microlending," *Psychological Science* (2015).

11. Malmendier, U. and Nagel, S., 2011, "Depression Babies: Do Macroeconomic Experiences Affect Risk-Taking?" *Quarterly Journal of Economics* 126(1), 373–416.

12. Kuhnen, C. M., "Asymmetric Learning from Financial Information," *Journal of Finance*, 70 (5) 2015, 2029–2062.

13. S. Asur and B. Huberman, "Predicting the Future with SocialMedia," *Web Intelligence and Intelligent Agent Technology* 1 (2010), 492–499.

14. Mao, H., Counts, S., and Bollen, J. (2015). Quantifying the effects of online bullishness on international financial markets. In ECB Workshop on Using Big Data for Forecasting and Statistics, Frankfurt, Germany.

15. J. A. Russell, "A Circumplex Model of Affect," *Journal of Personality and Social Psychology* 39(6), (1980), 1161–1178.

16. R. M. Yerkes and J. D. Dodson, "The Relation of Strength of Stimulus to Rapidity of Habit-Formation," *Journal of Comparative Neurology and Psychology* 18 (1908), 459–482.

17. D. M. Diamond, A. M. Campbell, C. R. Park, J. Halonen, and P. R. Zoladz, "The Temporal Dynamics Model of Emotional Memory Processing: A Synthesis on the Neurobiological Basis of Stress-Induced Amnesia, Flashbulb and Traumatic Memories, and the Yerkes-Dodson Law," *Neural Plasticity* (2007).

18. L. Schwabe and O. T. Wolf, "Stress Prompts Habit Behavior in Humans," *The Journal of Neuroscience* 3 (29), (2009), 7191–7198.

19. D. Hirschleifer and A. Subrahmanyam, "Investor Psychology and Security Under- and Overreactions." *Journal of Finance* 53(6), (1999), 1839–1885.

20. P. Winkielman, B. Knutson, M. Paulus, and J. Trujillo, "Affective Influence on Judgments and Decisions: Moving Towards Core Mechanism," *Review of General Psychology* 11(2), (2007), 179–192.

21. P. Winkielman, K. C. Berridge, and J. L. Wilbarger. "Unconscious Affective Reactions to Masked Happy versus Angry Faces Influence Consumption Behavior and Judgments of Value," *Personality and Social Psychology Bulletin* 31(1), (2005), 121–135.

22. J. S. Lerner, D. A. Small, and G. Loewenstein, "Heart Strings and Purse Strings: Carry-over Effects of Emotions on Economic Transactions," *Psychological Science* 15 (2004), 337–341.

23. J. S. Lerner and D. Keltner, "Fear, Anger, and Risk," *Journal of Personality and Social Psychology* 81 (2001), 146–159.

24. Lerner, Small, and Loewenstein, 337–341.

25. Lerner and Keltner, pp. 146–159.

26. Hirschleifer and Subrahmanyam, pp. 1839–1885.

27. Lerner, Small, and Loewenstein, 337–341.

CHAPTER 3

Information Processing

[I]n the biggest and most violent protest since riots shook the country in 2008, some 50,000 Greeks marched in Athens and clashed with police in pitched street battles. A petrol bomb attack killed three workers in a local bank branch.
                              —Reuters UPDATE, May 6, 2010,19:00 UTC[1]

On the morning of May 6, 2010, mayhem was erupting on the streets of Athens, Greece. Television financial news networks looped video of Greek police battling Molotov-cocktail-hurling protestors. News commentators speculated that the euro might not hold together, leading to Europe's "Lehman moment," or perhaps worse. U.S. stock markets opened down and trended down for most of the day as worries swelled.

At 2:42 p.m., with the S&P 500 down more than 2.7 percent for the day, the stock market began to fall rapidly, dropping 5.5 percent in 5 minutes. By 2:47 p.m., the S&P 500 showed a 9 percent loss for the day—a daily decline equivalent to $1 trillion in market wealth.

Then, just as suddenly as the dramatic slide had begun, prices reversed. Twenty minutes later, by 3:07 p.m., U.S. equity markets had regained most of the 5.5 percent drop. This historic decline and rapid recovery was called the *flash crash*.

The preliminary CFTC-SEC investigation of the crash noted that on May 6, 2010, markets had been depressed by "unsettling political and economic news" and "growing uncertainty in the financial markets."[2] In a follow-up report several months later, regulators blamed a large sell order as the triggering event of the price crash: "Around 1:00 p.m., broadly negative market sentiment was already affecting an increase in the price volatility of some individual securities."[3] The CFTC-SEC report went on:

> *By 2:30 p.m., the S&P 500 volatility index ("VIX") was up 22.5 percent from the opening level, yields of ten-year Treasuries*

fell as investors engaged in a "flight to quality," and selling pressure had pushed the Dow Jones Industrial Average ("DJIA") down about 2.5%.[4]

Regulators noted that risk aversion (flight to quality) was increasing in the hours before the sharp price decline.

To the thinking brain, emotion-driven behavior itself is not a sufficient explanation for a concrete event like a market panic. And the thinkers at the SEC and CFTC went and hunting for a cause more concrete than investor psychology. On page 2 the report explained that despite the aforementioned market stress, it was a single sell algorithm that triggered the crash. Per the report, an unnamed asset manager (later found to be Waddell and Reed) placed a 75,000 contract ($4.1 billion) S&P e-mini futures sale order at 2:32 p.m., minutes before the crash. This order and the dynamics of its execution triggered the rapid price slide.[5] On page 3 and for its remaining 90 pages, the report described the mechanics of market microstructure and how a relatively small sell order could cause a price crash. Less than one page was devoted to information flow, events, and psychology. This 2010 CFTC-SEC report was widely regarded as worthless.[6] While regulators had hoped to restore trust in markets by laying bare the causes of the crash, their thoughtful focus on market microstructure failed to achieve that goal.

Given the tenuous conclusions reached by the CFTC-SEC, the hunt for a concrete cause continued. In early 2015, the CFTC-SEC announced an indictment against Navinder Sarao, who was living in and trading from his unassuming row house in west London. In a Bloomberg article, "Guy Trading at Home Caused the Flash Crash," journalist Matt Levine lays out the CFTC-SEC's case against Sarao, who used spoofing robots—algorithms that enter large buy or sell orders near the bid or ask price but then withdraw those orders before they are executed—to fool market participants. Sarao's fake sell orders on S&P futures at one time equaled the entire buy-side of the order book. He changed or canceled his orders 19,000 times the day of the crash.

> *Those orders were never executed, or intended to be executed, but they tricked people into thinking that there was a lot more selling interest than there actually was. ... It's a pretty straightforward spoofing story.[7]*

Yet Sarao stopped his robots from spoofing, and he stopped trading, at 1:40 p.m. on May 6, 2010, more than 30 minutes before the crash. Despite the flash crash moving prices more than $1 trillion in notional value, Sarao earned $879,018 on the day of the flash crash.[8] The CFTC indictment implied that Sarao started his spoofing career with a bang, causing the flash crash in the early days, and then went on spoofing for another five years. Bloomberg's Levine pondered, "If his behavior on May 6, 2010, caused the flash crash, and if he continued it for much of the subsequent five years, why didn't he cause, you know, a dozen flash crashes?"

Humans feel some relief if they believe that a concrete, controllable trigger caused a painful chain reaction of events. Regulators can legislate away (or imprison) such a trigger. When the CFTC-SEC blamed a single mutual fund sell order in 2010, then a spoofer in 2015, a logical and actionable explanation for the flash crash was the goal. Unfortunately, these actors were only part of a diverse market landscape.

MEDIA AND THE FLASH CRASH

If it bleeds, it leads.
> —Eric Pooley, "Grins, Gore, and Videotape—The Trouble with Local TV News," New York Magazine, 1989.

It is possible to investigate whether media, and the information in it, correlated (or even instigated) panic selling on the day of the flash crash using sentiment and fear indexes. The Sentiment and Fear TRMI were built by quantifying real-time comments about the largest 500 companies by market capitalization in the United State and the S&P 500 itself. The TRMI scores were first aggregated into 60-second blocks, which were themselves averaged over 60 minutes. Figure 3.1 depicts the Sentiment TRMI derived from both news and social media superimposed on the intraday S&P 500 price.

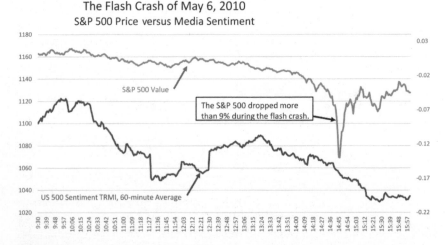

FIGURE 3.1 Sentiment about the S&P 500 expressed in news and social media, simple 60-minute average, on May 6, 2010.

Note that the flash crash was preceded by a significant decline in media sentiment. Researchers have identified that half-hour changes in media sentiment about the S&P 500 correlate with future half-hour price action.[9] After plummeting throughout the day, the value of the Sentiment TRMI was at its 2010 low in the minutes before the flash crash.

A specific type of negative sentiment—fear—indicated increasing risk perceptions before the selloff. Figure 3.2 depicts a large surge in media fear 1 to 2 hours before the crash. A second spike in fear followed the event itself. Figure 3.2 is a simple 60-minute average of fear, so it takes some minutes for the event itself to register.

Fear is a marker of risk-aversion. In experimental markets induction of fear leads to lower asking prices and lower bid prices.[10] When fear spikes, prices are expected to—and in this case did subsequently—fall.

From a psychological perspective, the flash crash was a dramatic example of emotional priming by the media portrayal of the events in Greece. A surge in fear and negativity in the media may have increased investors' risk perceptions and facilitated an outright price panic.

In the field of medicine, when someone dies, physicians determine the official cause of death. The cause of death is defined as "the disease or injury which initiated the train of morbid events leading directly to death."[11] In order to understand events like death—or market price movements—it helps to examine the proximate causes. The flash crash was triggered in the context of dramatically negative media, price feedback effects, and panicked crowd behavior. It occurred in the context of electronic markets, where most market makers went offline when volatility spiked. If it is necessary to settle on a single proximate cause of the flash crash, using the medical model, that cause would be investor panic.

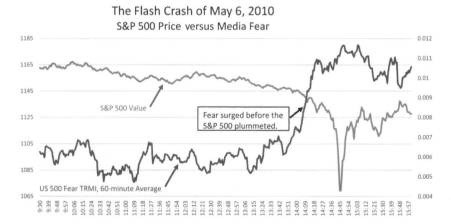

FIGURE 3.2 Fear about the S&P 500 expressed in news and social media, simple 60-minute average, on May 6, 2010.

Perhaps the CFTC-SEC flash crash report authors worried that blaming psychological causes—the feedback effect among Greek social unrest, the news cycle, and rapidly falling prices—would be too unempirical. Or perhaps regulators were concerned that such a cause would be unmanageable. In order to contain a panic triggered and inflamed by the media, regulators would be compelled to police provocative media messages or deploy an army of on-call market therapists to soothe investors' anxieties.

To understand the flash crash, it helps to explore how media content drives investor behavior. First such news must attract attention. After gaining investors' attention, three characteristics modulate its impact on decision making: how easily it can be accessed (availability), the ease of understanding it (fluency), and its emotional impact (vividness).[12] On the day of the flash crash, news of European financial catastrophe and stock market declines were easily available to investors, were easy to understand, and the vivid images of the riots were emotionally compelling. The remainder of this chapter explores the importance of diversity to price efficiency, the role of attention in driving prices, and impactful information characteristics such as availability, fluency, and vividness.

DIVERSITY BREAKDOWNS

[T]he issue is not whether individuals are irrational (they are) but whether they are irrational in the same way at the same time.
—Michael Mauboussin, *More Than You Know*[13]

Michael Mauboussin is managing director and head of Global Financial Strategies at Credit Suisse and a professor of finance at the Columbia Business School. He is also a polymath who has integrated elements of complex adaptive systems theory and behavioral finance into his investment philosophy. As Mauboussin points out, the stock market has no defined outcome and no defined time horizon. Prices in the financial markets both inform and influence participants about the future. Diversity (or efficiency) is lost in the markets when investors imitate one another or when they rely on the same "information cascades." Information cascades induce market participants to make similar decisions based on identical signals from the environment, without consideration that others are doing likewise.

From Mauboussin's work one can draw several conclusions. In order to find advantages in the markets, it helps to identify *diversity breakdowns*. Diversity breakdowns represent collective overreaction or underreaction to information. As Mauboussin puts it, "While understanding individual behavioral pitfalls may improve your own decision making, appreciation of the dynamics of the collective is the key to outperforming the market."[14] Diversity breakdowns might sound like a rare event, but in fact they occur daily in markets wherever collective attention is focused and information is compelling (in the case of price overreaction) or where attention is scattered and new information is complex (in the case of underreaction).

PRICE PATTERNS

Logic: The art of thinking and reasoning in strict accordance with the limitations and incapacities of the human misunderstanding.
—Ambrose Bierce

Sentiment-based price patterns are not entirely logical, which is perhaps one key to their continued existence. In general there are two well-known sentiment-based patterns in financial prices: overreaction and underreaction. A price movement is called *overreaction* in hindsight—if prices mean-revert (bounce) in a predictable way. If prices are pushed too far, the theory goes, then rational investors will take the other side of the trades and the opposing pressure of their orders will bring prices back toward fair value.[15] The mean reversion of the asset's price back toward its origin is sometimes predictable. When it occurs repeatedly and systematically, the price pattern is thought due to investor overreaction—perhaps to dramatic information.

A price movement is called *underreaction* if a trend (momentum) is born. In the case of underreaction, boring, routine, or complex information may be initially overlooked by investors. As they wake up to its meaning, they gradually buy (or sell), creating a gradual price trend. The concepts of overreaction and underreaction were coined retrospectively, to describe patterns observed in hindsight in price data. Importantly, the terms refer not only to the patterns of prices but also to the collective psychological reactions that fuel such patterns.[16]

If diversity breakdowns occur repeatedly in prices, creating underreaction and overreaction patterns, traders should be able to learn those patterns and dispassionately trade them, thus arbitraging them away. A confluence of forces appears to inhibit such arbitrage. For one, the presence of amateurs in the markets—who are likely to react emotionally—differs over periods. The percentage of professionals versus amateurs changes how prices will react. Second, humans have difficulty learning expected return patterns following gains, and especially, losses. Being active in markets interferes with learning patterns.[17] Third, the patterns emerge from unconscious processes. Traders are unaware that their thinking (and that of others) is biased.

Across stocks there are fairly consistent price patterns of overreaction at horizons less than one month, price momentum due to underreaction for horizons between 3 and 12 months, and price overreaction for periods longer than one year.[18] One obvious question is whether the price patterns described as overreaction and underreaction are really caused by psychological forces. Are traders in fact emotionally overreacting to news, and their subsequent trading creating a pattern in prices? This chapter starts exploring this question by first examining the proximate causes—whether feelings themselves, including those expressed in social media, predict collective buying and selling behavior.

INFORMATION CHARACTERISTICS

Researchers have found that media coverage affects investor sentiment and consequently alters stock returns and trading volumes.[19,20] Furthermore, this relationship is strengthened for young and growth stocks with small capitalization.[21,22] In fact, the impact of media on investor sentiment and stock returns appears prevalent across various asset markets.[23] The predictability of media sentiment on prices has been found to exist since at least 1905.[24] Given the preceding evidence, the next logical question is, what are the characteristics or content of information that affect trader behavior?

Information has many dimensions of meaning beyond sentiment. Characteristics such as information vividness, fluency, and novelty modulate the impact of a message. For example, investors tend to underreact to earnings surprises (which are fairly common) while overreacting after pharmaceutical company product news (which is more dramatic and vivid).[25] In the sports betting market, the more unexpected the ongoing score, the more likely bettors are to overreact in their bets, pushing prices away from actual odds.[26] Novelty is also an important characteristic, but in a surprising way. Prices respond with overreaction (reversals) more after stale news (old news) than after fresh, surprising information. According to professor Paul Tetlock, "Individual investors trade more aggressively on news when news is stale."[27] Based on such findings, it appears that characteristics of information unrelated to sentiment—those which attract or facilitate investor attention such as vividness, fluency, and novelty—exert a significant impact on investor behavior.

A SCARCE RESOURCE

[T]he media can sometimes foster stronger feedback from past price changes to further price changes, and they can also foster another sequence of events ... an attention cascade.
—Robert Shiller, 2015[28]

Unfortunately for investors, attention is a scarce resource, and when attention is consumed by vivid events in the media, it has little availability for focus elsewhere. In a TED talk, psychologist Mihály Csíkszentmihályi, a positive psychology researcher and author of *Flow*, noted that the human brain can only attend to 110 bits of information per second. A conversation consumes about 60 bits and two conversations consume 120 bits, which explains why most humans are unable to track two conversations simultaneously.[29] Such limited attention renders it nearly impossible to simultaneously consider both a potential catastrophe and sunnier possible outcomes in the markets.

A study by Paul Andreassen at Harvard University[30] examined the availability of information and its effect on investing returns. He asked two sets of subjects to manage an identical portfolio of stocks. One group was told to watch certain financial programs, read stock market articles, and stay on top of information regarding their holdings. The other group was explicitly told to avoid all information about their holdings—a news blackout of sorts.

When the gains and losses of the portfolios were later compared, the people who read articles and watched financial news programs did significantly worse compared to those who avoided the media. In fact, in more volatile times the gains of the "nonwatchers" were twice as good. Whether the (supposedly) relevant news was positive or negative made no difference. It wasn't the nature of the news that mattered; it was the consistently inappropriate response to information that proved to be the problem.

What is it about news that interferes with sound investment decisions? News captures attention. Across countries and regions, researchers have found that investors preferentially pay attention to and react to local news that is in their own language.[31] Additionally, investors are more likely to respond to news that is more prevalent (higher volume), leading to higher overall weekly stock returns for companies that are more often in the news with notably high or low sentiment.[32]

The rate of online searches for a company is a proxy for attention. Researchers using Google trends search data found that an increase in search volume predicts higher stock prices over the next two weeks and an eventual price reversal within the year, and it contributes to the large first-day return and long-run underperformance of IPO stocks.[33] Similarly, the frequency of search on Baidu for an individual stock name correlates with short-term outperformance and longer-term underperformance of that stock on the Chinese stock market ChiNext.[34]

Over the long run, stocks that are the most popular among investors—those that garner the most attention—tend to underperform those with less popularity. The effect of popularity is substantial, with the quartile of least popular stocks (least traded) outperforming the quartile of the most popular by more than 7 percent annually between 1972 and 2013.[35] News drives collective behavior, including of investors, but it only does so if they are aware of it. And too often, investors are paying attention to the wrong stocks (the popular ones) in the news. Additionally, news may be provoking inappropriate reactions among investors.

WHAT'S IN A NAME?

What information consumes is rather obvious: it consumes the attention of its recipients. Hence, a wealth of information creates a poverty of attention and a need to allocate that attention efficiently among the overabundance of information sources that might consume it.
—Herbert Simon, Nobel Laureate in Economics[36]

Some stock names are easier to remember than others, and research shows that investors more often invest in equities with catchy (easily remembered) or seductive (exciting) names. This is called the *fluency effect*.

Researchers found that for 296 mutual funds over the period 1994–2001, name changes associated with currently "hot" investment styles prompted increased net fund inflows of 27 percent for the year following the name change. This effect occurred regardless of whether the name change was only symbolic and without any underlying change in investment style or strategy. On average, investors who moved into renamed mutual funds lost money. According to the study authors, it appeared that the name changes were timed to trick investors into expecting better future performance than was actually delivered.[37]

Companies can change their stock tickers to be more compelling, such as Harley Davidson changing from HDI to HOG. Interestingly, such symbol changing stocks have increased returns, versus the overall market, following the change. Examples of evocative stock symbols include LUV for Southwest Airlines, BID for Sotheby's, and EYE for Advanced Medical Optics. From 1984 through 2004, stocks with clever symbols appreciated 23.6 percent compounded annually, compared with 12.3 percent for all stocks on the New York Stock Exchange and NASDAQ.[38] "One possible explanation for the results is that people prefer to work with information they can easily process."[39]

Further evidence for the "irrational" value of names came from a study by Princeton psychologists. They found that a basket of companies with pronounceable stock symbols gained 11.2 percent more in the first day of trading after their initial public offerings (IPOs) than other stocks.[40] "These results imply that simple, cognitive approaches to modeling human behavior sometimes outperform more typical, complex alternatives."[41] Catchy stock symbols and pronounceable names are more mentally accessible as investment decisions are formulated. They provide an easy processing shortcut, are often titillating (novel and rewarding), and are thus more attention-getting and easily available for recall. Beyond the importance of information fluency, researchers have also found that the vividness of information influences investor and market price responses.

"ALL THAT GLITTERS"

> *The psychologists Daniel Kahneman and Amos Tversky have shown when humans estimate the likelihood or frequency of an event, we make that judgment based not on how often the event has actually occurred, but on how vivid the past examples are.*
> —Jason Zweig, *The Intelligent Investor*

Attention is a limited resource, and it is attracted by the emotionally compelling traits of an asset—its *vividness*. The more vivid an event or its potential outcome, the more it influences judgment.

Since many investors observe content from the same limited pool of sources (CNBC, Bloomberg, Reuters, Dow Jones, *Financial Times*), there are often herds of buyers chasing the latest stocks in the news. News outlets such as the television network CNBC create emotionally compelling financial stories in order to engage viewers. One study found that stocks mentioned by journalist Maria Bartiromo on the *Midday Call* on CNBC experience almost fivefold increases in volume in the minutes following the mention.[42] It's not only Bartiromo's show that stokes investor buying.

The CNBC television program *Mad Money* with Jim Cramer creates a large one-day price move for stocks mentioned on the program, and the price move gradually reverses over subsequent weeks. The size of the initial stock price move is correlated with the show's Nielsen viewership ratings, directly demonstrating that the volume of investor attention is correlated with the strength of the price move.[43] In a similar vein, attention around earnings predicts the response of stock prices to earnings news, with greater underreaction among stocks with less investor attention.[44–48]

Finance professors Brad Barber and Terrance Odean found that, over a large sample of brokerage accounts, individual investors are net buyers of attention-grabbing stocks (e.g., stocks in the news, stocks experiencing high abnormal trading volume, and stocks with extreme one-day returns).

The authors analyzed data at two brokerage firms and discovered that stocks bought by individual investors on "high-attention days" (when they are in the news) tended to subsequently underperform stocks sold by those investors. "When calculated by number for the large discount brokerage, buy–sell imbalance is 2.70 percent for stocks out of the news and 9.35 percent for those stocks in the news. At the large retail brokerage, buy–sell imbalance is –1.84 percent for stocks out of the news and 16.17 percent for those in the news."[49]

No matter what the news, investors tend to buy stocks that are in the public eye. Individual investors buy following many attention-getting events: high-volume days, extremely negative and extremely positive one-day returns, and news releases. Investors even increase buying following earnings surprises, regardless of whether they are negative or positive.

While amateurs often fall into the attention-based buying trap, the same cannot be said for professional investors. Odean found that institutional investors (specifically value-strategy investors—presumably more savvy than individual investors) did not exhibit attention-based buying. From the studies above, it appears that most retail investors underperform when trading on news. For professionals, however, understanding shifts of attention opens up interesting opportunities.

PROFITING FROM SOCIAL INATTENTION

Understanding where crowd attention is focused allows fast-acting professionals to reap additional returns from news-based trading. Elijah DePalma, Senior Quantitative Research Analyst at Thomson Reuters, identified such trading strategies utilizing the Reuters newsfeed. He found highly positive and negative articles create trading opportunities for stocks, but they are fairly small. However, when he conditions these opportunities with social media attention to the news (buzz about the news article), he sees a significant boost in observed performance.

DePalma first examined the impact of pre-market news on the opening gap in large U.S. stocks. He found that Reuters news articles with high positive or negative sentiment are correlated with a large opening price gap. He then examined whether social media commentary picked up significantly before and at the time of the article's release. The news impact was modulated by the social media buzz (a proxy for investor attention) around the news release. DePalma notes, "The simple yet profound idea is that Social Media 'Buzz' (a.k.a. volume of chatter) can be used as a proxy for investor attention on news." Figure 3.3 demonstrates that news articles create a larger opening gap for stocks if attention (social media buzz) is focused on that stock.

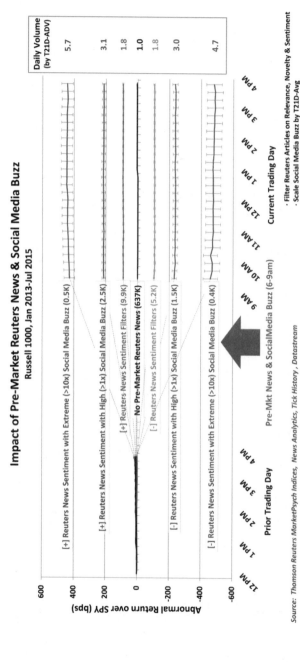

FIGURE 3.3 Price impact of pre-market Reuters news conditioned upon social media buzz.
Source: Thomson Reuters MarketPsych Indices, News Analytics, Tick History, Datastream.

Per DePalma, "The presence of pre-market, breaking Reuters news coupled with pre-market Social Media Buzz leads to significant increases in trading volume and price gaps at market open." This result is of particular interest to market makers, who try to predict daily trading volumes and volatility.

In a second set of research, DePalma found tradeable effects on stock price direction. DePalma identified intra-day Reuters news alerts about mergers, acquisitions, and takeovers (topic code MRG) for S&P 500 companies from June 2014 through May 2015. He aggregated each stock's TRMI social media buzz over a 6-minute window (the minute of the news alert and the trailing 5-minutes around the news event. For the 1178 MRG events identified, he classified the strength of the social media buzz relative to its average level as low (966 events) or high (212 events). He also identified an extreme level of social media buzz as a subset of high buzz (49 events). Figure 3.4 demonstrates the buy-and-hold-average-return (BHAR) to be gained in the minutes before and after the MRG news event.

The price impact following low social media buzz was approximately 15 basis points (0.15 percent). Higher levels of social media buzz preceded an average 40 basis point (0.40 percent) increase in the stock price. A significant average positive drift of 150 basis points (1.5 percent) occurred following the news events associated with extreme spikes in social media buzz (49 total events). The most significant price drift occurs over the 10 minutes following the news release, especially if social media lights up with commentary.

DePalma has preliminary findings that the level of social media buzz around natural gas and crude oil news correlates with the price impact of relevant news. DePalma explained, "By identifying which news items coincide with large spikes in commodities social media buzz I am able to determine whether that news event will impact futures prices over the following 1–3 hours (Crude Oil & Natural Gas)." Short-term momentum traders may benefit from buying on news events conditioned on the volume of attention being paid to them (measured via social media buzz).

Despite DePalma's impressive results, most individual investors trade with longer horizons in mind, and they ought to avoid trading on the news. Longer-term investors who manage their attraction to vivid news and who are prepared to trade against the herd during attention-grabbing events may do better. Most retail individual investors lose money when trading on news. While this chapter examined the role of information characteristics and sentiment in influencing individual financial behavior; the next chapter explores how different types of sentiment systematically influence market prices. Like this chapter, the next chapter reviews significant academic research.

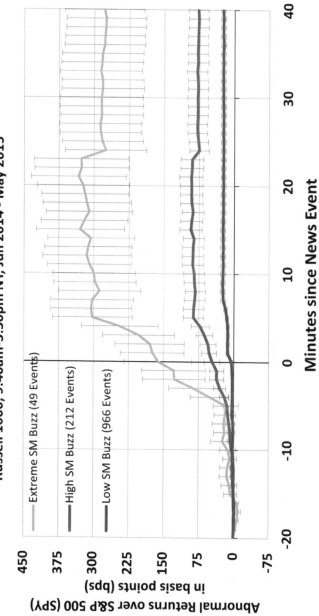

FIGURE 3.4 Price impact of intraday Reuters MRG news alerts conditioned upon social media (SM) buzz.

IN SUMMARY

- The flash crash of May 6, 2010, illustrated how investor emotions, when inflamed by a positive feedback loop between news media and price action, can cascade into market prices.
- The CFTC-SEC reports on the flash crash identified concrete triggers in order to restore confidence.
- Psychology-based price patterns occur when collective investor attention is riveted, causing an attention cascade and a "diversity breakdown."
- Overreaction and underreaction are two types of price pattern reflecting price mean reversion and trends, respectively. Each of these names makes reference to a psychological process driving investor behavior.
- Three cognitive characteristics of information—availability, fluency, and vividness—significantly bias investor judgment.
- Less popular investments outperform those that attract the most attention, implying that attention provokes overreaction in prices.
- News-based trading can be profitable for fast-acting professionals who identify which news articles generate a response from investors in social media.

NOTES

1. "UPDATE 3—Greek Parliament Backs Tough Austerity Bill," Reuters. May 6, 2010, 19:00 PM GMT.
2. SEC, "Preliminary Findings Regarding the Market Events of May 6, 2010." Report of the Staffs of the CFTC and SEC to the Joint Advisory Committee on Emerging Regulatory Issues. May 18, 2010. Downloaded May 20, 2015, from: https://www.sec.gov/sec-cftc-prelimreport.pdf.
3. SEC, "Findings Regarding the Market Events of May 6, 2010." Report of the Staffs of the CFTC and SEC to the joint advisory committee on emerging regulatory issues. Downloaded May 20, 2015, from: https://www.sec.gov/news/studies/2010/marketevents-report.pdf.
4. Ibid.
5. Ibid.
6. Mark Buchanan, "Flash-Crash Story Looks More Like a Fairy Tale," Bloomberg, May 7, 2012. http://www.bloomberg.com/news/articles/2012-05-07/flash-crash-story-looks-more-like-a-fairy-tale.
7. Matt Levine, "Guy Trading at Home Caused the Flash Crash," Bloomberg, April 21, 2015. Downloaded from http://www.bloombergview.com/articles/2015-04-21/guy-trading-at-home-caused-the-flash-crash.
8. U.S. District Court of Northern Illinois, *U.S. Commodity Futures Commission vs. Nav Sarao Futures Limited PLC and Navinder Singh Sarao*, April 17, 2015, http://www.cftc.gov/ucm/groups/public/@lrenforcementactions/documents/legalpleading/enfsaraocomplaint041715.pdf.
9. Sun, L., Najand, M., and Shen, J. (2015). "Stock Return Predictability and Investor Sentiment: A High-Frequency Perspective." Available at SSRN.

10. J. S. Lerner and D. Keltner. "Fear, Anger, and Risk," *Journal of Personality and Social Psychology* 81 (2001), 146–159.

11. Underlying cause of death is defined as "the disease or injury which initiated the train of morbid events leading directly to death, or the circumstances of the accident or violence which produced the fatal injury" in accordance with the rules of the International Classification of Diseases. Retrieved July 20, 2015, from the World Health Organization: http://www.who.int/healthinfo/cod/en/.

12. Daniel Kahneman, *Thinking, Fast and Slow* (New York: Farrar, Straus and Giroux, 2011).

13. Michael Mauboussin, *More Than You Know* (New York: Columbia University Press, 2006).

14. Ibid.

15. Andrew Wen-Chuan, Lo, ed. *Market Efficiency: Stock Market Behaviour in Theory and Practice*, Vol. 3 (Cheltenham, UK: Edward Elgar Publishing, 1997).

16. Barberis, N., Shleifer, A., and Vishny, R. (1998). A Model of Investor Sentiment. *Journal of Financial Economics*, 49(3), 307–343.

17. Kuhnen, C. M. (2014). "Asymmetric learning from financial information." *Journal of Finance*, 70 (5): 2029–2062, October 2015.

18. Hersh Shefrin, *Beyond Greed and Fear: Understanding Behavioral Finance and the Psychology of Investing* (Oxford: Oxford University Press, 2000).

19. Baker, M. and J.Wurgler, "Investor Sentiment and the Cross-Section of Stock Returns," *The Journal of Finance* 61(4), (2006), 1645–1680.

20. Tetlock, P. "Giving Content to Investor Sentiment: The Role of Media in the Stock Market." *The Journal of Finance* 62(3), (2007), 1139–1168.

21. Baker and Wurgler, 1645–1680.

22. L. Fang and J. Peress, "Media Coverage and the Cross-section of Stock Returns," *The Journal of Finance* 64(5), (2009), 2023–2052.

23. Yu Yuan, "Market-Wide Attention, Trading, and Stock Returns," *Journal of Financial Economics* 116(3), (2015): 548–564.

24. Diego Garcia, "Sentiment during Recessions," *Journal of Finance* 68(3) (2013), 1267–1300.

25. Dov Fischer, "Investor Underreaction to Earnings Surprises and Overreaction to Product News in the Drug Industry," *Journal of Business and Economic Studies* 18(2) (2012), 82.

26. Darwin Choi and Sam K. Hui, "The Role of Surprise: Understanding Overreaction and Underreaction to Unanticipated Events Using In-Play Soccer Betting Market," *Journal of Economic Behavior & Organization* 107 (2014), 614–629.

27. Tetlock, Paul C. "All the News That's Fit to Reprint: Do Investors React to Stale Information?" *Review of Financial Studies* 24(5) (2011), 1481–1512.

28. Robert J. Shiller. *Irrational Exuberance* (Prineton, NJ: Princeton University Press, 2015)., pp. 121–122.

29. Mihaly Csikszentmihalyi, "Flow, the Secret to Happiness," TED (February 2004), http://www.ted.com/talks/mihaly_csikszentmihalyi_on_flow?language=en.

30. Paul Andreassen, "Judgmental Extrapolation and Market Overreaction: On the Use and Disuse of News," *Journal of Behavioral Decision Making* 3 (1990), 153–174.

31. Nicky J. Ferguson, "Investor Information Processing and Trading Volume," *Asia-Pacific Journal of Financial Studies* 44(2) (2015): 322–351.

32. Michal Dzielinski, "Abnormal News Volume and Underreaction to Soft Information." In Eds. Gautam Mitra and Xiang Yu, *Handbook of Sentiment Analysis in Finance*. In Press.

33. Zhi Da, Joseph Engelberg, and Pengjie Gao, "In Search of Attention," *The Journal of Finance* 66(5) (2011), 1461–1499.

34. Fang Xianming Yu Jiang and Zhijun Qian, "The Effects of Individual Investors' Attention on Stock Returns: Evidence from the ChiNext Market," *Emerging Markets Finance and Trade* 50(3), (2014), pp. 158–168.

35. Roger G. Ibbotson and Thomas M. Idzorek, "Dimensions of Popularity," *Journal of Portfolio Management* 40(5) (2014), 68–74.

36. Martin Greenberger, "Designing Organizations for an Information-Rich World," *Computers, Communication, and the Public Interest* (Baltimore, MD: The Johns Hopkins Press, 1971), 40–41.

37. M. Cooper, H. Gulen, and P. R. Rau, "Changing Names with Style: Mutual Find Name Changes and Their Effects on Fund Flows." *Journal of Finance* 60(6) (December 2005), 2825–2858.

38. Alex Head, Gary Smith, and Julia Wilson, "Would a Stock by Any Other Ticker Smell as Sweet?" *Quarterly Review of Economics and Finance* 49(2) (2009), 551–561.

39. J. Valentino, "Does Stock by Any Other Name Smell as Sweet?" *Wall Street Journal* (September 28, 2006), p. C1.

40. A. A. Alter and D. M. Oppenheimer, "Predicting Short-Term Stock Fluctuations by Using Processing Fluency," *Proceedings of the National Academy of Sciences* 103: 9369–9372 (published online before print June 5 2006, 10.1073/pnas.0601071103).

41. Ibid.

42. Jeffrey A. Busse and T. Clifton Green, "Market Efficiency in Real Time," *Journal of Financial Economics* 65(3), (2002), 415–437.

43. Joseph Engelberg, Caroline Sasseville, and Jared Williams, "Market Madness? The Case of Mad Money," *Management Science* 58(2) (2012), 351–364.

44. Asher Curtis, Vernon J. Richardson, and Roy Schmardebeck, "Investor Attention and the Pricing of Earnings News," available at SSRN 2467243 (2014).

45. Barbara A. Bliss and Biljana Nikolic, "The Value of Crowdsourcing: Evidence from Earnings Forecasts," available at SSRN 2579402 (2015).

46. Brad M. Barber and Terrence Odean, "All that Glitters: The Effect of Attention and News on the Buying Behaviour of Individual and Institutional Investors," *Review of Financial Studies* 21(2), (2008), 785–818.

47. David, Hirshleifer, James N. Myers, Linda A. Myers, and Siew Hong Teoh, *Do Individual Investors Drive Post-Earnings Announcement Drift?* (Columbus: Ohio State University, 2002).

48. Yu Yuan, "Market-Wide Attention, Trading, and Stock Returns," *Journal of Financial Economics* 116(3), (2015), 548–564.

49. Brad M. Barber and Terrence Odean, "All that Glitters: The Effect of Attention and News on the Buying Behaviour of Individual and Institutional Investors," *Review of Financial Studies* 21(2), (2008), 785–818.

CHAPTER 4

Sentimental Markets

Rothschild coaches careered down highways; Rothschild boats set sail across the Channel; Rothschild messengers were swift shadows along the streets. They carried cash, securities, letters and news. Above all, news—latest, exclusive news to be vigorously processed at stock market and commodity bourse.

—Frederic Morton (1962), "The Rothschilds: Portrait of a Dynasty"

The Rothschild dynasty descended from Mayer Amschel Rothschild. He established an international banking family through his five sons, whom he sent to the five major financial centers of Europe. From London in 1813 to 1815, Mayer's son Nathan Mayer Rothschild was instrumental in almost single-handedly financing the British war effort against Napoleon, organizing the shipment of gold bullion to the Duke of Wellington's armies across Europe. His family's information network provided Nathan Rothschild with political and financial information ahead of his peers, occasionally giving him an information and time advantage in financial markets.

When Wellington fought Napoleon at the Battle of Waterloo in 1815, the outcome of the battle was of extreme importance to securities traders, and news of the battle's outcome was eagerly awaited. Frederic Morton relates the story dramatically in his authorized 1962 biography of the Rothschild family. In Morton's account, the 'Change is the Exchange and consols are British government debt certificates:

> *For days the London 'Change had strained its ears. If Napoleon won, English consols were bound to drop. If he lost, the enemy empire would shatter and consols rise. For thirty hours the fate of Europe hung veiled in cannon smoke. On June 19, 1815, late in*

the afternoon a Rothschild agent named Rothworth jumped into a boat at Ostend. In his hand he held a Dutch gazette still damp from the printer. By the dawn light of June 20 Nathan Rothschild stood at Folkstone harbor and let his eye fly over the lead paragraphs. A moment later he was on his way to London (beating Wellington's envoy by many hours) to tell the government that Napoleon had been crushed. Then he proceeded to the stock exchange.

There are multiple accounts of how the news of Napoleon's defeat reached London.[1] In one, Nathan Rothschild received the news through his network of fast carrier pigeons, which one of his agents released from Waterloo when the battle was known to be won. Once informed of the victory, Rothschild took the information directly to the British government.[2] From there, Rothschild proceeded to the exchange, where he bought British government consols (bonds).

There are many legends surrounding the Rothschild family, and perhaps most are untrue. In the nineteenth century, a legend spread that accused Nathan Rothschild of having used his early knowledge of victory at the Battle of Waterloo to manipulate the market. At that time, investors and financiers were generally scorned (despite their services being essential to the functioning of government). In fact, sentiment about bankers was so negative that some sentiment dictionaries such as the *Harvard General Inquirer,* which was first developed using nineteenth-century British Literature, categorized the words *financier* and *investor* as negative sentiment words.

Morton's authorized biography tells the dramatized legend of Rothschild's trading prowess as if it were truth. As a trader, it's a fascinating story of investing genius. Regardless of its ultimate veracity, it contains useful insights into the role of market perceptions:

> *Another man in his position would have sunk his worth into consols. But this was Nathan Rothschild. He leaned against "his" pillar. He did not invest. He sold. He dumped consols. ... Consols fell. Nathan leaned and leaned, and sold and sold. Consols dropped still more. "Rothschild knows," the whisper rippled through the 'Change. "Waterloo is lost." Nathan kept on selling, his round face motionless and stern, his pudgy fingers depressing the market by tens of thousands of pounds with each sell signal. Consols dived, consols plummeted—until, a split second before it was too late, Nathan suddenly bought a giant parcel for a song. Moments afterwards the great news broke, to send consols soaring.[3]*

Not only did Nathan Rothschild have one of the fastest information networks, he also understood market psychology and was skilled in disguising his intentions. "One cause of his [Nathan's] success was the secrecy with which he shrouded, and the tortuous policy with which he misled those who watched him the keenest."[4] As he was seen on the floor of the exchange selling bonds, he sparked a panic in those traders who imagined Napoleon was on his way across the Strait of Dover. In truth, after his purchase of consols, two years later Nathan Rothschild sold them at a 40 percent profit (with leverage, it was a substantial profit).[5]

Today, as two centuries ago, it is differences in perceptions that give rise to trading opportunities. This legend serves to illustrate that there are two primary ways to profit as an investor: (1) Receive important information faster than others, and (2) know the context of the information. If one understands what the investing herd believes, fears, and expects, then one may predict how the herd is likely to react to new information and events.

Rothschild wasn't the only trader accused of manipulating the herd around highly anticipated events. The *Wall Street Journal* reported on how high-frequency traders (HFTs) manipulate natural gas prices in the low-volume seconds before inventory data releases. This manipulation is called "Banging the Beehive."[6] Anxious traders are led to believe—via aggressive trading by HFTs—that the news has been released (or someone knows more than they) during the moments before the official news release. Pandemonium ensues. Limit orders and stops are hit in the seconds of pre-announcement volatility. Then when the announcement occurs, prices move and quickly stabilize, but the damage has already been done. It's not only events that affect prices; sometimes markets react to invisible information, with traders under the sway of biological forces outside of their conscious awareness.

REFLEXIVITY

[George Soros] realised that investor sentiment didn't affect just share prices, it could actually change economic fundamentals.[7]
—Richard Evans

George Soros is well known not only for the $24 billion net worth he earned through trading (as of 2015), but also for his trading prowess. He also has useful insights into the role of sentiment in driving market prices. Soros asserts that two factors—the complexity of the business world and the fact that it reacts to investor sentiment—lead to inevitable mis-pricings of assets.[8]

Sentiment interacts with stock prices and economic activity through a feedback loop. For example, if stock prices rise because of improved economic sentiment, investors will feel wealthier due to the price rise, and they will be more inclined to spend on consumer items. This spending improves the earnings of companies in various parts of the economy, including retailers and leisure firms. When they report higher earnings, their stock prices will rise, reinforcing the positive sentiment. Positive emotional responses lead to more of the behaviors that contributed to the events that caused the original positive feelings.

That social sentiment impacts asset prices is not only a hypothesis put forward by a great investor empirical evidence now supports it. Studying large datasets, academic researchers have found that group-level shifts in emotional and thought patterns impact market prices, leading to a positive feedback effect. For example, when a country is defeated in a major athletic event, stock prices in that country are directly affected. A loss in a World Cup football (soccer) elimination round leads to an average next-day stock market decline of 0.49 percent in the team's country of origin.[9] While athletic losses are dramatic and rare examples of the power of sentiment to move stock prices, more subtle effects occur regularly.

Humans are profoundly influenced by the natural environment, and nearly 40 percent of daily mood variation can be explained by the weather.[10] Natural influences on market prices arise from six types of environmental events: the degree of daily sunshine versus cloud cover, disruptions in sleep patterns due to daylight savings time shifts, temperature extremes, lunar cycles, electromagnetic storms, and daily wind strength.

Professor Hirshleifer at the Ohio State University found that morning sunshine correlates with stock returns. He examined 26 stock market indices around the globe for the period of 1982 to 1997. He identified the forecast for sunshine versus some cloud cover in the city of a nation's largest stock exchange. "In New York City, the annualized nominal market return on perfectly sunny days is approximately 24.8 percent per year versus 8.7 percent per year on perfectly cloudy days." He cites evidence that sunshine improves investors' moods. When their moods are elevated, investors are less risk averse and are more likely to buy.[11]

Interestingly, changes in market-maker behavior may be the cause of the sunshine effect. Goetzmann and Zhu (2002) analyzed trading accounts of 79,995 investors from 1991 to 1996, and they found that individual investors do not trade differently on sunny days versus cloudy days. However, the bid–ask spread was significantly impacted by the degree of cloud cover: Wider bid–ask spreads on cloudy days were hypothesized to represent risk aversion among market makers. Other researchers discovered that morning cloud cover and wind speed in Chicago correlate with wider bid–ask spreads in the afternoon.[12] The weather in the exchange's home city affects market-maker behavior, but investors in other cities who place orders on the exchange are probably unaffected.

The gradual waxing and waning of daylight as seasons change creates a seasonal pattern in stock prices. Kamstra, Kramer, and Levi (2003) examined stock market performance during the six months between the fall equinox (September 21) and the spring equinox (March 21) for the northern hemisphere and the opposite six-month period for the southern hemisphere. They found that stock markets underperformed in the seasonal summer and outperformed in the winter. As an example, the authors cite the returns of a portfolio invested 50 percent in each of Sydney, Australia (the most southerly major market with the most daylight during the northern winter), and Stockholm, Sweden (the most northerly major market with the most daylight during the summer). From 1982 to 2001, this equal-weighted portfolio earned 13.1 percent annually. If the entire investment followed the darkness across hemispheres, investing in Stockholm from September to March and Sydney from March to September, the annual returns were 21.1 percent (versus 5.2 percent if doing the opposite strategy). The researchers hypothesized that emotional shifts, related to the biology underlying seasonal affective disorder (SAD), alter risk preferences and subsequent investment behavior on a collective level.[13]

It's not only sunlight and season that affect mood and investment behavior. The psychology literature demonstrates a correlation between the two weeks following geomagnetic storms (a surge of ionic radiation from the sun) and signs of depression in the general population. Depression is an emotional disorder characterized in part by risk aversion, and researchers found that severe geomagnetic storms caused global stock market underperformance over the six days following the event.[14]

In addition to sunshine and geomagnetic storms, researchers found that poor sleep quality leads to subpar market returns. In this research, daylight savings time changes are a proxy for sleep disruption (because they cause desynchronosis). Kamstra, Kramer, and Levi (2002) found that on the time-change weekends of daylight savings time there are below-normal stock returns from the Friday market close to the Monday open (two to five times larger than normal). The authors hypothesize that this underperformance is due to impaired judgment secondary to sleep disruption. Expanding this hypothesis, the average weekend desynchronosis may explain the "Monday effect," where prices rise less on average on Mondays than on other days of the week.[15]

There is even a lunar effect on stock prices. Yuan, Zheng, and Zhu (2001) find this effect on stock prices worldwide. The authors report that stock market returns in 48 countries are lower during the days surrounding a full moon than during the days around a new moon. The superior returns around the new moon amount to 6.6 percent annually.[16] The light of the full moon may contribute to more frequent nocturnal awakenings, sleep disruption, and subsequent next-day risk aversion.

These natural market anomalies tell a compelling story about the impact of the natural world on collective investor behavior and market prices. Seasonal and meteorological factors may contribute to market price anomalies via collective changes in emotional states (and thus risk preferences). Importantly, such market patterns are predictable and significant, and they result from unconscious influences on collective behavior. It is the unconscious that both fuels such patterns and renders trading against them so individually challenging.

SENTIMENT

> *Contrariwise, if it was so, it might be; and if it were so, it would be; but as it isn't, it ain't. That's logic.*
>
> —Lewis Carroll

If investors' emotional states (sentiment) can predict market price movements, is there a way of reliably measuring investors' sentiment in advance to predict market prices? The aforementioned research investigated environmental stimuli such as sunlight and magnetism, which are known to influence mood and behavior. In the finance literature, the most widely accepted metrics of sentiment are surveys. Such surveys include the University of Michigan Consumer Sentiment Index (CSI), which is based on a monthly telephone survey of 500 consumers who are asked to answer five core questions, including this one: "Now turning to business conditions in the country as a whole—do you think that during the next 12 months we'll have good times financially, or bad times, or what?"[17] The value of the CSI for predicting longer term asset prices is still debated.

Since 1963, the weekly Investor Intelligence survey has quantified the bullishness of 100 independent financial newsletter writers. This index is the basis for several academic studies, but the overall findings have been unimpressive. Perhaps because of the infrequent nature of these surveys, or the rather subjective construction (surveys or impressions), or the lack of actionable findings, these have not been widely utilized in strategy development.

In academic research, the Baker–Wurgler sentiment index is considered the sentiment gold standard at the time of this writing. This index is a composite for the entire equity market "based on the common variation in six underlying proxies for sentiment: the closed-end fund discount, NYSE share turnover, the number and average first-day returns on IPOs, the equity share in new issues, and the dividend premium."[18] By its nature, this index is limited to a composite view of positive versus negative sentiment across an entire stock market. It is based on market data, but it is complex to construct. According to behavioral finance expert Hersh Shefrin, "Baker–Wurgler sentiment mediates the time series of investors' judgments of expected return and the cross-section of their judgments about risk." Using this sentiment index, Shefrin finds in his research that "investors' judgments of risk and return, both mediated by sentiment, influence market prices."[19] Several significant investment results have emerged from the Baker–Wurgler sentiment index, which are cited in this book.

Other measures of sentiment used by traders include put–call ratios,[20] TRIN (a measure of advancing versus declining issues), VIX (the *fear gauge*),[21] and the commitment of traders (used in commodity markets to detect retail, institutional, and corporate hedging behavior). These metrics are based on past behavior, not current sentiment itself. Nonetheless, they do show some predictive power, especially the commitment of traders report.[22] Some complex models find value in multiple sentiment measures used together.[23] Within this variety of potential sentiment metrics, investor surveys have emerged as the most widely tested, despite their limitations.

Surveys are vulnerable to numerous biases. Researchers found that both newsletter writers[24] and individual investors[25] show increased optimism about future stock market gains (bullishness) following high recent returns. Additionally, as the S&P 500 declined over a 12-month period, investor optimism about the stock market's future declined in tandem with prices. Investors' projections of future market action reflect their feelings about recent price trends. Perhaps paradoxically, Fisher and Statman (2000) noted that the percentage of investors who believed the market was overvalued was correlated with expectations of future returns from 1998 to 2001.[26] That is, even though investors knew that the market was "overvalued," their expectations of future gains actually increased the more they thought it was overpriced. Based on this surprising finding, it appears that investors' intellectual assessment ("overvalued") is decoupled from their underlying feeling of optimism ("it's going up!"). In general, survey-based sentiment levels do appear to be negatively correlated with (and somewhat predictive of) future market price changes, but the magnitude of the excess returns to be gained is not large.[27]

Using a variety of sentiment indexes, academics have found that overall investor sentiment inversely forecasts returns for small stocks[28] and for stocks with high idiosyncratic volatility.[29] These researchers attribute the contrarian relationship to overreaction during periods of high sentiment, which soon reverts. This observation is supported by evidence that the short side outperforms the long side for stock market anomalies that can be arbitraged. The increased profitability of the short side is likely due to greater overreaction to the upside during periods of high positive sentiment.[30] It's not only stock returns that are forecast by investor sentiment. Baker and Wurgler (2012) demonstrate that investor sentiment explains the bond risk premium.[31]

So far this chapter reviewed a variety of sentiment tools and limited evidence that sentiment predicts market prices. The following section explains the sentiment data series most referenced in this book—the Thomson Reuters MarketPsych Indices (TRMI). The TRMI were designed to identify specific market-moving sentiments reflected in news and social media.

UNDERSTANDING MEDIA

Though this be madness, yet there is method in't.
—William Shakespeare, *Hamlet*

Constructing an accurate sentiment index from media—news and social media—requires an intimate understanding of the goals and constraints of communication in each medium. Social media is generally unstructured, opinionated, and unfiltered content. Professional news sources include those with third-party editors and a journalistic responsibility to avoid slanderous or libelous commentary. News journalists ultimately are responsible to their publisher, who in turn is responsible to generate useful or actionable content for readers (true of premium feeds such as Reuters and Bloomberg) or, more commonly, publishers are incentivized to attract eyeballs for their advertisers. Editors and fact-checkers ensure not only that news journalists uphold the brand's journalistic standards, but also that they do not commit libel or publish inaccurate information.

The journalistic brand certifies the credibility of the published content. As a result, people will on average believe the content of articles published under a trusted brand, even if those articles contain dubious content. They offload critical thinking when they trust the source of a news article.[32] This book discusses the financial predictive evidence in the three information types in Table 4.1.

The TRMI data feed was constructed on social and news media due to the large volume of these sources and the presence of established research on both types of media. Beyond the TRMI, results from earnings conference call transcripts, product reviews, and Google Trends (search) data are also cited in this book. There are three broad classes of text information not discussed here, although they also appear to have some merit for trading: corporate press releases (these are predominantly company spin), SEC and

TABLE 4.1 Three Distinct Classes of Investment Media

Information Sources	Distinguishing Characteristics
Professional news	Third-party editors and fact-checkers review content. There is a journalistic and legal responsibility to avoid slanderous or libelous commentary.
Social media	Unstructured, opinionated, and unfiltered content. Often includes argumentation and dialogue.
Earnings conference call transcripts and executive interviews	Initially structured. Also contains a Q&A that contains challenging questions and ad-lib responses.

regulatory filings (these use strict legalistic templates), and financial analyst reports (these contain arguments supporting a specific recommendation). Other promising types of text for which there is little substantive financial markets predictive data include corporate email and text messages.

THE THOMSON REUTERS MARKETPSYCH INDICES

In an era of high-frequency trading, it is differences in perception that offer opportunities.
—John Kay, *Financial Times,* May 28, 2013[33]

In order to derive more insights about sentiment, since 2004 MarketPsych has developed and honed a unique (patented) methodology for extracting detailed, relevant concepts from a variety of business and investment text. At its most basic, such text-analysis software uses an extensive, expert-curated lexicon of English-language words and phrases of potential interest for traders, investors, and economists, which is called a "bag-of-words" approach. Financial domain customization is an important feature of such lexicons, as academics have found significant ambiguity in word meanings across domains of expertise. For example, almost three-quarters of words classified as negative in academic dictionaries such as the *Harvard Psychosociological Dictionary* are not considered negative when used in financial contexts.[34]

Specific lexicons are not useful unless deployed in conjunction with natural language processing software. Such software employs grammatical templates and part-of-speech recognition to extract relationships among concepts. With this custom design, qualities known to influence financial risk taking can be quantified in text. The TRMI data feed is based on such software.

The news media articles processed in order to construct the TRMI include more than 2,000 global sources each with more than 7,000 external web links, which is a measure of credibility and readership. The social media content used in the TRMI is derived from stock forums, tweets, comment streams, and blogs and includes over 700 primary sources. In collecting and aggregating social media, the software does not distinguish by follower count or other influence metrics. All included content is English language only.

References to a broad range of entities are tracked, with commercial publication of data on over 8,000 equities, 52 equity indices, 32 currencies, 35 commodities, and 130 countries. Billions of social media and news articles, dating to 1998, underlie the feed.

The construction of the TRMI using text analytics is not trivial. TRMI is derived using a three-step process. In step 1, the software obtains news and social media articles as quickly as possible. In step 2, the software quantifies various emotions, topics, tones, and macroeconomic concepts. In step 3, the software creates time series to be used in data analysis applications such as quantitative models and charting tools. The infographic in Figure 4.1 simplifies the task undertaken by the analytics software.

The TRMI include sentiment scores along dimensions evident in the affective circumplex depicted in Figure 2.4. In addition, the TRMI include an array of one- and two-directional scores on asset-specific topics. Examples include litigation and layoffs about equities, inflation and budgetDeficit about countries, productionVolume for commodities, and priceForecast for currencies. Finally, MarketPsych's language processing can quantify complex sentiment-topic combinations such as governmentAnger (for countries) and marketRisk (for countries and individual equities). A list of the available TRMI, as well as a detailed description of TRMI construction, is available in Appendix A.

Three key TRMI types are produced for the major tradable global assets:

1. Emotional indexes such as fear, joy, and trust.
2. Fundamental perception indexes, including earningsForecast, interestRateForecast, longShort positioning, and more.
3. Buzz metrics that indicate how much market-moving topics—such as litigation, mergers, and safetyAccident—are being discussed.

Given its coverage of diverse topics, macroeconomic indicators, and sentiments, TRMI data may be used for generating indicators on a broad spectrum of assets. For example, pessimistic and optimistic countries and

The average adult reads 250-300 words per minute.
The average news article length is 1200 words.

1200 / 300 = 4 minutes per article

Big Data: How to read 2,000,000 articles daily?

Traditional
Conventional, small-scale
human monitoring.

Bleeding Edge
LInguistic analysis paired with
behavioral economics for asset and
risk forecasting.

Vast dimensionality

Best human analyst

4,000
sentiments
& topics

40,000
entities and
assets
monitored

200,000
data points
per minute

Extracted from
news and social media

See entity and
asset list below

Real-time analysis of
2,000,000 articles daily

Market Psych's Macro matrix in numbers

Sentiments	Countries	Commodities	Currencies	Stocks
30	130	35	30	8,000

FIGURE 4.1 Infographic explaining large-scale text analytics.

sectors where value and momentum factors differ in impact are evident (Chapters 11 and 12). Sentiment-driven mis-pricings across currencies and commodities are studied (Chapters 20 and 21). And governments can monitor national business risk and economic sentiment using the macroeconomic country-level variables (e.g., Chapter 22). The remainder of this book demonstrates that media-derived sentiment indexes such as the TRMI are opening up a new way of understanding (and profiting in) financial markets.

IN SUMMARY

- Crowds move markets. Such crowds are made up of individuals—individuals who invest, trade, or manage portfolios. Since the trading behaviors of individuals combine to form a market, their collective emotions manifest in observable market behavior.
- Behavioral finance researchers have demonstrated that certain events, social moods, and natural phenomena are correlated with market price patterns.
- Traders have long factored market psychology into their strategies. Baron Nathan von Rothschild is an example of such an investor.
- Academic literature demonstrates how unconscious sentiments predictably affect market prices through the study of environmental phenomena such as, sunshine, seasonality, and sleep disruption.
- Market sentiment indexes have been developed in several variations, with surveys and the Baker–Wurgler sentiment indexes being the most widely utilized.
- The Thomson Reuters MarketPsych Indices (TRMI) were constructed to capture real-time news and social media sentiment about stocks, equity indexes, currencies, commodities, and countries (macroeconomic indicators).

NOTES

1. Lewis Jones, "The News from Waterloo: The Race to Tell Britain of Wellington's Victory by Brian Cathcart, review," *The Daily Telegraph* (29 April 2015).
2. Victor Gray and Melanie Aspey, "Rothschild, Nathan Mayer (1777–1836)," *Oxford Dictionary of National Biography* (Oxford: Oxford University Press, September 2004); online edition, May 2006. Retrieved 21 May 2007.
3. Frederic Morton, *The Rothschilds: A Family Portrait* (London: Secker & Warburg, 1962), pp. 53–54.
4. John Reeves, *The Rothschilds, Financial Rulers of the Nations* (1887), p. 167.
5. Niall Ferguson, *The Ascent of Money: A Financial History of the World* (London 2008), p. 78.

6. Jerry A. Dicolo and Geoffrey Rogow, "Gas Market Stung by Rapid Traders," *Wall Street Journal* (Oct. 16, 2012). Retrieved May 5, 2015, from: http://www.wsj.com/articles/SB10000872396390444657804578053153939092668.

7. Richard Evans, "How to Invest Like ... George Soros," *The Telegraph* (April 8, 2014). Downloaded from: http://www.telegraph.co.uk/finance/personalfinance/investing/10749558/How-to-invest-like-...-George-Soros.html.

8. Evans.

9. A. Edmans, D. Garcia, and O. Norli, "Sports Sentiment and Stock Returns," *Journal of Finance* 62 (2007),1967–1998.

10. M. Persinger and B. F. Levesque, "Geophysical Variables and Behavior: Xii: The Weather Matrix Accommodates Large Portions of Variance of Measured Daily Mood," *Perceptual and Motor Skills* 57 (1983), pp. 868–870.

11. D. Hirshleifer and T. Shumway, "Good Day Sunshine: Stock Returns and the Weather," *Journal of Finance* 58 (3), (June 2003), pp. 1009–1032.

12. P. Limpaphayom, P. Locke, and P. Sarajoti, "Gone with the Wind: Chicago Weather and Futures Trading." 2005 FMA Annual Meeting conference paper. www.fma.org/Chicago/Papers/gloom doom weather futures trading.pdf.

13. M. Kamstra, L. Kramer, and M. Levi, "Winter Blues: A SAD Stock Market Cycle," *American Economic Review* 93(1), (March 2003), pp. 324–343.

14. A. Krivelyova and C. Robotti, "Playing the Field: Geomagnetic Storms and the Stock Market." 2003 Working paper, Federal Reserve Bank of Atlanta.

15. Kamstra, M. J., Kramer, L. A., and Levi, M. D. (2002). "Losing Sleep at the Market: The Daylight Saving Anomaly: Reply." *American Economic Review*, 1257–1263.

16. K. Z. Yuan, L. Zheng, and Q. Zhu, "Are Investors Moonstruck? Lunar Phases and Stock Returns," September 5, 2001. http://ssrn.com/abstract=283156 or http://dx.doi.org/10.2139/ssrn.283156.

17. Question A4. Surveys of Consumers, Questionnaire. The University of Michigan Survey Research Center Institute for Social Research. Retrieved November 12, 2015 from: https://data.sca.isr.umich.edu/fetchdoc.php?docid=24776.

18. Baker, Malcolm, and Jeffrey Wurgler. "Investor Sentiment and the Cross-Section of Stock Returns." *The Journal of Finance* 61, no. 4 (2006), 1645–1680.

19. Hersh Shefrin, "Investors' Judgments, Asset Pricing Factors and Sentiment," *European Financial Management* 21(2) (March 2015), pp. 205–227. Available at SSRN: http://ssrn.com/abstract=2577046 or http://dx.doi.org/10.1111/eufm.12059.

20. Yul W. Lee and Zhiyi Song, "When Do Value Stocks Outperform Growth Stocks?" *Investor Sentiment and Equity Style Rotation Strategies* (January 2003). EFMA 2003 Helinski Meetings. Available at SSRN: http://ssrn.com/abstract=410185 or http://dx.doi.org/10.2139/ssrn.410185.

21. Durand, Robert B., Dominic Lim, and J. Kenton Zumwalt, "Fear and the Fama-French Factors," *Financial Management* 40(2), (2011), pp. 409–426.

22. Devraj Basu and Oomen, C. A. Roel, and Alexander Stremme. "How to Time the Commodity Market," *Journal of Derivatives & Hedge Funds* 16(1), (June 1, 2006), pp. 1–8. Available at SSRN: http://ssrn.com/abstract=910907 or http://dx.doi.org/10.2139/ssrn.910907.

23. Patrick Houlihan and Germán G. Creamer. "Can Social Media and the Options Market Predict the Stock Market Behavior?" In *Proceedings of the 21st International Conference on Computing in Economics and Finance*, Taipei, June 2015. Available at SSRN: http://ssrn.com/abstract=2611210 or http://dx.doi.org/10.2139/ssrn.2611210.

24. R. Clarke and M. Statman. "Bullish or Bearish?" *Financial Analysts Journal* (May/June. 1998).

25. K. Fisher and M. Statman. "Investor Sentiment and Stock Returns." *Financial Analysts Journal* (March/April2000).

26. Ibid.

27. Fisher and Statman, pp. 10–21.

28. M. Lemon and E. Portniaguina, "Consume Confidence and Asset Prices: Some Empirical Evidence," *Review of Financial Studies* 19 (2006), pp. 1499–1529.

29. X. Gao, J. Yu, and Y. Yuan, 2010. "Investor Sentiment and Idiosyncratic Volatility Puzzle." Unpublished Working Paper, University of Hong Kong.

30. Robert F. Stambaugh, Yu Jianfeng, and Yu Yuan, "The Short of It: Investor Sentiment and Anomalies," *Journal of Financial Economics* 104(2), (2012), pp. 288–302.

31. M. Baker and J. Wurgler, "Comovement and Predictability Relationships Between Bonds and the Cross-section of Stocks," *Review of Asset Pricing Studies*, 2(1), (2012), pp. 57–87.

32. M. Deppe, W. Schwindt, J. Kramer, et al. "Evidence for a Neural Correlate of a Framing Effect: Bias-Specific Activity in the Ventromedial Prefrontal Cortex during Credibility Judgments," *Brain Research Bulletin* 67(5), (November 15, 2005): 413–421 (Epub July 25, 2005).

33. John Kay, "Enduring Lessons from the Legend of Rothschild's Carrier Pigeon," May 28, 2013, 5:58 p.m. Retrieved May 5, 2015, from http://www.ft.com/cms/s/0/255b75e0-c77d-11e2-be27-00144feab7de.html#ixzz3S9QOSemU.

34. Loughran, T., and McDonald, B. (2011). "When Is a liability Not a Liability? Textual Analysis, Dictionaries, and 10-Ks." *The Journal of Finance*, 66(1), 35–65.

CHAPTER 5

Finding Signal in the Noise

All through time, people have basically acted and reacted the same way in the market as a result of: greed, fear, ignorance, and hope. That is why the numerical formations and patterns recur on a constant basis.

— Jesse Livermore, *How to Trade in Stocks*, 1940

On August 13, 2007, the *Financial Times* reported that two large hedge funds managed by Goldman Sachs had lost over a quarter of their value in a week, requiring the injection of $3 billion in emergency liquidity. Goldman Sachs's CFO David Viniar stated of the market price gyrations that caused these losses, "We were seeing things that were 25 standard deviation moves, several days in a row."[1] If one assumes that market price changes are normally distributed, which Viniar's risk models did (and is common practice), then a 25-standard-deviation move implies odds comparable to winning the UK lottery 21 times in a row[2] or finding a 30-foot-tall human.[3] The statistical models referenced by Viniar were not only useless, but actually dangerous.

There are several schools of thought on the best modeling techniques for financial data. Nobel Laureate Robert Shiller noted, "Theorists like models with order, harmony and beauty" while "Academics like ideas that will lead to econometric studies." By contrast, behavioral economists speak of the influence of human psychology, and this focus on the softer side can be off-putting to economists. According to Shiller: "People in ambiguous situations will focus on the person who has the most coherent model."[4] This search for coherence often misses the interesting nooks and crannies of financial market behavior, where some actual predictability may lurk.

In the midst of competing views on modeling, the volume of data awaiting analysis is swelling rapidly. IBM estimates that global data volume doubles every 18 months.[5] If computers could make sense of it, then this volume of data would not be problematic. But computers need human assistance to discover truths within this mass of data. Finance is littered with examples of stubborn assumptions, irrelevant correlations, and spurious self-deceptions made by those who wield statistical tools carelessly on large datasets. This chapter begins with an exploration of statistical self-deception. It then focuses in on statistical methods for modeling information flow and, just perhaps, for accurately predicting market prices.

CAN INVESTMENT RESEARCH BE BELIEVED?

> *Most of the empirical research in finance, whether published in academic journals or put into production as an active trading strategy by an investment manager, is likely false.*
>
> —Campbell Harvey and Yan Liu,
> "Evaluating Trading Strategies," 2014[6]

Making predictions is an exercise fraught with risks ranging from biased assumptions to the wielding of inappropriate statistical tools. In precipitating the global financial crisis of 2007–2009, many modelers performed self-serving mistakes. Some advantageously tweaked mortgage-lending models to improve forecasts of individual creditworthiness. Others used inappropriately short data histories in long-term pricing models. Even more employed statistical tools that could not account for tail risk (i.e., VaR models and multiple regressions). These pre-crisis modelers typically used their judgment, but as described throughout this book, human judgment is sometimes subject to biases.

In 2005, Dr. John Ioannidis wrote an academic article that has become the most widely read paper on *PLoS One* (Public Library of Science) and the first to surpass one million views. The paper contains a proof that the majority of published medical research results are false positives (i.e., untrue).[7] Dr. Ioannidis's statistical insights have been extended to finance by Marcos Lopez Del Prado, Campbell Harvey, Yan Liu, and others.[8–11]

If a test result is considered true at a 95 percent confidence interval (two sigma), then that confidence interval must be expanded as additional tests are performed on the dataset to achieve a similar level of confidence that the result is not a random coincidence. Unfortunately, such tightening of significance criteria is often neglected. "[I]n finance, we routinely accept discoveries where the *t*-statistic exceeds two—not five. Indeed, there is a hedge fund called Two Sigma."[12] It is tempting to believe in strategies that do not meet solid statistical thresholds because (1) it is difficult to find novel and outperforming investment strategies, and (2) the thrill of thinking one might have found such a strategy is more compelling than the repeated frustration of intellectual honesty. As a result, investigator biases undermine the applicability of many predictive models.

DATA BIASES

I've often said that, you know, whatever back test you'd like to see, I can certainly produce it for you. If you torture the data long enough, it will basically tell you anything you want ...
—Andrew Lo[13]

Essential to identifying useful predictive relationships in data is avoiding the psychological biases that plague data analysis. The majority of statistical fallacies arise out of the *desire* to find a positive result. The incentive to find a good result often leads to short-cuts in testing hygiene and spurious correlations.

Throughout the twentieth century, a variety of stock market leading indicators achieved notoriety. In the 1920s, the "hemline" indicator was popular. The market was said to rise as the length of women's skirts retreated—this was thought due to liberal attitudes during economic booms. Another, the Super Bowl indicator was so called because the U.S. stock market was said to rise in years that an NFL team won the American football Super Bowl, was 90 percent accurate in predicting the annual stock market direction from 1967 to 1997. However, both the Super Bowl and hemline indicators are random coincidences, the results of overfitting to a limited dataset.

When a function is too closely fit to a limited set of data points, statisticians say that *overfitting* has occurred. Some statistical methods can be so precise and processing power so powerful that, using a historical dataset, analysts can fit virtually every nook and cranny of the data into a statistical model. This model will appear impressively predictive on the in-sample (a.k.a. training) set of data. But when attempting to predict data on which the model wasn't trained (a.k.a. the out-of-sample set), then the forecast will likely be random. John von Neumann, a brilliant mathematician who, among many other accomplishments founded the field of game theory, noted of overfitting: "With four parameters I can fit an elephant, and with five I can make him wiggle his trunk."[14]

Overfitting is a problem that many companies experience when developing text analytics software. In 2010, I met an entrepreneur who had built a predictive model of housing prices based on text analysis. His best single word to predict home prices? The word *Obama*. His model had learned that the frequency of the word *Obama* in the news was a negative predictor of housing prices during its training period from 2005–2009. In subsequent years as the housing market recovered, the word *Obama* became a positive predictor of prices, and his model fell apart. In the text analytics process that underlies the TRMI, most specific nouns were not given sentiment tags. Instead only universal concepts—such as adjectives and nouns with enduring meaning—underlie the indexes.

Another common data analysis bias is throwing away unfavorable data without sound logical reasons. A strategist at a major quantitative asset management firm explained to me that including the financial crisis years in a predictive model was a bad idea: "It'll never happen again, and it ruins all our results, so why include it?" He had extracted those years from his models in order to achieve a better statistical fit, and he will be more vulnerable when the next crisis arrives.

Frustrating to investors, the confusion of statistical significance with practical significance is a significant flaw in many academic papers. If academics have not considered trade execution, timing, liquidity, transaction costs, and other practical matters, then it is unclear if their results are the equivalent of brain candy—fun to contemplate in the moment, but without enduring value.

This book itself exhibits some of the same data biases described in this chapter. Note that transaction costs are not included in the equity curves in this book, due to the large number of assets examined, and each model should be judged with that constraint in mind. For the most part, the assets studies include only liquid investments with relatively low transaction costs, except where noted. Furthermore, this book presents many of the best results, while volumes of weak results were excluded.

In order to establish the robustness of the results presented in this book, they are validated with out-of-sample sets and forward tests when possible. Additionally, each model is supported by anecdotal historical observation (thus accounting for the numerous historical quotes in the book) as well as psychological research on information processing biases. Finally, they were tested with several tweaks in statistical parameters and methodology. If a model held up through various stress tests, it was considered a worthy finding.

NONLINEAR CHARACTERISTICS

> *[Social scientists'] statistical tools do not work for what we call fat tails, as defined as something prone to black swan events. They can write whatever narrative they want. But we call that journalistic. That's not statistical.*
>
> —Nassim Taleb[15]

Models directing the flow of trillions of dollars in capital are based on linear predictive models. Linear predictive models assume normal (Gaussian) distributions of prices and information, and they are the basis for the most widely used statistical risk models in finance (e.g., VaR models). Some pundits attribute the financial crisis in part to faulty assumptions of normality, as models built with this assumption encouraged investors to pile into AAA-rated mortgage bonds and their derivatives as safe assets. Unfortunately the foundations of those models—the assumptions of human rationality and the linear behavior of market prices—stand on behavioral quicksand.

Academic researchers have found that asset price returns are distributed with fat tails, meaning that large declines (especially), but also large gains, happen more frequently than would be expected from a normal probability distribution. Such large gains and declines are nonlinear events, because they occur in a fashion that is incompletely modeled with linear tools such as regression.

Markets can be considered nonlinear systems because price action is not directly proportional to the information content coming into the market. For example, sometimes a stock will rally and stay up after a positive earnings surprise. Other times, in seemingly the same circumstances, the price will fall due to the high expectations already in the market before the event. It is very difficult to model financial markets when so many types of information—past price action, economic activity, earnings, interest rates, sentiment, context, market expectations, etc.—influence prices. The predictive variables behind valuable price patterns—those influenced by a convergence of multiple factors—are easily buried in the noise when linear modeling techniques are used.

Information is obtained by investors and hits the market in bursts and spikes. Visualization of sentiment data helps to put this reality into perspective. In 2013 the Turkish lira occupied little attention from the media. The Turkish lira declined in January 2014, following on the escalating Gezi Park protests of the preceding year. When the inept government response to the protests coupled with corruption revelations created economic and political instability in Turkey, the currency declined and the international business media increased coverage of the currency more than 20-fold. A chart of the Turkish lira versus the media buzz about that currency is depicted in Figure 5.1.

Like a forest that has been growing without periodic fires, after a lengthy period of calm in markets, when fear catches on, it may burn ferociously hot and fast. As seen in Figure 5.1, the value of the Turkish lira recovered substantially in the year after the panic (and later fell again). Of note to modelers of sentiment data, price returns become more predictable, and mean reversion becomes more likely, when fear is high.

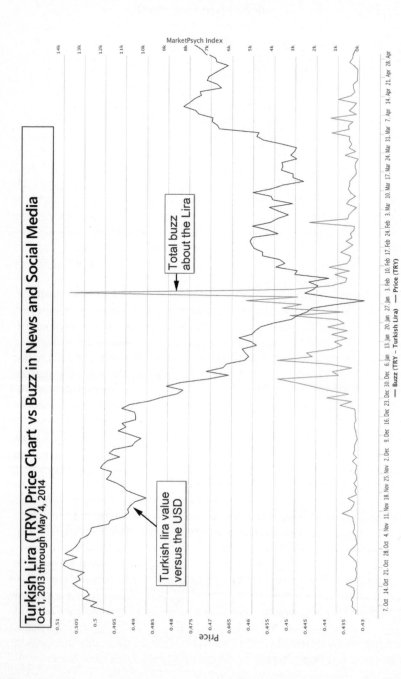

FIGURE 5.1 An image of the Turkish lira (TRY) price (dark line) versus the Buzz TRMI from October 1, 2013, through May 4, 2014.

Histogram of Fear Values

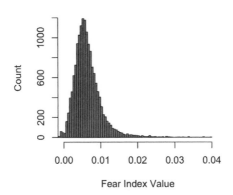

Fear Index Value

FIGURE 5.2 Histogram of daily Fear TRMI values for individual stocks from 1998 to 2015.

Fear is not an uncommon phenomenon across stocks. Figure 5.2 displays the distribution of fear as a percentage of all conversations about highly discussed stocks—those with a buzz value greater than 500 in a day. The values to the right demonstrate the "long tail" in the fear distribution.

Some stocks in Figure 5.2 experienced fear at 2 percent (0.02 on the x-axis) of all meaningful conversations in one day, which is approximately four times larger than the median level of fear. The gap is equivalent to the emotional difference between caution and terror. Caution does not lead to significant changes in behavior, but terror certainly does. On the left side of the distribution are stocks with very low expressed fear, including a few with negative fear. Negative fear is possible when most conversations regarding fear included negated expressions such as, "I'm not worried," or, "Their bad earnings don't scare me." Negated expressions count as negative values on unipolar (0 to 1) indexes.

It's not only emotions that affect price behavior. Extreme events may shift fundamentals. Severe weather, and its potential effects on commodity demand, is one example. During the series of polar vortices across the eastern and northern United States during the winter of 2013–2014, concerns arose about a shortage of natural gas for heating homes. Natural gas prices predictably rose in response to speculation of such a shortage. Figure 5.3 is a chart of the event using two moving averages of the supplyVsDemand TRMI.*

In Figure 5.3 a decreased supply of natural gas is increasingly discussed in the media. Shortage chatter reaches a crescendo in which the price of

---

*The supplyVsDemand TRMI is unique to commodity assets.

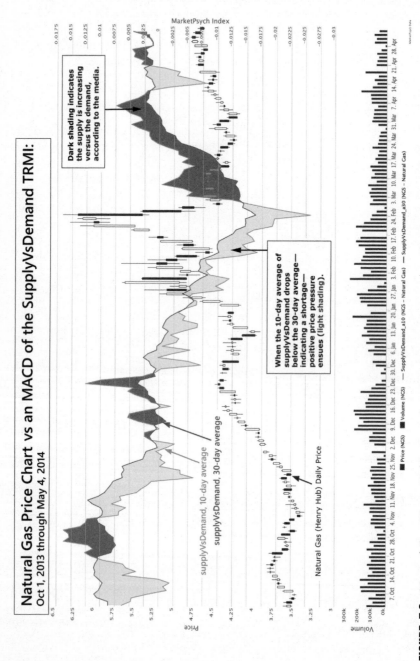

FIGURE 5.3 Natural Gas (Henry Hub) prices plotted against MACD 10–30 supplyVsDemand TRMI averages, October 1, 2013, to May 4, 2014.

natural gas has nearly tripled from its level four months prior. When the shortage conversations slowed, prices plunged. Figures 5.1, 5.2, and 5.3 demonstrate how significant events lead to spikes in sentiment data. Additional dynamics in the data are of interest to modelers, including differences between news and social media, seasonalities, and correlations.

EXPLORING SENTIMENT DATA

Sometimes social media sentiment data do not agree with news sentiment. Figure 5.4 displays two 500-day moving averages of the Sentiment TRMI for the US500 stocks. The US500 represents the largest 500 U.S. stocks by market capitalization point-in-time from 2006, and it was designed as a proxy for the S&P 500. One sentiment average is displayed for news and one for social media. These sentiment averages are plotted from 1998 to July 2015 with the weekly candlestick prices of the S&P 500.

Figure 5.4 shows that news sentiment occasionally diverges from social media sentiment. For example, while news sentiment about the US500 companies made frequent new highs after 2010, social media started at a very high level in 1998, and it only passed its tech-bubble level of sentiment in 2014, approximately coincident with the Nasdaq revisiting the price highs of the Internet bubble years.

It's not only during bull and bear markets that media sentiment changes. Figure 5.5 demonstrates seasonality in social media optimism. The plot was generated by fitting a line (light gray) to monthly average optimism from 1998 to 2014 (17 years). The horizontal dark lines represent the average level of optimism in a given month across all years.

Optimism has a clear seasonal pattern with a November peak, a springtime plateau, and a gradual slide from April into August. Over the 17 years studied, several crises occurred near the climax of pessimism in September, including the Russian debt default in 1998, the September 11 attacks in 2001, and the failure of Lehman Brothers (and other financial institutions) in 2008.

A correlation matrix is a simple technique for viewing how TRMI relate to one another in a linear fashion. The correlation matrix in Figure 5.6, with selected US500 TRMI (combined from both news and social media), demonstrates how many TRMI share valence values.

Positive correlations are shaded dark gray, while negative correlations are shaded more lightly. Sentiment, optimism, priceDirection, and marketRisk are correlated, while sentiment is inversely correlated with gloom, stress, and fear. Despite their correlations, each of these indexes conveys a different meaning. For example, sentiment is qualitatively different

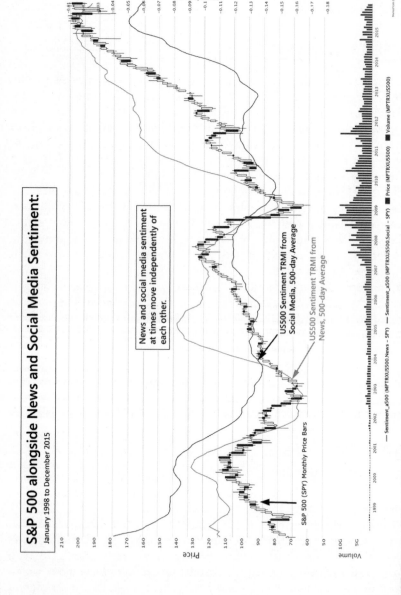

FIGURE 5.4 Weekly S&P 500 candlestick prices versus two 500-day moving averages of the US500 Sentiment TRMI for news and social media.

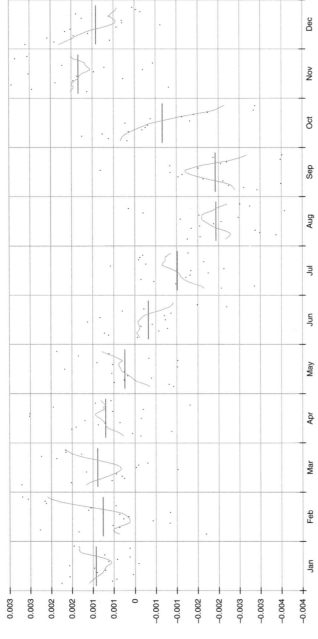

FIGURE 5.5 Monthly expressions of optimism in social media for the S&P 500. Horizontal bars represent the monthly 17-year average optimism. Wavy lines represent the month-by-month optimism from 1998 to 2014.

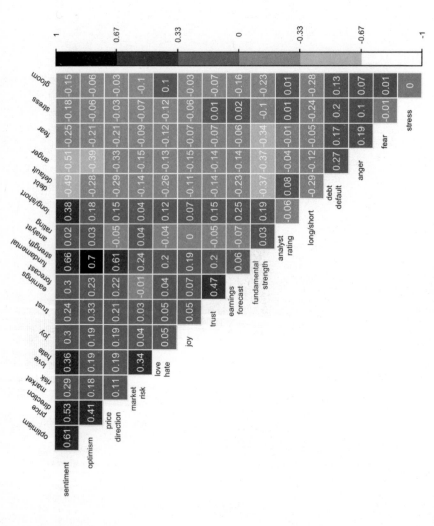

FIGURE 5.6 Correlation matrix for selected daily S&P 500 (US500) TRMI.

from speculative attitudes (marketRisk), which are themselves unique from references to the asset's price rising versus falling (priceDirection). There may be useful information in the deviations between such indexes.

STATISTICAL MODELS

Even if the market is efficient most of the time, we need to worry about the times when it is not. Academics and economists need to deal with the world as it is, not the world that is easily modeled.
—Economist[16]

Most of the studies in this book use the statistical tool R, its free libraries, and custom code. Other statistical tools of value include Python, MatLab, C++, and even Microsoft Excel. When deployed with sentiment data, some statistical techniques consistently show useful out-of-sample results across assets. Based on personal experience, regressions (OLS, bin, rolling), back-propagation neural networks (simple), support vector machines, and genetic algorithms yield inferior out-of-sample results in forecasting models using TRMI data. The techniques that the MarketPsych team identified as best capturing value in sentiment data include cross-sectional ranking models, decision trees, and moving average crossovers.

CROSS-SECTIONAL MODELS

Cross-sectional models examine the performance of tiers of assets over time. These models are also known as quantile or extremity rotational models, and they are frequently used in finance research. In an example from price momentum research, a stock portfolio is formed by first identifying the price performance of all stocks in the sample over a prior period of time. The stocks are then ranked by their historical performance, and a fixed percentage (top decile, for example) are bought, while the bottom decile (worst performers) are shorted. An equity curve is calculated as the positions go forward in time. After the period ends, the process of ranking and simulating investment in the top and bottom deciles is repeated. Rank, roll forward, and repeat, again and again, to the end of the study period.[17]

Using sentiment data instead of past price performance, a cross-sectional strategy ranks assets according to their average sentiment values. The equity curve in Figure 5.7 represents the returns generated by a cross-sectional rotation model applied to all U.S. stocks over a yearly time period for the Sentiment TRMI derived from the combination of both news and social media.

FIGURE 5.7 An equity curve derived by arbitraging the weekly average media Sentiment TRMI for individual U.S. stocks.

The top 20 stocks by buzz are selected for a given week. Those top 20 stocks are then ranked by their average value on the Sentiment TRMI over the study period. Absent sentiment values are not considered. The daily TRMI arrive at 3:30 p.m. New York time, 30 minutes before the close of stock trading on the NYSE. The top quartile (five stocks) are bought, and the bottom quartile (five stocks) are shorted on Friday market close. Those positions are held for one week, until the following Friday close, when the operation is repeated. The prior week's picks are exited, and new positions are entered. Zero transaction costs are assumed, and there is up to 100 percent turnover each week.

The equity curve in Figure 5.7 depicts a volatile 17-fold return from 1998 through July 31, 2015 for this simple strategy. The x-axis is time in years, and the y-axis is the appreciation of 1 dollar (the starting value) equally distributed among the positions: 20 percent in each of five long positions and 20 percent in each of five short positions, with 10 positions total and 200 percent of capital deployed, 100 percent long and 100 percent short.

Each cross-sectional equity curve described in this book was constructed in a similar fashion, but with variations in the minimum buzz limit, holding period, and the number of positions taken. The notation in the chart's title of "PnL (Sentiment -5/+5/20/W/US)" is aligned with a standard notation used in this book, where equity curve titles consist of Profit and Loss (PnL): (Source TRMI +long/-short/buzz filter/time period/country 2-letter ISO country code if equities). Note that when the source is news, the Source field indicates "News Media," and if social media, "Social Media" is written. If the source is the combination of both news and social media, as it is in Figure 5.7, no source is listed. TRMI refers to the single index tested. The next entries (-5/+5) refer to the direction and numbers of positions reweighted periodically. The leading −sign indicates the strategy shorts the five assets top ranked by average Sentiment TRMI. The buzz filter is the number of stocks ranked by buzz included in the analysis (20). The next field refers to the duration of both past TRMI averaging and future holding period, where durations are D for daily, W for weekly, M for monthly, and Y for yearly.

As far as the mechanics of each cross-sectional model, after each day the positions are reweighted to equal weighting. After each period the entire portfolio value is reinvested. Zero transaction costs, a highly impactful and unrealistic assumption, are factored in. Based on the equity curve in Figure 5.7, buying the most-talked-about stocks about which the media reports negative sentiment in a given week and shorting those with the most positive sentiment generates a sentiment arbitrage with overall positive but volatile returns. This strategy historically generated a positive equity curve because it, on average, identified stocks whose prices were likely to mean-revert over the following week. Mean reverting weekly stock patterns are described in detail in Chapter 8.

Cross-sectional models are featured in this book because of their simplicity. Cross-sectional models produce results that are often intuitive and aligned with historical market wisdom. Yet most sentiment indexes yield random results using this technique. Smoother and exponentially increasing equity curves give greater confidence in their validity.

DECISION TREES

Decision trees are a natural choice for modeling and predicting human choice behavior in markets. Decision trees resemble the process of human decision making. There are many varieties of decision trees, including random forest decision trees, classification trees, and association rules. To avoid overfitting, it is important to restrict the tree layers to a small number.

When applied to sentiment data, the association rule style of decision trees[18] appears most useful. Association rules are simple logical relationships. If the criteria in the association rule are met, then a prediction is made. An example association rule format follows:

1. If Fear > 0.9 (top 90th percentile of fear values), AND
2. Price < −0.1 (price has dropped more than 10 percent), THEN
3. Buy stock and hold for 5 days.

Such rules are selected by examining the thousands of times that stocks previously met these criteria. If the average return was acceptable, then such a rule may be selected for further analysis.

If the average risk-adjusted returns of data-mined rules are favorable in the training period, then further out-of-sample testing and human review may be performed. A human will examine the rule, and if it appears sustainable, universal, and generalizable, then it may be fit for forward testing (running it live in simulation) and ultimately, for use in trading.

MOVING AVERAGE CROSSOVERS

Moving averages are smoothed averages of data. When a noisy daily data series is smoothed with an average, trends may be visualized. When two moving averages—a longer term and shorter term one—are superimposed on a chart, gaps appear between them. The gaps represent recent changes in the values of the short-term versus the long-term averages. If a hugely positive earnings surprise occurs for a stock, the short-term sentiment average will increase more than the longer-term average. The gaps that form between the two averages are useful indicators of recent sentiment shifts, and they are less noisy (random) than plotting day-to-day fluctuations.

Academic literature shows mild support for using moving average crossovers (MACDs) of past price averages in forecasting future price direction, with a 200-day average being fairly standard.[19] MACDs can be used both to identify reversals from extremes as well as for following gradual trends. Figure 2.1 in Chapter 2 is an example of a MACD of sentiment about the US500 (a S&P 500 proxy), and it suggests value in predicting both important turning points as well as trends. Note that the number of trades resulting from the model in Figure 2.1 is too few for its outperformance to be considered statistically significant.

CAN SENTIMENT BE TRUSTED?

While trading MarketPsych's hedge fund, we adopted numerous data-mining hygiene techniques to avoid extracting false positives, including: rigorous data exploration of the training set only; using multiple out-of-sample sets and k-fold cross-validation; utilizing universal concepts and language in our concept dictionaries; visual inspection of output; and using a human filter to exclude strategies that are not empirically supported or based on "common sense." We are confident in the validity of our statistical hygiene and testing techniques because of these efforts to debias. However, without real-time performance and common-sense explanations, it is difficult to establish the robustness of quantitative sentiment-based investing strategies. To address these concerns, we have (1) an independently audited track record from our hedge fund, (2) live forward-tested strategies launched online in 2013, and (3) empirical support for the validity of our strategies from psychological research. Furthermore, we are occasionally emailed positive equity curves from happy clients. Each of those factors increases confidence, but nonetheless, modeling is very difficult to get right.

By extensively analyzing the TRMI dataset, several rules of thumb have been identified about media-derived sentiment data. For example, MarketPsych data scientists found that adaptive classification models which overweight recent data have more predictive power in out-of-sample sets. Additionally, models which select the best performing indexes (rather than selecting all TRMI) show superior performance. Furthermore, when examining TRMI with little activity, superior results are achieved when higher overall buzz levels are required (e.g., of 500 or more daily buzz). This last point explains the success of cross-sectional models that require a minimum buzz threshold, as will be seen in subsequent chapters.

Sentiment data is not simple to work with, and there is thus a temptation to overfit models, to throw out odd data, and to ignore practicalities such as transaction costs. Further, many statisticians have been trained to use only a few types of statistical modeling, most of them linear. Sentiment data are nonlinear, and modeling such data successfully requires an understanding of event impact, information flow, and herd information processing. The remainder of this book explores the predictive insights generated through the application of appropriate statistical tools to sentiment and information flow data.

IN SUMMARY

- Analyst biases often interfere with optimal predictive modeling of financial data.
- Most models in empirical finance are based on false assumptions, do not meet sufficient confidence intervals, or are overfit.
- Media-derived sentiment data are nonlinear, and they are characterized by data spikes and fat tails.
- The TRMI have numerous idiosyncrasies such as differences between news and social media derived data, spikes, seasonalities, and correlations.
- Optimal statistical techniques for finding predictive value in sentiment data include cross-sectional models, decision trees, and moving average crossovers.

NOTES

1. W. Bonner, "Goldman Sachs Fund Loses 30% Percent, Wall Street Math Fails to Predict Future," *The Daily Reckoning* (August 16, 2007). www.dailyreckoning.com.au/wall-street-math/2007/08/16/.
2. K. Dowd, J. Cotter, C. Humphrey, and M. Woods, "How Unlucky Is 25-sigma?" (Nottingham, UK: Nottingham University Business School, March 24, 2008). www.ucd.ie/bankingfinance/docs/wp/WP-08-04.pdf.

3. Buttonwood. "What's Wrong with Finance," *The Economist* (May 1, 2015). Downloaded August 10, 2015 from: http://www.economist.com/blogs/buttonwood/2015/05/finance-and-economics.

4. Ibid.

5. "Demystifying Big Data." IBM. Downloaded August 10, 2015, from: http://www-01.ibm.com/software/data/demystifying-big-data/.

6. C. R. Harvey and Y. Liu, "Evaluating Trading Strategies" (August 25, 2014). 2014b. Available at SSRN: http://ssrn.com/abstract=2474755 or http://dx.doi.org/10.2139/ssrn.2474755.

7. J. P. Ioannidis, "Why Most Published Research Findings Are False," *PLoS Medicine* 2, e124 (2005), pp. 694–701.

8. M. López de Prado, "What to Look for in a Backtest," Working paper, Lawrence Berkeley National Laboratory, 2013, http://papers.ssrn.com/sol3/papers.cfm?abstract_id=2308682.

9. Harvey and Liu, "Evaluating Trading Strategies."

10. C. R. Harvey and Y. Liu, "Backtesting," Working paper, Duke University, 2014a. Available at http://papers.ssrn.com/sol3/papers.cfm?abstract_id=2345489.

11. David H. Bailey, Jonathan M. Borwein, Marcos Lopez de Prado, and Qiji Jim Zhu, "The Probability of Backtest Overfitting," *Journal of Computational Finance* (Risk Journals), (February 27, 2015). Available at SSRN: http://ssrn.com/abstract=2326253.

12. Harvey and Liu, "Backtesting."

13. Michael W. Covel, *Trading the Trend (Collection)* (FT Press, 2012), pp. 272.

14. Attributed to von Neumann by Enrico Fermi, as quoted by Freeman Dyson in "A Meeting with Enrico Fermi" in *Nature* 427 (22 January 2004), p. 297.

15. Justine Underhill, "Nassim Taleb: World Is Not More Peaceful," Yahoo Finance (May 19, 2015). http://finance.yahoo.com/news/nassim-taleb-on-the-black-swans-of-war-194841536.html.

16. Buttonwood. "What's Wrong with Finance," *Economist* (May 1, 2015). http://www.economist.com/blogs/buttonwood/2015/05/finance-and-economics.

17. Yongchang Feng, Rong Chen, and G. W. Basset, "Quantile Momentum," *Statistics and Its Interface* 1 (2008), pp. 243–254. Retrieved May 20, 2015, from: http://stat.rutgers.edu/home/rongchen/publications/08SII_Q_MoM.pdf.

18. http://cran.r-project.org/web/packages/arules/vignettes/arules.pdf.

19. Mebane T. Faber, "A Quantitative Approach to Tactical Asset Allocation," *Journal of Wealth Management* (Spring 2007). Available at SSRN: http://ssrn.com/abstract=962461.

PART
Two

Short-term Patterns

CHAPTER **6**

Information Impact

Buys and sells are decided on emotion, not logic.
—Munehisa Homma, 1755[1]

Baron Nathan von Rothschild was not the first investor to use rapid long-distance communications to receive breaking news. During the reign of the Tokugawa family (1615–1867), Osaka, Japan, rose to become a key Asian commercial center, and merchants came to dominate the city's social scene. Commercial activity was so prevalent and socially sanctioned that people would sometimes greet each other with the question, "Are you making a profit?"

Osaka's Dojima Rice Exchange counted 1,300 rice dealers. Only physical rice was traded in Osaka's Dojima rice market until 1710, when a market emerged in which coupons, promising delivery of rice at a future time (futures contracts), were issued. Trading of futures coupons generated an active secondary market.

One of the greatest rice speculators of this time was Munehisa Homma (1724–1803). Homma was nicknamed the "god of the markets," and he was the wealthiest individual in Edo-era Japan, earning the equivalent of an estimated $10 billion to $100 billion via trading rice contracts and in business operations as a market maker.[2] He served as a financial advisor to the Tokugawa Shogunate, and he was named an honorary Samurai.

Homma wrote extensively about technical analysis, and he was the original developer of candlestick price charting. In 1755, Homma wrote (三猿金泉秘録,*The Fountain of Gold—The Three Monkey Record of Money*), with meaningful references to market psychology.[3] Homma noticed that traders' emotions significantly influenced the price of rice, and "the psychological aspect of the market was critical to his trading success."[4] Homma was also a student of fundamentals, but he noticed that often market prices did not reflect fundamental forces. He wrote, "Prices do not reflect actual value." He explained—with a classic contrarian observation: "When all are bearish, there is cause for prices to rise. When everyone is bullish, there is cause for the price to fall." Homma understood the importance of market information, its effect on crowd psychology, and the value of a contrarian outlook.[5]

The two major rice markets of Homma's time were in Osaka and Sakata, 600 km apart. Homma established a personal network of flag-signaling men stationed on rooftops approximately every 4 km between Sakata and Osaka to communicate market prices and facilitate a price arbitrage operation. Homma's most distinct advantage was information speed. His signaling network allowed him to rapidly arbitrage price differentials between rice markets and act as a market maker. Like Rothschild, Homma took advantage of both his information advantage and his understanding of market psychology.

As Homma, Rothschild, and today's high-frequency traders demonstrate, the greatest trading advantage is obtained with faster information flow. Yet much market moving information is conveyed in text, and as a result, many traders and market makers utilize real-time text analysis of news and social media to identify breaking high-impact news. Beyond the immediate impact of the facts in news, the tone of media and the expectations it sets are also influential on prices. And in addition to breaking news, broad changes in social media sentiment also correlate with future price action. This chapter examines the impact of short-term information flow such as that exploited by Homma, but with a modern twist—from millisecond trading on government data releases to daily swings in Facebook's Gross National Happiness.

THE NEED FOR SPEED

In the competitive business of ultra-high-frequency trading, speed and strategy fuel success. The names of the execution algorithms used by such traders—for example, *snipers, sniffers,* and *guerillas*[6]—reflect the highly competitive battle for each tick. *Algo wars* is a term coined to describe the expensive arms race for quicker information retrieval, greater processing power, superior message routing, and faster execution. On the competitive landscape of the algo wars, information retrieval is the prerequisite for all other activities. Without superior information, there is no value in higher speeds.

News providers such as Dow Jones and Thomson Reuters provide rapid releases of scheduled government data for algo warriors. Such data include unemployment statistics from the Labor Department and economic announcements. Because they are so valuable, these releases are scheduled and tightly choreographed. In order to transmit the data as rapidly as possible, reporters carry simple push-button circuits to send data at the moment a "lock-up" (press blackout) ends. The data is provided by the U.S. government to eager journalists, and it travels over dedicated high-speed networks from Washington, D.C., to New York City. It is then routed on to high-frequency trading clients.

It's not only macroeconomic data that is valuable at speed. A sentiment index—the University of Michigan Consumer Sentiment Index is received by Thomson Reuters' customers at 9:55 a.m. Eastern Time (ET), 5 minutes before the public press release at 10:00 a.m. ET. Some Thomson Reuters customers subscribed to receive the monthly survey results 2 seconds earlier than others, at 9:54.58 a.m. ET. When news of this information advantage caused a media uproar in 2013, the New York Attorney General requested a halt to the practice, and Thomson Reuters complied.[7]

The monthly nonfarm payroll numbers from the U.S. Labor Department factor into Federal Reserve (Fed) decisions to adjust monetary policy (interest rates). The Fed's decisions directly affect the prices of the most liquid asset markets in the world—the U.S. dollar and U.S. dollar–denominated bonds. Having a speed advantage in receiving and processing the nonfarm payrolls data release is thus potentially lucrative for high-frequency traders.

Elijah DePalma analyzed the millisecond impact of the nonfarm payrolls (NFP) release on the U.S. dollar future contract (DXZ4) on one day—December 5, 2014. A minutely chart of the December dollar index future contract in Figure 6.1 shows that the price impact was nearly instantaneous with the news release.

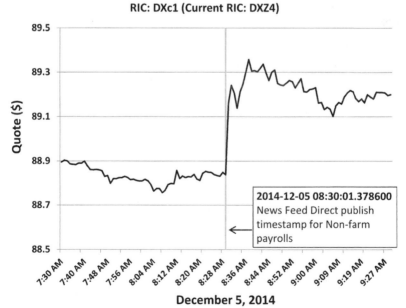

FIGURE 6.1 The impact of nonfarm payrolls on the U.S. dollar futures contract over minutes.
Source: Elijah DePalma PhD, Thomson Reuters, Personal Communication.

Dr. DePalma notes that on December 5, 2014, $5.7 million of USD contracts (DXZ4) were traded within 63 milliseconds of the NFP release, and $29 million was transacted within 100 milliseconds. On the one-second chart in Figure 6.2, the gray vertical line represents the moment of the NFP data release through Thomson Reuters, while the black bars are transaction volume on the DXZ4 contract in the milliseconds following.

Data such as nonfarm payrolls is numeric and structured data. The high-frequency trading computers processing such data use mathematical models to rapidly determine optimal positioning. Within microseconds preferred positioning is identified and trades are placed. Such structured, scheduled data can be easily understood by a machine, in contrast to the valuable information carried in press releases, news alerts, social media, and other text sources, which is more difficult—but still possible—for machines to process.

Information conveyed in text is called *unstructured data*. Although it is difficult to computationally determine the best course of action using unstructured data within milliseconds, it is not impossible. Technologists have figured out how to quantify and trade on some clearly meaningful corporate topics (e.g., bankruptcies, mergers) as well as political events (e.g., bombings).

BANKRUPTCY DEJA VU

Major news agencies not only compete to break macroeconomic data, they also sell millisecond-time-stamped breaking news. Such low-latency (ultra-fast) news delivery has been a robust part of trading since the mid-2000s. News providers label articles with sentiment scores and topics in a machine-readable fashion. Vendors in this space include Thomson Reuters News Analytics, RavenPack (republishing Dow Jones and Associated Press content), and Bloomberg. Beyond the major news vendors, some financial firms, such as Blackrock, collect and scan unstructured text for words and stories that suggest a clear market impact. Breaking news, filtered through text analytics algorithms, may be used to alert human or machine-traders to an important story. Based on the prevalence of such data services, it makes sense that evidence of the market impact of news-reading robots is increasing.

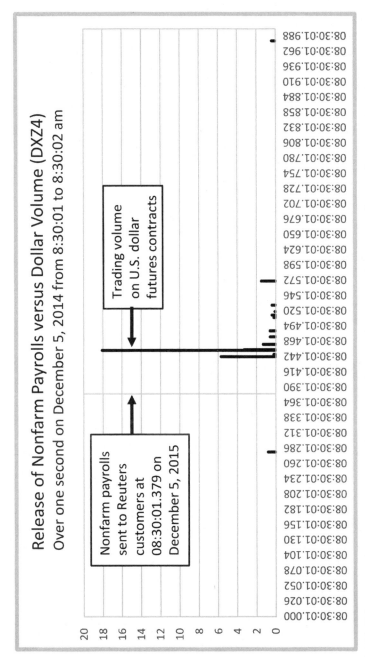

FIGURE 6.2 The impact of nonfarm payrolls on the U.S. dollar futures contract over milliseconds.
Source: Elijah DePalma PhD, Thomson Reuters, Personal Communication.

On September 8, 2008, a *South Florida Sun-Sentinel* article reported on a bankruptcy filing by United Airlines (UAUA). The article was picked up by the live Google News aggregator and republished widely. A human editor at Bloomberg was alarmed by the article, and quickly selected it to be distributed onto the Bloomberg news feed. The editor published the article over the Bloomberg at 10:53 a.m. Figure 6.3 depicts the intra-day price response in UAUA (United Airlines) stock.

High-frequency traders performing text analytics on the Bloomberg newswire may have sold shares and pressured down the price of UAL within seconds, with human traders following suit. Trading in United Airlines' stock was halted minutes later at 11:06 a.m. ET.

Ironically, the *South Florida Sun-Sentinel* article reporting on the bankruptcy was originally published in 2002. United Airlines was not suffering from financial difficulties in September 2008. Apparently one or more Internet browsers had recently retrieved the article on the *South Florida Sun-Sentinel website*, prompting it to be listed under the "Most Read" articles. The Google News aggregator picked it up, and a harried Bloomberg news editor passed it into the Bloomberg feed.

Trading resumed once the (mistaken) cause of the decline was understood. Shares resumed trading around 12:25 p.m., yet they closed the day with an 11.2 percent loss. Shares closed significantly down despite the republished article being 6 years old. United Airlines' shareholders were perhaps

Trading in United Airlines (UAUA) on September 8, 2008

FIGURE 6.3 News of United Airline's 2002 bankruptcy filing moved the stock price dramatically when republished in 2008 on Bloomberg.
Data Source: Thomson Reuters Tick History.

spooked by the unusual fragility of the stock. As described later in this book, negative news, regardless of its veracity, has short-term effects on prices. Additionally, the price damage from negative news is more severe in an already-weak sentiment environment.

The 2008 UAUA stock decline could have been profitably traded by an attentive human trader watching the Bloomberg newsfeed. In the past several years, however, the speed of text-based algorithmic traders has quickened. Now it is nearly impossible for human traders to outcompete algorithms, even around some complex events.

FASTER THAN A SPEEDING SPECIALIST

They're buying everything within like 3 seconds of it coming out, which is not possible for a human.
— Anonymous market maker[8]

On March 27, 2015, the Dow Jones Newswire published a news alert that Intel was in talks to purchase Altera, a semiconductor maker. After publication, robotic traders sent orders into the options market in less time than it takes a human to read a headline.[9] A $110,530 call purchase by one robotic trader resulted in a $2.4 million profit for the savvy algorithm (and its author).[10]

According to a human market maker trading in Altera options at the time of the announcement, humans are no match for such algorithms: "It would be impossible for me to do. By the time you could read the news, process it, and press the 'buy everything' button, it would take too long. The speed is unbelievable."[11] As a result of these superfast news-reading robots, the jobs of some human market makers are being outsourced to fast servers.

Although the previous example is from a newswire dedicated to breaking financial news, it's not only news moving markets. Social media is being exploited by algorithms as well. Credible tweets, regardless of their veracity, can have an immediately market-moving impact.

A REHASH OF THE #HASHCRASH

The stock-market selloff Tuesday shows how quickly social media such as Twitter can spread false information. U.S. stocks and the dollar briefly slid Tuesday afternoon and U.S. Treasury bonds and gold prices soared following the tweet.
— Shira Ovide[12]

Social media sites like Twitter often contain public postings about major events before they hit the newswires, and some companies—EOTpro and Dataminr being the most prominent—are working to develop their own predictive analytics services using the tweets published by global Twitter users. One key challenge in identifying valuable news communicated via social media lies in filtering out the useless noise.

On April 23, 2013, at 1:07 p.m. ET, the Associated Press's Twitter account published the following: "Breaking: Two Explosions in the White House and Barack Obama is injured." Within seconds, the S&P 500 dove, and within a few more minutes market prices recovered. Figure 6.4 is a minutely price chart of the S&P 500 on the day of this infamous #HashCrash.

The tweet was a hoax perpetrated by representatives of the Free Syrian Army, and it resulted in a brief evaporation of $136 billion in market capitalization from the S&P 500 index. The dust cleared quickly, and all executed trades were considered final. Within 2 minutes the S&P 500 had restored its pre-tweet gains.

If the Twitter account of the Free Syrian Army published such a tweet, the market would not have noticed, but the Associated Press is far more credible. For fairly obvious reasons, credible news sources have greater influence over market prices than less credible ones.

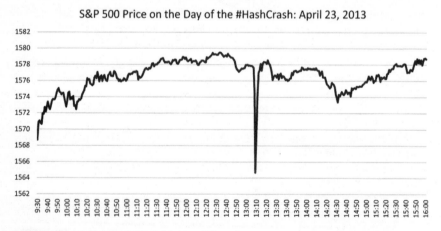

FIGURE 6.4   The S&P 500 on April 23, 2013, the day of the #HashCrash. Data Source: Thomson Reuters Tick History.

Looking in detail at who is publishing, at journalists individually, the credibility and historical tone of the journalist communicating the information also matters. Academic research shows that generally bullish journalists have a more positive impact on prices, while articles by generally bearish journalists have a more negative impact.[13]

The previous examples—a corporate bankruptcy (United Airlines), a buyout (Intel and Altera), and a bomb in the White House—were all instantaneously market-moving. But these are only single cases. To understand how news predictably moves markets, hundreds of examples are needed. Fortunately, the tools of news analytics allow such research.

BREAKING NEWS

The news article announcing Intel's intention to buy Altera was highly significant and positive for Altera's share price. As described previously in Chapter 3, Elijah DePalma examined the stock price impact of articles about such corporate mergers, acquisitions, and takeovers. His sample included the relatively liquid stocks in the Russell 1000 (the largest 1000 stocks in the United States by market capitalization). Figure 6.5 represents the average stock price return for stocks with the merger (MRG) topic code during

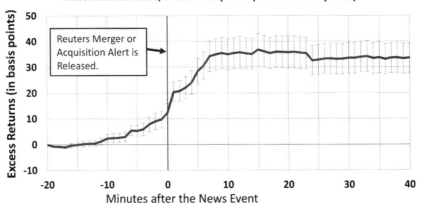

Returns over the S&P 500 Following Reuters M&A Alerts
Russell 1000 universe, 9:40am-3:50pm NY (June 2014 - May 2015)

FIGURE 6.5 Merger news impact and stock price returns.
Source: Elijah DePalma, PhD, Thomson Reuters, Personal Coimmunication.

the 1,178 times that code appeared in Reuters articles during New York market hours (9:40 a.m. to 3:50 p.m. ET) from June 2014 through May 2015. The excess returns in Figure 6.3 were derived from stocks tagged as relevant in MRG articles and with (1) positive sentiment greater than 0.5 and (2) novel article content (no linked news items over the trailing 12 hours).[14]

Merger-related news stories precede an approximately 20 basis point (0.20 percent) stock price return over the following 10 minutes versus the S&P 500 as a whole. This return is higher if more precision (positive sentiment and novelty) is demanded in the results, with average returns near 40 basis points over the following 10 minutes. DePalma also studied the Russell 2000 stocks (small caps), and he found post-news returns around 200 basis points (2 percent) using the filters noted above. Also notable on Figure 6.5 is that some of the price impact of merger news occurs in advance of the news release, as if it is leaked or appears in other news sources. This pre-announcement price drift is much less among the Russell 2000 stocks as opposed to the Russell 1000 stocks displayed in Figure 6.5. DePalma's similar result on mergers for companies in the S&P 500, conditioned on social buzz, was displayed in Figure 3.4.

LEAKING NEWS

When news is not locked-up in advance of its release, it may leak into market prices before any formal announcement. Note in Figure 6.5 that stock price movement begins before the formal Reuters news alert. Whether that movement is due to other news outlets reporting the story, or leaking in advance of any publication, is unclear.

Researchers have identified news leakage in many contexts. In particular, news that involves many parties or is political in nature, such as sovereign debt upgrades or downgrades, often leaks in advance of announcement. For example, the downgrade of U.S. sovereign debt by Standard and Poor's in 2011 was preceded by an 11 percent fall in the value of the S&P 500 index over 10 days, prompting an SEC investigation into leakage of the downgrade news.[15] Alexander Michaelideas and colleagues found that the intentions of ratings agencies to upgrade or downgrade sovereign debt are regularly leaked into the media in advance of the event. In fact, they find that such leakage can be detected in the TRMI. "We find negative abnormal sentiment before downgrades preceded by rumors."[16] News that is not embargoed and is highly significant—such as sovereign debt upgrades and downgrades—often leaks into the media, especially in regions with weaker institutions.

So far in this chapter, it appears that more structured, more credible, and more significant news has a greater impact on market prices. For news that hasn't leaked—novel news—there is a period of time over which it is absorbed into prices.

NEWS MOMENTUM

Shifts in media sentiment impact prices. Remarkably, this effect is consistent not only for news about individual stocks, but also for 30-minute shifts in the aggregated media sentiment tone about the U.S. stock market in general. Researchers Licheng Sun, Mohammad Najand, and Jiancheng Shen at Old Dominion University studied the effect of changes in the Sentiment TRMI (combining both news and social sentiment) regarding the S&P 500. They found that half-hour changes in S&P 500 sentiment predict the following half-hour price change in the S&P 500.[17]

Over longer periods, such as 24-hour windows, specific types of news have a prolonged impact on stock prices. Chapter 5 described the cross-sectional rotation style of analysis. When cross-sectional models are utilized to study the TRMI, it appears that specific topics and tones in the news create price momentum over the following 24 hours. Among U.S. stocks, the Optimism TRMI (a future-tense subset of sentiment) and earningsForecast (the expectation of whether a firm's earnings will rise versus fall) have both been drivers of daily returns across U.S. stocks. The following figures display the equity curves that result from a cross-sectional rotation strategy on those two TRMI.

Thirty minutes before the New York Stock Exchange (NYSE) close, this strategy selects the top 20 stocks by news Buzz in the United States over the past 24 hours. The top 20 stocks are then ranked on each TRMI, and an equity curve is derived by going long the top 25 percent (5 stocks) and shorting the bottom 25 percent (5 stocks) and holding the positions for 24 hours. Long and short positions in individual stocks are taken at the closing price on the current day and held through the close of the following day. The process is repeated every trading day, and the simulated portfolio returns are visible in Figures 6.6, 6.7, and 6.8. Returns were not adjusted for transaction costs, and there may be no realistic profit remaining once those are factored in. The equity curves start at a theoretical $1 in 1998.

Figure 6.6 shows the effect of news optimism (future-tense sentiment) on individual United States stocks. News optimism is generally useful for

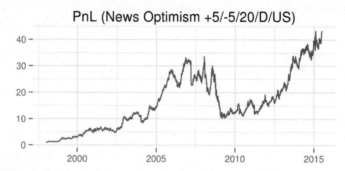

FIGURE 6.6 An equity curve derived by arbitraging the daily average news optimism TRMI for individual U.S. stocks.

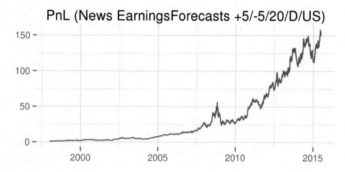

FIGURE 6.7 An equity curve derived by arbitraging the daily average news earningsForecast TRMI for individual U.S. stocks.

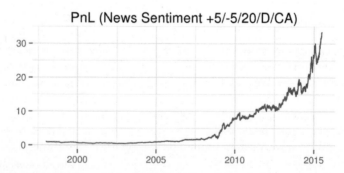

FIGURE 6.8 An equity curve derived by arbitraging the daily average news sentiment TRMI for individual Canadian stocks.

the next 24 hours, creating momentum in prices. There is a broad pattern—when the news tone reflects optimism or pessimism, prices subsequently rise or fall consistent with the tone.

Beyond news tone, specific topics may have a differential impact on prices. An arbitrage of a specific brand of optimism, about the topic of earnings—earningsForecast—is more striking in its historical predictive power, as seen in Figure 6.7.

Only a small number of stocks report earnings on any given day, but the above model is repeated every day, regardless of the presence of an earnings report. Perhaps when the news expresses optimism (or pessimism) about the future, it is most impactful when earnings are the topic. As will be described in Chapter 10, anticipation of future events leads to price momentum until the event. Following the event, a price reversal typically unfolds. In each case, expectations expressed in news media are positively correlated with the following 24 hours of price activity.

The daily momentum effect appears to be global. Similar to U.S. stocks, Canadian stocks respond to positive and negative news followed by price momentum. Patterns such as this are not reliably international. At least one study indicates that different types of news create characteristic patterns across global markets, and sentiment correlates with some broadly consistent results as well as findings that are unique to local markets.

The equity curve in Figure 6.8 is based on the top 20 Canadian stocks in the news, traded only on the Toronto Stock Exchange, and rotated daily. The 20 stocks selected were ranked by the Sentiment TRMI, and the model bought the top quintile (e.g., the five with the most positive sentiment) and shorted the bottom quintile. The Sentiment TRMI is computed by quantifying the net difference between positive references to company versus negative references. In Figure 6.8, it appears that Canadian stocks respond with momentum to news sentiment over the past 24 hours.

For Canadian stocks, positive news sentiment precedes price outperformance, while negative news sentiment indicates underperformance is likely. This arbitrage yields theoretical returns (before transaction costs) of more than 30-fold. Canadian stocks appear to incorporate positive and negative news over 24 hours, giving investors an opportunity to trade with this momentum (depending on transaction cost impact).

In studying the TRMI, social media content did not generate significant daily momentum; however, it should be noted that only absolute levels of daily sentiment, not changes in daily sentiment, were tested. Researchers who have tested such changes in broad social media sentiment find predictive power. For example, changes in a country's happiness level, as measured in Facebook status updates, appear to precede stock market price movements.

GROSS NATIONAL HAPPINESS

Facebook developed an index of *Gross National Happiness* (GNH) by counting happy keywords in user status updates. Using this data, researchers found—no surprise—that holidays are the happiest days of the year. The Facebook researchers also found—again, little surprise here—that Fridays are twice as happy as Mondays. The least happy day prior to the GNH's 2009 launch was the day that actor Heath Ledger died, and the second-to-least happy day was the day Michael Jackson died.[18] Clearly GNH does reflect investors' primary concerns. Despite this link with popular rather than business culture, researcher Yigitcan Karabulut found a robust predictive relationship between the GNH index and global stock market returns.

Karabulut discovered that a one standard deviation increase in Gross National Happiness was predictive of an estimated 11 basis point (0.11 percent) increase in next-day stock market performance in the United States. A positive relationship also appeared in the United Kingdom and Germany using those countrie's Facebook GNH indexes. A surge in the GNH is also predictive of increased trading volume the following day. Even more remarkably, dual-listed shares (stocks listed in two countrie's stock markets, such as Rio Tinto and Unilever) show a wider price disparity after a one standard deviation increase in the GNH of one country versus the other.[19]

SOCIAL SENTIMENT

Results from social media research are typically not so robust as that identified in Facebook's GNH. In one of the earliest studies of social media sentiment, Antweiler and Frank (2003) quantified positive and negative tone in Yahoo! Finance message board postings. The researchers found predictability over market volatility but not price direction.[20]

Following Antweiler and Frank's paper with negative results on message boards, subsequent analyses showed positive relationships between sentiment and price direction from blogs and Google searches. In one study, researchers used over 20 million posts from the *LiveJournal* blogging website to create an index of the United States national mood, which they called the Anxiety Index. Over the period of the financial crisis, they found that when this index rose sharply, the S&P 500 ended the day lower.[21] Other researchers found that the frequency of Google searches for economically negative words had predictive power. Google Trends data for words related to general economic concerns (e.g., *recession, unemployment,* and *bankruptcy*) contributed to what the authors termed a "FEARS" index. The FEARS index was correlated with a current-day decline in the stock market as well as positive stock market moves for the following two days (a bounce). The authors also found that a rise in their FEARS index predicted mutual fund outflows.[22] It appears that an increase in anxious blog posts and Google searches correlates with one-day price overreaction (followed by a price bounce).

Twitter sentiment has been more thoroughly studied than Google Trends data, and it reveals similar sentiment momentum patterns. In a 2011 study, researchers found that the general level of emotionality in Twitter on one day predicted stock returns the next day: "When the emotions on twitter fly high, that is when people express a lot of hope, fear, and worry, the Dow goes down the next day. When people have less hope, fear, and worry, the Dow goes up.[23] Other researchers found a similar result.[24] However, the results of those authors may have been biased by the short period of testing and the economic events in their study period (the 2007–2009 global financial crisis) during which expressed emotions were running atypically high.

In a more thorough analysis, Forbergskog and Blom (2013) demonstrated that positive and negative investor sentiment from Twitter predicts positive and negative returns of individual S&P 500 stocks the following day.[25] Most significantly, a one-standard-deviation increase in the percentage of positive tweets preceded a 0.18 percent increase in a stock's price the following day. A one-standard-deviation increase in the share of negative tweets preceded an average 0.44 percent reduction in stock returns over seven days.[26] Also, an increase in the percentage of generally emotional tweets (all positive and negative tweets together) predicted a decline in stock price two and three days later.

Some social media authors and sources have a more immediate impact on stock prices. The number of followers of a Twitter user determines how quickly their positive or negative sentiment filters into stock prices. Sul, Dennis, and Yuan (2014) discovered that Twitter users with a greater number of followers have a more rapid influence on stock returns, while users with fewer followers generate a slower effect that propagates up to 10 days ahead. And like the Google Trends researchers cited above, they found that tweet sentiment is positively correlated with daily returns of S&P 500 constituent stocks.[27]

Beyond social media and Google search volume, online product reviews and page views have also been studied. Company-relevant product reviews on the top 10 most viewed blogs are more impactful on stock prices than Google search results or page view numbers.[28] Additionally, the more widely a message is seen, the faster its sentiment is priced into markets.[29] Sentiments are incorporated into prices regardless of whether they are expressed in Facebook status updates, about products on blogs, about individual stocks on Twitter, or through searches on Google.

From these results it appears that stock price reactions are mixed depending on the social media source and nature of the references. From Twitter, stocks react positively to positive social media sentiment and negatively to negative sentiment over one to three days. However, at extreme levels of sentiment, reversals are evident. A higher level of emotionality predicts negative price action over the following day, and a highly positive or negative day is often followed by a price reversal. Additionally, little-followed sources and authors have a slower impact on prices.

THE HUMAN ADVANTAGE

Despite ever-faster and more intelligent machines reading media, humans have a better grasp of information context and an advantage in interpreting and understanding the longer-term implications. A human trader who uses a predictive model based on sentiment—and who takes the time to understand the nature of the sentiment—could potentially develop a much deeper understanding of which stocks are likely to move. For example, trading on daily earnings forecast consensus may be profitable for some securities but not for others (e.g., those far away from their earnings). Humans are well-suited to understand such nuances.

This chapter explored the short-term price momentum caused by news impact, extreme levels of sentiment, and changes in such sentiment. From social media data there is evidence of both short-term momentum (underreaction) and reversals (overreaction), such as the price bounce following an increase in the FEARS index. In the next chapter, social media–based reversal patterns are examined through the lens of a specific type of sentiment—that expressed as price forecasts.

IN SUMMARY

- Munehisa Homma (1724–1803), one of the wealthiest men of his day, profited through an understanding of information flow and market psychology.
- Some modern high-frequency traders profit from millisecond differences in processing speed around events such as nonfarm payrolls.
- Some topics in news and social media—bankruptcies, bombings, mergers—impact market prices faster than a human trader could trade.
- News with high or low sentiment impacts prices immediately and also over the subsequent 10-minute period of price drift.
- News that conveys future expectations, especially about company earnings, affects U.S. stock price action over subsequent 24-hour intervals.

- Academics have found that daily changes in social media tone, as well as the volume of Internet searches on negative topics, both correlate with future stock market price direction.
- Human traders may continue to outperform computers when interpreting nuanced and context-dependent information.

NOTES

1. "Munehisa Homma—Father of Japanese Candlesticks." December 12, 2013. http://www.mutiara-damansara.com/news/homma-munehisa-father-of-japanese-candlesticks.
2. Nial Fuller, "The 'Most Successful' Price Action Trader in History: Munehisa Homma." Downloaded from: www.learntotradethemarket.com/forex-articles/most-successful-price-action-trader-in-history-munehisa-homma#sthash.DFORwuoy.dpuf.
3. "Munehisa Homma—Father of Japanese Candlesticks."
4. A. W. Lo and J. Hasanhodzic, *The Evolution of Technical Analysis: Financial Prediction from Babylonian Tablets to Bloomberg Terminals,* Vol. 139. (Hoboken, NJ: John Wiley & Sons, 2011), p. 11.
5. Ibid., p. 46.
6. Jennifer Ablan, "Snipers, Sniffers, Guerillas: The Algo-Trading War," Reuters (May 31, 2007). Downloaded May 20, 2015 from: http://www.reuters.com/article/2007/05/31/businesspro-usa-algorithm-strategies-dc-idUSN3040797620070531.
7. "REFILE—Thomson Reuters suspends early distribution of consumer data" (July 8, 2013). Retrieved on May 7, 2015, from http://www.reuters.com/article/2013/07/08/thomsonreuters-consumerdata-idUSL1N0FE04S20130708.
8. Seth Stevenson, "The Wolf of Wall Tweet," Slate.com (April 20, 2015). Downloaded from: http://www.slate.com/articles/business/moneybox/2015/04/bot_makes_2_4_million_reading_twitter_meet_the_guy_it_cost_a_fortune.html.
9. Saqib Iqbal Ahmed, "Tweet on Altera-Intel Talks Came After Options Trades," Reuters (April 6, 2015). Downloaded from: http://www.reuters.com/article/2015/04/06/us-altera-options-idUSKBN0MX1BJ20150406.
10. Stevenson.
11. Ibid.
12. Shira Ovide, "False AP Twitter Message Sparks Stock-Market Selloff," *Wall Street Journal* (April 23, 2013).
13. Casey Dougal, Joseph Engelberg, Diego Garcia, and Christopher A. Parsons, "Journalists and the Stock Market," *Review of Financial Studies* (2012), p. hhr133.
14. Events Restricted to First News Alert per RIC per Day.

15. Jean Eaglesham, "U.S. Probes Rating-Cut Trades: Regulators Subpoena Hedge Funds, Others Over Actions Ahead of S&P Downgrade," *Wall Street Journal* (September 20, 2011).

16. Alexander Michaelides, Andreas Milidonis, George P. Nishiotis, and Panayiotis Papakyriakou, "The Adverse Effects of Systematic Leakage Ahead of Official Sovereign Debt Rating Announcements," *Journal of Financial Economics* 116(3) (2015), pp. 526–547.

17. Sun, L., Najand, M., & Shen, J. (2015). "Stock Return Predictability and Investor Sentiment: A High-Frequency Perspective." Available at SSRN.

18. "Facebook's 'Gross National Happiness Index' Measures How Happy We Are," HuffPost (March 18, 2010).

19. Yigitcan Karabulut, "Can Facebook Predict Stock Market Activity?" Received via personal communication with author, May 20, 2105.

20. Werner Antweiler and Murray Z. Frank, "Is All That Talk Just Noise? The Information Content of Internet Stock Message Boards," *Journal of Finance* 59(3) (2004), pp. 1259–1294.

21. E. Gilbert and K. Karahalios, "Widespread Worry and the Stock Market." *4th International AAAI Conference on Weblogs and Social Media (ICWSM)*, 2010.

22. Zhi Da, Joseph Engelberg, and Pengjie Gao, "The Sum of All FEARS Investor Sentiment and Asset Prices," *Review of Financial Studies* 28(1) (2015), pp. 1–32.

23. X. Zhang, H. Fuehres, and P. Gloor, "Predicting Stock Market Indicators Through Twitter: I Hope It Is Not as Bad as I Fear," *Procedia—Social and Behavioral Sciences* 26 (2011), pp. 55–62.

24. J. Bollen, H. Mao, and X. Zeng. "Twitter Mood Predicts the Stock Market," *Journal of Computational Science*, 2 (1) (2011), pp. 1–8.

25. J. Forbergskog and C. Blom, "Twitter and Stock Returns" (2013). Retrieved from http://brage.bibsys.no/xmlui/handle/11250/94935.

26. Ibid.

27. H. Sul, A. Dennis, and L. Yuan, "Trading on Twitter: The Financial Information Content of Emotion in Social Media," *System Sciences* (2014), pp. 806–815.

28. Xueming Luo, Jie Zhang, and Wenjing Duan, "Social Media and Firm Equity Value," *Information Systems Research* 24(1) (2013), pp. 146–163.

29. Yang Yu, Wenjing Duan, and Qing Cao, "The Impact of Social and Conventional Media on Firm Equity Value: A Sentiment Analysis Approach," *Decision Support Systems* 55(4) (2013), pp. 919–926.

CHAPTER 7

Daily Reversals

I'd be a bum on the street with a tin cup if the markets were always efficient.

—Warren Buffett

From 1999 through August 2006, Whole Foods' co-founder and CEO John Mackey posted numerous messages on Yahoo! Finance stock forums under the username "Rahodeb." It isn't unusual for active investors to post their thoughts in social media, but presumably few CEOs do so under aliases.

Despite his inner knowledge of Whole Foods' operations, and without regard to prohibitions under SEC Regulation FD to sharing insider information in advance of public announcements, Mackey posted pro–Whole Foods messages to the online investor community. He was open about his bias, but not about his insider status, going so far as to speak about himself in the third-person: "While I'm not a 'Mackey groupie,'" he wrote in 2000, "I do admire what the man has accomplished."[1] He was also defensive of himself at times. When another message board poster poked fun at Mackey's hair in a photo in the annual report, he retorted, "I like Mackey's haircut. I think he looks cute!"[2]

Rahodeb celebrated Whole Foods' financial results, announced his gains on the stock, and criticized Wild Oats (even as Whole Foods was angling to buy the rival grocery chain). In January 2005, Rahodeb posted that no company would want to buy Wild Oats, a natural-foods grocer, at its price then of about $8 a share.[3]

> "Would Whole Foods buy OATS?" Rahodeb asked, using Wild Oats' stock symbol. "Almost surely not at current prices. What would they gain? OATS locations are too small." Rahodeb speculated that Wild Oats eventually would be sold after sliding into

*bankruptcy or when its stock fell below $5. A month later, Rahodeb
wrote that Wild Oats management "clearly doesn't know what it
is doing .... OATS has no value and no future."[4]*

Disparaging comments are typical of stock message boards. Interestingly, Whole Foods ultimately did buy Wild Oats, and the agreed purchase was $18.50 per share on February 21, 2007, showing that Mackey's attempts to manipulate OATS price lower (if one may call it that) had failed. In part due to Mr. Mackey's critical postings of Wild Oats, the Federal Trade Commission instituted a restraining order on the corporate merger.[5] In 2008, the order was removed and the merger proceeded.

It's unknown how many corporate insiders post on social media using pseudonyms. That said, the practice does occur, and Aleksander Fafula made interesting discoveries about the relationship between social media and stock prices as he pursued the trail of one presumed insider.

SOCIAL MEDIA AND INSIDER TRADING

In 2011, a Fortune 100 company requested that MarketPsych help them investigate a strange pattern in their stock price. Before major news releases, the stock moved significantly in the direction of the news. After the news was released, the stock barely budged. The company was concerned that an insider was leaking the news. Not having wiretaps on employees' cell phones, they requested that our team scan social media for evidence that traders were aware of company news before the release. When we asked what type of information was leaked and the dates of the suspected releases, we were told, "We can't tell you—just look for someone who is really good at predicting our stock price or earnings."

Using social media data, Aleksander Fafula examined the prior ten years of social media mentions of the company's stock—over 2.6 million messages from 2000 through 2010. He found that over 14,000 of those 2 million messages contained explicit stock price forecasts. Of those 14,000, if a social media user predicted that the stock would rise the next day, the message was classified as a "StockUp" prediction. If the author forecast a downward move in the price, it was classified as a "StockDown" message. Figure 7.1 demonstrates the breakdown of the messages into types.

Aleksander then analyzed the relationship between the specific forecasts of each of the top 10 forecasters and the next-day stock price action. None of the most frequent forecasters showed greater than 50 percent accuracy. In fact, the top 10 forecasters demonstrated an average of 45 percent directional accuracy for the following day. When Aleksander looked below the

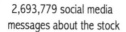

2,693,779 social media
messages about the stock

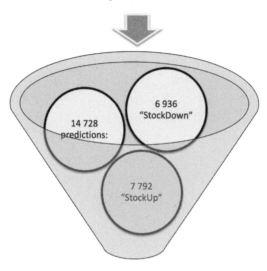

FIGURE 7.1 Breakdown of stock price
predictions in social media by positive or negative
direction.

top 10 forecasters by frequency, the overall group demonstrated yet lower accuracy, with an average 40 percent success rate for both "Price will GO UP" and "Price will GO DOWN" predictions, as depicted in Figure 7.2.

For this one stock, the average social media stock price forecast was wrong 60 percent of the time. On average, the next-day forecasts were so poor that a decent trading strategy could be built by going against the daily consensus. This phenomenon—of one-day forecasts being consistently and predictably wrong—is a one-day reversal effect. The prior chapter reported a similar reversal for the entire stock market in the FEARS study. Yet this result is not confirmed by others. Studies examining changes in the positive/negative sentiment tone of Twitter users and the happiness level of Facebook users predict price continuation. The best conclusion is that such effects are nuanced. The source and the type of sentiment—price forecasts, FEARS, positive/negative, and general happiness—all have statistically significant, but strikingly different effects on asset prices. From the available evidence, it appears that sentiments at a high absolute levels (as evident in the cross-sectional models) may precede next-day price momentum, while large one-day surges in sentiment precede price reversion.

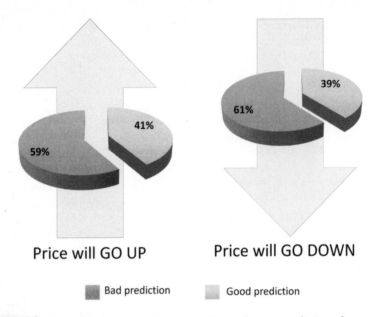

Price will GO UP   **Price will GO DOWN**

■ Bad prediction   ■ Good prediction

FIGURE 7.2 Next-day accuracy of social media stock price predictions for a Fortune 100 stock.

DAILY REVERSALS RESEARCH

Several years ago, the office across the hall from MarketPsych's belonged to one of the original Market Wizards, David Ryan.[6] David has studied the equity markets in detail, and on a gut level, he knows their idiosyncrasies better than almost anyone. One day in our break room I was explaining the sentiment analysis process to David. He noted that if we could track specific directional forecasts made by pundits in the media, then we ought to have one of the best, and most contrarian, indicators in the markets. When a pundit makes a big market directional call, especially if the stakes are high, that call is all too often followed by a fall from grace.

Price forecasts are a unique subset of sentiment. A price forecast is a very specific, and very confident, public prediction of the future. Making such a specific forecast is usually an indicator of overconfidence, which is evident in the poor results that typically follow. Such forecasts are often made after a big move in prices in the same direction, and the concordance between price moves and price forecasts is especially predictive, in a contrarian manner.

Professor Mark Seasholes and colleagues demonstrated that, on the Shanghai Stock Exchange, individual investors are net buyers the day after a stock hits an upper price limit. A larger percentage of purchases is made by first-time buyers on these days than on other days. The effect of individual investor buying is transitory, with reversion to pre-limit-day levels within 10 trading days. According to Seasholes, a small group of professional investors profit at the expense of individual investors by anticipating this temporary bump in share price and demand.[7]

On the New York Stock Exchange, researchers found a similar pattern to that in China.[8] Following a large one-day gain, the following day's gap up is typically overreaction. The morning gap up is called *overreaction* because the price tends to decline from the open throughout the remainder of the trading day. This overreaction pattern has been found to be stronger following bad news (negative open with daytime rally) than good.[9] Other researchers have found this pattern in Tokyo for the most actively traded stocks.[10] It appears that investors buy into the price momentum in a frenzy and then sell out the next day after the price momentum stalls. Perhaps the prior day's price action creates expectations of further price momentum.

Is there money to be made by fading (trading against) other investors' enthusiasm or despair? Professor Seasholes identified such a short-term trading strategy. Using a dataset of over 21 million matched transactions on the Shanghai Stock Exchange, Seasholes found that traders who buy nearly limit-up stocks at the market close and sell them at the next day's open make an average of 1.16 percent per day per trade.[11] Seasholes speculates that the opening gap may occur due to the influence of evening Chinese television business news programs. Individual investors who watch those programs then herd into the top-performing stocks in the morning. This reversal price pattern is present not only in Chinese stocks, to a lesser extent it is present in many global assets.

GLOBAL PRICE FORECASTS

Aleksander Fafula studied sudden changes in the TRMI priceForecast on a daily basis across assets using a Bollinger Band model. Using Bollinger Bands, if the current-day priceForecast value is more than one standard deviation from its 100-day average, then a buy or sell signal is triggered and implemented the following day. Because a priceForecast value at the high end of its range is thought to be a sign of positive overreaction, the model will go short (bet on a reversion) the following day. After a negative move in the priceForecast, a price bounce should follow.

TABLE 7.1   One-Day Returns Derived from Trading against One Standard Deviation Changes in the priceForecast TRMI in Global Stock Indexes and Crude Oil

Asset	Number of Trades	Average One-Day Return Following the One-Day Reversal Strategy
Nasdaq 100	830	0.11 percent
China Composite 300	355	0.08 percent
India 50	133	0.07 percent
Bovespa	340	0.21 percent
Crude Oil (lag 1 day)	670	0.11 percent

The results of the short and long positions was averaged together for periods when the priceForecast TRMI (combined from both news and social media) was more than one standard deviation from its 100-day average. Using this simple protocol for global stock indexes and crude oil over the period 1998 through 2014, Aleksander derived the results displayed in Table 7.1.

The returns displayed in Table 7.1 were generated by simulating shorting the asset at its open if, at 3:30 pm ET the prior day, the priceForecast was more than one standard deviation above its historical average. The assets were bought at the open if the prior day's priceForecast value was less than one standard deviation below the 100-day average. ETFs traded on the NYSE were used as price proxies, with FXI standing in for the Shanghai Composite, INDA for the Sensex, and EWB for the Bovespa. Positions were closed 24 hours later at the open. The returns were averaged for each asset. More speculative indexes such as the Nasdaq 100 show better returns using this rule than the S&P 500, although the S&P 500 shows a stronger pattern when the past price move is in line with the day's priceForecast index.

One explanation for the consistency of this strategy is that fear of another down day in the market after a prior down day frightens investors, and more sell orders are placed to execute at the open. But from that opening selloff, which is an overreaction, the market tends to rise over the course of the day. Market expectations are paradoxical. According to the research in this chapter, after a surge in the priceForecast, asset prices generally revert over the following day. Over the following week, reversion continues. It is at weekly time periods that the equity markets most consistently generate a gap between emotional perceptions and hard reality.

IN SUMMARY

- Financial social media contains opinions from investors with a range of expertise, from corporate CEOs (like Whole Foods' "Rahodeb") to those with no knowledge whatsoever.
- Individual stock forecasts posted in stock message boards are consistently wrong for many stocks.
- Across equity indexes and popular assets such as crude oil, historical evidence supports betting on a 1-day price reversal when the media (both news and social media) priceForecast is one standard deviation above or below the 100-day average.
- Conditioning price forecasts with recent price returns improves 1-day mean reversion results, as found in the S&P 500.

NOTES

1. David Kesmodel and John Wilke, "Whole Foods Is Hot, Wild Oats a Dud—So Said 'Rahodeb,'" *Wall Street Journal* (July 12, 2007). Downloaded May 20, 2015, from http://www.wsj.com/articles/SB118418782959963745.
2. Ibid.
3. Ibid.
4. Ibid.
5. Retrieved May 20, 2015, from: http://online.wsj.com/public/resources/documents/mackey-ftc-07112007.pdf.
6. Jack D. Schwager, *Market Wizards: Interviews with Top Traders* (Hoboken, NJ: John Wiley & Sons, 2012).
7. Mark S. Seasholes and Guojun Wu, "Predictable Behavior, Profits, and Attention," *Journal of Empirical Finance* 14(5) (2007), pp. 590–610.
8. Y. Amihud and H. Mendelson, "Trading Mechanisms and Stock Returns: Empirical Investigation," *Journal of Finance* 42(3)(1987), pp. 533–553.
9. A. Atkins and E. Dyl, "Price Reversals, Bid–Ask Spreads, and Market Efficiency," *Journal of Financial and Quantitative Analysis* 25 (1990), pp. 535–547.
10. T. J. George and C. Y. Hwang, "Transitory Price Changes and Price-Limit Rules: Evidence from the Tokyo Stock Exchange," *Journal of Financial and Quantitative Analysis* 30 (1995), pp. 313–327.
11. Seasholes and Guojun, pp. 590–610.

CHAPTER 8

Weekly Deceptions

We realise that you will think your own experience while watching magic is unique to you, but we know that, in general, everyone thinks in more or less the same way. Even as it gets harder to apply a technological edge, applying a psychological edge offers us nearly limitless possibilities.

—David Blaine, Magician and Illusionist[1]

In his TED talk "How I held my breath for 17 minutes," performer David Blaine recounts jaw-dropping feats of endurance and explains how the mind can overcome the biological urges to breathe and to eat for prolonged periods.[2] While investors are not faced with such daunting challenges of self-control, they are faced with a market and financial media—as seen in the prior chapter—that consistently fools them.

Magicians, like markets, fool their audiences by manipulating their perceptions. To deceive their audiences, magicians prey on mistaken assumptions, redirect attention, and punctuate their performance with emotional drama. Magician David Blaine said:

One of the wonderful things about the art of magic is that it doesn't really matter where the trapdoor is. That's not the secret. The secret is that magicians influence what you think by using your own preconceived ideas of the world around you to amaze you.

Gustav Kuhn is a cognitive psychologist and magician who studies how magic tricks work. In one study Kuhn threw a ball into the air. His eyes followed it up. When it came back down, he caught it. He then threw the ball back up into the air, his eyes again following it up. After the ball came down the second time, he pantomimed throwing it up into the air while his eyes tracked its invisible arc. Two thirds of the experimental subjects reported seeing the ball vanish in mid-air. But the ball had never left his hand. Subjects had assumed that the ball would rise on the third toss, and as a result, their minds perceived that this event actually happened.[3,4] In a second experimental condition, Kuhn pretended to throw the ball in the air on the third toss, but instead of tracking its potential course with his eyes, he stared at the actual ball in his hand. In that condition only one-third of the subjects believed he had thrown the ball into the air.

Kuhn set expectations with his gaze. When expectations were for the ball to rise, most subjects believed they had seen it rise. According to Kuhn, "Even though the ball never left the hand, the reason people saw it leave is because they expected the ball to leave the hand. It's the beliefs about what should happen that override the actual visual input."[5] Humans are hardwired to perceive patterns and develop predictions. Magicians learn how to set such expectations, misdirect attention, and generate false predictions among their audience. Magicians also manipulate audience emotion to improve their deception.

Magicians have noted that when subjects' emotions are provoked, they are more susceptible to being fooled. "Houdini engaged his audience emotionally, by playing to their hopes and fears. That is why it worked so well."[6] When emotion is engaged during a magic trick—regardless of whether it is a happy or tense moment—the audience is distracted. Consider the "saw a lady in half" trick.[7] During this performance, the victim is an attractive woman who rivets attention. The drama of sawing her in half— plus visual illusions with mirrors—blocks critical analysis of how the viewer could be deceived. It's not only fear that suspends disbelief, any variety of drama impairs critical thinking. According to the magician Teller, joy is also effective:

> It's hard to think critically if you're laughing. We often follow a secret move immediately with a joke. A viewer has only so much attention to give, and if he's laughing, his mind is too busy with the joke to backtrack rationally.[8]

In the markets, as in magic, high levels of emotion blind investors to rational considerations. Weekly stock price performance may provoke investor emotion, and weekend financial news summarizes and amplifies the exciting events of the week. In fact, researchers found that the best and worst performing stocks in a given week are vulnerable to a weekly reversal price pattern. This chapter explores this effect for equities, and notes how it is augmented, using two social media emotion-based sentiment indexes.

WEEKLY REVERSALS

> *Unexpected news arrives, and shareholders panic. Shares are sold,*
> *but shareholders soon feel a sense of despair; they feel mistaken,*
> *and after some time they discover that they were wrong in their*
> *dealings.*
>
> —Joseph De La Vega, 1688[9]

Good news makes a stock's price rise. Bad news leads to a price decline. That relationship is straightforward. New information is incorporated into prices over minutes to 48 hours. Investors learn this pattern and often follow it—buying on good news or selling after bad. But that is not the entire story. For one or two days, they may feel smart and prescient, but often the price unexpectedly rolls over in a reversal. The prior chapter described a pattern of daily reversals, but only when the media priceForecast has surged to a local extreme. This chapter describes a pattern of price movements followed by reversals over the course of a week.

In a seminal 1990 paper that first identified a weekly reversal price pattern in stock prices, Bruce Lehmann hypothesized that investor overreaction to information caused the pattern.[10] In his study, Lehmann tested all equity securities listed on the NYSE and AMEX from 1962 to 1989. He constructed a rotating weekly portfolio by setting the number of dollars invested in each stock proportional to the return in the prior week less the return of the equally weighted portfolio of the included securities. He found that:

> *Portfolios of securities that had positive returns in one week typi-*
> *cally had negative returns in the next week (−0.35 to −0.55 percent*
> *per week on average), while those with negative returns in one week*
> *typically has positive returns in the next week (0.86 to 1.24 percent*
> *per week on average).[11]*

Lehmann's portfolio demonstrated positive profits in roughly 90 percent of weeks and was positive in each of the 49 six-month periods he studied.[12]

While Lehmann showed that prices themselves are mean-reverting week after week, the cause of this pattern remained unclear. The reversals he identified fit a model of "noise traders" whose collective irrational behavior may drive asset prices to deviate from their fundamental value temporarily, after which they will mean-revert to their long-run average.[13]

Researchers have indirectly investigated the relationship between media and weekly price mean reversion. Columbia professor Paul Tetlock found that the tone of news influences short-term stock market price trends and reversals. Tetlock used simple positive and negative word counts to extract a sentiment factor from a *Wall Street Journal* column ("Abreast of the Market"). He found that negativity in the column predicted downward pressure on the Dow Jones index the next day, but on the subsequent four days a price reversal ensued: "I conclude that negative sentiment predicts returns throughout the ensuing trading day and subsequent reversals later in the week."[14]

Interestingly, Tetlock and colleagues also found price reversals in the week after *stale* news (news that is not novel to the market). This suggests that emotional reprocessing of news also drives prices, since there is no new information during the periods of stale news studied.[15] It is possible that news is emotionally digested by investors over several days. Investors, their beliefs reinforced and amplified by the resulting price trend, may grow to believe that the news was more significant than it actually was. After several days, the news is not only entirely priced in, but also overreacted to, and a price reversal (mean reversion) ensues.

EMOTIONS IN MARKETS

> [G]reater positive emotion in facial expressions before the market opens predicts higher prices and larger bubbles. Greater fear predicts lower prices and smaller bubbles. Those traders who remain the most neutral during periods of market volatility achieve the highest earnings.
> —Breaban and Noussair (2013), "Emotional State and Market Behavior"

Recent research on trading in experimental markets provides evidence that investor overreaction to information is the mechanism behind reversion price patterns. When examining the effects of fear, Lee and Andrade (2015) found that stimulating fear among investors in an experimental market induced early selloffs in stocks. Additionally, they found that social influences and beliefs—for example, believing oneself part of a fearful herd—provoked greater and earlier selling.[16] Employing facial recognition technology to recognize participant emotions, Breaban and Noussair (2013) set up an experimental market and found that positive investor facial expressions are associated with larger price bubbles, while fearful expressions correlate with decreased bubble magnitude.[17] Among positive emotions, Andrade, Odean, and Lin (2014) found that emotionally priming subjects with excitement (through movie clips) generates larger magnitude pricing bubbles among participants in an experimental market.[18] In fact, the authors found that priming investors with any emotional movie clip—fear, sadness, or excitement—led to larger pricing bubbles than when investors were unprimed.

These studies link the emotional impact of information and the emotional experiences of investors to subsequent price action in markets. Also of note is that emotion-fueled price overreactions (excessive fear or joy) are theorized to be correlated with larger weekly mean reversion in prices.[19] That's important to remember as the next section explores the effects of social media emotion in cross-sectional models.

TRICKY SENTIMENTS

> *In this respect the art of magic may carry a wider lesson for our*
> *technology-obsessed age. As in many professions in 2015 and*
> *beyond, it is the primitive skill of understanding people,*
> *perceptions and relationships that will increasingly matter.*
>   —David Blaine[20]

More often than not, traders' sentiments deceive. The Sentiment TRMI encompasses the net difference between overall positive and negative comments about an asset in the media. As noted in Figure 5.7, a weekly arbitrage strategy on sentiment yields a volatile equity curve. Importantly, that equity curve shows inverse predictive power. Stocks with the most positive sentiment ought to be shorted, and those with the most negative are better buying opportunities.

When that same arbitrage is repeated with the Sentiment TRMI limited to data derived from social media, the curve becomes more interesting. The equity curve in Figure 8.1 demonstrates a 30-fold return from this strategy, a result of social media sentiment arbitrage. Perhaps online investors are more

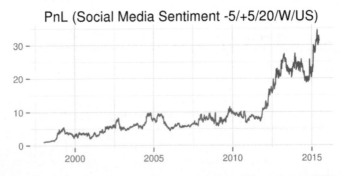

FIGURE 8.1 An equity curve representing weekly mean-reversion returns derived in a cross-sectional rotation model of the social media–based Sentiment TRMI.

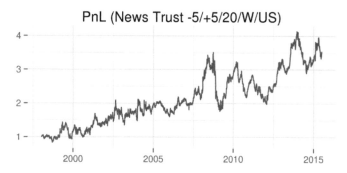

FIGURE 8.2 An equity curve representing weekly mean-reversion returns from a cross-sectional model of the news media-based Trust TRMI.

susceptible to swings in social media sentiment than the (I assume) longer term investors who consume the financial and business news.

In Figure 8.2, an equity curve derived from performing a weekly arbitrage of news-based trust, derived using the same process as that behind the sentiment result above, is displayed. More trusted stocks tend to decline the week following a high level of trust while those with less socially expressed trust tend to rise. This mean-reversion pattern is captured only in news media references.

The value of trading against trust speaks to the power of the news media to fool investors. When online investors express positive sentiment about a stock in a given week, or the news media associates the stocks with trust, the stock's price will on average fall the following week. The inverse is true of mistrust—the more mistrust expressed by the media, the more likely the stock will rise. These equity curves are volatile, and they are untradable without additional conditioning. Nonetheless, magicians could be envious of the consistency with which financial media fools its own customers.

THE LESSONS OF MAGIC

> *My chief task has been to conquer fear. The public sees only the thrill of the accomplished trick; they have no conception of the tortuous preliminary self-training that was necessary to conquer fear. No one except myself can appreciate how I have to work at this job every single day, never letting up for a moment.*
>
> —Harry Houdini

Consistent market price patterns—such as weekly mean reversion—are driven by emotional investors. The weekly mean reversion pattern is likely rooted in the brain's emotional centers, and as seen with the deceptive practices of magicians, it preys on the brain's misdirected attention, only to be whipsawed later as market prices magically reverse. Similar to the techniques used by magicians, it is shifts in attention, reliance on outdated assumptions, and emotions stimulated by the media that often lead traders astray. Different topics and types of media capture attention and subtly set expectations, often to investors' detriment. The studies in this chapter focused on social media, but the mean-reversion effect also occurs with global news media.

Traders who use social media tools such as Twitter are typically shorter term. Older adults, who are likely to manage more assets by virtue of age and experience, are less likely to be active on investing social media sites and more likely to respond to news media and hold positions for longer periods. Perhaps this demographic dynamic explains why—broadly speaking—news appears superior to social media for identifying both very short-term opportunities and longer term price patterns, as described later in the book.

The good news is that traders aren't doomed to forever fall into the same perceptual traps. According to some studies on magic, humans can improve in detecting perceptual foolery with practice.[21] Like magicians, investors can learn to manage their behavior for optimal effect. David Blaine said:

Whether you're shuffling a deck of cards or holding your breath, magic is pretty simple: It comes down to training, practice, and experimentation, followed up by ridiculous pursuit and relentless perseverance.[22]

Improving oneself is hard work—a topic picked up in the final chapter-but as seen so far in this book, it's a prerequisite to sustainable investment success. The next chapter examines the emotion that most powerfully triggers misperception and behavioral overreaction—the feeling of fear.

IN SUMMARY

- Similar to the psychological techniques of magicians in misdirecting attention, setting expectations, and provoking emotions, market prices fool many investors by displaying counterintuitive patterns.
- Researchers have identified a pattern of weekly mean reversion in stock prices.
- The cause of this price pattern is presumed to be investor overreaction to information, and this hypothesis is supported by experiments involving emotion-induction in experimental market environments.
- Social media emotions also precede weekly mean reversion in prices.

- U.S. stocks associated with the lowest levels of sentiment in one week in social media are more likely to experience a price rise in the following week.
- U.S. stocks associated with high levels of social media trust are more likely to decline in the following week.
- Through hard work, investors can learn to avoid being fooled and to take advantage of such patterns in markets.

NOTES

1. David Blaine, "The Future of Magic," The World in 2015, an *Economist* Magazine Supplement (November 18, 2014).
2. http://www.ted.com/talks/david_blaine_how_i_held_my_breath_for_17_min?language=en.
3. Gustav Kuhn, "Cognitive Illusions," *New Horizons in the Neuroscience of Consciousness* 79 (2010), p. 139.
4. Anthony S. Barnhart and Stephen D. Goldinger, "Blinded by Magic: Eye-Movements Reveal the Misdirection of Attention," *Frontiers in Psychology* 5 (2014).
5. http://www.livescience.com/1138-study-reveals-magic-works.html.
6. Blaine.
7. An explanation of that trick is on Wikipedia: http://en.wikipedia.org/wiki/Sawing_a_woman_in_half.
8. Teller, "Teller Reveals His Secrets," *Smithsonian Magazine* (2012), http://www.smithsonianmag.com/arts-culture/teller-reveals-his-secrets-100744801/?all&no-ist
9. Joseph De La Vega, *Confusion De Confusiones*, 1688. (Paragraph 69, translated and excerpted from: Corzo, Teresa, Margarita Prat, and Esther Vaquero, "Behavioral Finance in Joseph de la Vega's Confusion de Confusiones," *Journal of Behavioral Finance* 15(4), (2014), pp. 341–350.
10. B. Lehmann, "Fads, Martingales, and Market Efficiency," *Quarterly Journal of Economics* 1(55), (February 1990), pp. 1–28.
11. Ibid.
12. Ibid.
13. J. Bradford De Long, Andrei Shleifer, Lawrence H. Summers, and Robert J. Waldmann, "Noise Trader Risk in Financial Markets," *Journal of Political Economy* (1990), pp. 703–738.
14. P. C. Tetlock, "Giving Content to Investor Sentiment: The Role of Media in the Stock Market," *Journal of Finance* 62(3), (2007), pp. 1139–1168.
15. P. C. Tetlock, "All the News That's Fit to Reprint: Do Investors React to Stale Information?" *Review of Financial Studies* 24(5), (2011), pp. 1481–1512.
16. C. J. Lee and E. B. Andrade, "Fear, Excitement, and Financial Risk-Taking," *Cognition and Emotion* 29(1), (2015), pp. 178–187.

17. Adriana Breaban and Charles N. Noussair, "Emotional State and Market Behavior" (June 10, 2013). CentER Discussion Paper Series No. 2013-031. Available at SSRN: http://ssrn.com/abstract=2276905 or http://dx.doi.org/10.2139/ssrn.2276905.
18. Andrade, E. B., Odean, T., and Lin, S. (2015). Bubbling with Excitement: An Experiment, *Review of Finance*, rfv016.
19. D. Hirschleifer and A. Subrahmanyam, "Investor Psychology and Security Under- and Overreactions," *Journal of Finance* 53(6), (1999), pp. 1839–1885.
20. Blaine.
21. Barnhart and Goldinger.
22. Blaine.

CHAPTER 9

The Only Thing to Fear

A simple rule dictates my buying: Be fearful when others are greedy, and be greedy when others are fearful. And most certainly, fear is now widespread, gripping even seasoned investors.
—Warren Buffett, October 16, 2008[1]

In 1996 I took an overland trip across Zaire (now Congo). I was attempting to travel across central Africa by road, but the road became impassable due to the rainy season. Wanting to keep moving, with two fellow travelers I assembled a raft to float down the Congo River and across the African continent, Joseph Conrad–style.

We had left on our raft trip from the eastern Zaire city of Kisangani in a hurry—to avoid corrupt police shakedowns—and our canoe had capsized in the process, losing some provisions to the river rapids. We quickly ran out of food. To restock, we bought bush meat from local hunters. Unfortunately, we soon ran out of coal for our cooking stove, which was difficult to find.

In order to replenish our charcoal and food supplies, we decided to make a pitstop in Bumba, a city on the northern bank of the Congo River. We were floating near the southern bank, but visually the northern bank of the river looked only about a mile away on the morning we decided to cross. Unfortunately, what we thought was the northern bank of the river was actually an island. It turned out to be seven miles across the river, and after an exhausting and hungry paddle, we arrived at the far edge of the city at sunset.

We tied up our raft near an open-air market, and the first food stall we encountered was surrounded by a boisterous group of men dipping into a metal vat full of bubbling stew. One man placed a bowl of meat stew in my hands and encouraged me to eat up. I was half-starving, they were friendly, and the stew smelled delicious.

It was a wonderful dish—smooth with lightly textured meat and spiced exquisitely. The men were asking me questions in broken, heavily accented

French, and it took me a few minutes to understand—as I scraped the last bits from my bowl—that they were asking me if I'd eaten chimpanzee before.

Chimpanzee is a delicacy in central Africa, said to increase strength and virility. Unfortunately, I was also aware that the body fluids of infected chimpanzees were the vector that caused the 1995 outbreak of Ebola virus in Zaire, in that same region, the prior year.

I put down my empty bowl with a grim expression, concern gripping my mind. I interrogated the men in urgency—"Where did you get this chimpanzee?!" "Was the chimpanzee found dead in the forest or killed while alive!?" "Haven't you heard of Ebola fever?!" The men were baffled why I was inquiring about the premorbid state of my dinner, and I was unable to get a satisfactory response.

I developed a fever a few days later, and I was seriously worried that I had contracted Ebola. Perhaps, I thought, my death was imminent. I made plans for my pathetic passing ("I leave my journal to my mother ... "). We delayed our trip downriver while I searched in vain for a decent doctor. I was in a state of panic.

At its worst, fear can dominate behavior, leading individuals to make decisions they later regret. This chapter focuses on investors' propensity to overreact to danger, the patterns this phenomenon creates in markets, and how self-controlled investors can take advantage of such panics.

ESTIMATES OF FEAR

> *We go out of our course to make ourselves uncomfortable; the cup of life is not bitter enough to our palate, and we distill superfluous poison to put into it, or conjure up hideous things to frighten ourselves at, which would never exist if we did not make them.*
> —Charles Mackay, *Extraordinary Popular Delusions and the Madness of Crowds*, 1841

Fear differs from other negative emotions—such as anger and stress—in important ways. Fear is characterized by anticipation of a future threat, and it contains an element of uncertainty about whether the feared event will actually transpire. When the threat passes, fear abates. In this chapter the words *fear*, *anxiety*, and *nervousness* refer to different intensities of the same emotion. Stress is a cousin of fear, but unlike its cousin, stress is not focused on the future, but rather on the present. Stress is typically a response to negative events careening out of one's control, and it will not be examined in detail in this book.

Fear is aroused by the mere possibility of a future negative event. Academic research shows that a small probability of an emotional event occurring—such as an oil supply shock or a military assault—are overweighted in human probability assessments.[2] This cognitive bias—the overweighting—is called probability neglect, and it is characteristic of the fear response. As a result of this bias, humans overvalue actions that may eliminate low-probability risks. Even when the probability of a good outcome is 20 times more likely than that of a bad outcome, humans will focus their efforts on eliminating the possibility of the negative event.[3]

Researchers explored people's willingness to pay money to avoid pain.[4] Participants were asked to imagine taking part in an experiment involving some chance of a "short, painful, but not dangerous electric shock." In another scenario they were told that the experiment entailed some chance of a $20 penalty. Some participants were told that there was a 1 percent chance of receiving the bad outcome (either the $20 loss or the electric shock); others were told that the chance was 99 percent.[5] The differences in probability affected subjects facing the $20 penalty far more than they affected people facing the painful electric shock. The median subject was willing to pay $7 to avoid a 1 percent chance of a painful electric shock, and $10 to avoid a 99 percent chance of the shock. That difference represents an increase of 1.43 times in willingness to pay despite a 99 times increase in probability of being given the shock. The difference in willingness to pay to avoid the $20 penalty showed a much greater spread of 18 times.[6]

When a hazard stirs strong emotions, most people will pay a similar amount to avoid it, regardless of extreme differences in its probability. Dreadful possibilities activate emotions that render humans insensitive to the probability of harm.[7]

What does this mean for investors? Any vivid, frightening risk, regardless of the actual probability, may provoke mass selling of affected stocks. Investors, as long as they tune out the hysterics of the media, can confidently assess the actual risks and engage as appropriate. However, tuning out others' fear is difficult. Even with an intellectual understanding of its irrationality, it can be exceedingly difficult to self-regulate fear. Recent research on genetics is pinpointing the locus of fear among traders and is challenging cherished notions of free will.

TO CATCH A FALLING KNIFE

> *Avoiding fear is no safer in the long run than outright exposure.*
> *The fearful are caught as often as the bold.*
> —Helen Keller

Fear-based overreactions frequently occur in markets. In fact, in 2014 the U.S. stock market experienced a fear-based selloff based in part on Ebola fears.[8] Since 2002, investors have traded through outbreaks of mad cow disease, H1N1 (bird) flu, SARS, swine flu, and other pandemics. Rumors of a potential new epidemic disease erupt approximately every two years and prompt global waves of fear across markets. These fears drive stock price declines in industries ranging from meat producers to tourism, while sparking rallies in some health-care and biotech stocks. Sometimes the declines hit entire national stock markets or individual commodity prices. Historically, each epidemic is gradually brought under control, and prices rebound.

Buying shares during a panic is a bet that the panic will ultimately subside and shares will rise—a bet that markets are overreacting. For example, entertainment and airline stocks typically overreact during infectious epidemic scares as it is feared that consumers will stay home (who wants to be stuck in an airplane for five hours with a sneezing viral vector?). Stocks usually rally back once the fear begins to abate. In the worst case, the disease may spread, leading to massive global death rates, but in every historical case since the Spanish flu in 1917, the worst case has not emerged. Public health departments acted quickly to contain the risk, yet stocks still behaved as if the epidemic would cause significant damage.

The aphorism that refers to buying shares during a panic is "to catch a falling knife." This saying implies that traders may buy too early, causing financial pain. Fortunately, when panic abates, there is typically a pause before asset prices bounce. Fear has a refractory period in which—after the danger has passed—the afflicted appear to take time to catch their collective breath.

When we ran our MarketPsy Long Short Fund, we found the swine flu scare to be an excellent trading opportunity. I'll illustrate an actual trade we made to demonstrate how fear-based trading operates. We used fear- and price-based association rules to trigger trades in a purely quantitative model. A typical rule is: If (1) a stock price declines rapidly, and (2) fear spikes and then plateaus, then buy and hold for five days.

In April and May 2009, our quantitative systems indicated that investors were overreacting to swine flu by inappropriately selling off airlines and other leisure stocks in a panic. For example, American Airlines stock (AMR) had declined, and we received a signal to buy AMR once the panic appeared to be abating.

The events proceeded as follows:

- On April 25, 2009, the World Health Organization (WHO) director declared a "public health emergency" regarding swine flu.
- Anxiety rose in American Airlines stock (AMR) social media over the weekend. On Monday April 27, 2009, AMR stock gapped down.
- On April 27, 2009, the WHO pandemic level was raised to Phase 4, indicating the virus was self-propagating its spread, and a general selloff ensued across most entertainment and travel stocks.

- On April 30, 2009, it became clear that the spread was contained, and anxiety began to fall. MarketPsy purchased AMR shares at $4.81.
- On May 6, 2009, five trading days later, MarketPsy sold its AMR position for $5.95 per share.

The effects of the swine flu panic can be seen in the Leisure and Entertainment ETF (PEJ) at the same time as it affected American Airlines. The PEJ price gapped up substantially on the Monday open, but swine flu fear took hold, and by the end of the day the ETF was down more than 10 percent from the opening price, as depicted in Figure 9.1.[9]

Before further examining techniques for trading on fear, the next section explores the genetic nature of anxiety, which explains why most investors are doomed to repeatedly fall into the panic trap. Given its basic genetic origins, and the propensity of media to grab viewers' attention with potentially catastrophic risks, the panic-overreaction price pattern is likely to remain robust for decades to come.

GOOD NEWS FOR PEOPLE WHO LOVE BAD NEWS

> *Cowards die many times before their deaths;*
> *The valiant never taste of death but once.*
> —William Shakespeare, *Julius Caesar*

The fever I came down with after eating chimpanzee in Bumba abated quickly, and it was probably a benign tropical virus. Upon returning to the United States, I read that the particular strain of the Ebola virus I feared was then called the "Bumba strain," sharing a name with the city where I had eaten the vector. Having feared I would die from Ebola in Zaire, I know how easy it is to overreact to the danger of an infectious disease. As humans, we're genetically programmed to overreact to such risks. As the research data accumulates, it is clear that the ability to trade against fear is in large part genetic.

Several traits influence how humans take investment risk, including personal background, life experiences, age, and gender. Gene-environment interactions are also important. But primary among these influences over investment risk-taking is one's personal genetic endowment.

One of the most influential genetic determinants of fear during financial decision making is a polymorphism of the serotonin transporter gene: 5-HTTLPR. Individuals carrying the short polymorphism of this gene are more likely to develop depression in response to negative events and are more likely to experience a long-term emotional impact from financial losses.

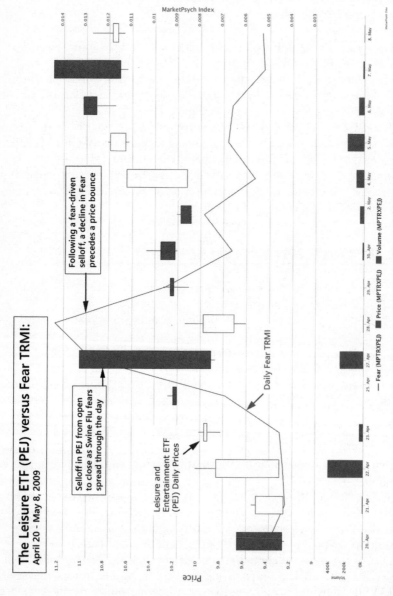

FIGURE 9.1 Fear TRMI versus the candlestick price chart of the Leisure and Entertainment ETF (PEJ) during the swine flu scare in 2009.

Kuhnen and Chiao (2009) found that this polymorphism biased investment preferences among a sample of university students. Students who are homozygous for the short form of the transporter—the s/s allele— took 28 percent less investment risk in their study.[10] Building on this work, Samanez-Larkin, Kuhnen, and Knutson examined the investing habits, genetics, and beliefs of a group of 60 retail investors. The researchers found that all three factors have some explanatory power over investment risk-taking, but genes appear to be the strongest contributor.[11] The contribution of the personality trait neuroticism to risk taking is accounted for by the 5-HTTLPR variant. Genes—an element out of personal control—determine the majority of human financial risk taking.

This is a dramatic conclusion, and it's important to qualify that it hasn't been replicated on other genes. It's disturbing to discount the valuable notion of free will. But it's only when traders recognize that much of what they *think* is in their control actually is not, that they can then accurately forecast and plan for errant investing behaviors.

Meanwhile, the vast herd of investors is reading news and reacting in a knee-jerk biological manner. Yet the savvy (and self-controlled) investor can take advantage of the surges of market fear and relief. Such investors take the time to ascertain whether a disease is as contagious as fearful commentators indicate, and they calmly consider the optimal timing for trading against the frightened herd.

PANICS AND BOUNCES

I tell my sincere environmentalist brothers, please withdraw from there and leave us to deal with the fringe terrorist groups. We will clean Gezi Park of them.
Recep Tayyip Erdoğan, President of Turkey, June 13, 2013

The Gezi Park protests in Turkey during the summer 2013 exposed corruption entrenched in the ruling AK party and led to economic and political instability in the country. As global investors became more attuned to the increasingly autocratic tendencies of the Turkish government, money began fleeing Turkey at a rapid clip. As the currency declined, the international business media increased coverage of the Turkish lira more than 20-fold, to over 20,000 relevant comments in 24 hours in January 2014 (as measured in the TRMI Buzz). As news and social media focused on the currency's decline, feedback effects and contagion turned the rout into an outright capitulation. Figure 9.2 depicts the value of the Turkish lira versus the U.S. dollar. Following the panic low in the lira, the value bounced over the following months.

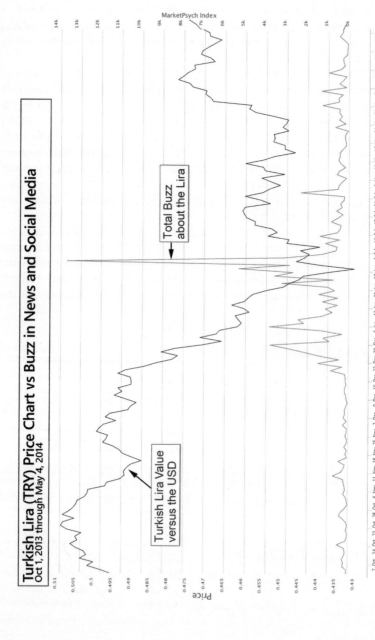

FIGURE 9.2 The decline of the Turkish lira versus the Buzz TRMI, 2013–2014.

When investors panic, prices drop steeply, climaxing in a frenzy of selling. A V-bottom is characteristic of panic in asset prices. At the point of climax, media attention is focused on the panic, and it is reflected in high levels of buzz. If precipitating causes are not addressed, such panics will be repeated as conditions deteriorate (e.g., the Turkish lira hit a new anxiety-fueled low in 2015).

Due to falling oil prices and Western sanctions over the Ukrainian social unrest, the Russian economy experienced an accelerating slowdown in 2014. As traders sold rubles and bought hard assets, severe pressure ensued on the ruble's value. During the climax of the panic in December 2014, wealthy Russians purchased record numbers of luxury automobiles as a stable store of value. As with the Turkish lira in 2013–2014, the Buzz TRMI is the most dramatic representation of the selling climax in the ruble, and it is depicted in Figure 9.3.

Note the spike in the black line, which represents the Buzz TRMI. Up to 40,000 relevant news and social media mentions of the ruble occurred in one 24-hour period during the panic.

Policy makers face a communications conundrum during market panics. Most policy makers assume they should communicate more information and be more transparent about their reasoning. In fact, based on recent research into Federal Reserve speeches amid fearful market climates, the deeper the arguments explained, the more uncertainty is introduced into the market.[12] Governmental leaders ought to keep their explanations short and sweet during periods of market anxiety.

In Alexander Michaelides and colleagues' research on information leakage in advance of sovereign debt downgrades, the authors found that rumors of such downgrades entered into the media (as reflected in the TRMI) in advance. Often such rumors stoked fearful overreaction among investors. In their paper, the authors showed "evidence that the post-announcement reversal is consistent with an over-reaction to downgrade rumors before the announcement."[13]

Just as investors fearfully overreact to potential threats like epidemics, social unrest, war, and debt downgrades, they may also overreact to the upside when anticipating positive news. We explore this "buy on the rumor and sell on the news" price pattern in the next chapter.

THE FEAR FACTOR IN MARKETS

Aleksander Fafula performed a simple test to identify the daily impact of spikes in fear (and days of low fear). When the daily value of fear is greater than one standard deviation above the 100-day average, then a buy signal is triggered and held for one day. When daily fear is one standard deviation or more below the 100-day average, then a sell signal is triggered.

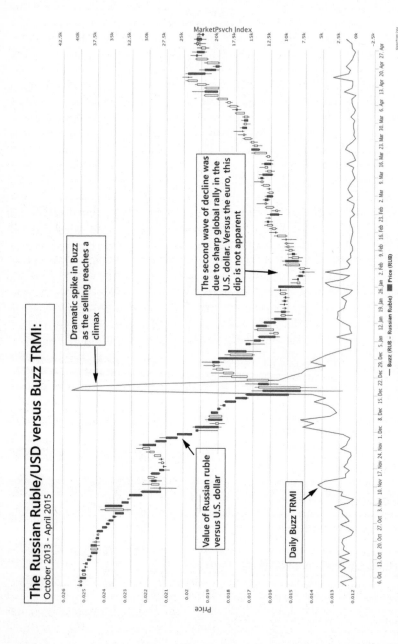

The Russian Ruble/USD versus Buzz TRMI:
October 2013 – April 2015

Dramatic spike in Buzz as the selling reaches a climax

The second wave of decline was due to sharp global rally in the U.S. dollar. Versus the euro, this dip is not apparent

Value of Russian ruble versus U.S. dollar

Daily Buzz TRMI

MarketPsych Index

— Buzz (RUB – Russian Ruble) ■ Price (RUB)

Price

6. Oct 13. Oct 20. Oct 27. Oct 3. Nov 10. Nov 17. Nov 24. Nov 1. Dec 8. Dec 15. Dec 22. Dec 29. Dec 5. Jan 12. Jan 19. Jan 26. Jan 2. Feb 9. Feb 16. Feb 23. Feb 2. Mar 9. Mar 16. Mar 23. Mar 30. Mar 6. Apr 13. Apr 20. Apr 27. Apr

FIGURE 9.3 Value of the Russian ruble versus the U.S. dollar and the ruble's Buzz TRMI.

Using the Fear TRMI for both news and social media for the Dow Jones Industrials, on 1,117 days from 1998 through 2014, the daily fear value was more than one standard deviation from the 100-day fear average. The Fear TRMI is published 30 minutes before the New York market close. Taking a position at the day's close and holding it through the next day's close—buying when the daily fear level is one standard deviation above average, and shorting when it is one standard deviation below average—yielded an average return of 0.10 percent daily. A similar strategy on the S&P 500 yields 0.06 percent daily. These are simplistic strategies, but nonetheless they show a significant value to buying when fear is high and selling when it is low over more than one thousand days since 1998.

Fear is best used as an occasional marker of price overreaction. In a short-term cross-sectional model, there is little benefit from buying stocks with high fear, and shorting those with low fear. When Ebola fear was associated with biotech stocks during the epidemic, it preceded a price rise (and later decline). When fear was associated with travel stocks, it indicated prices were likely to fall (and later bounce). As a result of the differential impact of fear across stocks, in which some stocks benefit from fear and others suffer, fear is a poor candidate for the cross-sectional style of analysis.

However, one year cross-sectional models of fear do show value across countries—buying the major stock indexes of the most fearful countries and shorting the least fearful. Fear is often tied to specific threats, as seen in the examples of disease epidemics and political risks in Turkey and Russia. Arbitrage of fear—buying fearful stocks and shorting the least fearful—relative to their home sector or country indexes, is a useful long-term strategy.

IN SUMMARY

- Disease epidemics like Ebola stimulate considerable fear among investors, which is evident in asset prices.
- Investor overreaction to threatening events like epidemics is predictable, and successful trading strategies may be built around it.
- Probability neglect is a cognitive bias that leads to overestimating the chances of catastrophic events.
- A polymorphism in the serotonin transporter gene is correlated with risk-averse (anxious) behavior in individual investors.
- Among global assets, media Buzz is often a correlate of panic, as seen in the Turkish lira and the Russian ruble in 2014.

- Changes in fear correlate with next-day price action in the U.S. stock markets.
- In a cross-sectional model, there is only benefit from buying stocks with high fear, and shorting those with low fear in specific industries or across countries.

NOTES

1. Warren Buffett, "Buy American. I Am," *New York Times* (October 16, 2008).
2. Yuval Rottenstreich and Christopher K. Hsee, "Money, Kisses, and Electric Shocks: On the Affective Psychology of Risk," *Psychological Science* 12(3) (2001), pp. 185–190.
3. Cass R. Sunstein and Richard Zeckhauser, Chapter 14: "Dreadful Possibilities, Neglected Probabilities." From *The Irrational Economist: Making Decisions in a Dangerous World*, Michel-Kerjan Erwan and Paul Slovic (eds.) (New York: Public Affairs Press, 2010), pp. 116–123.
4. Rottenstreich and Hsee, pp. 185–190.
5. Ibid.
6. Ibid.
7. Sunstein and Zeckhauser.
8. Tom Huddleston Jr., "Big Sell-off on Wall Street as Fears of Global Crises Weigh," *Fortune* (October 1, 2014). Downloaded May 20, 2015, from: http://fortune.com/2014/10/01/dow-jones-down-market-sell-off-october/.
9. Leisure and Entertainment ETF. https://www.marketpsych.com/c-v2/chart?feedty=CMPNY_GRP&ticker0=MPTRXPEJ+&startdate=04%2F20%2F2009&enddate=05%2F08%2F2009&topic=fear&price=candlestick&a=1.
10. Camelia M. Kuhnen and Joan Y. Chiao, "Genetic Determinants of Financial Risk Taking," *PloS One* 4(2) (2009), pp. e4362.
11. Camelia M. Kuhnen, Gregory R. Samanez-Larkin, and Brian Knutson, "Serotonergic Genotypes, Neuroticism, and Financial Choices," *PloS One* 8(1) (2013), pp. e54632.
12. Derek Harmon, "Federal Reserve Speech Structure and Market Uncertainty." Working paper. Obtained vis communication with the author on June 24, 2015.
13. Alexander Michaelides, Andreas Milidonis, George P. Nishiotis, and Panayiotis Papakyriakou, "The Adverse Effects of Systematic Leakage Ahead of Official Sovereign Debt Rating Announcements," *Journal of Financial Economics* 116(3) (2015), pp. 526–547.

CHAPTER 10

Buy on the Rumor

*OK, first rule of Wall Street—nobody—and I don't care if you're
Warren Buffett or Jimmy Buffet—nobody knows if a stock is
going up, down or fucking sideways, least of all stockbrokers. But
we have to pretend we know.*
          —Mark Hanna (played by Matthew McConaughey),
                                            Wolf of Wall Street[1]

Two days before receiving a subpoena from the SEC, 15 year-old Jonathan
Lebed posted the following pitch 200 separate times on Yahoo! Finance
stock message boards. He was promoting the stock of a company called
Firetector (ticker symbol FTEC):

> *Subj: THE MOST UNDERVALUED STOCK EVER*
> *Date: 2/03/00 3:43 PM Pacific Standard Time*
> *From: LebedTG1*
> *FTEC is starting to break out! Next week, this thing will
> EXPLODE. ...*
> *Currently FTEC is trading for just $2 1/2! I am expecting to see
> FTEC at $20 VERY SOON....* [2]

According to Michael Lewis, author of *Moneyball* and *Flash Boys*, Lebed
gradually honed the appeal of his promotional messages. Through a
trial-and-error process, Lebed learned which aspects of his stock appeals
unconsciously drove investors to buy in spite of their conscious misgivings.

In a 2001 press release, the SEC accused Lebed of touting stocks so that
he could make a quick profit on the price jumps he himself had engineered:

> *On eleven separate occasions between August 23, 1999 (when
> Lebed was 14 years old), and February 4, 2000, Lebed, of Cedar*

Grove, New Jersey, engaged in a scheme on the Internet in which he purchased, through brokerage accounts, a large block of a thinly traded microcap stock. Within hours of making the purchase, Lebed sent numerous false and/or misleading unsolicited e-mail messages, or "spam," primarily to various Yahoo! Finance message boards, touting the stock he had just purchased. Lebed then sold all of these shares, usually within 24 hours, profiting from the increase in price his messages had caused.

Jonathan Lebed settled out of court, reportedly for a minor fine, and kept the bulk of his trading profits. He continued operating as a paid stock promoter through the 2000s at lebed.biz.

It's not only stock promoters who have engineered their pitches. Foods can now be engineered to incite cravings, prevent the feeling of satiety, and thus drive humans to eat more.[3] Cheese puffs are the ultimate example of an engineered food that feels satisfying in the moment, thus driving repeat usage. Similarly, some media reports on stocks appeal to human brain circuitry, but too often they lead investors astray in the markets.

There is big money to be made from investor gullibility. In the effort to create the high quality sentiment data, the MarketPsych team found themselves wrestling with tremendous amounts of spam in financial social media. Most of the spam messages were stock promotions, and much of it consisted of duplicate messages posted by robots (bots). As the team dug deeper, it became apparent that bot networks were cultivating relationships with real humans. Pump-and-dump artists had set up dozens to hundreds of non-human users on various social media sites. These users would start following human traders and, once they were followed in kind, would post friendly and innocuous messages to their followers—messages like "I like your ideas," "Good point," and "Makes sense." Over time these bots built trust and gathered a real human following. After one year cultivating human relationships, the bots simultaneously recommended the same stock to all of their human followers. This was a sophisticated pump-and-dump scam. Such schemes rely on the psychological tricks of the stock promoters' trade to instill excitement (the pump) and then sell (the dump).

Broadly speaking, this book explores the phenomena of short-term momentum (underreaction) and mean-reversion (overreaction) in prices. Momentum generally follows good news (e.g., mergers) as well as positive expectations set by the news media (e.g., the earningsForecast research described in Chapter 6). Mean reversion is seen following investor overreaction (e.g., in the daily priceForecast examples in Chapter 7, and the weekly sentiment and trust examples in Chapter 8). Chapter 9 reviewed how fear affects investors, first driving prices to a panicked selling climax, which is then followed by a bounce.

This chapter looks at a very specific, and potentially lucrative, inversion of fear-related price bounces: the enthusiasm that accompanies event anticipation ("buy on the rumor") and the selloff that frequently follows the event itself ("sell on the news"). Perceptions of potential price returns are amplified as the event approaches, and after the event, cold reality sinks prices back to their pre-excitement level.

PRICE FORECASTS

The expectation of an event creates a much deeper impression on the exchange than the event itself.
—Joseph De La Vega, 1688[4]

Fear and optimism are anticipatory states. They are aroused when investors are focused on potentially painful (or lucrative) events. They help investors prepare for threats or opportunities, respectively. Other emotions, such as anger or joy, are more often reactions to events. The distinction between anticipatory and reactive emotions is important. Amateur investors often buy stocks based on anticipation of something good—a price move, an earnings surprise, or as seen in recent years at Apple, a product release.[5]

Sensational forecasts get the reader's attention, but they may be destructive to the readers' wealth. The "buy on the rumor and sell on the news" (BRSN) price pattern describes a phenomenon in which an asset price rises in anticipation of a positive event, and then falls immediately after the event happens.[6] Many traders buy shares in anticipation of a positive event, such as a "better-than-expected" earnings report, a hyped product release, or good economic news. It is said that traders are "buying on the rumor" because the good event has not yet occurred. When the expected event does occur, prices often fall, which is the opposite of what was expected.

SWEET ANTICIPATION

We find that whole communities suddenly fix their minds upon one object, and go mad in its pursuit; that millions of people become simultaneously impressed with one delusion, and run after it, till their attention is caught by some new folly more captivating than the first.
—Charles Mackay, *Extraordinary Popular Delusions and the Madness of Crowds*, 1841

Steve Jobs mastered the art of capturing the public's attention and enthusiasm at both Pixar and Apple. This section describes a BRSN pattern around the release of Pixar studio's (PIXR) widely anticipated computer-animated films, as well as one surrounding Apple's (AAPL) product releases. The collective insanity that accompanies such widely anticipated events usually ends poorly for investors.

Journalist Pui-Wing Tam identified a pattern in Pixar stock in a 2001 *Wall Street Journal* piece, "Pixar Takes Investors on Rocky Ride: Studio's Shares Rise Before Release of Films, Then Decline." The release of the Pixar film *A Bug's Life* was followed by a 40 percent decline in Pixar's share price. A Fool.com piece titled "Don't Buy on the Rumor" describes the event:

> *Prior to the 1998 Thanksgiving release of A Bug's Life, rumor was spreading around about the potential for the film. Upon this speculation, Pixar's stock rose from a low of $20 a share at the beginning of 1998 to $53 right before the film opened. When A Bug's Life did open, it broke all the box-office records for an animated film opening on Thanksgiving weekend. And yet the stock quickly lost about 40 percent of its value over the next month.[7]*

Naturally, Steve Jobs was one of the world's best at appealing to human emotions. As a result, Apple stock (AAPL) has historically been one of the most psychology-driven stocks in the market, especially around trade shows and product releases.

The following excerpt is from a *Wall Street Journal* article titled "Apple's Stock May Tumble after New Products Debut." While the article appeared in 2002, the pattern continues through this writing (2015) as seen later in the chapter. On January 3, 2002, four days before Apple's anticipated iMac unveiling at the 2002 MacWorld trade show in San Francisco, the author wrote:

> *The Cupertino, Calif., company's stock increasingly has been caught in a strange cycle: In recent years, the shares have run up strongly in advance of product debuts—and declined thereafter. In a December study from Morgan Stanley, analyst Gillian Munson found that in three of five cases after Apple launched a new computer since 1997, its shares slipped. Of those three occasions, the stock fell an average 19 percent in the ensuing six months, she noted.[8]*

AAPL shares peaked at a six-week price high on the morning of the new iMac release at the San Francisco *MacWorld* trade show on Monday January 7, 2002. The *Wall Street Journal* article describing this situational BRSN pattern did not prevent the pattern from recurring. AAPL shares declined more than 15 percent during the five days following the trade show.

This pattern has persisted for AAPL, often in more volatile form, particularly around releases of new iPhone versions.[9]

The marketRisk TRMI (a.k.a. the bubbleometer) was developed to quantify and measure the presence of speculative excess. Speculative excitement around 2013's iPhone 5 release is reflected in this index, and both the marketRisk index and AAPL price reversion following the iPhone 5 debut is visible in Figure 10.1. The darker shading between the averages signals speculative risk-taking (revealed in investors' language) due to overexuberance in advance of the product launch.

Figure 10.1 is a bit misleading. Despite the fall in AAPL shares over the week following the announcement, a large share rally occurred once the phone went on sale and the customer response—extensive lines formed outside stores—beat expectations. When there were no solid sales numbers to back investor enthusiasm, anticipation built to unrealistic levels and was subsequently disappointed by the product unveiling. A similar pattern to that in Figure 10.1 was evident before the iPhone 6 was released in 2014. Despite high levels of excitement, the stock price of AAPL slid in the week following both launches. This pattern of APPL stock price appreciation based on hype, and a slide when reality sets in, is characteristic of BRSN.

Beyond product releases, the BRSN pattern also appears around highly anticipated IPOs and corporate earnings during periods of optimism.

EARNINGS AND IPOS

The pattern identified in Apple shares has been identified systematically across many types of anticipated events. Cornelli et al. (2006)[10] utilized the pre-trading (gray market) prices related to European IPOs to proxy for retail investors' sentiment for the IPOs, uncovering that in good times the sentiment measure is valid in predicting first-day after-market prices of the IPOs, yet not in bad times. Since price action isn't the same as media sentiment, others have extended the research using Google search volume (SVI) and Twitter sentiment metrics to identify IPOs likely to overreact. Researchers on Google search volume found that, "Increased retail attention as measured by SVI during the IPO contributes to the large first-day return and long-run underperformance of IPO stocks."[11] In a first-of-its-kind exploration of social media, Professor Jim Liew and colleagues found that positive pre-IPO sentiment expressed on Twitter predicted post IPO price reversals. That is, sentiment about an IPO in Twitter one, two, and three days before an IPO is inversely correlated with first-day open to close returns of the IPO.[12] When excited investors bid the IPO open price higher, the price is more likely to mean revert on subsequent days due to overreaction.

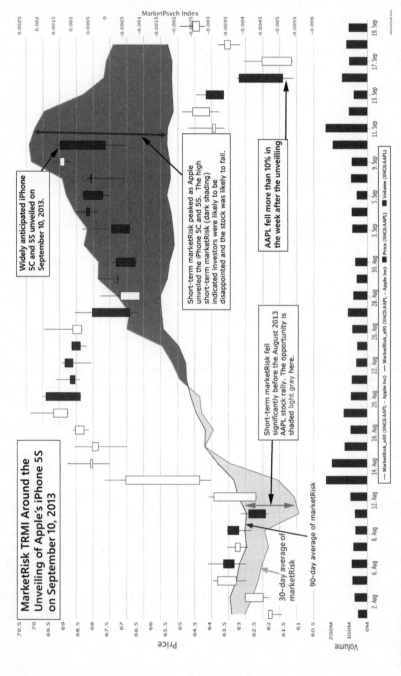

FIGURE 10.1 Speculative excitement around the iPhone 5 release in 2013, evident in this MACD 30−90 of the marketRisk TRMI for Apple Inc.

It's not only individual stock sentiment that drives prices higher. The overall sentiment climate appears to mediate the BRSN pattern as well. Professor Brett Trueman and colleagues at the University of California at Berkeley identified the BRSN pattern around the earnings announcements of Internet stocks. The authors analyzed earnings announcements for 393 Internet firms over 1,875 firm-quarters between January 1998 and August 2000. They found that purchasing an Internet stock five days prior to its earnings announcement and then selling that stock at the open on the day immediately following the earnings release yielded an average market adjusted return of 4.9 percent. Shorting the same stock at the open the day after its earnings release yielded an average market-adjusted return of 6.4 percent when the short was covered at the market close five days later.[13] The optimism brewing around Internet stocks was channeled into excitement around their anticipated events—in this case, their earnings reports.

THE NEUROSCIENCE OF DISAPPOINTED EXPECTATIONS

> *Oft expectation fails and most oft there*
> *Where most it promises, and oft it hits*
> *Where hope is coldest and despair most fits.*
> —William Shakespeare, from *All's Well That Ends Well.*

Investors' positive expectations for an anticipated event trigger activation in the brain's nucleus accumbens (NAcc). The NAcc is a structure in the brain's reward system, and its activation itself predicts future excessive financial risk taking.[14] As a positively anticipated event approaches in time, investors' expectations for "better-than-expected" news are amplified, confirming the wisdom of buying on the rumor. However, escalating alongside optimism and prices is the probability that, once the event occurs, investors will be disappointed.

Research demonstrates that when positive expectations are thwarted—such as when an expected reward or opportunity does not appear—dopamine secretion slows dramatically in the brain's reward system. The cooling of dopamine transmission is the biological correlate of feeling disappointed. Investors whose positive expectations of an event are no longer confirmed by price action after the event are forced to reset their expectations downwards. Such a decline in expectations reduces risk-taking and increases the propensity to sell, leading to the "sell on the news" side of the equation.

TRICKS OF THE STOCK PROMOTERS' TRADE

What gets us into trouble is not what we don't know. It's what we know for sure that just ain't so.

—Mark Twain

This chapter described the BRSN effect around product announcements for Apple, across industries (Internet stocks), and how sentiment is a clear amplifier of the effect (e.g., Twitter sentiment before IPOs). The chapter then suggested neuroscientific evidence for the role of overreaction in driving prices higher and mean reversion after the event due to disappointed expectations. Additionally, there are predisposing conditions which increase the likelihood that a BRSN pattern will emerge.

Stock promoters are experts at working investors into a state of unrealistic optimism. This optimism causes investors to buy at the high, sometimes from the promoter who may themselves be selling. In these cases, stock promotions occasionally cross the line into illegal pump-and-dump schemes.

How do promoters convince so many naïve investors to buy? First, they ease the prefrontal cortex offline with confident guarantees. Then, like the mythic Sirens, they appeal to the brain's limbic system, luring them into buying without interference from rational analysis. Often, stock promoters use some combination of the following psychological tricks:

1. *Positive sentiment*: Promoters create an environment of positive sentiment around the asset in the media, often spreading rumors to fan the public's excitement.
2. *Vividness and fluency*: They boil the concept behind the company into a simple, emotionally exciting, and memorable phrase or image.
3. *Confirmation*: They buy some shares of the company to move the price upward. The positive trend is price confirmation, and it engenders confidence.
4. *Authority*: They convince a canned expert—even an insider such as the company's own CEO—to make a positive public statement about the company. The authority effect lulls the brain's loss avoidance system into trusting submission: "He knows best!"
5. *Huge potential*: Unlimited projections of potential profits are made: "Could go even higher than 10×!"
6. *Inevitability*: A tone of confident certainty and inevitability infuses the messages about the asset.
7. *Lack of specifics*: There is insufficient information available to use typical valuation metrics. "Initial data indicate this goldmine will be the richest in history!" But the data is vague.

8. *Time pressure*: Investors need to act quickly: "Get in quick before the stock *rockets*!" There is no time for rational analysis; increased stress leaves the limbic system unmonitored and more vulnerable to jumping on the bandwagon impulsively.

Those eight ingredients, plus some bold type and exclamation points, are the chief tools of the stock promotion tradecraft. These characteristics are applicable whether or not a paid stock promoter is involved—sometimes the media itself is the promoter.

There is also a "Sell on the rumor, buy on the news" scenario in advance of feared events, but the dynamics of that strategy differ somewhat from BRSN.[15] The following chapter explores how the BRSN pattern is often only a short-term speedbump during a longer-term trend. As seen in Apple stock during the 2000s, a buildup of enthusiasm may evolve slowly over time, contributing to powerful price momentum.

IN SUMMARY

- Investors' collective event anticipation ("buy on the rumor") and the selloff that frequently follows the event itself ("sell on the news") creates a price pattern around widely anticipated events (herein called BRSN).
- Stock promoters utilize several psychological tools that engage investors' cognitive biases and render them more likely to buy in anticipation.
- Savvy marketers and CEOs such as Steve Jobs used product launch events to provoke a similar response in their stock prices.
- The BRSN pattern is common around many types of anticipated events including earnings announcements during speculative bubbles and around IPOs that are positively regarded in social media (Twitter).
- Disappointment-fueled selling follows the event.
- Neuroscientific evidence indicates that dopaminergic activity in the brain's reward system drops after results do not meet investors' (excessively high) expectations.
- At least eight information characteristics about a widely anticipated event—frequently employed by stock promoters—stoke the BRSN pattern.

NOTES

1. "Wolf of Wall Street." (2013). Paramount Pictures.
2. Michael Lewis, "Jonathan Lebed's Extracurricular Activities," *New York Times* (February 25, 2001). Retrieved May 20, 2015, from: http://www.nytimes.com/2001/02/25/magazine/jonathan-lebed-s-extracurricular-activities.html.

3. Michael Moss, "The Extraordinary Science of Addictive Junk Food," *New York Times Magazine* (February 20, 2013).

4. Joseph De La Vega, 1688. *Confusion De Confusiones* (in *Portions Descriptive of the Amsterdam Stock Exchange*, ed. H. Kellenbenz, Boston, 1957, pp. 10 and 12).

5. Pui-Wing Tam, "Apple's Stock May Tumble after New Products Debut," *The Wall Street Journal* (January 3, 2002).

6. R. Peterson, "Buy on the Rumor and Sell on the News," Chapter 30 in *Risk Management* (Amsterdam: Elsevier Publishing, 2005).

7. FOOL'S SCHOOL DAILY Q&A. "Don't Buy on the Rumor." Retrieved May 20, 2015: http://www.fool.com/foolu/askfoolu/1999/askfoolu990901.htm.

8. Pui-Wing Tam, "Apple's Stock May Tumble after New Products Debut," *The Wall Street Journal* (January 3, 2002).

9. Peterson, pp. 218–226.

10. F. Cornelli, D. Goldreich, and A. Ljungqvist, "Investor Sentiment and Pre-IPO Markets," *Journal of Finance* 61 (2006), pp. 1187–1216.

11. Zhi Da, Joseph Engelberg, and Pengjie Gao, "In Search of Attention," *Journal of Finance* 66(5) (2011), pp. 1461–1499.

12. Jim Kyung-Soo Liew and Garrett Zhengyuan Wang, "Twitter Sentiment and IPO Performance: A Cross-Sectional Examination" (February 19, 2015). Available at SSRN: http://ssrn.com/abstract=2567295 or http://dx.doi.org/10.2139/ssrn.2567295.

13. B. Trueman, F. M. H. Wong, and X-J. Zhang, "Anomalous Stock Returns around Internet Firms' Earnings Announcements," *Journal of Accounting and Economics* 34(1) (January 2003), pp. 249–271.

14. Camelia M. Kuhnen and Brian Knutson, "The Neural Basis of Financial Risk Taking," *Neuron* 47(5) (2005), pp. 763–770.

15. Peterson, pp. 218–226.

Three

Long-term Patterns

CHAPTER 11

Trends and Price Momentum

Trading has taught me not to take the conventional wisdom for granted. What money I made in trading is testimony to the fact that the majority is wrong a lot of the time. The vast majority is wrong even more of the time. I've learned that markets, which are often just mad crowds, are often irrational; when emotionally overwrought, they're almost always wrong.

—Richard Dennis

In 1983, fueled by a bet with his commodity-trading partner, William Eckhardt, Richard Dennis set out to answer a question: "Can trading be taught?" Dennis was already a celebrity in trading circles, and by the early 1980s he had earned the moniker "the Prince of the Pits" for having turned $5,000 into over $100 million trading commodities through the 1970s and into the early 1980s.

Dennis and Eckhardt placed a newspaper advertisement seeking candidates for their trader training program, and they hand-selected 21 potential traders from the more than 1,000 candidates who responded to their ad. In a two-week session, Dennis taught the 21 Turtles (Turtle Traders) a trend-following trading system with fairly simple and systematic principles. He educated the new traders in how to define entry and exit criteria, how to pyramid bet size, how to limit drawdowns, and how to utilize technical entry and exit rules. The strategy he taught them was rule-based, and it required discipline in its execution—not unlike systematic CTA strategies of today.

Richard Dennis's Turtles were seeded with $250,000 to $2 million each, and they performed spectacularly at first. According to former Turtle Russell Sands, as a group, the two classes of Turtles personally trained by Dennis earned more than $175 million in five years. As a result of the Turtles' outperformance, Dennis won his bet with Eckhardt that excellence in investing could be selected and trained—that *nurture* is more important than *nature* in driving trading success.

Over two weeks, Richard Dennis had taught the Turtles a trading system with defined rules, and as a group they performed exceptionally well for several years—but then markets changed. By 1986, his system was much less profitable, and from 1996 to 2009, the system generated no profits at all according to a thorough analysis.[1] Another report indicates good results for the surviving Turtles, who apparently adapted the rules and changed their styles over time in order to achieve high returns.[2]

It was hoped that the rules Dennis taught the Turtles would be perpetually profitable, but like many hopes left at the mercy of the markets, the rules didn't pan out. (*Note*: There are significant differences in interpretation among the sources that describe the Turtles' subsequent trading results.) Dennis himself no longer manages money, having closed his two funds after large losses in 1987–1988. He reopened a fund in 1997 but hit a 40 percent drawdown limit in 2001 and subsequently closed his fund. After a long period of outstanding performance, Dennis's trading rules stopped working. The Turtles demonstrate that while concrete trading rules can be taught, their performance doesn't persist.

Although Dennis's performance was uneven, some of his acolytes have continued to perform well as they adapted their trading styles to new market realities. Academic research indicates that investors who change their styles to take advantage of opportunities that appear outside of their usual domain perform better over time.[3] Such "style drift" among mutual fund managers—e.g., switching from value investing to growth investing during a bull market—leads to long-term outperformance according to that research (but this result is still hotly debated).

Trend-following strategies such as those practiced by the Turtles have proven to be—in aggregate—successful, with long periods of gradual declines punctuated by dramatic gains. For example, after a good run from 2008 to 2010, most modern systematic CTA strategies—similar in spirit to the Turtles' rules—had negative performance from 2010 to mid-2014.[4] Then in late 2014, they again exploded in profitability.

WHAT CAUSES TRENDS?

> *Merchant: In this chaos of opinions, which one is the most prudent?*
>
> *Shareholder: To go in the direction of the waves and not to fight against the currents.*
>
> —Joseph De La Vega, 1688[5]

In the academic literature, price trends are called *momentum,* in homage to the tendency of prior months' stock movements to continue into future months, as if driven by physical momentum. Stock price momentum tends

FIGURE 11.1 Momentum returns from a long-only momentum strategy based on the top 5 percent by past price performance of the S&P 500 constituents.

to follow prior 2- to 12-month returns. For example, after high price performance over the prior 2 to 12 months, a stock will typically continue to experience such excess performance for the following 6 months. After low price performance, momentum continues in the negative price direction for a similar period.[6]

There is significant value to be captured through investment strategies that take advantage of momentum. The equity curve in Figure 11.1 shows the returns from an extreme long-only momentum strategy generated by CJ Liu. Selecting only from stocks in the S&P 500, the strategy first identifies the top 25 stocks by past price performance over the past 12 months. It then buys and holds those 25 top-performing stocks for the following 12 months. The strategy is long-only and is updated monthly with one-twelfth of the portfolio. Without transaction costs, it shows a near fourfold return from 1999 through 2014 using this extreme (top 5 percent) momentum strategy.

The peaks and troughs of the simple equity curve in Figure 11.1 are comparable to those produced by momentum investors such as asset manager AQR (Applied Quantitative Research). However, CJ's overall results are higher, perhaps due to survivorship bias. The long-only momentum strategy returns are also comparable to the S&P 500 return over the period using the available constituent mapping from Thomson Reuters Tick History dataset.* The TRMI for each stock were calculated point in time since

---

*For reference, over the January 1, 1999, through the June 30, 2015, period, a S&P 500 simulation using the index's constituents available in the Thomson Reuters Tick History database showed a 357 percent return, while the same sample intersected with the constituents available in the TRMI dataset demonstrated a 382 percent return, excluding dividends.

January 2006, but in prior years, companies that went bankrupt or otherwise delisted may not be included in the sample.

Researchers have investigated the specific characteristics of momentum stocks in order to refine and improve predictions. For example, investigators found that the top-performing and worst-performing stocks often experience price reversals in the initial weeks after they are identified, but after those first weeks, the momentum resumes for up to 12 months.[7]

Researchers also found that stock price momentum is stronger when associated with news. Using monthly frequency price data and measuring the tone of news headlines, Chan (2003) found evidence of one-month post-news momentum in prices following negative news. If price changes are not associated with news, mean reversion over the following month is more likely.[8] Using news sentiment data, Nitish Sinha found that the sentiment tone of news articles predicted whether stock prices would develop momentum over subsequent months. Price underreaction to news tone generated a predictable momentum in prices contributing to a theoretical 8.6 percent excess annual return.[9] Since investor underreaction is thought to be a proximate cause of the momentum effect, investors might expect that low buzz about an asset (implying that the news is not being widely processed or discussed) may itself be a predictor of price momentum. Further study confirmed that momentum returns are higher if a stock's price has not yet responded to new information.[10]

Researchers have also found that stocks with greater public attention (using Google search volume as a proxy for attention) are more likely to develop price momentum.[11] Interestingly, Google Trends search volume also predicts trading by unsophisticated investors, implying that such "noise traders" may be significant drivers of price momentum, and tracking how such investors pay attention may improve momentum strategies.[12]

Complicating the picture of investor attention driving momentum returns, researchers report that price momentum occurs only following periods of overall market optimism.[13] Perhaps disclosure of bad news during optimistic periods generates cognitive dissonance—happy investors disbelieve negative information about their investments, preferring to wait for confirmation of the bad news rather than immediately selling. The authors investigated and verified this hypothesis in individual transactions: "An analysis of net order flows from small and large trades indicates that small investors are slow to sell losers during optimistic periods."[14] The role of cognitive dissonance in fueling momentum is similarly supported by evidence around earnings surprises. Following negative earnings surprises, negative price returns are larger if there was higher sentiment before the negative surprise.[15] For example, in Taiwan, negative price momentum following revenue disappointments accounts for the majority of the earnings-related price momentum effect.[16]

Price momentum is a universal phenomenon across assets. Asset management firm AQR frequently publishes research on the momentum effect, and an AQR paper published in the *Journal of Finance* demonstrates that momentum is ubiquitous, occurring across asset classes including bonds, global equities, currencies, and commodities.[17]

INVESTOR UNDERREACTION

Every body continues in its state of rest, or of uniform motion in a right line, unless it is compelled to change that state by forces impressed upon it.

—Sir Isaac Newton

When people receive information that contradicts their underlying beliefs, they tend to underreact to it. Price trends occur because of this underreaction. Wisdom passed down by stock traders includes the saying, "The first bad news is not the last bad news," an aphorism intended to goad investors into acting quickly when bad news breaks during an otherwise positive trend.[18]

In an effort to understand why such underreaction occurs, it helps to turn back to psychology. Psychologist Leon Festinger observed that individuals confronted by new information that conflicts with their existing beliefs, ideas, or values disregard the new information in an effort to reduce their psychological discomfort. An individual who experiences inconsistency (dissonance) will actively avoid situations and information likely to increase it.[19] Festinger called this effect *cognitive dissonance*. As investors slowly identify the implications of new information that is contrary to their expectations, a trend forms. In addition to "price momentum," academics also refer to such trends as *price drift*.

During the crude oil bear market of summer 2014 through 2015, the *Wall Street Journal* noted on August 20, 2015, "When oil prices started to edge down a year ago, most energy mavens thought the drop would be small and short-lived. Instead, the price of crude has plunged by almost 60 percent from its 2014 peak—and suddenly looks likely to stay low for months and maybe years to come."[20] The first sentence identifies the thought process behind underreaction. The second sentence indicates the slow adaptation to the new reality.

As noted in the prior section, underreaction is especially common when investors are bullish. Positive investors initially dismiss or ignore information that contradicts their optimism. Then as a negative trend becomes apparent, beliefs coalesce around the idea of an imminent rebound, and only after a prolonged slump do opinions begin to soften. Moving averages of sentiment facilitate the visualization of changing information tone. Given investor underreaction to such shifts in tone, charts of such averages could provide useful leading indicators.

TIMING TRENDS WITH MOVING AVERAGES

Chapter 5 suggested a role for TRMI moving average crossovers (MACDs) in forecasting asset prices. Shifts in media content are easily visualized using MACDs of specific sentiments, and this technique has potential forecasting power for both price trends and turning points. Consistent with the cognitive dissonance theory of underreaction driving trends, overall media sentiment about S&P 500 stocks produces a powerful predictive signal for the S&P 500. In the case of crude oil, the priceDirection TRMI reflects oil price trends and reversals.

S&P 500 Trends

Sentiment is a catchall term for all positive versus negative references to an asset, and it is a blunt categorization. Yet such simplistic metrics often show a striking utility in forecasting major swings in asset prices. In Figure 11.2, a simple moving average crossover of sentiment from news and social media was in hindsight useful in predicting major swings in the S&P 500. A short term increase or decrease in news tone about the constituents of the US500 leads the S&P 500 index both higher and lower.

Aleksander Fafula found that media sentiment is broadly predictive of the S&P 500 over the lifetime of the TRMI data. One simple crossover strategy depicted in Figure 11.2 is: (1) Buy when the short-term (200-day) average of sentiment is above the longer-term (500-day) average, and (2) sell short when the 200-day is below the 500-day. This simple strategy earned 314 percent from January 1, 2000 (when the 500-business-day average was fully populated and the trading began) through July 31, 2015 with a maximum drawdown of 33 percent. The S&P 500 itself, adjusted for dividends, earned 91 percent over that period with a maximum peak-to-trough drawdown of 57 percent. Importantly, investors would have been short stocks during the drawdowns associated with the 2000–2002 tech stock crash and the 2007–2009 financial crisis.

The Sentiment TRMI is simple, intuitive, and illustrates the nature of investor underreaction to shifts in media sentiment. However, in real-world experience moving averages appear more useful for equities when timing short-term tops, when investors are underreacting to a negative turn in the information flow. MACDs appear less useful in timing market bottoms, which are often characterized by overreaction panics.

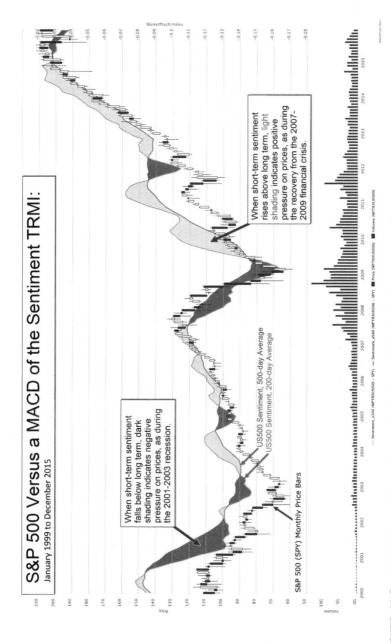

FIGURE 11.2 S&P 500 candlestick chart with Sentiment TRMI MACD 200–500 from January 1, 2000 through July 1, 2015.

Crude Oil

Measuring media sentiment around commodities is a difficult exercise. Producers and consumers of commodities have polar-opposite perspectives on events that affect the commodity's price. Rather than using sentiment itself to identify trends in perceptions around commodities, the priceDirection TRMI appears to be a useful stand-in. This TRMI was derived by quantifying references to the price of an asset increasing net of references to the price decreasing. The predictive value of the priceDirection TRMI for crude oil was first noted in 2012, and it has remained impressively predictive since it was first identified, including forecasting the more than 50 percent oil price slide from mid-2014 through 2015, as depicted in Figure 11.3.

From 1998–July 21, 2015, the moving average crossover (MACD) depicted in Figure 11.3 yielded a 7 percent average annual return, turning a hypothetical $1 at the beginning of the period into $3.12, excluding any borrowing or transaction costs. MACDs show unique power both in following the topics and sentiments that drive price trends, as well as in identifying turning points in such information flow. Furthermore, the predictive value of MACDs is evident across asset classes.

AUGMENTED MOMENTUM

The world as we have created it is a process of our thinking.
It cannot be changed without changing our thinking.
—Albert Einstein

Innovative companies develop new solutions to formerly intractable problems. Such companies are typically described in the media as having "creative," "dynamic," and "innovative" approaches to their products and their customers. Innovation perceptions can be quantified in text, and they are represented for individual companies in the Innovation TRMI.

When CJ examined the intersection of innovativeness and momentum, the original momentum plot demonstrated in Figure 11.1 improved significantly, with fifteen-fold returns from January 1999 through July 2015, as depicted in Figure 11.4.

The equity curve in Figure 11.4 was derived from the 12-month rotational model used to generate Figure 11.1. The equity curve represents the long-only returns derived from holding stocks at the intersection of the top 5 percent of past price performers in the S&P 500 and the top 25 stocks ranked on the Innovation TRMI (out of the top 100 most-discussed stocks in the S&P 500 by buzz). While the equity curve represents a small subset of momentum stocks, the finding that innovative momentum stocks

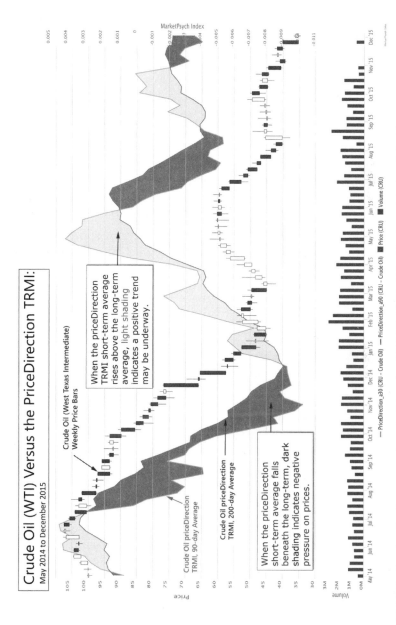

FIGURE 11.3 Crude oil price versus the priceDirection TRMI MACD (30–90), May 2014 to July 2015.

FIGURE 11.4 The returns of momentum strategies are boosted by innovation perceptions. The light gray line is the equity curve of Figure 11.1, included for comparison.

outperform their low innovation momentum peers remains consistent in larger samples. As stock prices of innovative companies rise higher and higher, investors nonetheless underreact to the positive developments within innovative companies.

GOING WITH THE FLOW

This chapter explored the phenomenon of price trends (momentum) across assets. Price trends form based on investor underreaction to new information which is rooted in the psychological process of cognitive dissonance. In cognitive dissonance, new information that conflicts with preexisting beliefs or expectations is initially underweighted. This bias is especially powerful during optimistic periods, when uncomfortable negative information is ignored or discounted. Prices develop a trend as investors gradually become aware of the new information's significance.

Research cited in this chapter demonstrates how the momentum effect strengthens or weakens depending on the sentiment climate of the entire market. For example, single-stock negative momentum is more pronounced during an overall optimistic period. Optimistic investors grudgingly come to believe the unpleasant information they have been receiving, and this delay is likely a function of cognitive dissonance.

Some moving averages of sentiments appear to lead price trends, both as the price trends gradually evolve and at significant turning points as they dissipate—as seen for both the S&P 500 and crude oil. Among individual stocks, adding the Innovation TRMI to a standard long-only momentum model improved momentum returns. Investors may underreact to the value of corporate innovation in driving share prices that are already undergoing price momentum.

The next chapter explores how asset prices occasionally trend downward into a wasteland of pessimism. Such pessimism provides opportunity under the aegis of value investing.

IN SUMMARY

- Richard Dennis was a trend-following trader with a profitable set of trading rules in the 1970s and 1980s. His trend-following trading rules initially worked well for himself and his trainees.
- Trends are called momentum in the academic literature, and they are a persistent pattern across markets.
- Trends are hypothesized to originate in investor underreaction to new information as a result of cognitive dissonance.
- The saying "The first bad news is not the last bad news" reminds investors to react more quickly.
- Tools such as moving average crossovers of sentiment indexes appear useful indicators of price trends and trend reversals.
- Simple equity momentum strategies may be augmented by identifying the most innovative companies with positive price trends.

NOTES

1. "Were the Turtles Just Lucky? ... " Au.Tra.Sy blog (March 8, 2010). Downloaded from: http://www.automated-trading-system.com/Turtles-just-lucky/.
2. "Richard Dennis, Bill Eckhardt, and the Turtle Traders." RCM Alternatives (April 9, 2013). Retrieved from: http://www.attaincapital.com/alternative-investment-education/managed-futures-newsletter/investment-trading-education/510.
3. Russ Wermers, "Matter of Style: The Causes and Consequences of Style Drift in Institutional Portfolios." Available at SSRN 2024259 (2012).
4. "Tracking the Managed Futures Industry: Altegris 40 IndexSM," http://www.managedfutures.com/managed_futures_index.aspx.
5. Joseph De La Vega, 1688, *Confusion De Confusiones*. Paragraph 67, translated and excerpted from: Corzo, Teresa, Margarita Prat, and Esther Vaquero, "Behavioral Finance in Joseph de la Vega's Confusion de Confusiones," *Journal of Behavioral Finance* 15(4) (2014), pp. 341–350.
6. Narasimhan Jegadeesh and Sheridan Titman, "Returns to Buying Winners and Selling Losers: Implications for Stock Market Efficiency," *Journal of Finance* 48(1) (1993), pp. 65–91.

7. Roberto C. Gutierrez and Eric K. Kelley, "The Long-Lasting Momentum in Weekly Returns," *Journal of Finance* 63(1) (2008), pp. 415–447.

8. Wesley S. Chan, "Stock Price Reaction to News and No-News: Drift and Reversal after Headlines," *Journal of Financial Economics* 70(2) (2003), pp. 223–260.

9. Nitish Ranjan Sinha, "Underreaction to News in the U.S. Stock Market." Available at SSRN 1572614 (2010).

10. Jungshik Hur and Vivek Singh, "Reexamining Momentum Profits: Underreaction or Overreaction to Firm-Specific Information?" *Review of Quantitative Finance and Accounting* (2014), pp. 1–29.

11. Zhi Da, Joseph Engelberg, and Pengjie Gao, "In Search of Attention," *Journal of Finance* 66(5) (2011), pp. 1461–1499.

12. Ibid.

13. Constantinos Antoniou, John A. Doukas, and Avanidhar Subrahmanyam, "Cognitive Dissonance, Sentiment, and Momentum," *Journal of Financial and Quantitative Analysis* 48 (2013), pp 245–275. doi:10.1017/S0022109012000592.

14. Ibid.

15. N. Seybert and H. I. Yang, "The Party's Over: The Role of Earnings Guidance in Resolving Sentiment-Driven Overvaluation," *Management Science* 58 (2012), pp. 308–319.

16. Fu Hsiao-Peng and Sheng-Hung Chen. "Investor Sentiment and Revenue Surprises: The Taiwanese Experience" (2013). Downloaded April 9, 2015, from: http://www.efmaefm.org/0EFMAMEETINGS/EFMA%20ANNUAL%20MEETINGS/2013-Reading/papers/EFMA2013_0505_fullpaper.pdf.

17. Clifford S. Asness, Tobias J. Moskowitz, and Lasse Heje Pedersen, "Value and Momentum Everywhere," *Journal of Finance* 68(3) (2013), pp. 929–985.

18. Hui Leong Chin, "3 Pieces of Useful Investing Advice for the Singapore Stock Market," Fool.com (June 25, 2015). https://www.fool.sg/2015/06/25/3-pieces-of-useful-investing-advice-for-the-singapore-stock-market/.

19. L. Festinger, *A Theory of Cognitive Dissonance* (Stanford, CA: Stanford University Press, 1957).

20. Russell Gold, "No End in Sight for Oil Glut: Crude-Price Plunge Is Deepening, Yet Producers Keep Pumping," *Wall Street Journal* (August 20, 2015).

CHAPTER 12

Value Investing

THE MANIC-DEPRESSIVE MR. MARKET

Often … Mr. Market lets his enthusiasm or his fears run away with him, and the value he proposes seems to you a little short of silly.

—Benjamin Graham[1]

Over recent decades, many of the top-performing stock investors used a style of investing pioneered by Benjamin Graham called *value investing*. Warren Buffett is the most recognizable of Graham's many successful acolytes. First editions of Graham's book *The Intelligent Investor* are revered at some mutual funds, with framed first editions placed in recessed alcoves like rare artifacts.[2] Graham's aphorisms are passed out to money management trainees as investing (and life) lessons.

Although some academics argue that market prices are always efficient, investors such as Graham believed that the herd of investors is driven more often by sentiment than reason. Their herd-like behavior is evident as they collectively panic out of shares in good companies, allowing more objective value investors, such as Graham himself, to snap them up at bargain prices. The opportunity to sell the shares at a profit would occur later after market sentiment reversed.[3]

Graham believed that stockholders should not be overly concerned with erratic fluctuations in stock prices. He suggested that in the short term the stock market behaves like a voting machine (the most popular stocks rise to the top), but in the long term it acts like a weighing machine (the intrinsic value of a company will be reflected in its stock price over years).[4]

Graham recommended that investors take the time to analyze the financial state of companies and determine their intrinsic value. Among many other metrics, intrinsic value can be seen in a company's earnings-to-price ratio. That is, when there are greater earnings relative to the share price, the ratio is higher, and the stock has greater intrinsic value to shareholders.[5]

When a company is available on the market at a price that is at a discount to its intrinsic value, a *margin of safety* exists, and such stocks are low-risk, high-potential-reward opportunities for investment. Graham wrote: "The margin of safety is always dependent on the price paid. For any security, it will be large at one price, small at some higher price, nonexistent at some still higher price." This concept is not to be taken lightly. Warren Buffett described *margin of safety* as the "three most important words in investing."[6]

In order to illustrate the effects of psychology on market prices, Graham told an allegory of Mr. Market, a fellow who turns up every day at the stock owner's door offering to buy or sell his shares at a different price. Usually, the price quoted by Mr. Market is reasonable, but occasionally it is silly. The investor is free either to agree with his quoted price and trade with him, or to ignore him completely. Mr. Market doesn't require any action on his suggested price. He will be back the following day to quote another.

Graham referred to Mr. Market as manic-depressive—sometimes subject to emotional price swings during fits of irrational optimism or pessimism. According to Graham, the erratic moods and behavior of Mr. Market often bear no relation to the state of the underlying business. As a result, his mood swings provide opportunities for patient investors. If investors can wait to buy when Mr. Market is in a pessimistic mood and offers a low sale price, they can increase the expected return of their investments dramatically. Similarly, investors can sell to Mr. Market for an irrationally high price when he is unduly optimistic.

Graham's systematic approach to valuing stocks gave birth to the discipline of *value investing*. To summarize the previous paragraphs: If there is a discrepancy in which the stock's value is lower than the intrinsic value of the company's assets and potential, then there is a margin of safety, and the stock is a good "value." The historical performance of value investing strategies is impressive. Graham put his ideas into practice in a partnership with Jerome Newman, which lasted from 1926 until his retirement in 1956. The partnership delivered average returns to investors of 17 percent annually.

Interestingly, Graham's emphasis on rational analysis and a margin of safety allows practitioners of his technique some emotional distance from Mr. Market's mood swings. Value investors attempt to take advantage of emotional cycles in the markets, but they utilize unemotional and lagging fundamental data to ascertain how Mr. Market feels (price-to-earnings ratios, book-to-market ratios, and other metrics). This chapter explores whether the already-stellar returns of value practitioners could be improved using the psychological insights of Benjamin Graham combined with modern sentiment analytics.

VALUE INVESTING

The market is a pendulum that forever swings between unsustainable optimism (which makes stocks too expensive) and unjustified pessimism (which makes them too cheap). The Intelligent Investor is a realist who sells to optimists and buys from pessimists.
> —Jason Zweig, *The Intelligent Investor*

Academics were late to the game of researching value investing, perhaps hobbled by an assumption of investor rationality and efficient markets. Despite this academic neglect, practitioners such as Benjamin Graham, Warren Buffett, and David Dremen[7] have written about the practice of value investing for many decades. As far back as the 1700s, investors propounded value-style techniques for selecting outperforming stock investments: "Defoe warned against buying shares above their intrinsic value, while Sir Richard Steele elaborated a contrarian investment strategy involving the suppression of hope and fear."[8]

In 1987, a systematic study examined stock price returns in relation to the book-to-market ratio, where book-to-market price represents a measure of intrinsic value. The authors found that the highest book-to-market quintile (the best value stocks), sampled every two years from 1969 to 1983, yielded a cumulative average excess return of more than 10 percent annually.[9] In 1992, University of Chicago professors Eugene Fama and Kenneth French analyzed returns of U.S. stocks from 1963 to 1990.[10] They divided stocks into deciles based on book-to-market ratios. The average return of those stocks with the highest book-to-market ratio (*value* stocks) was 1.53 percent per month higher than the average return on the highest price-to-book ratio tier (*glamour* stocks). When they analyzed stocks by E/P ratio, they found a 0.68 percent per month outperformance by the highest E/P stocks (value) versus the lowest E/P (glamour) stocks. Since those two landmark studies, value stock outperformance has been found across global stock markets using a variety of value-based accounting metrics.[11,12]

Metrics like net current asset value, liquidation value, book value, earnings (as E/P ratio), EBITDA, and cash flow multiples are all used to find value stocks. Each measure correlates with historical stock price outperformance.[13] According to some quantitative researchers, of all the available measures of intrinsic value, the best historical value factor is the enterprise multiple.[14]

Professor Kenneth French maintains an online database of hypothetical portfolio returns constructed using three factors correlated with stock price outperformance: value (based on the book-to-price and earnings-to-price ratios), momentum (discussed in Chapter 11), and size (small versus large stocks). Those three factors are now called the Fama–French factors, and stocks with one or more of those features demonstrated consistent outperformance over prior decades.

In order to replicate a traditional value strategy as designed by Kenneth French, CJ Liu used Thomson Reuters Tick History (TRTH) earnings data to generate value portfolios. His portfolio returns paralleled the monthly returns evident in data downloaded from Dr. French's online portal.[15] Like French, CJ excluded all companies with zero or negative earnings from his analysis. Unlike Dr. French, CJ explored only the long side of value investing, which is relevant to most buy-and-hold investors and long-only mutual funds.

CJ's model examined only the deepest value stocks. Each stock was ranked by earnings-to-price ratio (E/P), adjusted for index membership point-in-time since 1998. His long-only strategy bought the 25 stocks (top 5 percent) of the S&P 500 constituents with the highest E/P values and held them for one year. Each month he redeployed one-twelfth of the portfolio to new annual positions in a rotational model. The equity curve derived from this approach is visible in Figure 12.1, unadjusted for dividends.

Figure 12.1 shows that an extreme value strategy peaked with a 7-fold return (excluding transaction costs and dividends) over the period January 1999 through August 2015 using stocks for which TRMI are available.[16]

Benjamin Graham occasionally referenced moods while describing stock selection, and academic researchers have found that value returns can be increased when a broad market sentiment component is included in the analysis.[17] CJ tested whether value strategy returns could be boosted when single-stock sentiment is incorporated, and his results show that some sentiments—especially fear—boost value returns.

FIGURE 12.1 Equity curve of a long-only value strategy based on the S&P 500.

SELLING TO OPTIMISTS

> *Buy when most people, including experts, are pessimistic, and sell when they are actively optimistic.*
>
> —Benjamin Graham[18]

In his study "All That Glitters," described in Chapter 3, Berkeley professor Terry Odean found that news about a company, regardless of the positive or negative tone of the information, increased the rate of share purchasing.[19] Odean also found that one group in particular—institutional value investors—did not increase their share-buying on bad-news days. In this way, value investors demonstrated that they are a different breed from other investors—they are less likely to be caught up in the media frenzy. But this evidence also suggests that value investors do not buy more when pessimism is high. Value investors are still human, and at the extremes of fear they may be susceptible to excessive risk aversion to a greater degree than their growth-investing peers.

When Warren Buffett is asked to give advice to investors, he often refers to the value of buying on fear. In Buffett's words, if investors insist on timing their participation in equities, then "they should try to be fearful when others are greedy and greedy when others are fearful."[20] In order to test Buffett's advice, CJ examined the returns of stocks that are both value and have relatively high scores on the Fear TRMI. CJ first selected the top 5 percent of S&P 500 stocks by value. He then identified stocks that were both in that top 5 percent and also among the top 25 most fearful stocks (from the top 100 in the S&P 500 by buzz). The equity curve of this subset is displayed in Figure 12.2.

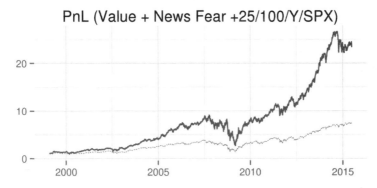

FIGURE 12.2 Equity curve of a long-only value strategy based on the intersection of value (high E/P) and high news fear. The light gray line is the equity curve from Figure 12.1, included for comparison.

Importantly, this is a fairly simple strategy conceptually, and the strategy has itself been described anecdotally by Buffett and other distressed-asset and value investors, lending further support to its legitimacy. While Buffett often speaks of fear as a useful buy signal, Graham relied on the less specific feeling of "pessimism." In studies of the Optimism TRMI (low optimism values are pessimism), value strategy augmentation was not found. That is, Graham's conjecture was not confirmed. Another negative emotion that has—like fear—been correlated with risk aversion is anger, and anger does boost value strategies. Importantly, anger's signal is one of the most robust value-boosters identified.

VALUE TRAPS AND CATALYSTS

Some stocks that fall out of favor, despite having inexpensive shares, never recover. These stocks are called *value traps*. Benjamin Graham acknowledged that there is no easy way to predict when or why stocks would revert to a normal valuation. He said, "It is a mystery to me as well as to everybody else. We know from experience that eventually the market catches up with value. It realizes it one way or another."[21]

Waiting for value to be recognized requires patience, and patience is often in short supply among investors dealing with performance targets and others' expectations. To decrease their odds of moving into a stagnant value trap, some value investors look for an event in the future that will expose the company's intrinsic value. Events such as product releases, investor road-shows, and earnings reports are such *catalysts*.

This chapter has so far focused on yearly returns. CJ's research also examined monthly returns from value strategies intersected with various sentiments. The sentiment-enhanced monthly value returns are impressive, and they tend not to be contrarian in nature. That is, if buying value stocks on a monthly basis and selling a month later, the best value-enhancers are positive sentiments such as a positive priceForecast. This finding broadly indicates that (1) many stocks enter value territory in the short term (one month) but quickly rebound, and—more speculatively—that (2) positive sentiments and events drive month-to-month recoveries in share prices.

As noted in Chapter 1, the gap between perceptions and reality provides many of the profit opportunities in markets. While fear and innovation are useful in annual value and momentum strategy augmentation, they are not profitable in cross-sectional arbitrage across the entire universe of stocks. Fear and innovation seem to derive much of their power via *conditioning* on (1) past price action (momentum) and (2) corporate fundamentals (value). Conditioning is an important technique for extracting outperforming strategies from sentiment data. While sentiment reflects perception, fundamentals represent reality. The gap between fundamentals (E/P) and perception (fear) confirms the presence of long-term investor overreaction and unfairly discounted stock prices. Catalysts are events that collapse the gap between perception and reality, ideally toward more positive perception. The key to identifying catalysts and timing price reversals is looking ahead before others. Investors can identify catalytic events that will collapse the perception versus reality chasm. It is thus helpful to document a plan of action in advance of potential catalysts.

Identifying specific sentiments conveyed by the media that marks overreaction—the sentiments that would lead investors to "throw the baby out with the bathwater"—is the subject of the next three chapters. The sentiments reviewed next—trust, leadership quality, and uncertainty—are correlated with each other. For example, a corporate leadership scandal may trigger investor anger and a decline in trust in a company. Despite their correlation, each sentiment contains independent predictive value.

IN SUMMARY

- Benjamin Graham was a pioneer of value investing. He imagined the character of a manic-depressive Mr. Market who creates the deep discounts occasionally available to investors.
- Academic research identifies that value investing has generated outperformance for hundreds of years.
- Warren Buffett postulated that fear indicates a good time to buy value stocks.
- When an extreme long-only value strategy, using earnings-to-price (E/P) ratio, is augmented with the Fear TRMI, performance is doubled.
- Many value investors wait for catalysts to avoid value traps, and on a monthly basis, positive sentiments and topics appear to drive value returns in a noncontrarian fashion.

NOTES

1. Graham, B., and Zweig, J. (2003). *The Intelligent Investor: The Definitive Book on Value Investing*. New York: HarperBusiness Essentials, p. 42.
2. https://www.brandes.com/us/individuals/corporate-overview/about-brandes.
3. Richard Evans, "How to Invest Like … Benjamin Graham," *The Telegraph* (March 31, 2014). Downloaded from: http://www.telegraph.co.uk/finance/personalfinance/investing/10749558/How-to-invest-like-…-George-Soros.html.
4. Graham, B., and Zweig, J. (2003). *The Intelligent Investor: The Definitive Book on Value Investing*. New York: HarperBusiness Essentials. p. 18.

5. Benjamin Graham and David L. Dodd, *Security Analysis: Principles and Technique* (New York: McGraw-Hill, 1934).

6. "Berkshire Chairman's Letter to Shareholders, 1981." From *Benjamin Graham Lecture Number Four*, from the series titled "Current Problems in Security Analysis."

7. David. Dremen, *Psychology and the Stock Market: Why the Pros Go Wrong and How to Profit.* Warner Books: New York, 1977.

8. Edward Chancellor, *Devil Take the Hindmost: A History of Financial Speculation* (New York: Plume, 2000), pp. 57.

9. Werner F. M. DeBondt and Richard H. Thaler, "Further Evidence on Investor Overreaction and Stock Market Seasonality," *Journal of Finance* 42(3) (1987), pp. 557–581.

10. E. Fama and K. French, "The Cross-Section of Expected Stock Returns," *Journal of Finance* 47(2) (1992), pp. 427–465.

11. E. Dimson, S. Nagel, and G. Quigley, "Capturing the Value Premium in the UK 1955–2001," *Financial Analysts Journal* 59 (2003), pp. 35–45.

12. "Value vs. Glamour: A Global Phenomenon," *The Brandes Institute* (November 2012). Retrieved May 20, 2105, from http://www.brandes.com/docs/default-source/brandes-institute/value-vs-glamour-a-global-phenomenon.pdf.

13. T. E. Carlisle, *Deep Value: Why Activist Investors and Other Contrarians Battle for Control of Losing Corporations* (hardcover, 240 pages, Hoboken, NJ: Wiley Finance, 2014) and T. E. Carlisle and Wesley Gray, *Quantitative Value: A Practitioner's Guide to Automating Intelligent Investment and Eliminating Behavioral Errors* (hardcover, 288 pages, Hoboken, NJ: Wiley Finance, 2012).

14. Tim Loughran and Jay W. Wellman, "New Evidence on the Relation between the Enterprise Multiple and Average Stock Returns," *Journal of Financial and Quantitative Analysis* 46(6) (2012): 1629–1650.

15. http://mba.tuck.dartmouth.edu/pages/faculty/ken.french/Data_Library/det_port_form_ep.html.

16. For reference, over the January 1, 1999, through the June 30, 2015, period, an S&P 500 simulation using the index's constituents available in the Thomson Reuters Tick History database showed a 357 percent return, while the same sample intersected with the constituents available in the TRMI dataset demonstrated a 382 percent return, excluding dividends.

17. San-Lin Chung, Chi-Hsiou Hung, and Chung-Ying Yeh, "When Does Investor Sentiment Predict Stock Returns?" *Journal of Empirical Finance* 19(2) (2012), pp. 217–240.

18. Evans.

19. B. M. Barber and T. Odean, T. "All That Glitters: The Effect of Attention and News on the Buying Behaviour of Individual and Institutional Investors," *Review of Financial Studies* 21(2), (2008), pp. 785–818.

20. Warren Buffett, 2004 Berkshire Hathaway Shareholders Letter.

21. Evans.

CHAPTER 13

Anger and Mistrust

After four and a half intense and wonderful years as CEO of Groupon, I've decided that I'd like to spend more time with my family. Just kidding—I was fired today. If you're wondering why ... you haven't been paying attention.
      —Andrew Mason, founder and former CEO of Groupon

Groupon, during its 2011 IPO roadshow, was a darling of the media. The company's CEO—Andrew Mason—was young, relaxed, and unconventional. The company's financials were phenomenal, and it sported a growth rate said to be the fastest in history in the year prior to its IPO: 2,241 percent full-year revenue growth from 2009 to 2010.[1]

Inevitably, Groupon's growth slowed, and investors grew increasingly angry at CEO Andrew Mason's inability to revive growth. Following a series of media gaffes (or humorous faux pas, depending on the perspective), investors began to call for Mason's ouster. The anger at Mason peaked just before December 18, 2012, when investor trust was at a low. Mason was named "Worst CEO of the Year" by Herb Greenberg of CNBC. Greenberg wrote:

> *Mason's goofball antics, which can come off more like a big kid than company leader, almost make a mockery of corporate leadership—especially for a company with a market value of more than $3 billion. It would be excusable, even endearing, if the company were doing well (think Herb Kelleher of Southwest Airlines) but it's not. Sales growth is through the floor ...[2]*

Mason was dismissed as Groupon's CEO on February 28, 2013, a day after the company missed analysts' earnings expectations. In his resignation letter, Mason stated, "After four and a half intense and wonderful years as

CEO of Groupon, I've decided that I'd like to spend more time with my family. Just kidding—I was fired today. If you're wondering why... you haven't been paying attention."[3]

Ironically, the Groupon (GRPN) price low following Herb Greenberg's snarky commentary preceded a more than 400 percent gain in the stock over the following 12 months, as depicted in Figure 13.1.

While anger at Groupon started falling after the price bottomed, the departure of Mason—the focus of investors' anger—reduced the stock's anger-fueled risk premium.

Frustrated investors—including professional activist investors—sometimes take to news and social media outlets to shame companies into changing their operations. But such open conflict may not lead to positive change in the near-term. Anger is a sign that belief has become rigid and cannot tolerate doubt. Fortunately for investors who can maintain equanimity, public anger at a company, and the mistrust it fuels, is a sign of opportunity.

ANGER UNDER THE MICROSCOPE

> My tongue will tell the anger of my heart, or else my heart
> concealing it will break.
> —William Shakespeare, *The Taming of the Shrew*

Anger is a uniquely powerful emotion in its influence on trading. Experiments on anger during financial transactions in an experimental marketplace revealed that angry subjects reduced both their bid and offer prices for consumer items.[4,5] Angry traders tend to both (1) sell shares and (2) feel more reluctant to repurchase them even after the provocation has passed.

Online communities and social media have made anger more virulent. A study on the social media site Weibo found that anger disseminates faster through the network and farther across social connections than joy, disgust, and sadness.[6] Additionally, psychological research has found that sharing anger is self-perpetuating. Venting anger (catharsis) increases innate feelings of anger,[7] thus increasing the overall angry tone in online environments where anger is vented.

Individually, anger is associated with predictable distortions in perception and decision making. Anger assigns blame, taking control of the situation out of the hands of the one who is angered. Anger can linger for months or years, and it is characterized by a sense of certainty that the target of the anger is deeply flawed. Anger is characterized by defensive optimism—the angry person feels justified in their anger and is optimistic about the future. The optimism renders the angry person more likely to hold "a grudge." Based on the evidence in the paragraphs above, anger about a company

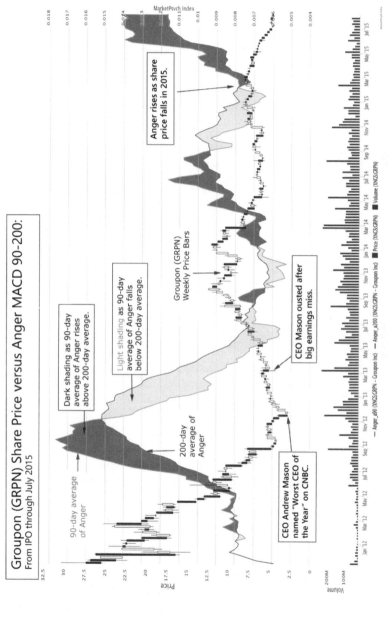

FIGURE 13.1 A depiction of the Groupon (GRPN) share price versus a MACD (90–200) of media anger. Surges in anger are correlated with a falling share price, while declines are associated with price rises.

is likely to be inflamed online, and it should be a consistent predictor of investors undervaluing stocks that provoke their anger.

There are cultural disparities in how anger may affect prices. In many Asian cultures, open displays of anger are disdained as evidence of poor self-control, and if anger is expressed by one party during negotiations, there are fewer accommodations from the opposing party. In contrast, in most Western cultures, open displays of anger are useful as a negotiation tactic to achieve greater concessions.[8] As a result, if anger is indeed predictive of price action, we may see cultural differences in anger's effects on global stock markets.

In order to study the effects of anger on prices, the Anger TRMI was developed. It encompasses angry sentiments ranging in intensity from disgust (low-level anger) to rage (intense anger). Anger is measured from news media via direct references to others' anger, such as the statement, "Enraged shareholders demanded a cut in the CEO's pay." In social media anger is more often expressed as insults toward the company or others in the community, "I'd tell the CEO to go screw himself," and "Shorts are such morons!"

THE VALUE OF ANGER

> *In time we hate that which we often fear.*
> —William Shakespeare, *Antony and Cleopatra*

Angry investors believe they are right, they do not investigate opposing viewpoints, and they become inflexible and unwilling to reverse course even when evidence contradicts their stance. Despite such obvious cognitive biases rooted in anger, cross-sectional studies designed to arbitrage anger across stocks have weak results. However, like fear, anger is much more useful when conditioned with value characteristics. When stocks that are high in both value and anger are selected, such stocks outperform a simple value strategy substantially on a yearly turnover strategy.

When investor anger hardens into the belief that there are permanent fundamental flaws in a company, it creates a buying opportunity for those who can examine both sides of the argument dispassionately. Ultimately prices—on average—drift higher as anger abates or bargain-hunters with less emotional sensitivity step in to buy discounted shares. The mental rigidity and mistrust that anger spawns is destructive to stock investors.

A more complex cousin of anger is trust. Trust itself takes time to build, but like anger's ability to explode onto the scene, trust can be broken in seconds. The next section explores how violations of trust, and chronic states of mistrust, provoke asset price overreaction and create arbitrage opportunities.

TRUST

[Animal Spirits] refers also to the sense of trust we have in each other, our sense of fairness in economic dealings, and our sense of the extent of corruption and bad faith. When animal spirits are on ebb, consumers do not want to spend and businesses do not want to make capital expenditures or hire people.
  —Robert Shiller, 2013 Nobel Laureate in Economics[9]

As Robert Shiller noted, interpersonal trust underpins the animal spirits of the economy. Without trust, there is no credit given. Without credit, there is little economic activity beyond physical barter.

Trust as a state of mind is a complex emotion, and measuring it in text is a challenge. Trust is embodied in such descriptors as confidence, belief, and faith. It is an abstract state of mind reflected through stated beliefs and behavior. The Trust TRMI was designed to quantify the trusting references toward a company, its management, and its products versus mistrustful references. A trusting reference includes phrases such as "Their new product is reliable" and "The CEO is an upstanding individual." Mistrustful references include "Their customer service department is underhanded and sneaky" and "The product warranty is deceptive." The difference between trusting and mistrustful references over time is quantified in the index.

Corruption scandals bring to light a darker side of human nature, and it should be no surprise that they instill mistrust. When the Trust TRMI is low, it represents such mistrust, often prompted by the criminal behavior of companies or their management teams.

Petrobras (PETR4) started 2014 with among the highest media sentiment of all Latin American companies. By the end of that year, its media sentiment was near the lowest. This reversal in fortunes can be traced to a scandal involving kickbacks for construction contracts, implicating involvement near the top of the Brazilian government.[10] As the weeks passed after the scandal broke in the media, it became apparent that more than $2 billion had been funneled to pay bribes in order to secure lucrative contracts for the company.[11] The fallout from the scandal was projected to shave up to 1.5 percent off of Brazil's GDP for the year 2015.[12] Considering these sobering facts, the selloff of the stock following this scandal was somewhat predictable.

Figure 13.2 depicts how the trust investors expressed in Petrobras fell as revelations of the company's misdeeds spread. As details of the Petrobras corruption scandal were unearthed throughout fall 2014, the stock slid along with each sordid new indictment.

Trust underpins functioning markets. Researchers found that countries with lower levels of interpersonal trust have slower economic growth,[13] while increasing levels of trust predict greater economic activity.[14] The mechanism by which trust increases growth is long-term in nature: "[T]rust affects schooling and the rule of law directly. These variables in turn affect the investment rate (schooling) and provide a direct effect (rule of law) on the growth rate."[15] The Petrobras scandal had far-reaching implications for Brazil's economy, and as a result, international investors exited their Petrobras (and Brazilian) investments.

As seen earlier in the book, investors overreact to events with vivid, possibly catastrophic consequences. Similarly, investors underprice assets in which they have lost faith. In the case of Petrobras, the stock's 75 percent rally over the two months from March to May 2015 (visible in Figure 13.2) should not have been wholly unexpected based on investors' short-term overreaction.

WHO TRUSTS BANKERS?

> *A critical aspect of animal spirits is trust, an emotional state that dismisses doubts about others.*
> —Robert Shiller, 2013 Nobel Laureate in Economics[16]

In the aftermath of the global financial crisis, during a period when trust in banks was only just beginning to recover, a particularly damaging scandal broke. LIBOR (London Interbank Offered Rate)—used to value over $350 trillion in derivatives contracts[17]—was being rigged by the banks tasked with assigning its daily value. Bankers were falsely adjusting their submitted rates to increase trading profits or to give a rosy impression of their creditworthiness. While egregious, the negative implications of this scandal were exaggerated in the media, and populist rants against banks arose with renewed vigor. Figure 13.3 demonstrates the dramatic decline in trust in Barclays Bank, despite (or perhaps because of) Barclays' transparency about its employees' involvement in LIBOR-rigging.

Remarkably, trust in Barclays recovered rapidly, driving a more than 100 percent stock rally from the low within 12 months. For both Petrobras and Barclays, major scandals precipitated dramatic stock slides, and the mistrust-fueled lows were followed by price recoveries (fully in the case of Barclays, but stillborn in the case of Petrobras as of this writing).

Given these rebounds, is it possible that high media mistrust systematically marks investor overreaction? Cross-sectional studies provide insights.

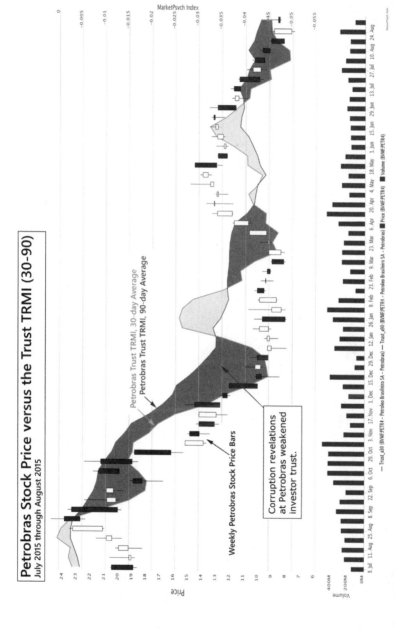

FIGURE 13.2 A depiction of the declining media trust in Petrobras following revelations of corruption at the company; a simple 90-day and 200-day average of trust are superimposed on the stock price.

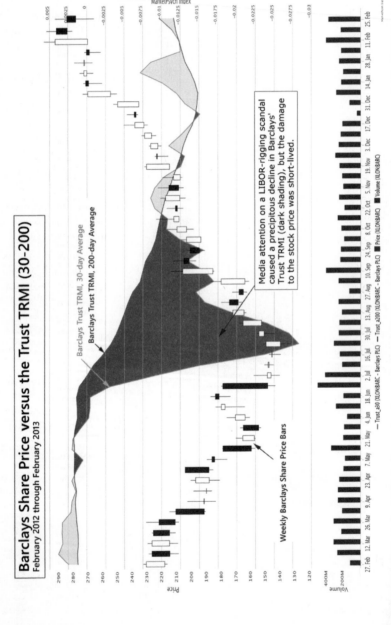

FIGURE 13.3 A chart of Barclay's stock price with a MACD (30–200) of the Trust TRMI superimposed. The LIBOR-rigging scandal caused a sharp fall in stock price and trust, both of which quickly rebounded.

THE TRUST FACTOR

As Dr. Shiller suggests, trust is a key "animal spirit," and its effect on investor behavior is both profound and surprisingly contrarian over the year following a trust-damaging event. This section reviews the results of trust arbitrage across U.S. stocks and global stock markets to establish when mistrust (and high trust) precede asset price reversals.

A cross-sectional study of the Trust TRMI for individual U.S. equities was performed. The potential value of arbitraging trust was seen to a limited extent in the weekly model of Figure 8.2. Trust presents arbitrage opportunities on monthly and yearly horizons across stocks as well. This section demonstrates two monthly equity curves. Figure 13.4 shows a monthly equity curve derived from arbitraging trust in the news about the top 100 U.S. stocks by buzz—going long the quintile (20) least trusted and shorting the quintile (20) most trusted.

Note that the equity curve in Figure 13.4 is uninteresting until the global financial crisis. Perhaps trust in stocks became an issue conducive to overreaction among U.S. stock investors after the crisis. Global markets also show benefits from trust arbitrage.

The equity curve in Figure 13.5 was derived using a monthly holding period cross-sectional model. Global stock index prices came from Thomson Reuters Tick History database. The strategy shorts the top quartile (5) of highest trust countries and goes long the bottom quartile (5) of lowest trust countries using each country's principal stock index.

According to this model, stock markets in the most trusted countries have underperformed those in the least trusted countries since 1998. While it is emotionally more comfortable to invest in a country whose government

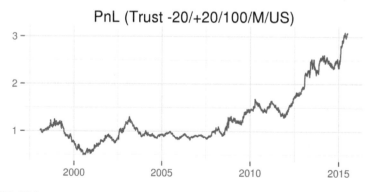

FIGURE 13.4 An equity curve derived from arbitraging monthly news trust across U.S. stocks.

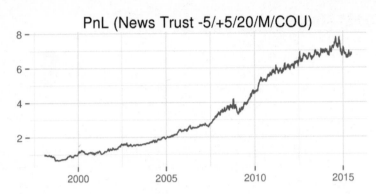

FIGURE 13.5   An equity curve derived from arbitraging trust across global stock indexes in a monthly rotation model.

and business conditions are trustworthy, such comfort has a cost. Lower long-run returns result from trusted countries' stock markets. This model has benefited from increasing fund flows into markets with less established legal and governance systems (emerging markets) in the past two decades, and there are likely to be periodic flights to quality that cause the returns to decline (as in 2015).

TRUST AND FORGIVENESS

> *The stupid neither forgive nor forget; the naive forgive and forget; the wise forgive but do not forget.*
>
> —Thomas Szasz

Investors have much to learn in the repeating pattern of overreaction to scandal. In the case of Petrobras, after 4 to 5 months sideways price movement characterized by very low trust, the stock price rapidly reversed upward more than 75 percent in less than 2 months, from March to May 2015. It subsequently slumped again. For Barclay's a 100 percent reversal in share price occurred more rapidly, and it endured. Such rebounds are a common occurrence. As a result, trust may be arbitraged in a contrarian manner in cross-sectional models over weeks, months, years, and across countries.

Two key lessons emerge from this chapter. First, scandals and mismanagement that provoke public anger present opportunity for investors. Second, investors benefit from a strategy of rational forgiveness. While anger may achieve short-term goals, in the long term forgiveness leads to greater investing flexibility (and a happier and healthier life).[18]

In these cases there is a specific corollary to Warren Buffett's assertion, "We buy when others are fearful, and we sell when others are greedy."

One could rewrite that saying as, "Buy when others have lost faith, and sell when confidence is complete." The next chapter examines a specific type of trust that suggests stronger predictability over prices—trust in leadership.

IN SUMMARY

- When investors collectively feel angry or mistrustful, stocks become mispriced, and investment opportunities emerge.
- Investors primed with anger avoid buying and are more motivated to sell (purge) assets associated with this emotion.
- Groupon CEO Andrew Mason provoked significant anger among investors and in the media.
- A long-only stock investment strategy that buys stocks which are high in earnings to price (E/P) and high in anger leads to superior long-term returns versus either strategy alone.
- While anger is a simple emotion, trust is a complex feeling that underlies freely operating financial markets.
- Levels of interpersonal trust are correlated with economic growth on a country level.
- A corruption scandal in 2014–2015 at Petrobras and the 2012 LIBOR-rigging scandal at Barclays illustrate how investor mistrust drives price overreaction.
- Perhaps because trust is such an important element of a functioning financial system, there appear to be systematic opportunities to arbitrage trust across individual stocks—buying the least-trusted equities and shorting the most trusted leads to consistent absolute returns over weekly, monthly, and yearly horizons
- Cross-sectional trust arbitrage is valuable not only among U.S. stocks, but also across global stock indexes using the Country-level Trust TRMI.
- A nonjudgmental temperament is needed to buy into scandalous (but likely profitable) corporate turmoil.
- Forgiveness helps to release anger and improve investment decision making.

NOTES

1. Shira Ovide, "Groupon IPO: Growth Rate Is 2,241%," *Wall Street Journal*, June 2, 2011. Retrieved November 20, 2015, from: http://blogs.wsj.com/deals/2011/06/02/groupon-ipo-growth-rate-is-2241/7.
2. Herb Greenberg and Patti Domm, eds., "Greenberg: Worst CEO of 2012," *Market Insider* (CNBC) (December 18, 2012).

3. Michael J. de la Merced, "Remembering the Long, Strange Trip of Groupon's Now-Fired Chief," *The New York Times* (February 28, 2013).
4. J. S. Lerner and D. Keltner, "Fear, Anger, and Risk," *Journal of Personality and Social Psychology* 81 (2001), pp. 146–159.
5. J. S. Lerner, D. A. Small, and G. Loewenstein, "Heart Strings and Purse Strings: Carry-over Effects of Emotions on Economic Transactions," *Psychological Science* 15 (2004), pp. 337–341.
6. R. Fan, J. Zhao, Y. Chen, and K. Xu. 2014, "Anger Is More Influential Than Joy: Sentiment Correlation in Weibo," *PLoS ONE* 9(10), p. e110184.
7. B. J. Bushman, "Does Venting Anger Feed or Extinguish the Flame? Catharsis, Rumination, Distraction, Anger, and Aggressive Responding," *Personality and Social Psychology Bulletin* 28(6) (June 2002), pp. 724–731.
8. Hajo Adam and Aiwa Shirako, "Not All Anger Is Created Equal: The Impact of the Expresser's Culture on the Social Effects of Anger in Negotiations," *Journal of Applied Psychology* 98(5) (2013), p. 785.
9. Robert J. Shiller. "Animal Spirits Depend on Trust: The Proposed Stimulus Isn't Big Enough to Restore Confidence," *Wall Street Journal* (January 27, 2009). Downloaded from: http://www.wsj.com/articles/SB123302080925418107.
10. Stephen EIisenhammer. "Petrobras Scandal Shakes Up Brazil's Presidential Race," *Reuters* (September 7, 2014). Retrieved May 20, 2015 from: http://www.reuters.com/article/2014/09/07/us-brazil-election-petrobras-idUSKBN0H20PZ20140907.
11. Wyre Davies, "The Real Losers in Brazil's Petrobras Scandal," *BBC* (April 23, 2015). Retrieved May 20, 2015, from: http://www.bbc.com/news/world-latin-america-32428954.
12. Jen Blount, "As Petrobras Scandal Spreads, Economic Toll Mounts for Brazil," *Reuters* (April 20, 2015). Downloaded May 20, 2015, from http://www.reuters.com/article/2015/04/20/us-brazil-petrobras-impact-idUSKBN0NB1QD20150420.
13. Paul. J. Zak and Stephen Knack, "Trust and Growth," *Economic Journal* 111(470) (2001), pp. 295–321.
14. Christian Bjørnskov, "How Does Social Trust Affect Economic Growth?" *Southern Economic Journal* 78(4) (2012), pp. 1346–1368.
15. Ibid.
16. Robert J. Shiller, "Animal Spirits Depend on Trust: The Proposed Stimulus Isn't Big Enough to Restore Confidence," *Wall Street Journal* (January 27, 2009). Downloaded from: http://www.wsj.com/articles/SB123302080925418107.
17. "Libor Scandal Explained and What Rate-Rigging Means to You," *USA Today* (July 2012). Retrieved August 3, 2012.
18. Emiliano Ricciardi, Giuseppina Rota, Lorenzo Sani, Claudio Gentili, Anna Gaglianese, Mario Guazzelli, and Pietro Pietrini, "How the Brain Heals Emotional Wounds: The Functional Neuroanatomy of Forgiveness," *Frontiers in Human Neuroscience* 7 (2013).

CHAPTER 14

The Psychology of Leadership

They grumbled and complained of the long voyage, and I reproached them for their lack of spirit, telling them that, for better or worse, they had to complete the enterprise on which the Catholic Sovereigns had sent them. I cheered them on as best I could, telling them of all the honors and rewards they were about to receive. I also told the men that it was useless to complain, for I had started out to find the Indies and would continue until I had accomplished that mission, with the help of Our Lord.
—Christopher Columbus, Wednesday, October 10, 1492

Christopher Columbus had set out 68 days before he wrote the lines above, confident that he could reach Cathay (China) on his first voyage across the Atlantic Ocean. Unfortunately a series of bad omens had spooked his sailors over the course of the journey, and by October 10 they had still not sighted land. His crew was on the verge of mutiny, and they demanded that Columbus turn back to Spain.

To understand the sailors' mutinous attitude, it helps to contemplate the voyage's uneven progress. After originally setting out from Spain, they had arrived in the Canary Islands to pick up supplies. There they received word that the Portuguese king had ordered the crew captured and imprisoned. After hastily embarking from the Canaries, the rudder of the *Pinta* broke and they were forced to return to the islands for repairs. While awaiting repairs on Tenerife, the island's volcano began to violently erupt—a new and frightening experience for the Spanish sailors. Repair finished, they took to the Atlantic again, and as the shores of the last of the Canary Islands faded out of sight, many sailors burst into tears, saying that "they were sailing off—off—off—upon the awful Sea of Darkness and would never see land any more."[1]

The ships slowed in the Sargasso Sea—where there are few winds or currents—and drifted lazily through beds of seaweed and still waters for a week. The sailors became concerned that they would die, adrift. Mirages of land raised hope and then dashed the crews' spirits.

In addition to the crew's increasing fragility, Columbus soon realized that his calculations were incorrect—they had not found land where he had anticipated. If Columbus returned to Spain without having reached land, he would face disgrace, imprisonment, or even death. Columbus made a decision to doctor the distances traveled in his logs, keeping one log of the true distance and one for his crewmen which showed less distance traveled.

The sailors then noticed that their magnetic compass no longer oriented itself properly to the North Star. To quiet their fears, Columbus lied and told the crew that the North Star had changed its position.

On October 10, 1492, the anxiety of the crew turned into mutinous fervor. To temporarily calm his sailors' frustration, Columbus took a gamble. He promised that if they did not sight land within three days, the ships would turn back to Spain. Columbus appealed to duty, cajoled, threatened, practiced deceit, and finally made a last-ditch gamble, all to maintain his leadership in the pursuit of his vision. Fortunately for Columbus and the sailors, landfall was made on the morning of October 12, 1492.

Like Columbus, corporate executives often face restive investors as they pursue their goals. Sometimes they gamble their leadership on a specific outcome. Columbus' "just three more days" becomes their bet that they can turn around earnings "next quarter" or that a new product launch will be a hit. If they achieve their goal, they are acclaimed, but if not, their reputation is damaged.

The social psychology of how humans perceive and respond to leaders has deep roots in the psyche. Powerful positive social emotions about leadership—such as adoration and acclaim—may rapidly turn to blame and scapegoating. This chapter examines unfairly blamed leadership teams and their opposite—the superstar CEOs. Research in this chapter demonstrates how individual stocks are influenced by perceptions of management instability and dishonesty. Additionally, executive communications on earnings conference call transcripts influence stock prices.

BLAMING MANAGEMENT

It's too easy to criticize a man when he's out of favour, and to make him shoulder the blame for everybody else's mistakes.
—Leo Tolstoy, *War and Peace*

Reid Hastings, CEO of Netflix, experienced widespread news and social media criticism following the company's launch of a new DVD/streaming subscription model in 2011.[2] Hastings had led Netflix to raise prices up to 60 percent for a standard subscription, which severely dented customer confidence, and rumors spread that he was unfit to lead the company. The stock price plummeted from over $40 to $9 per share (split-adjusted) over the 5 months following the shift in strategy. A chart depicting Netflix (NFLX) stock price, and the managementTrust TRMI during 2011 appears in Figure 14.1. Despite the initial media excoriation of Hastings' leadership, in 2013 Hastings' reputation (and stock price) recovered to new highs.

Media denigration of CEO judgment is commonplace and, too often, misplaced. There are numerous examples of heavily criticized CEOs returning to prove their detractors wrong. Most famously, Steve Jobs was ousted from Apple in 1985 under withering criticism of his leadership. After he was invited back to run the company in 1997, he grew Apple into the world's most valuable company. Such scapegoating of leaders is commonplace in the media, and based on anthropological research, it holds an important socio-psychological function.

THE EMOTIONAL VALUE OF HUMAN SACRIFICE

> *Scapegoat:*
>
> a) *one that bears the blame for others.*
> b) *one that is the object of irrational hostility.*
> —*Merriam Webster Dictionary*[3]

Scapegoating emerges when a society or organization is in distress, and it provides both an explanation for the distress ("He caused this!") and an easy solution ("Throw the bum out!"). In pre-modern societies, animal sacrifice (from which the word *scapegoat* derives) satisfied the emotional needs of the group without upending the social order. Sacrifices established a feeling of control over uncertain circumstances (weather, crop yields, war, and other unpredictable events). In honor of the value of the scapegoating process to stabilizing the society, the chosen victim was sometimes first elevated to a near-god-like status and—during human sacrifice among the Aztecs—groomed with a year of luxurious living prior to their execution.

In modern societies ritualistic sacrifice no longer occurs, yet the social need to place blame remains, and episodic paroxysms of social violence appear to serve a similar psychological purpose. Witch hunts, pogroms, or ethnic cleansing are often instigated by the politically or economically

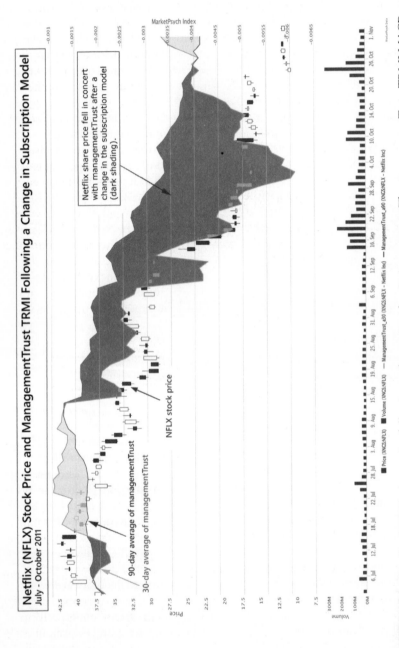

FIGURE 14.1 Netflix (NFLX) share price following a change in subscription strategy. The managementTrust TRMI MACD (30–90) is plotted against the share price.

powerful to bolster their status and reduce simmering class tensions. Evidence of the economic link between socially sanctioned group-on-group violence is seen in the correlation of cotton prices with anti-black violence (lynchings) in the U.S. South between 1882 and 1930. "The correlation between the price of cotton (the principal product of the area at that time) and the number of lynchings of black men by whites ranged from −0.63 to −0.72, suggesting that a poor economy induced white people to take out their frustrations by attacking an outgroup."[4]

Modern references to workplace scapegoats acknowledge the social-emotional benefits of scapegoating, sometimes in a humorous way, as in Scott Adams' Dilbert cartoons.[5,6] However, for the scapegoats themselves, the process is anything but enjoyable. In the business world, a peanut gallery of analysts and investors is watching for strategic blunders by management teams, and scapegoating is often inappropriately intense, as seen in the Reid Hastings example above.

In 2010, one year prior to the precipitous decline in Netflix's stock price, Reid Hastings was named the Top Businessperson of the Year by *Fortune* magazine. His photo graced *Fortune*'s monthly magazine cover.[7] Hastings's fall from media grace should not have been entirely unexpected. According to academic research, after CEOs are recognized as "superstars" in the media, their stock price underperforms over the subsequent three years.

SUPERSTAR CEOs

> *[A] person is a leader (good or bad) because others say so.*
> —James McElroy, describing the *Attribution Theory of Leadership*[8]

Hubris is one of the most dangerous emotional states that CEOs (and investors) can experience, as it often precedes the greatest losses. The business press has coined the term "CEO disease" to refer to the tendency of CEOs to underperform after achieving the top position in their organization.

In their 2009 paper, "Superstar CEOs," Ulrike Malmendier of Stanford and Geoffrey Tate of UCLA, using data collected by Stefano Della-Vigna, selected a sample of 283 companies whose CEOs had won prestigious nationwide awards from the business press.[9] From six days following the award to three years later, they found that the stocks of award winners underperformed those of predicted award winners (a similar cohort). In fact, the stocks of the 283 award winners studied in the paper underperformed the predicted award winners by 4 percent over the first year, 14 percent over two years, and 20 percent over a three-year window. From this result, it appears that hubris is one cause of the decline in fortunes for the most trusted companies. A second cause—moral corruption—may also be present.

Believing oneself to be a superstar manager may predispose managers to moral decline. Lord Acton's saying, "Power corrupts, and absolute power corrupts absolutely," has been borne out in an ingenious series of experiments.[10] The researchers emotionally primed subjects by asking them to remember a time that they felt powerful (one group) or felt powerless (a second group). When compared to the powerless, those primed to feel powerful condemned other people's cheating while cheating more themselves. The powerful were also more strict in judging others' moral transgressions but more lenient in judging their own transgressions.[11] Just as Christopher Columbus found it reasonable to doctor the ship's distance logs in order to pacify his crew, those who feel powerful believe they are entitled to break rules and behave less morally than others. They also judge others more harshly than they would judge themselves for the same moral lapse. These tendencies are an innate feature of human leadership psychology, and they predispose managers with high opinions of themselves to start down a slippery slope of scandalous behavior.

BUY MISTRUSTED LEADERSHIP

> *Leadership is a construct in the mind of human beings that does not exist independently from followers, but only in their perceptions.*
>
> —Bobby J. Calder[12]

In cross-sectional studies, CJ Liu arbitraged high management trust versus low management trust companies. The managementTrust TRMI is calculated by quantifying specific characteristics in references to a company's corporate management team (board, CEO, directors, and others). Trust was quantified in the presence of descriptors of managers with terms such as "reliable," "dependable," and "honest," while mistrustful associations were measured in words such as "scoundrel," "crook," and various expletives. The difference between the frequency of each type of reference was aggregated into a rolling index.

CJ's analysis identified the top 100 U.S. stocks with the highest buzz in the news over the past year and then ranked those 100 companies by their average monthly managementTrust value. To establish a broad effect, it simulated a portfolio that shorts the top 20 percent of most-trusted-leadership companies, and it goes long (buys) the bottom 20 percent. It holds each position for 12 months. This model is performing arbitrage

FIGURE 14.2 Equity curve derived from arbitraging managementTrust across the yearly news and social media about individual U.S. equities.

of management trust, generating an absolute return equity curve seen in Figure 14.2.

On an annual basis, when a company's management team is heavily featured in the news for incompetent behavior, investors should be buying that stock, and when they are praised for excellent work, investors should be selling. This positive equity curve also appears in weekly and monthly arbitrage.

There may be a scarcity effect driving the results. Major management implosions are uncommon, but when they happen, they are often deemed newsworthy. As Warren Buffett famously said, "It takes 20 years to build a reputation and five minutes to ruin it."[13] The media's perceptions of governments—and their overall level of instability—shows a similar pattern to that seen with management teams.

BUY UNSTABLE GOVERNMENTS

> *Il faut acheter au son du canon et vendre au son du clairon.*
> *[One must buy to the sound of cannons and sell to the sound of trumpets]*
>   —Attributed to Baron Nathan Rothschild, 1812

Nathan Rothschild's above comment was uttered during the Napoleonic Wars, hence its reference to cannons (countries at war) and trumpets (to celebrate victory). Today there is much less geopolitical conflict, yet a nation in political distress, such as one experiencing government instability, represents a modern application of Rothschild's maxim. For global investors, the risk of a legal contract not being honored by a change in government is real, and investors may avoid the perceived risk of countries with unstable governments. Based on recent research, such avoidance is typically overreaction.

The global map in Figure 14.3 depicts the frequency of media reports about government instability around the globe. Several countries in sub-Saharan Africa were not included in the analysis, and thus are colored white.

The countries that show the darkest shading—Libya, Venezuela, Cambodia, Syria—are not easily tradable. Among countries with easily tradable stock market indexes, government instability may take the form of a rapid succession of short-lived governments in a parliamentary system. Such democratic instability, which is characterized by rapid changes in the dominant party or threats of significant political turnover, appears to create investment opportunities in developed nations, as explained in the following pages.

To study whether Rothschild's stated global investment philosophy still holds true, CJ Liu performed an arbitrage using the governmentInstability TRMI. His code selected the top 20 most buzzed-about countries in the news over the past 12 months. Countries without tradable stock were excluded. The remaining countries were ranked by their average value of governmentInstability over the prior 12 months. A hypothetical portfolio was generated in which the top four (e.g., most unstable according to the news media) stock indexes were bought, and the bottom four (most stable) were shorted. The positions were held for 12 months. The portfolio was rolled forward monthly and updated with one-twelfth of the portfolio since 1999. Figure 14.4 depicts the equity curve derived from this research.

The positive results of this model are predominantly from buying the most unstable countries. Shorting stable countries alone does not yield positive returns. Currency fluctuations were not hedged out of this model, and interest rate yields, when included, actually boost the returns.

Given the high returns historically generated by this strategy, CJ performed a sensitivity analysis (a type of stress test) which showed superior returns at higher values of governmentInstability. All of the equity curve's returns come from buying stocks in countries with unstable governments. Shorting stocks of countries with stable governments in not a consistently profitable strategy. Importantly, there are a wide variety of countries chosen by this model. All of the model's constituents currently have publicly–traded ETFs representing their major stock indices.

Media reports about untrusted management teams and wobbly governments create investment opportunities. Yet if one is a corporate manager trying to establish credibility, how can one build a good reputation? Text

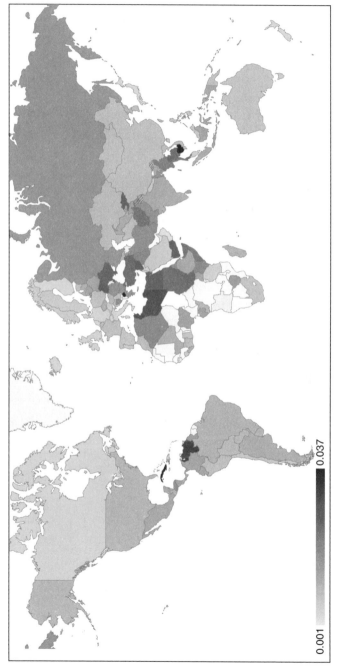

FIGURE 14.3 The value of the governmentInstability TRMI on a global heat map in 2014.

0.001

0.037

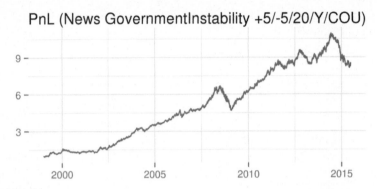

FIGURE 14.4 An equity curve derived via a 12-month rotating arbitrage of the primary stock indexes in the countries with the most unstable governments, as ranked by the governmentInstability TRMI, versus the most stable governments.

analytics of corporate conference call transcripts provides communication lessons for corporate executives.

USING TEXT ANALYTICS TO IMPROVE EXECUTIVE COMMUNICATION

A few years ago, a Fortune 500 company asked MarketPsych to help the CEO improve his investor communications. The CEO often said the wrong thing at the wrong time, especially during earnings conference calls, and the investing public was doubting his leadership capabilities. Using the Thomson Reuters Street Events database of earnings conference call transcripts, the CEOs comments were quantified over the 30 past quarterly conference calls. The analysis identified exactly what content was impacting the stock price in the three months after each call.

The initial results were self-explanatory. Naturally, negative accounting news and uncertainties expressed by the CEO led to stock price declines. But as a subset of those negative calls, it appeared that if the CEO announced a definitive plan to restore earnings despite the current setback, the stock was not negatively impacted in the long term. If he announced no plan or waffled, the stock fell and continued to fall. If he discussed new innovations at the company, the stock rose; if he did not, the stock underperformed. If he praised his team, the stock outperformed; if he did not, it declined. In fact, expressing appreciation for his team members was one of the most powerful independent factors driving the stock price in the three months following an earnings call. Perhaps there is a subtle social signal when a leader apportions credit. Such a leader may be less dazzled by his (or her) brilliance, and thus less likely to make mistakes rooted in hubris.

CONCLUSION

> *The search for a scapegoat is the easiest of all hunting expeditions.*
> —Dwight D. Eisenhower

Christopher Columbus was ultimately celebrated for his discoveries, but contemporaries shamed him for poor leadership. On his third and fourth voyages to the New World, Columbus was evicted from the colony he founded on Santo Domingo by mutineers who despised him. He was later banned from landing at Santo Domingo to obtain badly needed supplies, and he was forced to weather a hurricane in a nearby harbor.

After returning to Spain, Columbus spent decades attempting to persuade the Spanish crown to relinquish his contractual share of the wealth his discovery brought back to Spain. The Spanish crown, perhaps corrupted by power, did not honor its agreement with Columbus. The crown appropriated Columbus's share of the New World profits for themselves. He died with the Spanish crown having violated its commercial agreement with him (although it was later restored by his son).

Management of others is one of the most complex processes in business. As investors, it is beneficial to observe the cycle of adoration and scapegoating of CEOs and management teams. Managers who see themselves as more powerful than they actually are weaken their long-term performance (conversely, one shouldn't see oneself as lacking power—the middle ground is key). As Netflix's Reid Hastings put it while he accepted (yet another) leadership award from Stanford University in 2014—"There's this whole motif that to be a great CEO you have to be a great product person. That's intoxicating and fun, but you build in incredible amounts of dependence on yourselves. You're much stronger building a distributed set of great thinkers."[14] Such great thinkers shine during periods of uncertainty, which is the topic of the next chapter.

IN SUMMARY

- Corporate executives are the human face of companies, while government leaders are the face of countries.
- Such leaders embody the emotional hopes and expectations of the organization, and their media image may veer from that of a superstar leader to one of a scapegoat.

- Scapegoats serve important socio-psychological stabilizing functions during times of distress and unpredictability.
- Leaders who win awards experience average stock price underperformance following the award.
- Investor risk aversion related to changes in leadership perceptions create arbitrage opportunities across stocks.
- Buying stocks with mistrusted management teams and shorting those with stable or trusted teams is an exploitable arbitrage opportunity.
- Buying stocks in countries with unstable governments and shorting stocks in countries with stable governments creates a historically successful arbitrage.

NOTES

1. Elbridge S. Brooks, "The True Story of Christopher Columbus: Called the Great Admiral" (1892). From: http://www.gutenberg.org/files/1488/1488-h/1488-h .htm#link2HCH0005.
2. Jessie Becker, "Netflix Introduces New Plans and Announces Price Changes," July 12, 2011. http://blog.netflix.com/2011/07/netflix-introduces-new-plans-and.html.
3. http://www.merriam-webster.com/dictionary/scapegoat.
4. C. I. Hovland and R. R. Sears, "Minor Studies of Aggression: VI. Correlation of Lynchings with Economic Indices," *Journal of Psychology: Interdisciplinary and Applied* 9 (1940), pp. 301–310.
5. See this Dilbert comic strip for a humorous example: http://dilbert.com/dyn/str_ strip/000000000/00000000/0000000/000000/30000/5000/800/35831/35831 .strip.gif.
6. Other examples include this poster: http://fridayfunfact.files.wordpress.com/ 2011/12/scapegoat.jpg.
7. Michael V. Copeland, "Reed Hastings: Leader of the Pack," *Fortune* (November 18, 2010). Downloaded May 20, 2015, from: http://fortune.com/2010/11/18/ reed-hastings-leader-of-the-pack/.
8. James C. McElroy, "Leadership & Organization Development Journal Attribution Theory: A leadership Theory for Leaders," *Leadership & Organization Development Journal* 3(4) (1982), p. 413.
9. Ulrike Malmendier and Geoffrey Tate, "Superstar CEOs," *Quarterly Journal of Economics* 124(4) (November 1, 2009), pp. 1593–1638.
10. Joris Lammers, Diederik A. Stapel, and Adam D. Galinsky, "Power Increases Hypocrisy Moralizing in Reasoning, Immorality in Behavior," *Psychological Science* 21(5) (2010), pp. 737–744.
11. Ibid.

12. B. J. Calder, "An Attribution Theory of Leadership," in B. M. Staw and G. R. Salancik (eds.), *New Directions in Organizational Behavior* (Chicago: St. Clair Press, 1977), p. 196.

13. "Warren Buffett: His Best Quotes," *The Telegraph* (February 14, 2013). Downloaded July 25, 2015, from: http://www.telegraph.co.uk/finance/newsbysector/banksandfinance/8381363/Warren-Buffett-his-best-quotes.html.

14. Bill Snyder, "Netflix Founder Reed Hastings: Make as Few Decisions as Possible: The CEO of Netflix Discusses What He's Learned While Redefining Movie-Watching," *Insights from Stanford Business* (November 3, 2014). Downloaded July 25, 2015, from: https://www.gsb.stanford.edu/insights/netflix-founder-reed-hastings-make-few-decisions-possible.

CHAPTER 15

Navigating Uncertainty

The fundamental law of investing is the uncertainty of the future.
—Peter L. Bernstein

Chris "Jesus" Ferguson won more than $7 million playing poker, including three championship bracelets from the *World Series of Poker*.[1] Ferguson's background is notable not only for his success in the poker game Texas Hold 'em, but also for his immersion in game theory from a young age. Ferguson's father, Tom Ferguson, is a professor of mathematics at UCLA with a specialization in game theory, the mathematics of optimal behavior in strategic and competitive situations.

While playing poker professionally, Chris spent 13 years as a graduate student in computer science at UCLA. Relying on both his understanding of the mathematical odds and the lessons he learned from game theory, Chris became, in 2000, the first person to win a prize of more than a million dollars in a poker tournament.[2] According to his father, during that time in graduate school Chris "learned to think about playing and strategies and what other people know about what you know."[3]

The best poker players utilize a superior understanding of odds, as well as an understanding of the betting patterns employed by others:

> *From the pattern of their opponents' bets and behaviors, they work like detectives to determine their cards. They play opportune hands deceptively, and feckless ones, too, and shed unpromising ones before the cards cause them too much harm.*[4]

Chris Ferguson varied his play in order to confuse opponents and leave them with maximum uncertainty about his cards and his intentions. For players unfamiliar with game theory, Ferguson's play appears erratic. According to Andy Bloch, an MIT Electrical Engineering and Harvard Law graduate with over $4 million in poker tournament winnings, "They'll see a bluff and think he bluffs too much, because the bluff doesn't make sense." Through the use of game theory, Ferguson reduces his reliance on intuition and is less distracted by irrelevant information.[5]

There is anecdotal evidence that excellent strategic game players have an edge in investing. Warren Buffett is an avid bridge player, and many portfolio managers play poker.[6] Bridge and poker require a knowledge of odds and an assessment of fellow players. Like in markets, learning the pure mathematics of the games will allow one to approach the top echelons of performance, but to be a champion, it's essential to understand the behavioral patterns that drive the other participants.

This chapter reviews how strategic decisions are best made in the context of uncertainty—when players don't fully understand the odds and the potential payoffs. Usefully for this chapter, most investors seek to avoid uncertainty, and such avoidance creates long-term opportunities in equities.

HOW INVESTORS DEAL WITH UNCERTAINTY

> *Our doubts are traitors, and make us lose the good we oft might win, by fearing to attempt.*
> —William Shakespeare, *Measure for Measure*

Chris Ferguson's approach to poker is based on both an understanding of the fixed odds of poker hands as well as patterns in human behavior around risk and reward. The four rounds of betting in Texas Hold 'em provides considerable leverage for psychological game play and behavioral misdirection.

In the markets, the future is unknown, and for traders to hone optimal expected value assessments, they must do so in the midst of much noise. The odds that Ferguson assessed in poker hands were fixed—for example, the odds of being dealt two aces in the hole is 0.45 percent—while those faced by traders in the markets are more ambiguous. Uncertainty is endemic to markets.

In the first half of the twentieth century, Frank Knight developed the concept of Knightian uncertainty to differentiate between two types of uncertainty.[7] Knight noted that when potential future outcomes can be expressed probabilistically, they are called risk. When there is a lack of knowledge about potential probabilities, the outcomes are described as uncertain or ambiguous.

Excellence in investing depends on both the ability to find an edge and the ability to accurately assess potential downside. Taken together, these two abilities comprise strategic thinking. Strategic thinking is more precisely called *intuitive expected value assessment,* and it is defined by the ability to rapidly and unconsciously evaluate the odds, risks, and potential benefits of a gamble. Yet strategic thinking is not a deliberate mental process, as in solving mathematical problems, but rather, it is a subtle intuitive process that blends pattern recognition, risk assessment, and stress management.

MarketPsych has offered a variety of free online financial tests since 2004. These tests evaluate a range of cognitive and personality characteristics. In 2014, Paul Squires, an industrial psychologist and founder of Applied Skills & Knowledge, analyzed the test results. Dr. Squires cleaned the data extensively and found that among professional investor and traders, cognitive traits were more significant than personality traits in predicting investment performance. In particular, he found the strongest correlation with investor success came from the MarketPsych Gambling Task (MGT). In the MGT players are forced to make rapid and intuitive expected value calculations, and their performance correlates strongly with their reported historical market returns.

The MGT is a derivative of the Iowa Gambling Task. In the MGT, test-takers are asked to select between one of five card decks on each trial. They have five seconds to make a decision. After a deck is selected, the payoff of that deck and every other deck is displayed for one second. The payoffs vary on each trial but on average, two decks yield overall losses and two decks generate overall gains. One deck always gives a fixed small reward on each trial.

Test-takers' goal is to make the most money by finding the decks with the highest payoffs over time. The MGT gauges the accuracy of one's intuition and learning rate in a "noisy" and time-constrained environment. Test-takers who most rapidly learn the pattern in returns across the decks make the most money. Because the task cycles too quickly for writing down payoffs, it tests unconscious rather than conscious learning of the expected value of each deck.

Using self-reported data on five-year investment returns, Dr. Squires identified that the better one's performance on the MGT, the more likely that the user would report higher investment returns. A graphic of this finding is in Figure 15.1.

This correlation between test results and investment returns was the most significant of all such results from MarketPsych's various personality and cognitive tests. Interestingly, the origin of this cognitive skill may be partially genetic.

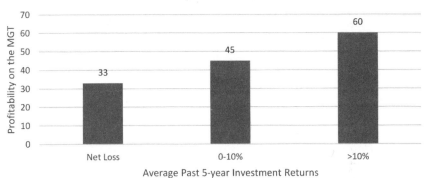

FIGURE 15.1 Investors who perform well on the MarketPsych Gambing Task (*y*-axis) on average report higher past investment performance (*x*-axis). Source: Paul Squires, PhD.

THE WARRIOR GENE

Markets are constantly in a state of uncertainty and flux and money is made by discounting the obvious and betting on the unexpected.

—George Soros

Academics call attempts to avoid uncertainty *ambiguity aversion*. Ambiguity-averse individuals excessively avoid situations in which they have inadequate information to make an informed decision. The neural basis for ambiguity aversion is activation in the brain's amygdala, part of the loss-avoidance system,[8] which fuels overreaction. Investors who can tackle—rather than shy away from—ambiguity are at a distinct advantage. Unfortunately, the ability to hone this skill may be partially hardwired.

Although genetic science is still primitive, there are fascinating preliminary findings relevant to finance. For example, the presence of the gene (MAOA-L) in an individual correlates with superior financial risk taking in multiple studies. The MAOA gene produces an enzyme involved in the catabolism (breakdown) of the neurotransmitters dopamine, norepinephrine, and serotonin. The abnormal variant MAOA-L is more active than the normal MAOA gene. The enzyme produced by MAOA is inhibited by some antidepressants (monoamine oxidase inhibitors), and the dopamine, serotonin, and norepinephrine that accumulates in the synapses as a result of this inhibition is thought to be responsible for the typical improvement in mood for those who take these medications. While the MAOA-L variant does not correlate with higher rates of depression, it may indicate greater sensitivity to neurotransmitters.

The behavioral traits associated with the MAOA-L gene variant include impulsive risk taking and aggression. Those with this gene variant take more risks, but importantly, they prefer risks with higher expected values. As a result of its profit-maximizing nature, the gene variant was nicknamed the *warrior gene*. In a study on the genetics of financial risk–taking biases, researchers note, "Our computational choice model, rooted in established decision theory, showed that MAOA-L carriers exhibited such behavior because they are able to make better financial decisions under risk, and not because they are more impulsive."[9] In summary, carriers of this gene perform better strategic financial decision making. This finding is significant because there are numerous sources of uncertainty in markets, and honing the skills underlying expected value computation is one key to trading success. Another key to success is to dive into—rather than avoid— uncertainty surrounding investments.

UNCERTAINTY ABOUT ASSET PRICES

> *The future is never clear, and you pay a very high price in the stock market for a cheery consensus. Uncertainty is the friend of the buyer of long-term values.*
>
> —Warren Buffett [10]

As Warren Buffett noted, investors occasionally overreact to uncertainty, creating opportunities for others. Uncertainty isn't clearly bad or good for assets—it depends on how the uncertainty is framed. Uncertainty about an earnings announcement in a high-growth sector is often greeted with giddy anticipation, while uncertainty about monetary policy during a financial crisis is cause for alarm. In the psychology literature, the term *probability collapse* refers to the resolution of uncertainty due to an event. For example, after an earnings report is released, uncertainty about that quarter's earnings collapses to zero. Yet despite such singular events, uncertainty is widespread about many issues and topics, and there also appear to be systematic effects of uncertainty.

Researchers found that ambiguity aversion systematically and predictably leads investors to mistakenly discount asset prices. High-uncertainty equities and country stock indices on average outperform their less ambiguous peers.[11] For example, ambiguity aversion is reflected in the returns of stocks of companies with ambiguous information on their balance sheets (e.g., research and development spending) that cannot traditionally be correlated with future valuations. Stocks with poorer earnings quality (having more ambiguous information) have greater long-term returns than those with better (more transparent) accounting.[12] As a result of aversion to ambiguous items on accounting statements, investors mistakenly avoid such stocks and miss out on greater long-term returns. However, there are some interesting exceptions.

High uncertainty typically amplifies negative sentiment and generates opportunity (as Warren Buffett notes above), but in speculative bubbles uncertainty has the opposite effect—magnifying the prevailing positive sentiment. During speculative bubbles, companies with valuation uncertainty outperform peers before earnings[13] and during IPOs.[14] When optimism is high, investors project an unfounded positive spin onto the unclear data. In the late 1990s, initial public offerings (IPOs) of Internet companies with negative cash flows had relatively higher initial trading prices. According to researchers, "The role of earnings in valuation of these firms ... completely disappeared in 1999."[15] Presumably, investors considered negative cash flows to be an investment in the future. The lack of concrete earnings information led to an exaggerated projection of investors' optimism. In such cases of "irrational exuberance," investors are ambiguity loving. In summary, investors are usually ambiguity averse, especially when they are pessimistic, but during periods of optimism, they overvalue ambiguity.

To investigate how overall market sentiment affects the returns of stocks with ambiguous or subjective information on their balance sheets, researchers examined general sentiment versus subsequent stock performance. Highly subjective stocks were considered to be small stocks, young stocks, high-volatility stocks, unprofitable stocks, non-dividend-paying stocks, extreme-growth stocks, and distressed stocks. The researchers discovered that when investors are optimistic, stocks with ambiguous, uncertain, and generally subjective information underperform over the subsequent period (one year). When investors are pessimistic, the opposite occurs. During periods of pessimism, it is best to buy high-uncertainty stocks, but during periods of optimism, one should stay away from such stocks.[16]

According to researchers, when information about a financial offering is vague, investors rely on feelings and imagination to evaluate stocks.[17] As evidence of ambiguity aversion among investors, during times of greater uncertainty in the markets, when prices are volatile and trading volume high, investors tilt their portfolios toward familiar local stocks.[18] Perhaps this preference is driven by a need for certainty and comfort, which are more likely to be found closer to home.

Supporting the initially damaging effects of uncertainty on stock prices, researchers into the effects of government policy uncertainty concluded, "Stock prices fall at the announcements of policy changes, on average. The price fall is expected to be large if uncertainty about government policy is large."[19] Later, a price bounce is likely to ensue.

Investors' behavioral biases are increased by uncertainty. When stocks are more difficult to value using objective accounting data, investors exhibit a stronger disposition effect (holding losing positions too long and cutting winners short). Even among executives, ambiguity in corporate accounting correlates with behavioral biases such as loss aversion and overconfidence among management.

An interesting reversal of ambiguity aversion occurs when people feel the need to make more money than that offered in a certain outcome. In one gambling experiment, when participants' financial need was greater than the known options' expected average payout, subjects preferred the ambiguous (high-volatility) option.[20] People are more willing to take a chance, and deal with the stress of uncertainty, when other options (not having enough money) are even more stressful.

UNCERTAINTY AT BOEING

Boeing's production of its Dreamliner was beset with production delays and mishaps. Investors and the media followed its manufacturing progress closely. One *Wall Street Journal* report was headlined, "Boeing, in Embarrassing Setback, Says 787 Dreamliner Will Be Delayed." The article noted, "Boeing Co. reversed itself after weeks of promising its new widebody jet would be delivered on time, saying the ambitious project now faces a delay of at least six months."[21] Such setbacks plagued the Dreamliner, and analysts were attuned to each rumor of further production issues. Each time the media reported uncertainty about production progress, the stock dropped significantly.

The Uncertainty TRMI measures expressions of ambiguity—Knightian uncertainty—encompassing a lack of knowledge about outcome probabilities. Words and phrases in the media conveying "doubt," "uncertainty," or "lack of clarity" about an asset contribute to the scores in this index. When a higher proportion of communications about an asset contain elements of uncertainty, the value of the Uncertainty TRMI rises.

Using a decision tree model over a six-year period, the Uncertainty TRMI was the primary driver of Boeing's stock price on a monthly basis

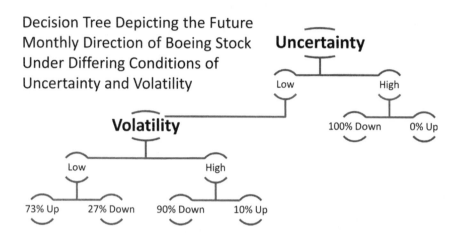

Decision Tree Depicting the Future Monthly Direction of Boeing Stock Under Differing Conditions of Uncertainty and Volatility

FIGURE 15.2 Decision tree depicting the future monthly direction of Boeing (BA) stock under differing conditions of uncertainty and volatility from 2007 to 2013.

from 2007 to 2013. When uncertainty about Boeing's production schedule, management, suppliers, and other factors rose into the top 10 percent of its historical range, the stock dropped 100 percent of the following months. Even when uncertainty was not in the top tier of its historical range, but references to volatility in the company, stock, or production process were high, then the stock dropped the following month. Boeing stock rose 73 percent of the remaining months in which neither uncertainty not volatility was in the top tier. Figure 15.2 displays a decision tree derived from this monthly decision tree study of the years 2007–2013.

Boeing investors were very sensitive to uncertainty during that crucial period for the airline producer. In this single case, high uncertainty preceded falls in the stock price on a month-to-month period. Decision trees are useful for identifying interesting historical relationships; however, those relationships do not always persist into the future. Boeing's case is unique. In cross-sectional analyses across thousands of stocks and over 12-month holding periods, uncertainty is more often precedes a stock price increase.

UNCERTAINTY ACROSS EQUITIES

CJ performed cross-sectional analysis of the Uncertainty TRMI across U.S. stocks. He found that annual and monthly media uncertainty correlated with stock price movement over the following month and year. The equity curve in Figure 15.3 was generated by identifying the top 100 stocks by buzz in the media (both news and social media) and buying shares in the 20 with the most uncertainty and shorting the 20 with the least uncertainty.

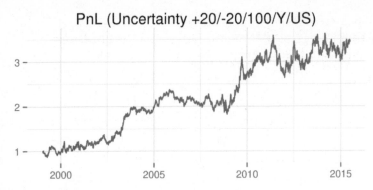

PnL (Uncertainty +20/-20/100/Y/US)

FIGURE 15.3 Equity curve derived by arbitraging annual uncertainty across the most buzzed-about U.S. stocks in the media.

While the concept of uncertainty arbitrage makes sense in the context of irrational ambiguity aversion, it is not stable. It the arbitrage opportunity is absent in daily and weekly data. There are many subtypes of uncertainty such as production delays, accounting ambiguity, and policy changes that are not subdivided in the Uncertainty TRMI. As noted in academic studies cited above, the effect of uncertainty is often regime-dependent and thus inconsistent over time.

CERTAINLY DOUBTFUL

Uncertainty is nuanced for stocks, and it is difficult to clarify its effects on asset prices. Sometimes uncertainty is associated with known future events, and other times it is chronic and pervasive. Uncertainty can also serve to amplify the momentum of positive stocks during optimistic periods and conversely to accelerate mean reversion of negative stocks during negative sentiment periods. As a result of these nuances, there are conflicting regime-dependent and event-dependent results in how uncertainty drives equity prices. In contrast to equities, for currencies there is a more robust story about the predictive value of uncertainty, which is described in Chapter 20.

For discretionary investors, the key to taking advantage of uncertainty is to identify where a broad "cheery consensus" exists and to tactically bet against it. Buffett's view was confirmed by regime-dependent research on individual equities. For global macro traders, uncertainty carrries a similar implication as it did in the case of Boeing. George Soros suggests taking advantage of uncertainty where unexpected events are not being properly anticipated. For Soros, uncertainty is a constant in markets, and the key to profitability is to identify where potentially destabilizing unexpected events are being discounted. Both Buffett's and Soros's approaches are valid, and their differences illustrate the challenge of systematically defining and taking advantage of uncertainty in markets.

The next section of the book examines how information flow impacts complex market events such as speculative bubbles. The book goes on to examine media sentiment for assets such as commodities and currencies as well as economic indicators.

IN SUMMARY

- The best investors have the skill of rapid intuitive expected value calculation. This talent may be partially genetic in origin.
- Equity investors benefit from buying equities associated with high level of uncertainty and companies with greater uncertainty around their balance sheets, especially when overall market sentiment is pessimistic.
- Global macro and event traders benefit from identifying event-related uncertainties that others are ignoring or discounting. For example, the numerous delays in the production schedule of the Boeing Dreamliner were heavily discounted, and the news of further production uncertainties predictably drove the stock price lower.
- Uncertainty is challenging to systematically arbitrage across equities. There is nonetheless evidence of yearly profitability from such arbitrage strategies, although the results are volatile.

NOTES

1. Alec Wilkinson, "What Would Jesus Bet? A Math Whiz Hones the Optimal Poker Strategy," *New Yorker Magazine* (March 30, 2009). http://www.newyorker.com/magazine/2009/03/30/what-would-jesus-bet.
2. Ibid.
3. Ibid.
4. Ibid.
5. Ibid.
6. Carrie Hojnicki, "The 22 Biggest Poker Players on Wall Street," *BusinessInsider* (July 10, 2012). Retrieved July 20, 2015, from: http://www.businessinsider.com/the-22-biggest-poker-players-on-wall-street-2012-7#carl-icahn-icahn-partners-9.
7. F. H. Knight, *Risk, Uncertainty, and Profit* (Boston: Hart, Schaffner & Marx, Houghton Mifflin Company, 1921).
8. Ming Hsu, Meghana Bhatt, Ralph Adolphs, Daniel Tranel, and Colin F. Camerer, "Neural Systems Responding to Degrees of Uncertainty in Human Decision-Making," *Science* 310(5754) (2005), pp. 1680–1683.

9. Cary Frydman, Colin Camerer, Peter Bossaerts, and Antonio Rangel, "MAOA-L Carriers Are Better at Making Optimal Financial Decisions under Risk," *Proceedings of the Royal Society B*. 278 (1714) (2010), pp. 2053–2059.

10. W. Buffett, "You Pay a Very High Price in the Stock Market for a Cheery Consensus," *Forbes Magazine* (August 6, 1979).

11. S. N. Erbas and M. Abbas, "The Equity Premium Puzzle, Ambiguity Aversion, and Institutional Quality" (October 2007). IMF Working Papers, 1–58. Available at SSRN: http://ssrn.com/abstract=1019684.

12. Alok Kumar, "Hard-to-Value Stocks, Behavioral Biases, and Informed Trading," *Journal of Financial and Quantitative Analysis* 44(6) (2009), pp. 1375–1401.

13. B. Trueman, F. M. H. Wong, and X-J. Zhang, "Anomalous Stock Returns around Internet Firms' Earnings Announcements," *Journal of Accounting and Economics* 34(1) (2003), pp. 249–271(23).

14. E. Bartov, P. S. Mohanram, and C. Seethamraju, "Valuation of Internet Stocks—an IPO Perspective," *Journal of Accounting Research* 40(2) (2002).

15. Ibid.

16. M. Baker and J. Wurgler, "Investor Sentiment and the Cross- Section of Stock Returns," *Journal of Finance* 61(4) (2006), pp. 1645–1680.

17. D. G. MacGregor, P. Slovic, D. Dremen, and M. Berry, "Imagery, Affect, and Financial Judgment," *Journal of Psychology and Financial Markets* 1 (2000), pp. 104–110.

18. Jennifer Francis, Ryan LaFond, Per Olsson, and Katherine Schipper, "Accounting Anomalies and Information Uncertainty," in AFA 2004 San Diego Meetings. 2003.

19. Veronesi, Pietro, and Lubos Pastor, "Uncertainty about Government Policy and Stock Prices." In 2011 Meeting Papers, no. 86, Society for Economic Dynamics, 2011.

20. Rode, C., L. Cosmides, W. Hell, and J. Tooby, "When and Why Do People Avoid Unknown Probabilities in Decisions under Uncertainty? Testing Some Predictions from Optimal Foraging Theory," *Cognition* 72(3) (October 26, 1999), pp. 269–304.

21. Lynn Lunsford, "Boeing, in Embarrassing Setback, Says 787 Dreamliner Will Be Delayed," *Wall Street Journal* (Oct. 11, 2007). Retrieved July 20, 2015, from: http://www.wsj.com/articles/SB119203025791454746.

Complex Patterns and Unique Assets

Optionality

[O]ne lucky break, or one supremely shrewd decision—can we tell them apart?—may count for more than a lifetime of journeyman efforts. But behind the luck, or the crucial decision, there must usually exist a background of preparation and disciplined capacity. One needs to be sufficiently established and recognized so that these opportunities will knock at his particular door. One must have the means, the judgment, and the courage to take advantage of them.

—Benjamin Graham, *The Intelligent Investor* (added to the 1971/1972 edition)

Despite being the scholar behind value investing, Benjamin Graham had unspectacular investment performance aside from one specific investment: GEICO. Per Graham (1976), "In 1948, we made our GEICO investment and from then on, we seemed to be very brilliant people." Graham initially declined to buy GEICO stock because its valuation exceeded his framework. With some difficulty, his investing partner Newmann persuaded Graham to make an exception to the rigorous valuation criteria encapsulated in his model.[1] As a result of this ill-disciplined investment, Graham and Newmann profited enormously. GEICO stock accounted for more profits to the Graham–Newmann investment partnership than all of their other investments *combined*.

It's not only Graham who became wealthy on the back of one key investment that captured enormous upside. Consider the world's billionaires, nearly all of whom are wealthy due to one very successful business (Jack Ma, Bill Gates, Lei Jun, Mark Zuckerberg, etc.). Aside from business owners, some investors who invest in others' businesses, such as Warren Buffett and Carlos Slim, have made three or four fantastic investments that generated the vast bulk of their wealth. Enormous gains are often obtained through an investment technique described by Mark Twain and repeated by Andrew Carnegie (a U.S. Steel baron) in his essay *How to Succeed in Life*: "Place all your eggs in one basket and then watch the basket...."[2]

As Indian billionaire investor Rakesh Jhunjhunwala puts it, "See, I'm a risk taker.... If I feel very opinionated, I can really put the money on the table. I don't think too much deep research is needed. I don't go into analysis paralysis." He says, "All you need is common sense."[3] As a Reuters article on Jhunjhunwala notes, he is an advocate of leverage, which he has often used in his career and perhaps best defines his big, bold-bet investment philosophy.[4] Such big bets can cut both ways, leading to massive losses when one gets the direction wrong.

Most financial advisers recommend that investors hold a diversified portfolio to grow their wealth gradually over time. Yet most extremely wealthy individuals did not diversify. This reality is dangerous to mention, since it contradicts a doctrine that is intended to protect investors from their bad ideas , biases, and tendency to gamble. Only professionals with superior planning and risk management skills should attempt to find investments with optionality. The vast majority ought to honor their human nature by diversifying and taking a hands-off approach.

Most investors make crucial mistakes when watching just one basket. Sometimes their attention is captured and shifted by the media, and they forget to tend to the basket ("poor planning and neglect"). Sometimes the basket drops, the eggs crack, and rather than moving on, they focus even more attention on trying to salvage the basket in an ultimately losing situation ("holding losers too long, sunk cost bias"). More often, they lose confidence in their bet after a setback, giving up and caving in to a pessimistic story told by the media. Other times, they simply sell their basket to the first and highest bidder, moving on to another basket, but never truly unlocking the potential value in it (e.g., "cutting winners short"). And sometimes, as occurred at 10:17 a.m. and 24 seconds on May 21, 2015, someone whose eggs are all in the same basket, such as Li Hejun, chairman of Chinese solar firm Hanergy, can watch as $14 billion in paper wealth evaporates in less than a second for no apparent reason.[5] Yet with proper judgment and by limiting the amount of capital invested in long shots, putting all of one's eggs in a single basket may yield impressive returns.

This chapter leaves the realm of information analytics to explore the tremendous potential that can arise out of uncertainty. This chapter prepares for the subsequent two chapters on price bubbles. Because investments with optionality are rare, empirical data on these phenomena is lacking.

OPTIONALITY AND WEALTH CREATION

Optionality is the property of asymmetric upside (preferably unlimited) with correspondingly limited downside (preferably tiny).

—Nassim Taleb, *Antifragile*[6]

Most investors have a story of "the one that got away"—a good investment that would have made them a fortune. Like most, I've had a few big misses. In 1992, the president of Dell Computer taught an undergraduate class of mine at the University of Texas, and he repeatedly told me, "If you want to get rich, buy Dell stock and hold on." But the stock's P/E ratio was too high for my valuation models, and I was a dogmatic value investor at the time, so I stayed on the sidelines. Dell stock was up 100× over the next six years.

Even worse, I initially dismissed the Internet. I had dinner with two professors who explained the Internet and wireless technology would change society (this was 1994). The professors outlined their vision of the future with such wonder. They were truly in awe of the world's upcoming transformation. At the time, I reflected on the painfully slow Mosaic browser and huge clunky cell phones, and I vocally disagreed.

I learned a few things from these missed opportunities. Each opportunity had enormous—even life-changing—upside and limited downside. To take advantage of such optionality, investors must cultivate the long-term vision to see over the horizon at the exponential changes coming their way. Moreover, investors need both the aggressiveness to act on a vision and the prudence to avoid sabotaging themselves as they pursue it.

HABITS ARE HARD TO BREAK

One of the greatest ironies about optionality is that—in hindsight—it was so obvious. It was obvious in 1995 that the Internet would change the world. It was obvious that the bitcoin blockchain would become a part of global financial transfers. But if such investments are so obvious, then how did their potential lie largely unrecognized for years?

Among professional investors and experts, there is often a psychological resistance to becoming involved in investments with nonlinear payoffs. Those who have seen many market cycles are typically skeptical and concerned about the risk inherent in such bets. This hesitancy is rooted in both habit (inertia) and the emotional evaluation of risk. One key to identifying optionality in an investment is to understand the biases that prevent other investors from seeing it.

Human learning is hypothesized to be a linear updating process.[7] Humans integrate new information, and they weigh it more heavily in their learning, depending on its relevance, impact, and recency. As a result, subtle, gradual changes are often missed. When breakthroughs are building on existing slow-but-steady progress, their significance is often overlooked. For example, in 1994 the Mosaic browser was just another way to access

Internet content; in 2008 bitcoin's blockchain innovation was simply a new feature among a half-dozen cryptocurrencies vying for attention. Each breakthrough started out as a new feature, but it quickly evolved into something much more powerful.

Humans are creatures of habit, and that's generally a good thing—habits are efficient behavioral plans in familiar situations. Humans tend to have three to four behavioral strategies (habits) easily available during their approach to a problem.[8] This limited number of strategies supplies a narrow decision space. When faced with breakthroughs, there is no precedent, and humans are uncertain how to act. Should one scoff, take risk and jump in, or wait and see?

The temptation to wait for confirmation (waiting to see others jump in) is due to risk aversion. Intellectually, taking a bet on a new breakthrough shouldn't be a difficult decision. If a potential payoff is 100 to 1, then losing 98 times out of 100 would still lead to doubling one's original capital. But it is emotionally painful to experience losses, much less a high frequency of small losses. Several experiments based on the Soochow Gambling Task have found that individuals will sacrifice large long-term returns to avoid frequent small losses, even when they are aware of the expected payoffs and the irrationality of their own behavior.[9,10]

The human tendency to be inattentive to obvious changes was best illustrated by a surprising study in which an experimenter posed as a lost pedestrian. The experimenter held a map and asked a random passer-by for directions. As the pedestrian provided directions to the experimenter, two people walked in between the experimenter and the passer-by holding a wooden door. As the door was moved between them, the experimenter switched positions with one of the door carriers, who proceeded to listen to the passer-by. The passer-by continued to explain the directions to this new stranger. The original experimenter was no longer there. He was replaced with a new experimenter who looked markedly different and had a distinctly different voice. However, nearly 50 percent of passers-by failed to notice that they were talking to a different person after the door passed and the person asking for directions switched.[11] "[I]t's counterintuitive that people can miss things that are substantial and right in front of them."[12] This phenomenon is known as *change blindness*. Change blindness and inattention compel investors to miss the breakthroughs that precede large price movements.

Finding investments with optionality requires coming to terms with one's habits of avoidance, concern about frequent small losses, and the simple inattention to fundamental breakthroughs. Once investors have identified potential optionality in an investment, they can alleviate some risk by identifying events that will increase public attention on the breakthrough and demonstrate its growing value. As in value investing, these events are called *catalysts*.

CATALYSTS

The Internet was used throughout the 1970s and 1980s for research purposes and communication. While Al Gore famously pioneered legislation opening the Internet to commercial use in 1992, it wasn't until web browsers such as Mosaic and Netscape emerged in 1994 and 1995, respectively, that the public was introduced to the novelty and usefulness of this new medium. A fundamental change or a new technology like the Internet may remain unrecognized by the market for many years or decades. In order to avoid the opportunity cost of waiting for exponential price movement, investors ought to identify triggers for an attention cascade.

Most catalysts are specific events. Investor roadshows, IPOs, product launches, favorable legislation, policy announcements, and other high-publicity events are common triggers. In the case of assets with optionality, catalysts must gather attention. The attention-getting event itself is the first condition. Second, the event must contain the psychological seeds of investor frenzy.

Because optionality is relatively rare, there is considerable hindsight bias in the examination of historical examples. The lessons presented in this section are general because optionality only occurs once in each situation. Trying to follow in Mark Zuckerberg's footsteps with a new social network or betting on the next bitcoin clone is unlikely to yield astronomical returns. However, optionality can be domain-specific. There are fields—such as biotechnology—where breakthroughs are different in specifics but follow the same hype and FDA approval cycle. A successful treatment for influenza, cancer, or even aging would all yield substantial payoffs, and each follows a similar roadmap.

To identify optionality in an investment, consider the following questions:

1. How likely is the breakthrough or transformation to dramatically change the world?
2. Is the innovation isolated to an esoteric community? Specialist advances are appreciated by people in that field, but initially ignored by outsiders.
3. What will be a catalyst for others to recognize the opportunity?
4. Does the investment have the intellectual pizzazz or emotional hook to attract others' attention?

Just as a virus that elicits sneezes from its human host is more likely to propagate—passing from person to person through the microscopic mist of a sneeze—an idea that stimulates its host to proselytize is more likely to survive and become popular.[13] Some ideas are so intellectually "sticky" or emotionally compelling as to appear to be shopping for humans to transmit them. Ultimately, a form of natural selection determines which ideas survive and propagate and which lose market share to the point of extinction.[14] Just as computer viruses may highjack a computer operating system, such viral ideas infect human thinking. These ideas improve their contagious properties as they pass from person to person, recombining into belief sets along the lines of "this time is different." Contagiousness is a key precursor of optionality.

In order to pass along the contagion—to infect others—there ought to be a metaphorical sneeze. The sneeze is a catalyst that garners attention. From a psychological perspective, catalysts should have the following characteristics in order to inflame investor excitement:

- A large potential payoff
- Novelty or newness
- Expectancy for more good things to come

The large potential payoff is better if enormous—and this is more likely if the breakthrough "changes everything." The breakthrough is typically technical or specialist enough that it is difficult to value, and thus it is more susceptible to hype as it takes off. And the breakthrough should be expected to generate downstream positive developments.

Timing investments around catalysts requires close attention, and often it is a better use of time to invest a small amount of capital in many such opportunities—like planting seeds in a field—and let nature do the germinating. Broadly speaking, this is the strategy followed by venture capitalists.

DETECTING OPTIONALITY

If you "have optionality", you don't have much need for what is commonly called intelligence, knowledge, insight, skills, and these complicated things that take place in our brain cells. For you don't have to be right that often. All you need is the wisdom to not do unintelligent things to hurt yourself (some acts of omission) and recognize favorable outcomes when they occur.

—Nassim Taleb[15]

At the beginning of the exponential upturn in an asset with optionality—investments such as the Nasdaq bubble, rare earths bubble, biotech bubble, or housing bubble—the media conveys doubts while experts express optimism. In retrospective analysis, it appears that the significance of many breakthroughs was recognized by experts well in advance of mass media attention.

When considering buying into optionality, keep in mind these lessons that Stanley Druckenmiller learned from George Soros: "It takes courage to be a pig. It takes courage to ride a profit with huge leverage. As far as Soros is concerned, when you're right on something, you can't own enough."[16] This comment also characterizes Jhunjhunwala's approach. Investors who pursue optionality in their investments (1) are willing to bet an inordinate amount on a limited number of opportunities, and (2) they watch those opportunities closely. This style is high risk/high reward, and it isn't for everybody.

For those who can't stomach the pain of loss inherent in most investments with optionality, Benjamin Graham's value investing allows for a *margin of safety*. Value investing is a systematic technique for identifying assets with the potential for large gains, in this case due to undervaluation. While the returns of most "value" companies are not characterized by optionality, some—such as in the case of Benjamin Graham's GEICO stock—do show massive gains, leading to superior average long-term returns. Investments with optionality often grow into speculative bubbles. The subsequent two chapters examine the ups, and downs, of such events.

IN SUMMARY

- Optionality, popularized by Nassim Taleb, refers to investments with the property of enormous potential upside and little potential downside.
- Several notable investors use a style of investing that takes advantage of optionality, including Benjamin Graham (with GEICO) and Rakesh Jhunjhunwala.
- Human biases, including habit, loss aversion, and change blindness, cause inattention to optionality, creating opportunities for attentive experts and investors.
- Catalysts bring attention to such investments. A psychological process of thought contagion and exponential price increases may ensue.

NOTES

1. John Huber, "Case Study: The Story of GEICO, Graham, and Buffett," SeekingAlpha (May 14, 2013). Retrieved May 20, 2015, from http://seekingalpha.com/instablog/677842-john-huber/1858211-case-study-the-story-of-geico-graham-and-buffett.

2. Napoleon Hill, *The Laws of Success in 16 Lessons* (Meriden, CT: The Ralston University Press, 1928). http://archive.org/stream/Law_Of_Success_in_16_Lessons/law-of-success-napoleon-hill_djvu.txt.

3. Rafael Nam and Abhishek Vishnoi, "'I'm Jhunjhunwala,' not India's Buffett," *Reuters* (June 15, 2012). Retrieved May 20, 2105, from http://in.reuters.com/article/2012/06/15/india-jhunjhunwala-buffett-idINDEE85D0JX20120615.

4. Ibid.

5. Jacky Wong and Scott Patterson, "Hanergy: Bulk of Stock Collapse Occurred in Less Than a Second," *Wall Street Journal* (May 22, 2015). http://www.wsj.com/articles/hanergy-bulk-of-stock-collapse-occurred-in-less-than-a-second-1432316315.

6. Nassim Nicholas Taleb, *Antifragile: Things That Gain from Disorder* (New York: Random House Incorporated, 2012).

7. Thomas L. Griffiths, Chris Lucas, Joseph Williams, and Michael L. Kalish, "Modeling Human Function Learning with Gaussian Processes," in *Advances in Neural Information Processing Systems,* pp. 553–560 (2009). Retrieved May 20, 2105, from http://cocosci.berkeley.edu/tom/papers/funclearn1.pdf.

8. Anne Collins and Etienne Koechlin, "Reasoning, Learning, and Creativity: Frontal Lobe Function and Human Decision-Making," *PLoS Biol* 10(3) (2012), p. e1001293. Retrieved May 20, 2105, from http://www.plosbiology.org/article/info%3Adoi%2F10.1371%2Fjournal.pbio.1001293.

9. Ching-Hung Lin, Yao-Chu Chiu, and Jong-Tsun Huang, "Gain-Loss Frequency and Final Outcome in the Soochow Gambling Task: A Reassessment," *Behavioral and Brain Functions* 5(1) (2009), p. 45.

10. Ania Aïte, Mathieu Cassotti, Sandrine Rossi, Nicolas Poirel, Amélie Lubin, Olivier Houdé, and Sylvain Moutier, "Is Human Decision Making under Ambiguity Guided by Loss Frequency Regardless of the Costs? A Developmental Study Using the Soochow Gambling Task," *Journal of Experimental Child Psychology* 113(2) (2012), pp. 286–294.

11. Daniel J. Simons and Daniel T. Levin, "Failure to Detect Changes to People During a Real-World Interaction," *Psychonomic Bulletin & Review* 5(4) (1998), pp. 644–649.

12. Zak Stambor, "Right Before Our Eyes: A Psychologist Finds That What We See Often Differs from What We Think We See," *Monitor* 37(9) (October 2006), p. 30. http://www.apa.org/monitor/oct06/eyes.aspx.

13. A. Lynch, "Thought Contagions in Deflating and Inflating Phases of the Bubble," *Journal of Psychology and Financial Markets* 3(2) (2002), pp. 112–117.

14. Aaron Lynch, "Thought Contagion in the Stock Markets: A General Framework and Focus on the Internet Bubble," in *Derivatives Use, Trading and Regulation* 6(4) (2001), pp. 338–362.

15. Nassim Nicholas Taleb, *Antifragile: Things That Gain from Disorder* (New York: Random House Incorporated, 2012).

16. Proinsias O'Mahony, "Buy Bubbles, Big Bet, and Backache—Soros's Secret," *Irish Times* (Aug. 12, 2014). http://www.irishtimes.com/business/personal-finance/buy-bubbles-bet-big-and-backache-soros-s-secrets-1.1893639.

CHAPTER 17

Blowing Bubbles

Evidence of bubbles has accelerated since the [2007–2009 world financial] crisis.

—Robert Shiller

The celebrated author and humorist Samuel Clemens (pen name Mark Twain) was the most widely recognized American in the last decade of the nineteenth century.[1] Clemens's documentation of his experiences in the Nevada mining stock bubble are one of the earliest (and certainly the most humorous) firsthand accounts of involvement in a speculative mania.

After a brief stint as a Confederate militiaman during the beginning of the U.S. Civil War, Clemens purchased stagecoach passage west, to Nevada, where his brother had been appointed Secretary of the Territory. In Nevada, Clemens began working as a reporter in Virginia City, in one of Nevada's most productive silver- and gold-mining regions. He enviously watched prospecting parties departing into the wilderness, and he quickly became "smitten with the silver fever."[2]

Clemens and two friends soon went out in search of silver veins in the mountains. As Clemens tells it, they rapidly discovered and laid claim to a rich vein of silver called the "Wide West" mine. The night after they established their ownership, they were restless and unable to sleep, visited by fantasies of extravagant wealth: "No one can be so thoughtless as to suppose that we slept, that night. Higbie and I went to bed at midnight, but it was only to lie broad awake and think, dream, scheme."[3]

Clemens reported that in the excitement and confusion of the days following their discovery, he and his two partners failed to begin mining their claim. Under Nevada state law, a claim could be usurped if not worked within 10 days. Clemens lost his claim to the mine, and his dreams of sudden wealth were momentarily set back.

But Clemens had a keen ear for rumors and new opportunities. Some prospectors who found rich ore veins were selling stock in New York City to raise capital for mining operations. In 1863, Clemens accumulated stocks in several such silver mines, sometimes as payment for working as a journalist. In order to lock in his anticipated gains from the stocks, he made a plan to sell his silver shares either when they reached $100,000 in total value or when Nevada voters approved a state constitution (which he thought would erode their long-term value).

In 1863, funded by his substantial (paper) stock wealth, Clemens retired from journalism. He traveled west to San Francisco to live the high life. He watched his silver mine stock price quotes in the newspaper, and he felt rich: "I lived at the best hotel, exhibited my clothes in the most conspicuous places, infested the opera .... I had longed to be a butterfly, and I was one at last."[4]

Yet after Nevada became a state, Clemens continued to hold on to his stocks, contrary to his plan. Abruptly the gambling mania on silver stocks ended, and without warning, Clemens found himself virtually broke.

> *I, the cheerful idiot that had been squandering money like water, and thought myself beyond the reach of misfortune, had not now as much as fifty dollars when I gathered together my various debts and paid them.[5]*

Clemens was forced to return to journalism to pay his expenses. He lived on meager pay over the next several years, and even after his great literary and lecture-circuit success in the late nineteenth century, he continued to have difficulty investing wisely. In later life he had very public and large debts, and he was forced to work, much more vigorously than he wanted, to make ends meet for his family.

Clemens had made a plan to sell his silver stock shares when Nevada became a state. His rapid and large gains stoked a sense of invincibility. Soon he deviated from his stock sales plan, stopped paying attention to the markets, and found himself virtually broke.

Clemens was by no means the first or last person to succumb to mining stock excitement. The *World's Work*, an investment periodical published decades later in the early 1900s, was beset by letters from investors asking for advice on mining stocks. The magazine's response to these letters was straightforward:

> *Emotion plays too large a part in the business of mining stocks. Enthusiasm, lust for gain, gullibility are the real bases of this trading. The sober common sense of the intelligent businessman has no part in such investment.[6]*

While the focus of market manias changes—mining, biotech, Chinese technology stocks, housing, etc.—the outline of speculative bubbles has remained remarkably similar over the centuries.

A BRIEF HISTORY OF BUBBLES

Taxi drivers told you what to buy. The shoeshine boy could give you a summary of the day's financial news as he worked with rag and polish. An old beggar who regularly patrolled the street in front of my office now gave me tips and, I suppose, spent the money I and others gave him in the market. My cook had a brokerage account and followed the ticker closely.
— Bernard Baruch, describing the environment before the
1929 stock market crash

The above quote was republished in a *Fortune* magazine article. In that article the author fretted that the U.S. stock market was in a bubble.[7] When was that *Fortune* article published? April 1996. Later in 1996, Alan Greenspan was also early to the bubble-spotting party, giving his infamous "irrational exuberance" speech on December 5, 1996.

The history of bubbles starts with the first recorded speculative bubble—the Dutch Tulip Mania of 1637[8]—is punctuated by the first bubble with truly global economic repercussions—the U.S. stock market bubble of 1926–1929—and it continues through today. Most readers lived through the dot-com bubble of 1996–2000, the housing bubbles of 2004–2006, the Chinese stock market bubbles of 2006 and 2015, the gold bubble of 2009–2011, and the bitcoin bubble of 2013. As trading has globalized, bubbles are expanding more frequently. In fact, they may be an inextricable feature of modern globalized markets.

The Merriam-Webster definition of a bubble is "a state of booming economic activity that often ends in a sudden collapse." The *Farlex Financial Dictionary* defines a speculative bubble as "a situation in which prices for securities, especially stocks, rise far above their actual value."[9] In the case of a bubble at its peak, the perceived risk is low while the actual risk is high.

Bubbles are complex market events in which individuals act together in exercising their collective right to poor judgment. Charles Kindleberger, an economic historian, notes in his book, *Manias, Panics, and Crashes*, that speculative manias begin with a displacement (such as increased profitability), which excites speculative interest. This is followed by positive feedback from rising share prices, the entrance of inexperienced investors into the market, and a climax of euphoria.[10]

Bubbles are notoriously difficult to invest into. If a bubble is defined as market prices widely exceeding fundamental valuations, then hindsight is the only real evidence of its existence (after the crash). A rise in prices may accurately anticipate or reflexively pull fundamentals higher, and the top of the process can be difficult to identify. Unfortunately investors don't have the luxury of hindsight.

Since there is both a massive creation and destruction of wealth during bubbles, the three questions of interest to most investors are:

1. How do I identify where and when a bubble will occur?
2. How do I identify when a bubble is underway?
3. How can I know when a bubble will go bust?

These questions are explored in this and the following chapter. To answer the first question, the preconditions for bubble emergence are examined. To answer the second question, the interaction between fundamentals, investor psychology, media attention, and price action is analyzed. For the third question bubble peaks and the signs of imminent collapse are explored. The third question is by far the most difficult, and—like Samuel Clemens—not having a clear plan has led many investors to participate in both the ride up and the freefall down. In order to understand bubbles, it helps to reference the wisdom of Robert Shiller.

IRRATIONAL EXUBERANCE

Irrational exuberance is the psychological basis of a speculative bubble. I define a speculative bubble as a situation in which news of price increases spurs investor enthusiasm, which spreads by psychological contagion from person to person, in the process amplifying stories that might justify the price increases and bringing in a larger and larger class of investors, who, despite doubts about the real value of an investment, are drawn to it partly through envy of others' successes and partly through a gambler's excitement.

—Robert Shiller

Before economist Robert Shiller was awarded the 2013 Nobel Prize in economics, he was best known for research on speculative bubbles popularized in his book *Irrational Exuberance*. In the first two editions of that book, he accurately predicted the tops of the U.S. technology stock bubble in 2000 and the U.S. housing market bubble in 2007, respectively. In his 2015 edition, Shiller outlined several preconditions and characteristics of speculative bubbles.[11] Shiller suggests that bubbles are increasingly commonplace across global stock markets, which makes understanding them especially urgent.

Shiller's book is a journey through past bubbles, his thoughts about how bubbles form, and ideas on asset price valuation. Precipitating factors for bubbles include positive price movement (by definition), media attention (storytelling and compelling memes), psychological factors (beliefs, emotions, and social pressures), and amplification mechanisms (positive feedback loops). As the media share compelling stories, positive price action reinforces an already-optimistic media tone. Investors revise their expectations upward, and new—often naïve—participants enter the bubbling market.[12]

Shiller suggests that the media's need to garner readership increases bubble attention and participation. The media tell stories that justify price movements, "thereby enhancing the salience of these movements and focusing greater attention on them." If those stories are catchy or exciting—such as stories of a new era—then the media stokes greater public optimism and market participation. This creates a positive feedback loop between the media and the investing public. "[T]he media can sometimes foster stronger feedback from past price changes to further prices changes." This feedback process drives an attention cascade.[13]

Like news media, some market gurus echo the public mood, reverberating with objective facts and figures that are fit to the current environment. For example, Harry Dent Jr. authored the October 1999 book *The Roaring 2000s*, which included concrete predictions, among them "a Dow that will reach at least 21,500 and possibly 35,000 by the year 2008." (As of 2015 it is near its all-time high of 18,000). In 2006, Dent published *The Next Great Bubble Boom* near the cyclical top of the financial markets, and in January 2009 he published *The Great Depression Ahead* two months before the U.S. stock market bottom. Those books gained significant attention at the time of publication, in part because they reflected the public mood. However, despite echoing the public mood, such books and media articles may contribute to the positive feedback effect driving prices.

Shiller notes that most people rely on *psychological anchors* (beliefs) to determine the appropriate level of stock prices. He distinguishes between quantitative anchors—those related to numerical levels—and moral anchors—based on beliefs about the best places to invest wealth. Occasionally beliefs of a market's fair value may be adjusted wildly higher based on emotional input into the reasoning process.

George Soros noted that every bubble has two components: an underlying trend that prevails in reality and a misconception relating to that trend. "A boom–bust process is set in motion when a trend and a misconception positively reinforce each other."[14] The misconception is fueled by emotional factors in a positive feedback loop: "As prices continue to rise, the level of exuberance is enhanced by the price rise itself."[15]

Shiller's and Soros's ideas are testable. In the following sections we explore sentiment patterns that underlie bubbles, starting with the role of the individual psychology that collectively inflates them.

LABORATORY BUBBLES

> *Even when traders in an asset market know the value of the asset, bubbles form dependably. Bubbles can arise when some agents buy not on fundamental value, but on price trend or momentum. If momentum traders have more liquidity, they can sustain a bubble longer.*
> —Steven Gjerstad and Vernon L. Smith[16]

Nobel-laureate Vernon Smith developed the most widely cited experimental model to elicit bubbles among laboratory participants.[17] Smith and his co-authors designed a set of experiments in which an asset gives a dividend with expected value $0.24 at the end of each of 15 periods. During each round, the market is open for trading shares. At the end of a round, each share pays the owner a dividend. The dividend per round is one of $0, $0.08, $0.28, or $0.60 with equal probability. At the end of the experiment, after 15 rounds, the assets are worthless.

Traditional economics theory—in which investors are rational agents—predicts that the asset would start trading near $3.60 (15 times $0.24) and decline by 24 cents each period. Smith and his co-authors found instead that prices started trading well below the fundamental value and subsequently rose far above it in later periods. The average transaction price peaked around periods 9 to 11 and crashed from periods 13 to 15. This experiment has been repeated hundreds of times in labs around the world with similar results.

Experimental bubbles emerge despite various manipulations to the experimental model, including allowing short-selling, margin buying, and insider trading.[18] Even when uncertainty about payoffs and asset values is eliminated, bubbles persist.[19] Bubbles arise regardless of whether participants are business students, managers, or professional traders.

Given the universality of valuation bubbles among various groups, it's apparent that a common psychological element—as yet unquantified—is a defining feature. Historical descriptions of bubbles often employ emotional terms such as *mania* and *irrational exuberance*. To describe the process of a bubble's collapse, words including *fear* and *panic* come into play.

Beyond the anecdotal, solid research supports an emotional component to the bubble-building process. When researchers provoke emotions in experimental market traders, they find that positive excitement among participants generates larger pricing bubbles,[20] positive facial expressions of investors correlate with larger bubbles,[21] and investor fear induces early selloffs in bubbles.[22] Investor self-control (or lack thereof) may be one of the key psychological factors in bubble formation in experimental markets,[23] although specific causes of self-control breakdown (social pressure, emotions, attention overload, media influences) have not yet been linked to this hypothesis.

STAGING A BUBBLE

But before we begin assuming that the market is revealing some truth about this new era, it behooves us to reflect on the real determinants of market moves.... Many of these real determinants are in our minds.

—Robert Shiller

Many bubbles arise due to a *fundamental trigger*. This trigger can be a technological breakthrough, monetary or fiscal stimulus, shortages (e.g., for commodities), or price changes alone. Bubbles are characterized by *rising prices*, accelerating higher. Every bubble has a *story* associated with it, usually insinuating the possibility of earning great wealth in a short time, perhaps with several individual cases representing that possibility. *Investor psychology* describes how investors perceive the market in each stage. The *tone of the media* may contribute to bubbles and their inflation—is media supportive or critical? As bubbles inflate, many more *amateurs* enter as speculators. All of these factors may work together in a positive feedback loop to *amplify* the current trends of the market. The conditions of a bubble are described in more detail in Table 17.1.

Fundamental triggers are typically new technologies. In fact, new technologies as diverse as fire engine and burglar alarm companies in the 1690s and machine gun and perpetual motion machine manufacturers in the 1720s experienced investment bubbles.[24]

New technologies are difficult to value. As a result, there is greater emotional input into the valuation process. As an extreme example, how would one value an unprofitable biotech company that claimed to hold a cure for human aging? Traditional metrics would indicate not to invest (it is profitless), but emotional metrics say "Go for it!" There are also bubbles in commodities, currencies, and housing. For such non-equity bubbles, fundamental triggers may include shortages and excess liquidity.

TABLE 17.1 Conditions Fueling a Speculative Bubble

Conditions	Characteristics
Fundamental Triggers	Breakthrough technological change, new government policy, scarcity, macroeconomic shocks such as interest rate, credit availability, or supply changes (such as shortages).
The Story	How big, vivid, and emotionally compelling is the story? Are there compelling narratives of others who struck it rich?
Investor Psychology	As prices continue higher and the story is seemingly confirmed by the price movement, optimism hardens into firm beliefs (e.g., "This time is different").
Media	Media reports on fundamental triggers. The emotion of the story spun is gripping and inspires urgency.
Participants	Amateurs enter the market. These new participants have less education about valuations and less self-control.
Amplifiers	News and social media spread rumors, techniques, and advice for investing. Trading the asset becomes cheaper. Leverage is easy to obtain.

Figure 17.1 shows a positive trend in which fundamentals are improving following a technological breakthrough—the Internet (smooth gray line). Gradually, psychology turns from optimism to greed, and prices rise (jagged gray line).

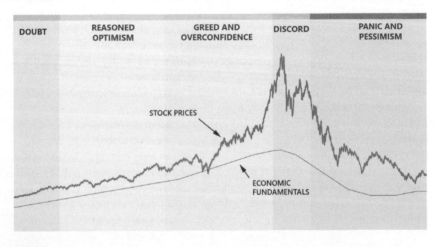

FIGURE 17.1 The anatomy of a bubble based on the Nasdaq bubble of 1996–2002.

As represented in Figure 17.1, bubbles have fundamental trends (the initiating factor), price trends, and psychological aspects that broadly define stages. In stage 0, at the very beginning of a positive fundamental trend, doubt is prevalent. Such doubt was also seen in Vernon Smith's experimental bubbles. In the early stages of Smith's bubbles participants undervalued the dividend-paying asset. As investors analyzed the fundamentals and others' behavior and found them supportive, reasoned optimism set in (stage 1). In stage 2, greed and overconfidence grow as prices rise and fortunes were made and described in the media. In stage 2, the valuation of the asset far exceeds reasonable expectations of earnings justification. In stage 3, the information flow turns negative. Discord, disagreement, and price volatility erupt. In stage 4, investor psychology devolves into panic, pessimism, and a price crash.

In the initial stage 0 of doubt, the technical press supports the emerging trend, although it is likely ignored in the popular press. Growth will be fairly tepid, and significant uncertainty characterizes the fundamental transformation. Investors will be fearing the ambiguity of the new information, and concerned they may regret any investment without more confirmation of a trend. They may think to themselves, "No need to invest now, I'd rather wait and see." Biologically their brains' loss-avoidance systems are active. This period is an important contributor to equity performance, but it is missed by most investors. Gradually, doubt gives way to reasoned optimism.

In stage 1 of a bubble—reasoned optimism—the price is trending upward at a fast pace as fundamentals continue to improve. Psychologically, investors feel rationally optimistic. They have done their due diligence and found that the potential earnings from the new breakthrough are significant. They may think, "Wow, this is going to be big." Biologically, they are balanced in their assessments of risks, and they are pleased to see news of the improving fundamentals beginning to jump from technical publications to the popular press. As profits accumulate, cases of wealthy earlier investors will be picked up by the media, kick-starting the second stage of the bubble.

In stage 2 of a bubble—greed and overconfidence—the price has surged far ahead of reasonable expectations for earnings. Psychologically investors feel the need to chase prices higher so they will not miss out. Hubris sets in for some, and the mantra of "This time it's different" is often repeated. There is a widespread failure to be aware of, much less to manage, risks. Biologically, dopamine is surging through investor reward systems, and they are focused on the next opportunity, accumulating riskier and riskier positions. As profits accumulate, surges in testosterone increase risk taking. While investors should be even more diligent about examining risks in such a climate, they are unable to do so.

Bubbles eventually end when there is no new money available to enter the market, the price trend peters out, and the media coverage becomes more critical, thus reversing the feedback loop. News of negative price action saturates the media and the decline accelerates. Stages 3 and 4 describe the peak-to-end stages of a bubble, and they are discussed in the next chapter.

THE BUBBLE CHECKLIST

When I see a bubble forming I rush in to buy, adding fuel to the fire .... That is not irrational."

—George Soros[25]

Understanding how bubbles arise and propagate is important, but it isn't adequate for investors. Investors ought to understand where prices are in the bubble cycle in order to ascertain if it is safe to enter. Additionally, such an understanding improves one's timing for an exit (or inverse position). To diagnose the stage of an active bubble, the questions in Table 17.2 serve as a diagnostic tool. Stage 1 corresponds to reasoned optimism, stage 2 corresponds to greed and overconfidence, stage 3 corresponds to discord, and stage 4 corresponds to panic and pessimism.

The three potential responses for each question in Table 17.2 (e.g., "accelerating, plateaued, or reversing" for question (1) mirror the stages of a bubble. In the first stage there is a growing bubble, while in the second stage there is an imminent reversal, and the third stage is the crash.

It's important to note whether the above five conditions are aligned and amplifying each other. Often answers are not entirely aligned, with different questions having answers in both stage 1 and stage 2 or in both stage 2 and stage 3. Be careful not to force personal impressions onto the table. To reduce bias, detach yourself by asking the market, "What are you telling me—what stage are you in right now?" Such a perspective allows a more intuitive response.

Table 17.2 may not accurately describe niche bubbles. For example, the 2008 Rhodium bubble saw prices of that rare earth element increase from $500 per ounce in late 2006 to $9,500 per ounce in July 2008, before falling even more rapidly back to $1,000 per ounce by January 2009. That bubble was unknown to most investors, and it did not have wide public participation. (In fact, it may have been an example of a large trader cornering the market rather than a true speculative bubble.) The next chapter describes quantitative research into identifying bubbles and timing their tops.

TABLE 17.2 Checklist for Bubble Staging

Bubble Stage/ Question	Stage 1: Reasoned Optimism	Stage 2: Greed and Overconfidence	Stage 3: Discord and Dissonance	Stage 4: Panic and Pessimism
1. Fundamental trigger?	Present	Accelerating	Hitting unexpected roadblocks	Reversing
2. Prices?	Rising steadily	Accelerating upwards (parabolic)	Faltering, large intraday price swings	Hitting monthly lows
3. Compelling story?	Minimal or highly technical	Seeming to confirm	Setbacks contradict the original optimism	Clearly negative
4. Investor psychology?	Rationally optimistic	Esctatic, "This will change the world!"	Confusion, denial of contrary evidence	Concern, fear, and panic.
5. Media tone?	Optimism in technical/ specialty press	Enthusiasm and "rags-to-riches" cases in popular press	Popular press enthusiastic, professional press turning sour	Popular press conjectures a rebound at first, then blames external forces
6. Amateur participation?	Non-existent	Growing	Frenzied	Plateaued
7. Amplifiers?	Disengaged	Increasing	Highly coordinated	Correlating to the downside

IN SUMMARY

- Bubbles are direct evidence of the impact of investor psychology on asset price behavior.
- Despite the evidence of frequent bubbles, they are one of the least systematic price patterns.
- Bubbles arise from a breakthrough in technology or policy that creates a profitable business opportunity.
- As news of this breakthrough and the profits derived from it spreads, amateurs invest, driving up share prices.
- Leverage allows investors to amplify their gains, while the mass media cheerleads prices higher in a positive feedback loop.

- Eventually the psychological tone shifts to a consensus of doubt, and prices come crashing down, aggravated by the prevalence of leverage in the market.
- Like other investments with optionality, bubbles generate great wealth for those who enter early and exit at the top.
- The chapter concludes with a checklist to help investors identify when they are involved in a speculative bubble.

NOTES

1. R. Powers, *Mark Twain: A Life* (New York: Free Press, 2005), p. xi.
2. Mark Twain, *Roughing It* (1872), Chapter 26. Free Public Domain Books from the Classic Literature Library. http://mark-twain.classicliterature.co.uk/roughing-it/.
3. Ibid.
4. Ibid.
5. Ibid.
6. M. Statman, "A Century of Investors," *Financial Analysts Journal* 59(3) (May/June 2003). Excerpted from *The World's Work*, 1907a, pp. 8383–8384.
7. John Rothchild. "When the Shoeshine Boys Talked Stocks, It Was a Great Sell Signal in 1929. So What Are the Shoeshine Boys Talking about Now?" *Fortune Magazine*, April 15, 1996. Retrieved December 11, 2015, from: http://archive.fortune.com/magazines/fortune/fortune_archive/1996/04/15/211503/index.htm
8. Charles Mackay, *Extraordinary Popular Delusions and the Madness of Crowds* (Start Publishing LLC, 2012).
9. "Speculative Bubble," *Farlex Financial Dictionary* (2009). Farlex 3 May 2015, http://financial-dictionary.thefreedictionary.com/Speculative+Bubble.
10. Charles P. Kindelberger and Robert Z. Aliber, *Manias, Panics and Crashes: A History of Financial Crisis* (Palgrave Macmillan, 2005).
11. R. J. Shiller, *Irrational Exuberance* (Princeton, NJ: Princeton University Press, 2015).
12. Ibid.
13. Ibid. From Chapter 6, "The News Media" (pp. 121–122).
14. Richard Evans, "How to Invest Like … George Soros," *The Telegraph* (April 8, 2014). Downloaded from: http://www.telegraph.co.uk/finance/personalfinance/investing/10749558/How-to-invest-like-...-George-Soros.html.
15. R. J. Shiller, *Irrational Exuberance* (Princeton, NJ: Princeton University Press, 2015), p. 97.
16. Steven Gjerstad and Vernon L. Smith, "From Bubble to Depression?" *Wall Street Journal* (April 6, 2009). Retrieved May 20, 2015, from: http://www.wsj.com/articles/SB123897612802791281.
17. Vernon L. Smith, Gerry L. Suchanek, and Arlington W. Williams, "Bubbles, Crashes, and Endogenous Expectations in Experimental Spot Asset Markets," *Econometrica* 56 (5) (1988), pp. 1119–1151.

18. Ronald R. King, Vernon L. Smith, Arlington W. Williams, and Mark V. van Boening, "The Robustness of Bubbles and Crashes in Experimental Stock Markets," in R. H. Day and P. Chen, *Nonlinear Dynamics and Evolutionary Economics* (New York: Oxford University Press, 1993).

19. Smith, Suchanek, and Williams, "Bubbles, Crashes, and Endogenous Expectations in Experimental Spot Asset Markets," *Econometrica* 56 (5) (1988), pp. 1119–1151.

20. Eduardo B. Andrade, Terrance Odean, and Shengle Lin, "Bubbling with Excitement: An Experiment," *Review of Finance* 19(3) (May 2015).

21. Adriana Breaban and Charles Noussair, *Emotional State and Market Behavior* (Center for Economic Research 2013-031, Tilburg University, 2013).

22. Lee, C. J., and Andrade, E. B. (2015). "Fear, Excitement, and Financial Risk-Taking," *Cognition and Emotion* 29(1), 178–187.

23. Martin Kocher, Konstantin E. Luck, and David Schindler, *Unleashing Animal Spirits—Self-Control and Bubbles in Experimental Asset Markets* (June 11, 2014), http://www.edge-page.net/jamb2014/papers/Kocher%20et%20al%20%20(2014)%20-%20Unleashing%20Animal%20Spirits.pdf.

24. Edward Chancellor, *Devil Take the Hindmost: A History of Financial Speculation* (New York: Plume, 2000), p. 122.

25. Richard Evans, "How to Invest Like … George Soros," *The Telegraph* (April 8, 2014), http://www.telegraph.co.uk/finance/personalfinance/investing/10749558/How-to-invest-like-…-George-Soros.html.

CHAPTER 18

Timing Bubble Tops

[There is a] two-way reflexive connection between perception and reality, which can give rise to initially self-reinforcing but eventually self-defeating boom–bust processes, or bubbles.
—George Soros[1]

Sir Isaac Newton was one of the most influential scientists in history. He laid the groundwork for classical ("Newtonian") physics. He was the first to demonstrate that the motions of objects on Earth and the movements of the celestial bodies are governed by the same set of mathematical laws. His investigations into optics and sound formed the basis for centuries of research. Unfortunately, Newton's scientific acumen did not improve his investing decisions. On the contrary, he lost much of his wealth in the largest stock bubble of his age.

Like many members of the British aristocracy in the early 1700s, Newton owned shares of the South Seas Trading Company in 1720. The South Seas Company was organized with two missions: (1) as a monopoly over British trade with the Spanish colonies in America and (2) as a converter of British government annuities into long-term debt. The South Seas Company initially had a legitimate and profitable business monopoly courtesy of the British government. Furthermore, the Company was repeatedly successful in raising money on the British stock market for proposed expansions of its operations. As a result of their success, a series of corporate competitors arose and the Company's monopoly was placed in jeopardy.

Following the lead of the South Seas Company, joint-stock companies proposing a wide range of speculative ventures formed and began to raise money through share sales. Public enthusiasm for stock trading grew, and a price bubble formed among the traded shares. When the sometimes-fraudulent promotions of new joint-stock companies became apparent to legislators, a law was passed by the British parliament in June 1720 (the "Bubble Act") to prevent non-royal-endorsed joint-stock companies from issuing shares to the public. Even after the "Bubble Act" was passed, companies continued selling shares for absurd enterprises. One such offering advertised its business as follows: "For carrying on an undertaking of great advantage; but nobody to know what it is."[2]

In the midsummer of 1720, Newton foretold a coming stock market crash, and he sold his shares of the South Seas Company for a profit of 7,000 pounds. Subsequently, however, Newton watched the Company's stock price continue to rise. He saw others reap ever more wealth from their shares. Charles Kindleberger, an economic historian, noted, "There is nothing so disturbing to one's well-being and judgment as to see a friend get rich."[3] Newton couldn't resist, and he jumped back into the market, as depicted in Figure 18.1. Newton remained invested as prices started a precipitous decline. Soon panic ensued, and the bubble collapsed.

After the dust had settled from the stock market crash of August 1720, Newton had lost over 20,000 pounds of his fortune. As a result of these losses, he famously stated, "I can calculate the motions of heavenly bodies, but not the madness of people." Newton's fear of missing out on further gains drove him to buy shares as the price soared higher. His inertia during the panic led to the loss of most of his assets.

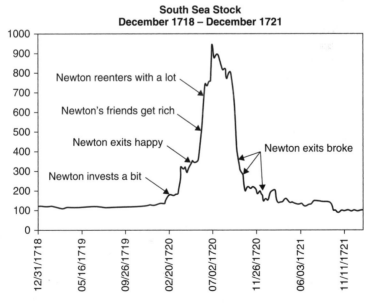

FIGURE 18.1 Sir Isaac Newton's investments during the South Seas bubble. Source: Marc Faber; *Gloom, Boom, Doom Report.*

As Newton became painfully aware, the ability to identify the top of a speculative bubble is a necessary skill for investors involved in speculative manias. There are two approaches to this pursuit—one lies in understanding the mechanics of market prices and fundamentals at a top, and the other relies on understanding the psychological cues of an imminent decline. Bubbles are rooted in human nature, and they pull in most investors. Only investors with rigorous risk management discipline should consider the strategies described in this chapter.

HOW BUBBLES POP

When the music stops, in terms of liquidity, things will be complicated. But as long as the music is playing, you've got to get up and dance. We're still dancing.

— Chuck Prince, then CEO of Citigroup, in an interview with the *Financial Times* published July 10, 2007

Economic historian Charles Kindleberger noted in his book *Manias, Panics, and Crashes*, that the euphoria of a speculative mania often migrates into proximate assets. New companies are floated to take advantage of the euphoria, investors leverage their gains, credit becomes overextended, and fraud proliferates. The economy enters a period of distress that is the prelude to a crisis.[4] In the prior chapter, Figure 17.1 described the stages of a bubble. The topping process is evident in stage 3, Discord, and Panic characterizes stage 4.

At the top of a bubble investors feel a sense of discomfort and discord. In the professional or specialty media, the fundamental trend is doubted and its flaws are exposed. Many investors express disbelief and denial about these doubts as a result of cognitive dissonance. They fear that if they exit, they will miss out on further gains. They may have trouble sleeping or feel restless, constantly distracted by their investments and the size of their accumulated wealth. As prices begin to retreat, they experience a sense of inertia. They may think, "It will turn back up soon." Biologically, the stress hormone cortisol is elevated, reducing their propensity to take risk. They freeze and become mentally rigid—*analysis paralysis*. It is at this time of freezing when they most need to sell, but few are able to. If the boom was built on credit, margin calls begin to come in, spooking investors into outright panic selling.

The final psychological stage of a bubble is panic and pessimism. This phase creates a downward price momentum of its own. Stress and frustration lead to bursts of panic selling punctuated by small price bounces, which again roll over into further declines. Investors are likely to hold on to their losers, watching frantically as they decline further. They may rationalize paying margin calls with thoughts such as, "I'm averaging down." Biologically investors are experiencing chronically elevated levels of cortisol, and the stress of the decline leads to increased detail-orientation and a propensity to impulsive action. Occasional short-term surges of norepinephrine (a.k.a. noradrenaline) precipitate panic. The best investment strategy in such an environment is to ride the bubble downward as a short seller. Longer-term, value bottom-fishers profit by getting in after panic and volatility has settled.

Some investors have a neurological early-warning system that quickly alerts them to a bubble's Siren song—to the speculative exuberance that is luring others onto the rocks. New research out of CalTech on experimental bubbles pinpoints the neurological mechanism behind the skill of exiting a bubble at its peak.

BRAINS OF STEEL

In an experimental bubble environment, CalTech researchers found that the best investors become aware of bubble danger earlier, based on activity in their brain's anterior insula, a part of the loss-avoidance system.[5] In earlier studies, the brain's anterior insula was found to be activated by disgusting smells, electric shocks, and financial losses. Researchers identified that activity in the anterior insula actually affected future behavior. Such activation *predicted* when investors would avoid investment risks.[6] In the context of market exuberance, anterior insula activity predicts selling at the bubble top. "[W]e report a signal in the anterior insular cortex in the highest earners that precedes the impending price peak, is associated with a higher propensity to sell in high earners, and that may represent a neural early warning signal in these subjects."[7] Investors who listen to honor their neural early-warning system make more money during an experimental bubble by exiting before the collapse.

Another brain region predicted underperformance of investors in experimental bubbles. The subjects who performed the worst in the CalTech experiment were those who bought during an activation signal in the brain's nucleus accumbens, part of the brain's reward center. Note that the nucleus accumbens is activated by many desires: expectations of making money, cravings for illicit drugs, seeing desired luxury goods (women), and the prospect of taking revenge (men). The reward system compelled the worst performers to "Buy-Buy-Buy!" right at the top of the bubble. They could not resist the temptation of trying to ride the trend higher.

Many of the best investors hate experiencing losses. When positions go against them, they may exit immediately while resuming their research. This intense focus on imagining and managing financial downside risk allows them to survive through market ups and downs.

THE PEAK-END RULE

> *You may be happy to sell out to him [Mr. Market] when he quotes*
> *you a ridiculously high price, and equally happy to buy from him*
> *when his price is low. But the rest of the time you will be wiser to*
> *form your own ideas of the value of your holdings....*
> —Benjamin Graham, Chapter II, *The Investor and*
> *Stock-Market Fluctuations*, p. 42

Benjamin Graham's quote seems reasonable, but as seen with Sir Isaac Newton, it is very difficult to resist believing the emotion-based valuations offered by Mr. Market. It turns out that how investors assess value depends on deep emotional circuits. Daniel Kahneman performed several behavioral experiments on the relationship between valuation and emotional states. In one study, Kahneman submitted experimental subjects to a painful exposure to very cold water.[8] Participants were asked to rate their preference between:

1. Exposure of one hand for 60 seconds to 14°C ice water followed by exposure to 30 seconds of 15°C ice water.
2. Exposure of one hand for 60 seconds to 14°C ice water.

Both exposures are very painful, and subjects would not have enjoyed them in the least. Yet subjects preferred a longer overall exposure to ice-water involving greater overall pain. The reason for this preference was the gradual increase in temperature after 60 seconds. Kahneman found that one's memory of pleasure or pain from an experience is the average of the peak experience and the ending experience, which he called the *peak-end rule*.

Kahneman and others went on to study exposure to positive experiences. The researchers found that television commercials that induce positive feelings are rated more highly if the commercials have high peaks of intensity and strong positive endings.[9] Others found that participants rated a wonderful life that ended suddenly as better than one with the addition of mildly pleasant years, which they termed the James Dean effect.[10]

The James Dean effect is rooted in a common perception that people should leave a party early, believing an early departure will increase their overall happiness (because their memories will be happier). In the financial markets, this is akin to the desire to cut winners short.

In the comedy series *Seinfeld*, George Castanza was one of Jerry Seinfeld's hapless friends with big dreams. In one episode, George found that if he left a social situation on a high note—following a joke or great idea—others were more appreciative of him in later interactions.[11]

Timing the exit on a high note is challenging. When on a roll, most want to keep going. And all too often, when George tried to follow one good joke with another, it fell flat and led to frowns. In his attempts to salvage the good feeling, he piled one bad joke onto another. George tried to add to his string of social successes, only to lose all of the social capital he had accumulated from his prior gut-busters. Too often investors press their luck out of fear of regret. They don't want to miss anything good, but they end up overstaying their welcome.

Researchers hypothesize that brain cortical-monitoring technology could ascertain whether markets are in a bubble by monitoring trader brain activity. If the majority of traders were preferentially using their limbic systems versus their reasoning prefrontal cortices when making trading decisions, then wearable functional near-infrared spectroscopy (fNIRS) technology could detect this biomarker and flash warning signal to market regulators.[12] But until the day of personalized bubble-detection helmets, using media-derived sentiment data may serve as a reasonable substitute.

THE BUBBLEOMETER

Markets can remain irrational a lot longer than you and I can remain solvent.[13]

—John Maynard Keynes

As Keynes alluded, prices can inflate indefinitely, and understanding the mere existence of a bubble isn't sufficient. Shorting a rising bubble is a dangerous game if there is no clear discipline behind it.

George Soros has done well investing into bubbles. But Soros has not always been fortunate with bubble timing. In 1999 Soros's Quantum Fund rose 37 percent, in part due to a jump into technology stocks early that year. However, timing the top proved tricky, and the fund suffered losses on those shares in 2000, perhaps precipitating the closing and reorganization of the fund.[14] Investors who aim to time both the rising and the popping of bubbles are taking a significant risk, and tools are needed to facilitate such trading.

In order to explore the psychology of bubbles, the MarketPsych team developed a custom sentiment index. Sentiments derived from text analysis such as anger, joy, and price forecasts can be combined—like puzzle-pieces —to construct more complex sentiment indexes. In 2009 the MarketPsych team reviewed the characteristics of speculative conversations in social media at the tops of six speculative stock bubbles in U.S. stock markets: the Internet bubble in 2000, biotech stocks in 2000, the homebuilding stock bubble in 2005, the Chinese ADR bubble in 2006, copper stocks in 2007, an oil stock bubble in 2008, and a grain stock bubble also in 2008. The team examined the differences between the language used at the price tops versus during the months before the bubble emerged.

Speculative language such as positive emotionality, positive price expectations, and a focus on short-term returns predominated during bubble tops. Before bubbles emerged, analytical, fundamentally focused, and often pessimistic conversations predominated in social media. The team developed an index called the "bubbleometer" to quantify the disparity between the predominantly speculative attitudes evident at bubble tops and the rational analysis that preceded the bubble emergence. The bubbleometer was subsequently renamed the marketRisk index. When marketRisk readings are high, there is more speculative conversation about an asset. When it is low, there is more rational discourse.

The marketRisk index is inversely correlated with asset prices on a one-year horizon. A 12-month average of country-specific marketRisk index based on global media shows an inverse correlation with future 12-month country equity returns ($p < 0.05$) after controlling for prior GDP change, stock market returns, and the country's World Bank development status. The marketRisk index is inversely correlated with 12-month currency price changes as well ($p < 0.001$). These correlations were tested over 1998 to 2012 using the TRMI version 1.1 TRMI dataset.[15]

Moving averages of the marketRisk index appear to capture trends in prices, and of equal importance, turning points. In Figure 18.2, the moving averages of the marketRisk index for the Nasdaq Composite during the period 1998–2002 are displayed. Note that the marketRisk index was high since early 1998. Alan Greenspan's famous "irrational exuberance" remark in December 1996 indicates that a bubble was mooted to be underway much earlier than 1998. The moving average crossed into the red zone just before the large Nasdaq price crash in April 2000. As the Nasdaq speculative frenzy deflated, the short-term average generally stayed under the long-term, leading prices lower.

How investors value assets changes from prior to during a bubble. During the Internet bubble of 1997–2000, "click-throughs" and "eyeballs" underpinned valuations. At the bottom of recessions investors watch cash flows. Both of these concepts are embodied in the marketRisk index.

A similarly prescient MACD of the marketRisk TRMI for China is visible in Figure 18.3, suggesting a leading relationship with the Shanghai Composite index during China's stock market mini-bubble of 2014–2015.

The examples of the Nasdaq and the Shanghai Composite bubbles above are not statistically significant due the infrequency of bubbles and few trades. However, given the correlations with future country stock returns, marketRisk appears to shows predictive potential.

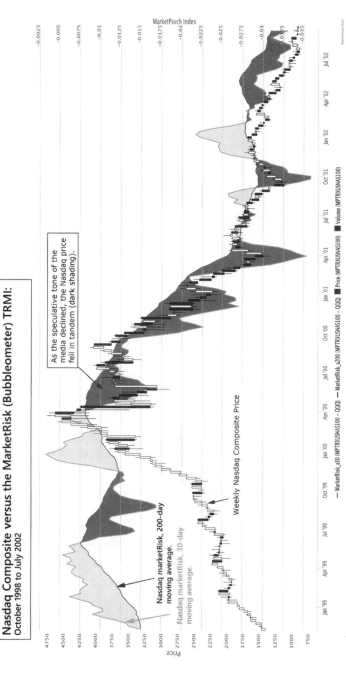

FIGURE 18.2 Nasdaq Composite candlestick chart versus a MACD (30–200) of the marketRisk TRMI (a.k.a. the Bubbleometer), 1998–2002.

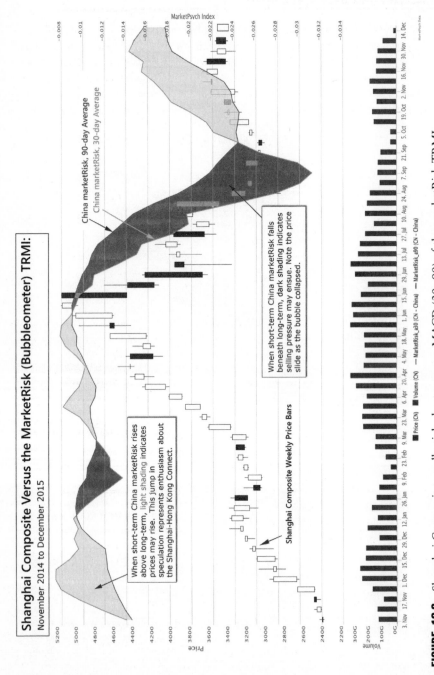

FIGURE 18.3 Shanghai Composite candlestick chart versus a MACD (30–90) of the marketRisk TRMI (a.k.a. the Bubbleometer), 2014–2015.

ARBITRAGING STOCK SPECULATION

Using cross-sectional analysis, it is possible to arbitrage speculative tone (marketRisk) across tiers of stocks. Such an analysis was performed by ranking all U.S. stocks by their past 12-month's average marketRisk values. The top 100 were selected by buzz, and the top 20 (most speculative) were shorted, while the bottom 20 (most analytical) were bought. The equity curve derived from this annual rotational model is visible in Figure 18.4.

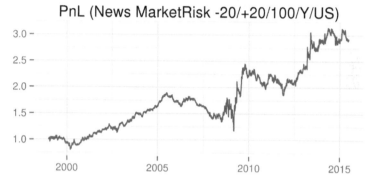

FIGURE 18.4 Equity curve derived from annual arbitrage of news-derived marketRisk TMRI across individual U.S. stocks.

This arbitrage is unimpressive for social media. It is possible that investment social media commentators are more savvy to the presence of a speculative bubble than the news media, who may profit through their cheerleading efforts. While news-derived marketRisk appears a valuable signal of speculative excess across individual stocks, it also holds value across global stock markets.

GLOBAL MEAN-REVERSION

When you buy a stock, because it has surplus assets or a good yield or a great safety margin, you are really making a bet on regression to the mean. We are really counting on the fact that current unpopularity will fade, that the current problems in the industry will dissipate, and that the fortunes of war will move back to normal.... The aggregate stock market of a country is more provably mean-reverting when mispriced than sectors. And great asset classes are provably more mean-reverting than a single country.
—Jeremy Grantham, April 2010[16]

Jeremy Grantham notes there is often mean-reversion in asset prices, which is more significant in larger asset classes. The investment returns to be gained from following such mean-reversion strategies are impressive, but also volatile. The following equity curves demonstrate the returns derived from arbitraging speculative risk across country stock indexes.

In order to derive these equity curves, the 20 countries with the highest news buzz and tradable stock indexes were selected for further modeling. Nontradable countries in the news—such as Libya, Afghanistan, and Iraq—were excluded. The top 20 countries were ranked by the average past 12-month marketRisk TRMI values. The primary stock indexes of the top five countries ranked on marketRiskTRMI were shorted, and the bottom five were bought. All positions were held for 12 months. The stock returns of the primary equity index for each country were averaged for the top five and bottom five countries to give a composite equity curve for each ranking. The model was rolled forward monthly and one-twelfth of the portfolio value was reinvested each month. As a result, the average holding period per position is at least 12 months.

Figure 18.5 depicts the annual cross-sectional results obtained with a marketRisk cross-sectional model across countries—a five-fold return from 1999 to 2014. The equity curve represents an absolute return model that is uncorrelated and somewhat, although not entirely, shielded from global events.

Shorting the major stock indexes of countries with the highest speculative fervor and buying the stock indexes of countries in a pessimistic funk was a historically productive arbitrage. Moving beyond stocks, other asset bubbles, such as commodity bubbles, have telltale signs of speculation visible in charts.

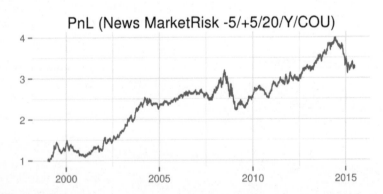

FIGURE 18.5 An equity curve produced from an annual marketRisk arbitrage across global stock indexes, based on shorting the quintile of countries with the greatest marketRisk and buying the quintile with the least, based on news media.

In a brief digression on speculation in commodities, shortages or excess demand lead to higher prices and may precipitate a bubble. In response to rising physical prices, commodity producers increase exploration and production, but there is a significant time lag before increased output will hit the market. As media reports on commodity price increase, public excitement may be stoked, fueling a speculative bubble. This pattern is evident in past commodity speculative bubbles, including in coffee, cotton, and natural gas.

KEEPING THE HOUSE MONEY

Trend followers only get hurt at inflection points, where the trend changes.
> —George Soros, in *Soros on Soros*

The psychology of the Looney Tunes cartoon character Wile E. Coyote represents the third stage of a bubble. In the third stage (discord), a reversing price forecast consensus is followed by price collapse. Consider that Mr. Coyote can run off a cliff and remain in empty space with his legs spinning until he looks down. Once he looks down he realizes he can no longer stay aloft, and he falls. In asset prices, a broad-based recognition that prices are too high relative to fundamentals that precedes collapse.

Most investors stay invested at the top of a bubble despite increasing doubts due to the phenomenon of cognitive dissonance (which fuels the underreaction in prices described in Chapter 11). In timing bubble tops, the goal is first to confirm that a speculative bubble exists using a checklist or other discipline, second to manage one's own emotional engagement with the bubble, and third to track the sentiment tone of the market for use in timing the top. This three-step process is easier said than done.

The philosopher St. Augustine wrote lengthy passages about his intense sexual desires in his book *Confessions*. As a Christian monk, he had taken a vow of chastity, and he struggled mightily to control his appetites. One of his prayers captures the struggle between his overwhelming physical desires and his moral intentions: "Lord grant me chastity and continence, but not yet."[17] Like St. Augustine, most bubble investors stay too long at the top, hoping to earn one last thrill. Unfortunately, when prices turn, it is often rapid and unexpected, and the exit is a costly one.

While some investors are inclined to leave the party early (cutting winners short), others (those with high expectations/reference points) play fast and loose with their gains. This excessive risk taking with gains is called the *house money effect* (a.k.a. the St. Augustine problem) and results in complacency and a failure to manage risk when the future looks bright.

When markets wobble at all-time highs, remember to reorient yourself to (1) what has been driving prices, and (2) your risk-management strategy.

Sometimes investors are torn by the fear of regret that they will leave the party early, missing out on further gains. Other times, they leave immediately, hoping to capture the peak experience and cutting a winner short. If engaging in investment during bubbles, always remember your time horizon, your strategy, the drivers of price action, and how to mitigate your personal weaknesses.

IN SUMMARY

- Many investors end up like Sir Isaac Newton, who lost his fortune in the South Seas stock bubble. Often, personal emotions and biases preclude investors from taking needed selling actions.
- Timing bubble tops is a dangerous game, but also one that can be very lucrative for those with appropriate tools and disciplined risk management.
- The best bubble traders have neural activations that compel them to sell out before others. This anterior insula activation indicates their brains are aware of the risk of bubble collapse.
- The peak-end rule describes how high positive emotion attracts investors to bubbles, and why investors stay invested too long.
- MACDs using the marketRisk index (a.k.a. bubbleometer) suggest that the speculative tone of the media could have been a useful tool in timing the top of the Nasdaq (1998–2002) and Shanghai Composite (2014–2015) stock bubbles.
- Commodity bubbles frequently have fundamental precursor events. Once those triggers have resolved, the bubble is at risk of collapse. In many cases, media priceForecast (a marker of speculation) and sentiment increase even after the fundamental trigger has abated, perhaps driving a positive feedback loop with prices.
- Investors who trade during bubbles benefit from using checklists to improve risk management.

NOTES

1. Proinsias O'Mahony, "Buy Bubbles, Big Bet, and Backache—Soros's Secret," *Irish Times* (Aug. 12, 2014), http://www.irishtimes.com/business/personal-finance/buy-bubbles-bet-big-and-backache-soros-s-secrets-1.1893639.
2. C. MacKay, *Extraordinary Popular Delusions & the Madness of Crowds* (London: Crown Publishing, 1841). www.historyhouse.com/book.asp?isbn=051788433X.
3. Charles P. Kindleberger and Robert Z. Aliber, *Manias, Panics and Crashes: A History of Financial Crises* (Palgrave Macmillan, 2011).
4. Ibid.

5. Alec Smith, Terry Lohrenz, Justin King, P. Read Montague, and Colin F. Camerer, "Irrational Exuberance and Neural Crash Warning Signals During Endogenous Experimental Market Bubbles," *Proceedings of the National Academy of Sciences* 111 (29) (2014), pp. 10503–10508.

6. Kuhnen, C. M., and Knutson, B. (2005). "The Neural Basis of Financial Risk Taking," *Neuron* 47(5), pp. 763–770.

7. Alec Smith.

8. Daniel Kahneman, Barbara L. Fredrickson, Charles A. Schreiber, and Donald A. Redelmeier, "When More Pain Is Preferred to Less: Adding a Better End," *Psychological Science* 4(6) (1993), pp. 401–405.

9. Hans Baumgartner, Mita Sujan, and Dan Padgett, "Patterns of Affective Reactions to Advertisements: The Integration of Moment-to-Moment Responses into Overall Judgments," *Journal of Marketing Research* (1997), pp. 219–232.

10. Ed Diener, Derrick Wirtz, and Shigehiro Oishi, "End Effects of Rated Life Quality: The James Dean Effect," *Psychological Science* 12(2) (2001), pp. 124–128.

11. Josh Thomas, "George Goes Out on a High Note," YouTube (Sept. 11, 2012), https://www.youtube.com/watch?v=8YaaZZN9VYs.

12. John L. Haracz and Daniel J. Acland, "Neuroeconomics of Asset-Price Bubbles: Toward the Prediction and Prevention of Major Bubbles" (2015). Online Working Paper.

13. A. Gary Shilling, *Forbes* 151(4) (1993), p. 236.

14. Martin Mitchell "Soros Shuffles Management as Big Funds Struggle," *New York Times* (April 29, 2000). Downloaded May 20, 2015, from: http://www.nytimes.com/2000/04/29/business/worldbusiness/29iht-soros.2.t.html.

15. Using TRMI v1.1.

16. Jeremy Grantham, *GMO Quarterly Letter* (1st Quarter, 2010).

17. Augustine of Hippo, *Confessions*, 8:7.

CHAPTER 19

Commodity Sentiment Analysis

Man: *"You talk as though you struck it rich sometime or other, Pop. How about it? Then what are you doin' in here, a down-and-outer?"*
Howard: *"That's gold, that's what it makes of us. Never knew a prospector yet that died rich. Make one fortune, you're sure to blow it in trying to find another. I'm no exception to the rule...."*
—*Treasure of the Sierra Madre* (1948)[1]

The 1948 movie *Treasure of the Sierra Madre*—in which the above scene was played out—examines the psychological effects of speculation on three American gold prospectors in Mexico. These Americans weren't the first foreigners seeking to strike it rich in Mexico. Spanish Conquistadors such as Cortes and Coronado spent their family fortunes and risked their lives searching for gold there. Coronado sought Cibola—the lost city of gold—and in the process explored as far north as the plains of present-day Kansas. Hernan Cortes, who is best known as the conqueror of the Aztec empire, informed envoys of emperor Moctezuma II, "I and my companions suffer from a disease of the heart that can be cured only with gold."[2] His allusion was figurative, although he may have intended it to be taken literally. Gold has an allure that drives some to take unfathomable risks in its pursuit—occasionally to the point of mental and physical ruin.

Returning to the *Treasure of the Sierra Madre:*

Howard: *Gold itself ain't good for nothin' except makin' jewelry with and gold teeth. Aw, gold's a devilish sort of a thing anyway. You start out to tell yourself you'll be satisfied with twenty-five thousand handsome smackers worth of it, "so help me Lord and cross my heart." Fine resolution.... But I tell you, if you was to make a real strike, you couldn't be dragged away. Not even the threat* *of miserable death would keep you from trying to add ten thousand more. Ten, you'd want to get twenty-five; twenty-five, you'd want to get fifty; fifty, a hundred. Like roulette. One more turn, you know. Always one more.*[3]

A speculative mentality among gold investors was apparent to George Soros following the global financial crisis. By the end of 2009 Soros had accumulated a $663 million stake in gold ETFs and mining stocks. Other well-known investors, including John Paulson, then famous for his "Big Short" of mortgage bonds before the financial crisis, also bought in. In January 2010 Soros noted that gold was becoming the "ultimate asset bubble," and he exited his gold positions before the gold bubble burst. In documents that his firm filed with the SEC, it appeared that he paid less than $1,225 an ounce for his gold positions and sold more than a year later for more than $1,300.[4]

Two years after the gold bubble had peaked, by Spring 2013, a confluence of events stoked a consensus that gold was overvalued. First, Goldman Sachs formally reversed a bullish forecast for gold.[5] Then a rumor spread that Cyprus was dumping its 14 tons of gold reserves onto the market. Nobel laureate Paul Krugman wrote an op-ed in the *New York Times* ("Lust for Gold") summarizing the evidence that there had been unsustainable investment in gold.[6] Krugman cited a 2011 Gallup poll in which one-third of Americans called gold the best long-term investment. Independent Wall Street guru Barry Ritholtz debunked some of the cult-like rationalizations of gold hoarders in an online interview.[7] The gold consensus rapidly turned bearish, and prices followed the consensus lower, as seen in Figure 19.1.

While sentiment often does lead prices higher and lower, it's not a perfect relationship. Gold prices are driven by multiple factors: the whims of jewelry buyers, the availability of supplies, trust in fiat currencies, and other factors. Precious metals often trade as currencies, and like currencies, their prices are stoked by perceptions.

Research performed on the TRMI version 1.1 by Aleksander Fafula found that the most predictive sentiment of the monthly price of gold from 1998 through 2012 was the average level of trust expressed in the U.S. dollar over the prior month. When a high level of trust was expressed in the U.S. dollar, the price of gold on average declined the following month. Similarly, when a low level of trust was expressed, the price of gold subsequently rose.

Commodities are unique assets in which investors, producers, consumers, and speculators vie in a zero-sum game. Their sentiment reflects such competing interests, where events that provoke joy in buyers conversely contribute to sellers' pain. There are also differences in time horizon that cloud the meaning of commodity sentiment. On a given day

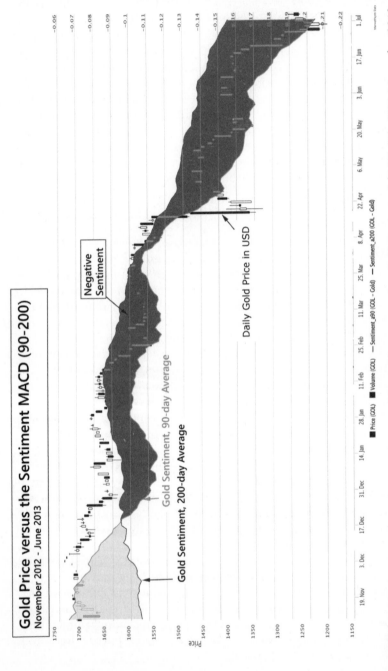

FIGURE 19.1 The beginning of the gold bear market. Gold prices versus a Gold Sentiment MACD (90–200), November 2012 through July 2013.

cattle ranchers may express negative sentiment about a drought, yet those who can maintain their herds will ultimately benefit from the higher prices. Meanwhile consumers may feel good about lower short-term beef prices, but complain about higher long-term prices after the cattle supply has been depleted and a shortage ensues. As a result of such competing perspectives, sentiment TRMI are often of less value for predicting commodity trends than measures of information flow around fundamentals (supplyVsDemand) and prices (priceDirection). In general, gold prices are not easily predictable with sentiment itself, but as seen in this chapter, "black gold" (oil) has experienced consistent price patterns in reaction to information and rooted in human psychology.

WHAT DRIVES OIL PRICES?

> *The Strait of Hormuz is the world's most important oil chokepoint due to its daily oil flow of about 17 million bbl/d in 2011 .... Flows through the Strait in 2011 were roughly 35 percent of all seaborne traded oil, or almost 20 percent of oil traded worldwide.*
> — U.S. Energy Information Administration[8]

Before oil was a ubiquitous energy source, it was used as a weapon of war. The image in Figure 19.2 is from a Greek manuscript, and it demonstrates the use of a petroleum-based fire-spraying weapon (Greek Fire) during naval combat. Such weapons came into use in the sixth century CE.

Economic warfare may be an effective weapon for the assertion of strategic power, and oil is one of the key armaments in such battles. When reviewing the information flow about crude oil, it appears that the Fear, Conflict, and Violence TRMI measure threats that affect oil prices. Ranging across incidents including the U.S. invasion of Iraq in 2003, the air war against Muammar Quaddafi in spring 2011, the Iranian–Israeli tensions over Iran's nuclear program in early 2012 (and after), and the Islamic State takeover of Mosul in 2014, the oil price is repeatedly driven high by conflict in oil-producing regions.

During Middle Eastern conflicts there is typically a fear of production disruptions. Such fears prompt panicked price hedging (buying) by refiners, airlines, chemical companies, and other price-sensitive oil consumers, all acting out the cognitive bias of probability neglect, where small probabilities of threats are overweighted. Granted, such fears are not entirely unfounded. Oil traders have prior experience with politics driving oil prices—for example, during the 1973 Arab Oil Embargo.

FIGURE 19.2 A depiction of a crude oil–derived weapon called Greek Fire. Source: Codex Skylitzes Matritensis, Bibliteca Nacional de Madrid, Vitr. 26-2, Bild-Nr. 77, f 34 v. b. (taken from Pászthory, p. 31). Image from an illuminated manuscript, the Madrid Skylitzes, showing Greek Fire in use against the fleet of the rebel Thomas the Slav. The caption above the left ship reads, στόλος Ρωμαίων πυρπολῶν τὸν τῶν ἐναντίων στόλον, i.e., "the fleet of the Romans setting ablaze the fleet of the enemies."

Fear is a measure of overreaction—an indicator that risk is being seen as greater than it actually is. So when fear is high, odds are that investors are overreacting to some vivid negative event, and prices are likely to revert to their pre-crisis level once fear begins to wane.

Tensions between the West and Iran repeatedly affected the oil price over the years 2010 to 2013. Rhetoric, like the following quote from Iranian Vice President Rahimi on December 27, 2011, if one explanation: "If they (the West) impose sanctions on Iran's oil exports, then even one drop of oil cannot flow from the Strait of Hormuz." Given that 20 percent of all oil produced flows through the Strait, Rahimi was effectively threatening economic warfare on oil-consuming nations. When the United States and Israel threatened to militarily dismantle Iran's nuclear program, the Fear and Violence TRMI around crude oil rose, as seen in Figure 19.3.

Having seen violence and fear rising in concert with prices, and falling before their declines, a statistical study was performed to establish whether significance—and related trading opportunities—exist in oil markets based on surges in such indexes.

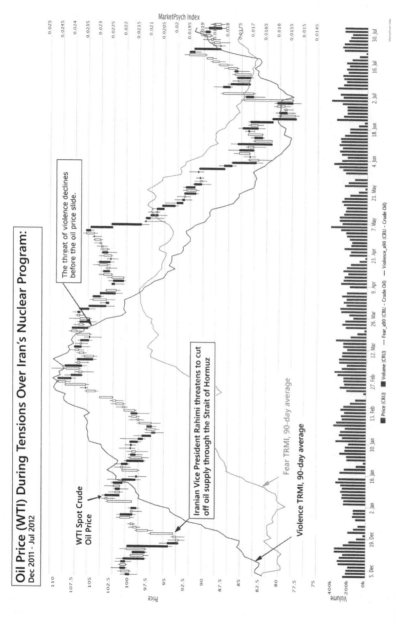

FIGURE 19.3 Threats to forcibly dismantle the Iranian nuclear program, and counter-threats from Iran to close the Strait of Hormuz, lead to surges in the crude oil fear index, violence index, and the price itself.

THE PREDICTABILITY OF FEAR, VIOLENCE, AND OIL PRICE VOLATILITY

The international energy market is dependent upon reliable transport. The blockage of a chokepoint, even temporarily, can lead to substantial increases in total energy costs.
— U.S. Energy Information Administration, August 22, 2012[9]

Aleksander Fafula ran a series of simple data mining experiments to understand how media references to conflict, violence, and fear preceded oil price moves over the past 15 years. The Conflict TRMI refers to high levels of dispute and disagreement surrounding the oil markets, fundamentals, prices, and other topics. The Violence TRMI encapsulates military threats and actions associated with the oil market. Fear is a measure of references to "worries," "concerns," and other symptoms of anxiety surrounding oil prices.

Using the TRMI as independent variables and price changes in the highest-volume futures contract of West Texas Intermediate Crude as a dependent variable, extreme levels and changes in media fear, conflict, and violence around crude were examined over the period 1998–2012 using association rules.

The monthly return patterns associated with these indexes create an interesting story. First, when the news of a conflict or potential war hits the newswires, it precedes a spike in oil prices. Importantly for traders, that spike has momentum—oil prices continue higher for the following one month. For example, a one-week spike in the crude oil Violence TRMI, which occurred 91 times in the study period, preceded an average +2.2 percent oil price return over the following month. One-week spikes in Conflict had a similar effect (94 events, +3.2 percent average one-month return). These "spikes" occur with a frequency of approximately 13 percent of weeks (about 6 weeks per year). There is a similar positive momentum effect for Fear, but only during extreme surges. A rise in one-week fear greater than 90 percent of all such spikes happened 19 times with average 3.2 percent next-month returns. A summary of monthly results is visible in Table 19.1.

Examining two variables together, such as when conflict rises *and* productionVolume drops, the next-month return averaged 8.2 percent (28 occurrences in the 15-year sample with 82 percent directional accuracy). This is an important result because it is reasonably common and it makes sense—both conflict *and* concerns about declining production together drive prices higher than either one alone. Importantly, oil prices seem to react sluggishly to new information. Oil traders have time to enter into positions based on these signals.

TABLE 19.1 Future One-Month Oil Price Returns Following One-Week Surges in Oil-Related Media with References to Violence, Conflict, Fear, and Production Volume

TRMI	Number of Signals	Average Next Month Return
Violence (weekly jump)	91	2.2%
Conflict (weekly jump)	94	3.2%
Fear (large weekly jump)	19	3.2%
Conflict (jump) and ProductionVolume (decline)	28	8.2%

If you've got an aversion to data-mining, then you'll have lots of bones to pick with this analysis. This is not a formal back-tested study, but rather the TRMI data was fit to a historical 15-year period (1998–2012) using the first version of the TRMI data to see if useful insights could be gleaned. Helpfully, the ensuing three years since these models were created support their value in oil price prediction. In summary, rising Conflict, Violence, and Fear TRMI typically lead average oil price rises over the following month. Oil traders may be underreacting to media reports, positioning themselves relatively slowly when tensions rise. Another theory for these results is that infrequent traders overreact to threat-related information, slowly driving prices higher as fear spreads. If such patterns truly represent overreaction, then a fallback in prices should occur following high levels of risk-related sentiments.

WHEN THE HEAT STAYS ON

While large jumps in media references to fear, violence, and conflict historically preceded oil prices higher, high absolute levels of such sentiments led price declines. On a monthly basis—over the interval (1998–2012)—when monthly crude oil fear was in the top 10 percent of historical values, the crude oil price declined every one of the following months with an average loss of 5.4 percent. For conflict values in the top 20 percent of the historical range, the average next-month drop is −3.2 percent (37 samples). See Table 19.2.

The most complex finding in the table indicates that when urgency declined (a crisis is not longer acute), but conflict remained high, there was a predictable opportunity to short oil and profit.

After the above patterns were identified in oil prices, there were several opportunities to test them in real-time. For example, after Islamic State routed Iraqi soldiers and seized Mosul in June 2014, fear rose and oil prices

TABLE 19.2 Monthly Oil Price Returns Following Periods When Monthly Average TRMI Values Are at the High End of Their Historical Range (Top X%) over the Past One Month

TRMI	Number of Signals	Average Monthly Return
Fear (top 10%)	19	−5.4%
Fear (top 20%)	37	−1.8%
Conflict (top 20%)	37	−3.2%
Conflict (High) & Urgency (Decline)	19	−5.5%

spiked. Throughout the remainder of 2014 no additional production disruption fears hit the market, and the oil price fell 60%. In another example, the Syrian government's use of chemical weapons on civilians prompted the West to threaten airstrikes against Syrian President Assad. Iran was a backer of Assad, and oil markets were put on edge in August 2013. The *New York Times* reported: "Iran's and Syria's defense ministers threatened on Friday to unleash attacks on Israel if Mr. Assad was in danger."[10] Yet the West did not engage in airstrikes against Assad, and crude oil prices predictably dropped in the subsequent month. While the aforementioned results are based on crude oil alone, groups of similar commodities such as precious metals, grains, and livestock have been studied with association rules and also yielded positive results.

This chapter has focused on specific examples of extreme information driving crude oil prices over shorter periods. Over the long term, and across commodities generally, cross-sectional models demonstrate few useful results. Perhaps the divergent influences on commodity prices prevent cross-commodity arbitrage.

COMMODITY PSYCHOLOGY

In *Treasure of the Sierra Madre*, Humphrey Bogart's character (Dobbs) and two companions set out together from their flophouse in Tampico, Mexico, to search for gold in the Sierra Madre mountains of Mexico. They find a vein, and after secretly mining the gold from their claim for several weeks, Dobbs begins to suspect his partners will kill him to steal his share. The excitement that accompanied striking it rich morphs into desperation and paranoia for Dobbs. He overreacts to perceived threats, and he becomes unhinged from reality.

As Dobbs grows increasingly paranoid about his partners' intentions, he tries to preemptively kill one while the other is away from camp. His victim survives, and shortly after the assault, bandits arrive on the scene.

Dobbs is killed by the bandits, and the bandits then steal the partners' gold. Ironically, the bandits don't know what the gold dust is. As they ride away, they dump the gold dust into the wind as if it were worthless sand. The gold blows away, and Dobbs' two partners—who are less consumed by the gold fever—live on, poorer and wiser for the experience.

There is something about gold—and commodities in general—that uniquely appeals to human psychology. Gold, oil, and other commodities are tangible. They have deep historical meaning. In many ways these commodities each soothe one or more primal psychological concerns: Security, currency, and beauty (jewelry) are provided by precious metals, life-giving nourishment is provided by agricultural commodities, and the energy that warms, lights, and sustains modern life is provided by the energy commodities. Whatever their psychological meaning, commodities news provokes significant repeating patterns in markets, including both the overreaction and underreaction patterns described in this chapter.

IN SUMMARY

- Perhaps because of the psychological meaning of unique physical commodities, each commodity demonstrates independent patterns in responses to information flow.
- Using association rules, on a weekly basis oil prices underreact to news containing frequent references to fear, violence, and conflict.
- Historically, high absolute monthly levels of fear, violence, or conflict preceded price declines in crude oil over the following month.
- Sentiment-based trend-following models perform well for commodities.
- Studies using cross-sectional analysis show no predictive power across commodities.

NOTES

1. *The Treasure of the Sierra Madre*, Warner Brothers, 1948. http://www.youtube.com/watch?v=EQyqvFVe4Y4.
2. "The conquest," *The Economist*, Millennium issue (December 23, 1999).
3. *The Treasure of the Sierra Madre*.
4. Richard Evans, "How to invest like … George Soros," *The Telegraph* (April 8, 2014). Downloaded from: http://www.telegraph.co.uk/finance/personalfinance/investing/10749558/How-to-invest-like-...-George-Soros.html.
5. Joe Wiesenthal, "It's Over: Goldman Calls the End of the Great Gold Bull Market," *Business Insider* (December 5, 2012). Downloaded May 20, 2015, from: http://www.businessinsider.com/goldman-calls-the-end-of-the-gold-bull-market-2012-12.

6. Paul Krugman, "Lust for Gold," *New York Times* (April 11, 2013). Downloaded May 20, 2015, from: http://www.nytimes.com/2013/04/12/opinion/krugman-lust-for-gold.html.

7. Stacy Curtin, "12 (Misguided) Commandments of Gold Bugs: Barry Ritholtz," *Daily Ticker* (April 19, 2013). Downloaded May 20, 2015 from http://finance.yahoo.com/blogs/daily-ticker/12-misguided-commandments-gold-bugs-barry-ritholtz-123507310.html.

8. "Factbox: Strait of Hormuz," Reuters (January 9, 2012). http://www.reuters.com/article/2012/01/09/us-iran-oil-hormuz-facts-idUSTRE8081BX20120109. Downloaded August 30, 2012 from: http://www.eia.gov/countries/regions-topics.cfm?fips=wotc&trk=p3&utm.

9. Ibid.

10. Anna Barnard and Alissa J. Rubin, "Experts Fear U.S. Plan to Strike Syria Overlooks Risks," *New York Times* (August 30, 2013).

CHAPTER 20

Currency Characteristics

There is no subtler, no surer means of overturning the existing basis of society than to debauch the currency. The process engages all the hidden forces of economic law on the side of destruction, and does it in a manner which not one man in a million is able to diagnose.

—John Maynard Keynes[1]

Over $5 trillion are traded in global foreign exchange markets every day, rendering currencies the most actively traded global asset class. Participants in the currency markets include central banks, multinational corporations, investment firms, banks, and retail speculators, among others. Each group may have coordinating or competing goals in the markets. For example, governments may take actions to boost their own export-based industries (via depreciation) or even to undermine others' (such as the 50 percent devaluation of the Iranian rial in 2013 following discussions of international sanctions). Retail and institutional investors may be pursuing a carry trade to earn higher yields in other nations' bonds. Speculators may trade based on macroeconomic announcements. Given these competing influences, and the difficulty of identifying both perception and reality in currency markets, how can investors determine the true, equilibrium value of a dollar? This chapter explores how media sentiment and perceptions may drive currency prices in systematic, predictable patterns.

THE VALUE OF UNCERTAINTY

"[I]t is uncertainty—far more than disaster—that unnerves and weakens markets."

—Alexander Hamilton[2]

Alexander Hamilton was a founding father of the United States and served as the first U.S. Secretary of the Treasury (1789–1795). Hamilton argued that a strong central government would serve to bolster business confidence, "[T]o give people faith in the financial structure of the country and in the soundness of the currency...."[3] As Secretary of the Treasury, Hamilton lobbied the U.S. government to issue bonds to bolster the government's finances. The goal of this debt issuance was to improve business confidence. Hamilton believed that a centralized and fiscally sound government would reduce uncertainty and thus boost economic activity following the U.S. Revolutionary War.

Confirming Hamilton's belief in the value of strong governance to stabilize market values, researchers found that monetary policy uncertainty creates a risk premium in currencies.[4] A country's currency remains weak until policy uncertainty passes, after which the currency rises in value. This discount in currency value is larger when the country is economically weak. Further academic research into the impact of uncertainty on bond prices finds that the bond risk premium rises (bond prices fall) as uncertainty about expected inflation rises.[5] Furthermore, price movements in currencies often occur as a result of sudden "flight to quality" (a euphemism for panic) among traders who engage in the same safety-seeking behavior simultaneously.[6] Such patterns in currency prices, based on changes in consensus price expectations and uncertainty, may be modeled using currency media sentiment data.

Previous chapters described the value of cross-sectional rotation models in identifying consistent mis-pricings—when perception deviates from reality—across assets. In an effort to test Hamilton's conjecture, CJ Liu used cross-sectional analysis of the Uncertainty TRMI to study the effects of uncertainty on 32 currencies. The Uncertainty TRMI is specifically quantified in currency-related media references to concepts including "doubt," "confusion," and "lack of clarity."

CJ started his testing with a weekly cross-sectional analysis of uncertainty. His model selected the top eight currencies in the news over the prior week and simulated going long the two with the highest uncertainty and going short the two associated with the most clarity (least uncertainty) at the open price on the first business day of the week. In order to prevent look-ahead bias, weekly models used prices opening on Monday and closing on Friday. The ranking was repeated and positions were reestablished each Monday. Rotating forward on a weekly basis, plotting the long-short returns yields the equity curve seen in Figure 20.1.

On a weekly basis, currency-related uncertainty provided an arbitrage opportunity from 1998 through July 2015. Over the course of an entire year, country-level uncertainty—a country's overall level of uncertainty

FIGURE 20.1   Equity curve derived from arbitraging currency uncertainty across the top eight currencies (top two long, bottom two short) in the media with 1-week look-back and prediction horizons.

(versus the uncertainty associated with the currency itself)—reveals an interesting arbitrage result. That is, similar to the weekly arbitrage, countries described with more uncertainty in the media have higher currency returns over the subsequent 12 months (and low uncertainty countries have lower relative currency returns). This result can be seen in the equity curve in Figurese 20.2. This equity curve was derived by selecting the top 8 countries in the news over the prior 12 months, buying the currencies of the 2 countries with the most uncertainty, shorting the currencies of the 2 countries with the least uncertainty, and holding for 12 months. The strategy is rotated forward at the end of each month with one-twelfth of the portfolio redeployed.

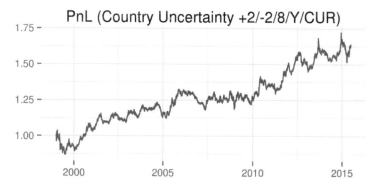

FIGURE 20.2   Equity curve derived from arbitraging country uncertainty across the top eight currencies (top two long, bottom two short) in the media with 12-month look-back and prediction horizons.

The value of the Uncertainty TRMI appears to be contrarian. When the media report uncertainty about a currency—such as its price direction, interest rates, or government policy—investors may overreact and require a greater risk premium to hold it. Such uncertainty distorts interest rate yields between currencies and fuels the profitability of carry trade strategies. In general, across various holding periods, currencies associated with uncertainty outperform those associated with a greater level of certainty.

INFORMATION FLOW

When the Federal Reserve unexpectedly raises interest rates, the value of the U.S. dollar may surge dramatically. When monetary policy deviates from expectations, prices adjust as expectations adjust.

While uncertainty represents a lack of clarity about the future, it does not carry a directional expectation. That is, uncertainty has no valence. If a news article contains the statements, "Investors are unsure where the yen is headed," then it conveys uncertainty. If a journalist writes, "Analysts foresee a surge in the yen over the next week," then that reference contains a positive expectation for the currency's direction.

One of the TRMI—the priceForecast TRMI—quantifies media expectations for the future direction of a currency's price. The TRMI priceForecast is the net balance of directional price forecasts in a given period of time, divided by the total volume of relevant references.

Using the same weekly cross-sectional analysis procedure described in the prior section, an arbitrage of the priceForecast TRMI across the top 10 currencies in the media was performed. The model went long the currency with the highest price forecast and shorted the one with the weakest. Rotating forward weekly, this model developed the equity curve depicted in Figure 20.3.

The average news price forecast of a currency's value—at extreme levels (deciles)—was borne out over the following week. While uncertainty appears to fuel investor overreaction, the priceForecast appears to capture investor underreaction. Many of the weekly indexes demonstrating profitable arbitrage show similar results at monthly and yearly horizons, and like this decile arbitrage, more extreme arbitrages have higher return/higher volatility equity curves.

Beyond annual country-level uncertainty, using the country Trust TRMI, it is also possible to arbitrage currency values. Buying the two most trusted and shorting the two least trusted country's currencies, year after year since 1999, yields the equity curve in Figure 20.4. Alexander Hamilton's goal to restore confidence (trust) in order to bolster the value of the nascent U.S. government's securities is supported by this research. High levels of

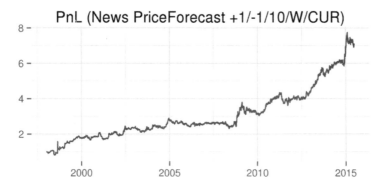

FIGURE 20.3 Equity curve derived from arbitraging currency priceForecast across the top 10 currencies (top one long, bottom one short) in the media with one-week look-back and prediction horizons.

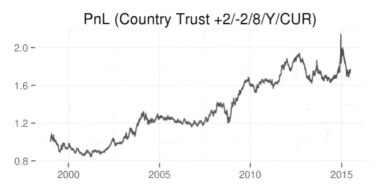

FIGURE 20.4 Equity curve derived from arbitraging country-level Trust across the top eight currencies in the media (top two long, bottom two short) with 12-month look-back and prediction horizons.

trust in a country predicted outperformance of its currency over a 12-month horizon.

High country trust implies very little risk premium in a currency, while high uncertainty implies the opposite, yet the equity curves both capture arbitrage opportunities. It appears that country-level trust and uncertainty contain orthogonal information for the prediction of currency values.

Based on a comprehensive analysis of historical currency sentiment data, currency investors should not only avoid countries with low levels of trust, but beyond uncertainty several sentiment indexes also inversely correlated with trust. For example, according to the data, investors should avoid currencies of countries with high levels of violence, government instability, or social unrest, and they should have preferred to hold the currencies of countries low on those indexes. Across countries, uncertainty was the only sentiment index that contributed to an arbitrage-able risk premium.

Cross-sectional arbitrage allows the identification of opportunities at extreme values of sentiment or on macroeconomic metrics, which is useful as a simple directional indicator. Unfortunately, blunt cross-sectional models do not allow fine-tuning of timing. Moving average crossovers, applied to sentiment data, may be an elegant solution to the problem of timing major currency trends and reversals.

TIMING CURRENCIES WITH MACDS

Based on the above cross-sectional results, currency values may be driven by country-level sentiments such as uncertainty and trust, and by media-embedded price expectations. Such sentiments may drive currency values through overreaction (uncertainty) and underreaction (trust and priceForecast).[7] Underreaction is already exploited by many traders using price momentum, while overreaction is arbitraged via the carry trade. Trading on price momentum in currency markets was found to earn surprisingly high excess returns, yielding an average annualized returns payoff of 4.4 percent, a standard deviation of 7.3 percent, and a Sharpe ratio of 0.60 in one study[8] and 10 percent annualized returns in another study.[9] In the foreign exchange markets, momentum strategies have demonstrated excess returns not only in the current period, but also back to the 1920s.[10] While price trends may be persistent, they are also, by their nature, lagging. If information flow is a leading indicator of price action, then changes in currency-related news might provide a useful signal on when to change directional bets.

Using moving averages of currency prices (price-based MACDs) to indicate currency buy and sell signals captures price momentum.[11] Others found that adaptive systems using customer behavior (order flows) as an input historically predicted future currency price direction.[12] Yet moving averages are lagging indicators, and they are susceptible to increased tail-risk as a result of extreme events.[13]

Amidst the whirl of thousands of contradictory opinions, the general average opinion is more evident, and the consensus opinion can be observed to shift over time. When a short-term sentiment moving average crosses over a longer term moving average, it may indicates that a trend has changed. In Figure 20.5 and the other MACDs profiled in this book, lighter shading between the average lines indicates when the short-term crosses above the long-term average (often placing upward pressure on prices) and darker shading is present when the short-term average falls below.

In 2012, the authors visually identified that the yen's priceForecast MACD seemed useful for timing trends in the Japanese yen (versus the U.S. dollar). Since first identified, that MACD has correctly forecast two major trends in the yen (both to the downside) in the intervening years. In order to explore this relationship further, a colleague used data mining to identify the optimal TRMI-based MACDs for predicting the yen's direction since 1998. He added 10-fold cross-validation to ensure the findings were consistent over time (and weren't only catching two or three large trends). According to this analysis, if one were to apply a constant position of either long or short the JPY/USD—going long when the 90-day average of the yen priceForecast MACD crossed above the 200-day average, and short when the 90-day average crossed below the 200-day average—then a 6.7 percent average annual return with a Sharpe ratio of 0.6 was historically achieved. A one-dollar stake would have theoretically grown to $3.14 during the simulation, which covered the period from October 1998 through July 31, 2015. An image of that strategy in the recent period is visible in Figure 20.5.

The MACD in Figure 20.5 provides an unusually robust result. In order to understand this finding, several forex traders were asked their opinions on the relationship. One yen trader remarked that he sees more herding and news-following among traders of the Japanese yen. Another suggested that the Bank of Japan is leaking price forecasts to business reporters. The bank would do this to share with investors the risk of moving the yen in the Bank's desired direction. If the bank itself is buying or selling yen on the open market, it may be more vulnerable to front-running or speculative attack.

Speculating on the motivations for an asset price move is inherently dangerous. Fortunately the priceForecast index is transparently constructed, and its role in predicting the yen's value since 1998, and especially during the premiership of Shinzo Abe, is interesting. When working with sentiment data, a dose of human discretion may improve the value of the TRMI in trading applications. If a new prime minister or head of the Bank of Japan changes monetary policy, it is possible that the value of the priceForecast index will remain only a historical curiosity.

USING CURRENCY SENTIMENT IN TRADING

Within our mandate, the ECB is ready to do whatever it takes to preserve the euro. And believe me, it will be enough.
—Mario Draghi, ECB President, July 26, 2012.

Since the Euro's launch in 2000, the optimal strategy for timing investments in the currency has been to await spikes in uncertainty about its future.

Similarly, when Mario Draghi at the European Central Bank asserted his intent to save the currency, he collapsed uncertainty and the value of the currency rallied sharply. Amareos, a sentiment consulting and research provider, noted in a client report, "[I]t turned out to be 'whatever it takes'; three words that marked a turning point in the Euro zone crisis. . . ." With those words Draghi restored confidence in European central bankers, deflated uncertainty, and kindled a months-long rally.

Before Mario Draghi, Alexander Hamilton assumed that perceptions and expectations create a self-fulfilling prophecy that plays out in exchange rates. Hamilton's ideas were corroborated on both weekly (and yearly) horizons with the Uncertainty TRMI. Other research similarly supports Hamilton's conjecture, for example, noting that monetary policy uncertainty increases the currency risk premium. Uncertainty may provoke risk aversion and overreaction, and such uncertainty appears to generate opportunities for exploitation of currency price movements and perhaps for taking advantage of the carry trade.

Weekly TRMI that demonstrate appealing equity curves in cross-sectional models include priceForecast (a measure of expectations). The priceForecast momentum result may reflect investor underreaction on a weekly basis. Longer term, yearly TRMI including country-level trust appears to hold predictive power over the following year's currency price action, perhaps providing evidence of investor underreaction to brewing monetary instability.

Using moving average crossovers of sentiment data provides a potentially leading indicator for forecasting prices. In studying the viability and stability of simple TRMI moving average cross over models, it is apparent that many currencies are influenced by unique TRMI. That is, there is no one single moving average crossover that shows value in forecasting currency prices. As in the case of the Japanese yen and the priceForecast TRMI, there may be unique local information that traders monitor. When the widely followed information rises or falls in intensity, currency prices follow.

While the yen MACD in Figure 20.5 is historically interesting, it was developed over a short historical window (17 years), and the rules it utilizes are not necessarily transferable to other currencies. Data mining renders models vulnerable to historical overfitting. Fortunately, in the authors' testing, data-mined MACDs show value rolling forward, both in out-of-sample sets and in forward-tested environments. Furthermore, cross-sectional models built on currency TRMI appear robust and generalizable.

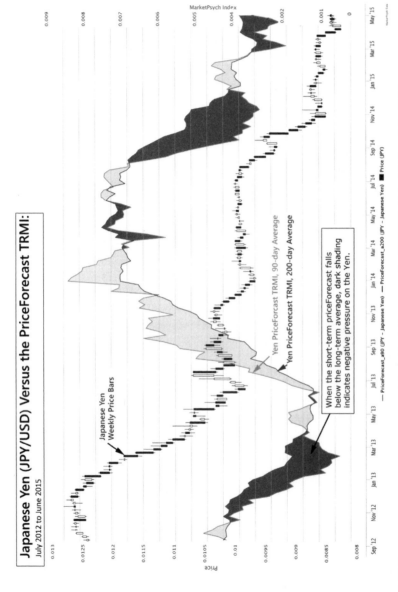

FIGURE 20.5 Japanese Yen priceForecast MACD (90–200) versus the JPY/USD, July 2012 to July 2015.

When developing predictive models for currencies based on cross-sectional arbitrage, a combination of TRMI such as Uncertainty and priceForecast may offer superior returns to either one alone. In a simulation performed by CJ Liu, higher and more stable (less volatility) equity curves were observed when multiple TRMI were combined into a single predictive model. Such combinatorial models have continued to perform well in forward-testing since 2013. This suggests that currency and country-related media contain diverse information characteristics with orthogonal value toward predicting currency prices.

IN SUMMARY

- Alexander Hamilton identified that uncertainty irrationally debases a currency and trust inflates its value.
- Researchers have since found that monetary policy uncertainty adds a risk premium (an excessive discount) in currency values.
- The Uncertainty TRMI shows significant historical predictive value over currency valuations in cross-sectional models at weekly and yearly horizons, likely due to investor overreaction to uncertainty.
- Weekly TRMI that demonstrate appealing equity curves for currency forecasting include priceForecast and economicGrowth.
- Yearly TRMI including country-level Trust and Violence may hold predictive power due to long-term underreaction to social and monetary changes.
- Moving average crossovers (MACDs) may help time reversals in influential information flow, as in the case of the Japanese yen priceForecast.
- Using a combination of orthogonal TRMI boosts model returns.

NOTES

1. John Maynard Keynes, *The Economic Consequences of the Peace*, 1919, Chapter VI, pp. 235–236.
2. J. S. Gordon, *The Scarlet Woman of Wall Street* (New York: Weidenfeld and Nicolson, 1988), p. 10. From Lo, 14, p. 62.
3. Ibid., p. 62.
4. Philippe Mueller, Paolo Porchia, and Andrea Vedolin, "Policy Announcements in FX Markets." Available at SSRN 2480131 (2014).
5. Ravi Bansal and Ivan Shaliastovich, "A Long-Run Risks Explanation of Predictability Puzzles in Bond and Currency Markets," *Review of Financial Studies* (2012), pp. hhs108.
6. Brunnermeier, M. K., and Pedersen, L. H. (2009), "Market Liquidity and Funding Liquidity," *Review of Financial Studies*, 22(6), pp. 2201–2238.

7. Menkhoff, L., Sarno, L., Schmeling, M., and Schrimpf, A. (2012), "Currency Momentum Strategies," *Journal of Financial Economics*, 106(3), pp. 660–684.

8. Burnside, C., Eichenbaum, M. S., and Rebelo, S. (2011), "Carry Trade and Momentum in Currency Markets" (No. w16942), National Bureau of Economic Research.

9. Menkhoff, L., Sarno, L., Schmeling, M., and Schrimpf, A. (2012), "Currency Momentum Strategies," *Journal of Financial Economics*, 106(3), pp. 660–684.

10. Accominotti, Olivier and Chambers, David, "Out-of-Sample Evidence on the Returns to Currency Trading (March 2014)." CEPR Discussion Paper No. DP9852. Available at SSRN: http://ssrn.com/abstract=2444873.

11. Schulmeister, S. (2008), "Components of the Profitability of Technical Currency Trading," *Applied Financial Economics*, 18(11), pp. 917–930.

12. Austin, M. P., Bates, G., Dempster, M. A., Leemans, V., and Williams, S. N. (2004), "Adaptive Systems for Foreign Exchange Trading," *Quantitative Finance*, 4(4), pp. 37–45.

13. Gyntelberg, J., and Schrimpf, A. (2011), "FX Strategies in Periods of Distress," *BIS Quarterly Review*, December.

CHAPTER 21

Economic Indicators

All economic movements, by their very nature, are motivated by crowd psychology.

—Bernard Baruch

This chapter explores the economic predictive power of sentiment from both microeconomic (corporate earnings) and macroeconomic (national economic activity) perspectives. News-derived measures of economic activity are faster predictors of earnings, stock price reactions to earnings conference calls, and economic growth than current standards. Before delving into the relationship between sentiment and macroeconomic activity, the chapter addresses how fundamentals and sentiments, as communicated in company earnings conference calls, lead stock price movement.

Earnings conference calls are legally mandated quarterly conversations between corporate executives and their shareholders. Every publicly traded company must hold these calls. The calls provide a window into the thinking of financial analysts and corporate executives. Challenging and aggressive questions for the corporate management team are typical, and the CEO's responses to such queries are telling.

In 2009, MarketPsych's then-CTO, Yury Shatz, performed text analysis of 120,000 conference call transcripts provided by Thomson Reuters StreetEvents. The transcripts spanned the years 2002 through 2009. A detailed analysis of the topics and tones expressed in the conference call transcripts was performed, and those that correlated with future stock price performance were identified.

The analysis found that among companies with over $1 billion market capitalization, those with the largest increase in negative accounting news (at the highest 2 percent level) had subsequent 0.5 percent price declines relative to the S&P 500 from the morning after the earnings call through the following five business days. The opposite effect occurred in case of good accounting news, which predicted an average 0.6 percent increase relative to the

S&P500. Changes in the tone of accounting news were directly correlated with future price action, implying underreaction by investors to both fundamental deterioration and improvement in corporate prospects.

While the sentiment around fundamental information reported in earnings conference calls was directly correlated with price action—positive fundamentals preceded positive price movement—the expression of fear, despite being negative in tone, was also correlated with positive price direction. In fact, both high levels of fear and large increases in fear (versus a prior 3 quarter average) were associated with average price increases of 0.7 percent and 0.5 percent, respectively, relative to the S&P 500 over the following five business days. It appears that—investors may predictably overreact to expressions of fear in earnings conference calls.

Interestingly, some of the best indicators of future stock price performance involved social graces. A higher percentage of politeness ("thank you"; "excuse me"; etc.) and praise ("Great numbers!"; "Good job!"; etc.) were associated with stock outperformance over the following week. Perhaps the optimism of complimentary analysts infected other investors on the call, or perhaps analysts inadvertently expressed verbal "tells" of future earnings estimate revisions.

EARNINGS FORECASTS

Earnings conference call transcripts reflect corporate presentations as well as a dialogue with investors and analysts. Accurately seeing beyond the layer of regulatory and public relations spin in such corporate presentations can be a challenge for Wall Street analysts. Yet developing superior corporate earnings estimates is a key value-add of stock analysts. Because such estimates influence asset allocation and stock prices, producing better estimates is a key source of alpha for some traders. Data from social platforms and media appears to significantly improve earnings estimate models.

The company Estimize collects earnings estimates via an online platform where analysts share their estimates, with the payoff being the ability to see the best guesses of others. Estimize receives a significant number of quarterly estimates for most companies, and academics studying earnings estimates published to Estimize report that the average earnings estimate from the company's users shows 58–64 percent superior accuracy over the I/B/E/S Wall Street consensus.[1] There appears to be a social advantage in forecasting earnings.

It's not only Estimize that can help analysts improve their accuracy. Online search frequency for product names predicts sales volume and subsequent corporate earnings. Researchers Da Zhi, Joey Engelberg, and Pengjie Gao studied the relationship between Google search engine volume (Google

Trends data) of company product names and stock price returns around earnings announcements. The authors found that an increased frequency of searching for product names on Google led to larger earnings surprises.[2]

Given the higher accuracy of crowd-sourced earnings estimates and the predictive value of Google Trends product search volume, a logical next step is to sample social and news media for explicitly stated earnings forecasts. Fortunately the TRMI contain an index for equities called "earningsForecast." The earningsForecast TRMI represents the aggregation of all expressions which assert that a company's earnings will either rise or fall going forward. When such individual expressions are aggregated together they form a time series of expectations about a company's earnings prospects (see Appendix A for a sentence-level example).

In order to study the predictive power of the earningsForecast TRMI, CJ Liu performed cross-sectional analysis of this index across U.S. stocks over several prediction windows. The equity curve for the daily arbitrage is visible in Figure 6.7 (in Chapter 6). CJ's weekly cross-sectional analysis demonstrated momentum value in this index. Importantly, a monthly cross-sectional study showed no value, and annual models demonstrated inverse value from the earningsForecast TRMI. That is, over an annual horizon investors appear to overreact to earnings forecasts published in the news media.

Elijah DePalma found that regardless of buzz level, the earningsForecast TRMI produces viable trading signals. DePalma examined all earningsForecast signals from the news about S&P 500 stocks over the period January 2012 to August 2015. He found 4,300 earningsForecast signals during this period. Following these signals, there was a price drift over the following three weeks. When he isolated the 1,000 signals (of the 4,300) that were associated with the lowest social media buzz, he noted significantly higher returns over the following 15 business days. When a positive earningsForecast appeared in the news media with little associated social media buzz (approximately 500 samples), the stock price outperformed the overall stock market an average of 120 basis points (1.2 percent) over the following 15 business days. For negative earningsForecast signals (approximately 500 samples), the outperformance was by approximately 80 basis points (0.80 percent) over the subsequent 15 business days. These results show that changes in earnings forecasts that are not noted by social media lead a 15-day drift in the stock price, and they are superior to CJ's weekly cross-sectional returns because they take advantage of low-buzz events that are little-noticed by others.

Wall Street analysts have an array of tools available for improving their earnings estimates. While Google product search frequency and social earnings forecasts (Estimize data) contribute to superior earnings forecasts, extracting earnings forecasts from the news flow using text analytics itself generates outperforming trading strategies. The next section explores how estimates of national economic activity can similarly be improved using data sources as diverse as Google search volume and media analytics.

PREDICTING ECONOMIC ACTIVITY

Accurate and timely measures of business activity are integral to economic forecasting. Policymakers use such metrics to set monetary policy, business-people follow economic growth in order to more wisely allocate resources, and traders and investors use economic growth numbers to guide their asset allocation decisions. Each group is thus heavily invested in using the most accurate and timely proxies of economic activity.

Global economic activity is currently measured using a variety of techniques. The most widely followed metrics of economic activity include the Purchasing Managers' Indexes (PMIs) released by the Markit Group, the Institute of Supply Management (ISM) survey, and quarterly GDP numbers released by individual governments.

Unfortunately the available data on economic activity is produced with a high degree of uncertainty. Many economic growth metrics are released following a delay, and they are often subsequently revised. In addition, the process of producing economic data contains inherent biases. PMI and ISM are based on survey and are released monthly, while GDP is published quarterly.

The construction of such indexes is inherently fragile. The use of paper surveys and telephone interviews leads to delays in compilation, calculation, or dissemination of the PMI and ISM indicators. Second, the surveys that underlie the PMI and ISM economic indicators are vulnerable to self-report bias and small sample sizes, both of which introduce noise into what is already an infrequent data release. Third, due to noise, significant revisions of these numbers are not uncommon on future release dates. Fourth, many countries are not covered by these commercial economic indicators. Finally, most economic indicators show a trivial correlation with future stock market, fixed income, and currency valuations, thus diminishing their utility as forecasting tools. Nonetheless, despite their flaws, monthly economic indicators such as the PMI and ISM are watched closely by global traders, economists, and central bankers, and they influence major asset allocation and monetary policy decisions.

In order to identify superior economic indicators, researchers have explored sources of real-time data as proxies for economic activity, an activity called nowcasting.[3,4] Data sources as diverse as credit card transaction data,[5] satellite images of retail store parking lots,[6] ambient nocturnal light measured from space,[7] credit spreads,[8] Internet search data,[9,10] and (theoretical) semantic analysis of news[11] have been investigated. In the search for a better economic indicator, Google search and media data produce significant advances over existing indicators.

QUANTIFYING ECONOMIC PRESSURES

Google Trends data records the volume of searches about specific terms through Google's search engine, which itself receives more than 70 percent of U.S.-based search queries.[12] Hal Varian, chief economist at Google, performed a number of economic studies using this data. Google's search data has the potential to describe interest in a variety of economic activities in real time, and Choi and Varian provide evidence that search data can predict home sales, automotive sales, and tourism.[13] Yet other sources of social data, such as Facebook, may not be so predictive. In one sentiment at least—the Gross National Happiness index provided by Facebook—daily changes in happiness do not correlate with future economic activity.[14]

Aleksander Fafula set out to explore whether the broad range of country TRMI could demonstrate predictive power over global economic activity. The country TRMI are real-time quantitative time series of 48 sentiments and macroeconomic topics quantified in the news and social media flow about 130 countries. The complete list of Country TRMI and a description of their construction is visible in Appendix A. These indexes are derived from textual analytics of global news and social media content. When such media refers to economic activity, political risks, or sentiments in specific locations (such as cities, regions, or provinces) or national entities (such as ministries or central banks) then those references are quantified and added to one or more of the relevant Country TRMI.

An example of the economicGrowth TRMI for the third quarter of 2015 is visible in the global heat map displayed in Figure 21.1. Darker shading indicates greater growth-related economic references about a country expressed in the media, while countries shaded lightly were experiencing economic contraction.

NEWS FLOW AS A LEADING ECONOMIC INDICATOR

Given the potential value of economic references in the media, Dr. Fafula set out to develop a predictive model of global PMI activity. The country-specific economic model he developed is called the MarketPsych Manufacturing Index (MPMI). In order to develop this model, he used the Country TRMI as in dependent variables, while Markit's PMI value served as the dependent variable of his 12 national models. Based on this study, it appears that the MPMI are both highly correlated with and predictive of PMI changes in the 12 countries modeled.

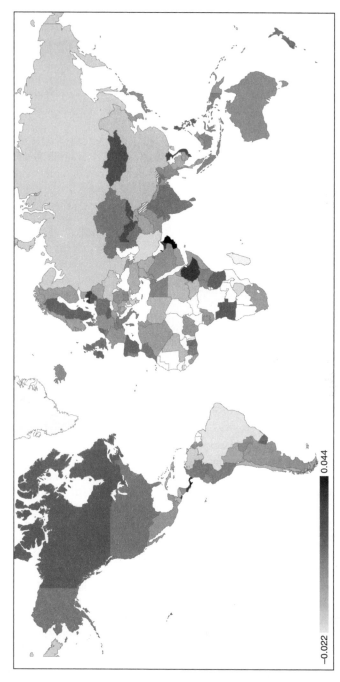

FIGURE 21.1 Interactive map displaying the economicGrowth TRMI for the third quarter of 2015, where dark shading indicates positive economic growth, and light represents economic contraction mentioned in the media.

0.044

−0.022

When compared to established economic indicators, such as PMI values, each TRMI demonstrates a different (although often correlated) significance in forecasting future PMI values. As might be expected, Markit's PMI is highly correlated with the economicGrowth TRMI. This TRMI, when smoothed with a 200-day moving average, shows striking similarity to the PMI time series, as seen in Figure 21.2. Such comparisons suggested that economicGrowth and similar TRMI derived from the media may reflect economic activity with little delay.

The relationship between Markit's PMI and each TRMI varies by country. Some of the TRMI are correlated with PMI over time, while others show periods of correlation that later dissipate, depending on economic and political events in a country. Over time, different TRMI reflect the economic activity in each country. For example, the United States TRMI that are positively correlated with the country's monthly PMI include economicGrowth, optimism, interestRates, and governmentCorruption (perhaps surprisingly for the latter). The U.S. PMI is negatively correlated with short-term average values of the unemployment, economicVolatility, gloom, and debtDefault TRMI. Long-term TRMI averages that are negatively correlated with monthly PMI include financialSystemInstability and stress. Appendix B describes in detail challenges, data transformations, and selection of statistical methods utilized for developing the MPMI. The next section skips ahead to results, but please do visit the appendix for more technical information if desired.

MPMI RESULTS

An adaptive learning model was used to generate the MPMI simulation. For the true out-of-sample comparison, model learning was frozen and forward-tested results compared to actual PMI values for five months. Specifically, absolute predicted values and directional accuracy were compared to the absolute PMI values for 12 countries and the monthly change from the prior month's PMI value, respectively. This approach demonstrates a practical economic application of using the MPMI for predicting PMI changes. The MPMI values the day before the flash PMI release (the flash PMI is a draft monthly value released on the third week of the month) were compared. Additionally, the MPMI value at the end of the month was compared to the monthly PMI (release 1–3 days later). Figure 21.3 presents the United States daily MPMI fit to PMI with a shaded five months of true out-of-sample period, which is magnified in Figure 21.4.

Based on Figure 21.4, the MPMI appears to capture significant turning points in the PMI's value. The flash PMI is a preliminary PMI value delivered 3 weeks into a month. The overall directional accuracy of the MPMI

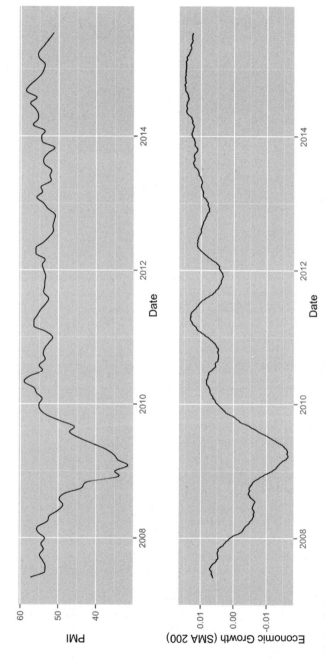

FIGURE 21.2 Plots of the U.S. PMI (top) and the 200-day simple average of the U.S. economicGrowth TRMI (from both news and social media).

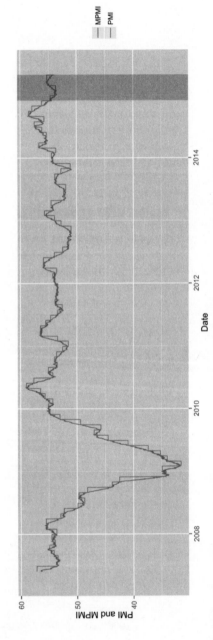

FIGURE 21.3 PMI and MPMI with true out-of-sample fit shaded in darker gray—entire time series.

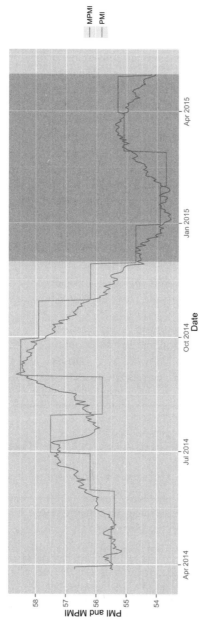

FIGURE 21.4 PMI and MPMI—detailed view of out-of-sample period in darker gray for the United States. Note that the high-frequency line represents the MPMI while the step function is Markit's PMI.

in predicting prior month's PMI to current month's flash PMI value (delivered three weeks into the month) was 69 percent for all 12 countries in the out-of-sample period. In this case, the model was not retrained monthly on the latest PMI release each month—however, that is a feature of the model that improves accuracy further. In the presented results it operates for five months without feedback. The overall the quality of the predictions is stable.

LIVE NOWCASTING

To facilitate its practical use, the MPMI model was implemented in a decision support system with a dashboard consisting of interactive maps and charts for viewers to quickly assess the current state of economic activity. Figure 21.5 is a partial view of the MPMI dashboard while Figure 21.6 displays a historical view.

NEW ECONOMIC INDICATORS

The MPMI model complements existing economic indicators by providing daily resolution and broad coverage of the unseen forces that drive the economy's "animal spirits" (specific sentiments, topics, and outlooks embodied in text communications). The MPMI model shows stable performance in both training and out-of-sample periods. The increased resolution and higher frequency of such an economic model could be useful for policymakers, currency traders, and brokerages who need faster access to country-level economic activity.

The MPMI model has several notable flaws, including the smoothing operations performed to improve stability—which may diminish the impact of sudden, important events. The MPMI model would further benefit from monthly recalibration using the latest PMI values. Furthermore, performance may benefit from periodic reshuffling of input TRMIs. Such rebuilding of the model would allow it to adapt more quickly to changes in media tone. Seasonal variations are another cyclical aspect of economic activity that was not considered in the MPMI. The TRMI are derived from English-language content only, and they would benefit from additional language capabilities for coverage of non-anglophone countries.

On the positive side, the MPMI model provides readings in daily (or shorter) frequency, has a robust data history, and operates on more than 130 countries. By reviewing each TRMI that contributes to the MPMI, predictive explanations of economic activity can be developed. Plots of model variables point to specific media trends, sentiments, and topics that drive or

DAILY-UPDATED MANUFACTURING FORECASTS FOR THE TOP 12 ECONOMIES:

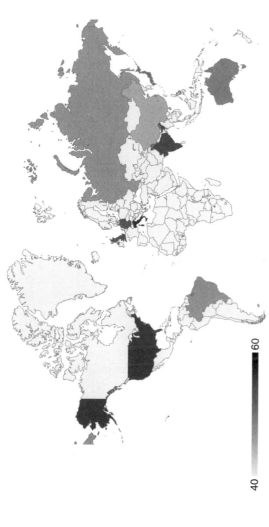

FIGURE 21.5 MPMI implementation as dashboard in a decision support system (current-day view of selected countries).

DAILY-UPDATED MANUFACTURING FORECASTS FOR UNITED STATES: [VIEW ALL COUNTRIES]

| MPMI
MarketPsych Manufacturing Index | Today's MPMI (2015-12-10)
greater than 50 is expanding, less than 50 is contracting | Change from last day of prior month (2015-11-30) | Toolbox |
|---|---|---|---|
| United States
(US) | 54.40 | 0.00 | [recent] [history] |

HISTORICAL VALUES, AT THE END OF THE MONTH:

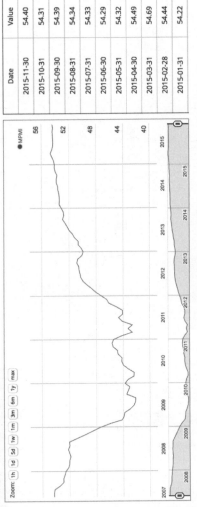

Date	Value
2015-11-30	54.40
2015-10-31	54.31
2015-09-30	54.39
2015-08-31	54.34
2015-07-31	54.33
2015-06-30	54.29
2015-05-31	54.32
2015-04-30	54.49
2015-03-31	54.69
2015-02-28	54.44
2015-01-31	54.22

Based on extraction of real-time manufacturing and sentiment data from news and social media articles, MarketPsych has created daily-updating predictive models for the top 12 economies.

FIGURE 21.6 MPMI historical view for a single country (United States).

reflect economic behavior. The MPMI model is not overly influenced by any political or financial institution, but rather, by the flow of information in news and social media.

There are at least four explanations for the role of media content in reflecting and, perhaps, forecasting economic activity. Economically relevant information in the news flow—such as winter weather closing factories—may appear in the TRMI more rapidly than the data encountered by purchasing managers surveyed for the PMI and ISM indexes. A second possibility is that economic forecasters who publish their opinions in financial news and social media are more informed about broad economic activity than the purchasing managers surveyed for the ISM and PMI indexes. A third interesting possibility is that sentiments relayed in the news flow predictably alter the economic activity of individuals. For example, individuals saddened or frightened by highly publicized news of a terrorist attack may be emotionally primed to risk aversion and subsequently spend less on consumer items. As a result of this media-inspired caution, economic activity will fall slightly. And finally there may be a "wisdom of the crowds" effect in which sampling millions of economic comments creates a more accurate composite picture of the current state of the economy than a limited survey of hundreds (400 plus) purchasing managers.

Like Google Trends and social media platforms, the MPMI model encapsulates a new way of understanding—and perhaps predicting—human behavior by modeling the fundamental drivers of business activity. Based on research into data provided by Estimize, Google Trends, and the TRMI, it appears that socially sourced and media-derived data can improve predictive models of fundamentals—including corporate earnings, economic activity, and stock prices.

IN SUMMARY

- Detailed characteristics of earnings conference call transcripts predict stock price overreaction and underreaction following an earnings announcement.
- Earnings forecasts from "wisdom of the crowds" platforms, such as the social tool Estimize, demonstrate superior predictive power over I/B/E/S estimates.
- The earningsForecast TRMI shows predictive power over daily stock price activity for up to 15 business days, regardless of whether a company's earnings are reported during the holding period. Over yearly periods a mean reversion effect is evident.
- Sources of data as diverse as ambient light and credit card transaction data demonstrate value in gauging current economic activity (called nowcasting).

- Predictive models of economic fundamentals are enhanced with socially sourced data such as Google search data.
- The MarketPsych Manufacturing Indexes (MPMI) are timely metrics of economic activity. They appear to demonstrate superior predictions of economic activity over common survey-based economic indicators.

NOTES

1. Barbara A. Bliss and Biljana Nikolic, "The Value of Crowdsourcing: Evidence from Earnings Forecasts." Available at SSRN 2579402 (2015).
2. Zhi Da, Joseph Engelberg, and Pengjie Gao, "In Search of Fundamentals." In AFA 2012 Chicago Meetings Paper, 2011.
3. Scott, S. L., and Varian, H. (2014), "Bayesian Variable Selection for Nowcasting Economic Time Series." In Economic Analysis of the Digital Economy. University of Chicago Press.
4. Banbura, M., Giannone, D., Modugno, M., & Reichlin, L., "Now-casting and the Real-Time Data Flow." Chapter 4 of Elliott, G., and Timmermann, A. (eds.), (2013), *Handbook of Economic Forecasting* SET 2A–2B. Elsevier.
5. Sobolevsky, S., Massaro, E., Bojic, I., Arias, J. M., and Ratti, C. (2015), "Predicting Regional Economic Indices Using Big Data of Individual Bank Card Transactions." arXiv preprint arXiv:1506.00036.
6. Hope, Bradley, "Startups Mine Market-Moving Data From Fields, Parking Lots—Even Shadows," November 20, 2014, *Wall Street Journal*.
7. Mellander, C., Stolarick, K., Matheson, Z., and Lobo, J. (2013), "Night-time Light Data: A Good Proxy Measure for Economic Activity." Royal Institute of Technology, CESIS e Centre of Excellence for Science and Innovation Studies.
8. Faust, J., Gilchrist, S., Wright, J. H., and Zakrajšsek, E. (2013), "Credit Spreads as Predictors of Real-Time Economic Activity: A Bayesian Model-Averaging Approach," *Review of Economics and Statistics*, 95(5), pp. 1501–1519.
9. Choi, H., and Varian, H. (2012), "Predicting the Present with Google Trends," *Economic Record*, 88(s1), pp. 2–9.
10. Artola, C., and Galan, E. (2012), "Tracking the Future on the Web: Construction of Leading Indicators Using Internet Searches," Banco de Espana Occasional Paper, (1203).
11. Sakaji, H., Sakai, H., and Masuyama, S. (2008), "Automatic Extraction of Basis Expressions that Indicate Economic Trends." In *Advances in Knowledge Discovery and Data Mining* (pp. 977–984), Springer Berlin Heidelberg.
12. "Google Makes the Search Volume Index (SVI) of Search Terms Public via the Product Google Trends" (http://www.google.com/trends).
13. Hyunyoung Choi and Hal Varian, "Predicting the Present with Google Trends," *Economic Record* 88(s1) (2012), pp. 2–9.
14. Yigitcan Karabulut, "Can Facebook Predict Stock Market Activity?" Working Paper. Received via personal communication with author, May 20, 2015.

CHAPTER 22

Sentiment Regimes

According to Darwin's Origin of Species, *it is not the most intellectual of the species that survives; it is not the strongest that survives; but the species that survives is the one that is able best to adapt and adjust to the changing environment in which it finds itself.*

—Leon C. Megginson[1]

In 2014, Nick Hassabis demonstrated software capable of teaching itself to play classic Atari video games—Pong, Breakout, and Enduro—with no instructions. The software was equipped only with access to the controls and the display, knowledge of the score, and instructions to make the score as high as possible.[2] In 15 minutes the software could move from having no understanding of a video game to beating a human expert. Google CEO Larry Page called the technology of Hassbis's company, Deep Mind, "one of the most exciting things I've seen in a long time," and Google bought the company one month later.[3]

As an adolescent, Hassabis founded a successful video game company. He later earned a degree in computer science. Despite early success in the video game industry, he wanted to better understand human intelligence, and in 2005 he enrolled in a neuroscience PhD program at University College London. Hassabis published a study in 2007 that was recognized by the journal *Science* as a "Breakthrough of the Year." He showed that the hippocampus—a part of the brain thought to be concerned only with the past—is also crucial to planning for the future.[4]

The feats of Hassabis' Atari-playing software were based on the theoretical work of Geoffrey Hinton. In 2006, Hinton, a University of Toronto computer science professor, developed a more efficient way to teach individual layers of neurons in an artificial neural network. In Hinton's neural algorithm, the first layer of neurons learns primitive features, like an edge in an image or the smallest unit of speech sound. It does this by identifying combinations of pixels or sound waves that occur more often than they should by chance. Once that layer accurately recognizes those features, they're fed to the next layer, which trains itself to recognize more complex features, like a corner or a combination of speech sounds. The process is repeated in each layer until the system can reliably recognize printed phonemes or objects.[5]

In addition to other innovations, Hassabis added a feedback loop to Hinton's work. Deep Mind's Atari-playing software replayed its past experiences over and over to make the most accurate predictions for the optimal next move. According to Hassabis, this function was inspired by the rumination on the day's events performed by the sleeping human brain: "When you go to sleep your hippocampus replays the memory of the day back to your cortex," all the while extracting and learning from the most relevant and useful patterns.[6]

Deep Mind's breakthroughs are based on algorithms that can learn not only precise details, but also context. Furthermore, the algorithms repeatedly review the intricate relationships between the present and the past to find clues that will improve future forecasts. Such algorithms mirror the learning style of history's great investors. Baron Nathan von Rothschild understood the importance of understanding the context of current events. He knew that British consol traders' fearful anticipation of news of the Battle of Waterloo in 1815 could easily give way to panic.

Context matters in financial markets. In the academic literature, differences in context are said to be a product of market regimes. A market regime is—in its most simplistic terms—a bull or a bear market. Recent academic research demonstrates that the performance of common investment strategies differs across market regimes, and these differences may be rooted in the divergent mental states of traders in each context (e.g., optimism in a bull market versus pessimism in a bear market). This chapter examines the phenomenon of market regimes and the differences in sentiment that fuel them.

REGIME DEPENDENCY

The studies described so far in this book focused on sentiment-based strategies that worked fairly consistently over the period 1998–2015. During that 17-year period, the U.S. stock market went through two bear and two bull markets. Given the ups and downs in stock markets, the consistent performance of sentiment-based strategies is surprising. In fact, according to recent academic literature, many common market anomalies perform well in only one market regime.

Finance professor Diego Garcia used text analysis to quantify the sentiment of two investment-themed columns in the *New York Times* from 1905 to 1958. He found that a daily one-standard-deviation increase in negative sentiment predicted a 0.11 percent fall in the Dow Jones Industrial Average the following day, but this effect only occurred during recessions.[7] Expansionary periods in the markets did not show any price predictability. Garcia's finding was dependent on the presence of an economic recession.

Some statisticians suspect that regime-dependent performance is a result of data-mining bias—torturing the data to yield the best results possible. Arguing against that view is evidence that regimes are characterized by unique and systematic differences in investor cognition and decision making. For example, investors respond to threatening information differently amidst a fearful climate versus during a gentle positive trend.

Two asset price patterns that show differential performance across regimes—the momentum effect and the value effect—were reviewed in Chapters 11 and 12. Several other market anomalies—such as the post-earnings announcement drift anomaly, the accruals anomaly, and the equity risk premium itself—have also been explored for regime dependency. This chapter will focus on research into these anomalies, and the role played by media sentiment, with sizable contributions from Thomson Reuters' Elijah DePalma.

STRATEGY-SHIFTING

All happy families are alike; each unhappy family is unhappy in its own way.

— Leo Tolstoy, *Anna Karenina*

As Tolstoy notes, there are systematic differences between the happy and the unhappy. Researchers have found that when bad earnings news hits a stock during pessimistic periods, prices tend to drop more than if equally bad news breaks within an overall optimistic market environment. Unhappy investors take bad news harder than happy investors. Conversely, positive earnings news leads to larger positive price reactions during positive sentiment periods.[8] Happy investors are more ecstatic about good news. It is as if traders are emotionally primed to overreact to bad news and underreact to good news during pessimistic periods. Conversely, during positive periods traders respond joyfully to good news while dismissing the significance of negative news. Hard-to-arbitrage stocks (smaller size, non–dividend paying, more volatile, and distressed) all exhibit evidence of this phenomenon more strongly.[9] Other researchers confirmed a similar relationship in the Chinese stock market.[10] Importantly, such news-based price reactions are not the entire story. There is a price drift after breaking news that provides significant profit opportunities, depending on the regime, which will be explored later in the chapter. In general, the effect of context-dependent responses is called *regime dependency*.

The phenomenon of regime-dependent performance is hypothesized to result from shifts in liquidity available to portfolio managers. According to an analysis by UCLA professor Avandir Subramanyam and colleagues, the profitability of published market strategies rises and falls in 3- to 5-year cycles based on liquidity. This liquidity-driven alpha cycle is characterized by 3 to 5 years of low liquidity and high performance for a strategy that follows a well-known price pattern, followed by 3 to 5 years of high liquidity and underperformance. As investors flock into the top-performing funds, they increase liquidity, oversaturating the available alpha and arbitraging it away in the process. The low returns they subsequently experience lead to capital withdrawals and, over time, to avoidance of the strategy. As the strategy lies unexploited, its intrinsic alpha increases, and the remaining practitioners exploiting it become top performers, thus attracting new capital again. The alpha to be harvested from such price patterns exists when they are largely ignored, but as capital is attracted to them, the excess returns dry up or even reverse.[11]

As investors learn what works in markets, they develop regime-specific beliefs. For example, before the global financial crisis of 2007–2009, many investors believed in the value of "buying on dips." When the equity markets dipped 15 percent and investors bought stocks, prices usually rebounded. However, during the global financial crisis, the U.S. stock market dipped 15 percent from its peak and continued to move a total of more than 55 percent lower before it bottomed. The wisdom of buying on dips was always questionable, but few investors conceived that a crash of that magnitude could occur ... until it did.

Investors gradually adapt to the prevailing climate (regime), developing a host of beliefs to justify why the current trend will continue indefinitely. As the regime changes, investors first act in surprise and underreact (as if disbelieving) and then overreact as they eventually jump onto the bandwagon.[12] Two price patterns support such a hypothesis: Market prices underreact to recent earnings surprises[13] but overreact to sustained extreme performance.[14] Investors are slow to learn patterns at first, but then overlearn them, as if expecting the trend to continue *ad infinitum*. In an experiment with MBA students asked to predict a random walk, subjects showed a strong tendency to predict reversion after seeing many reversals and to predict trending after seeing few recent reversals. Investors with a short history believe the current price trend will continue, but those with a longer history are more likely to believe that trends cannot last.[15] Investors overweight recent periods, learning how to predict the future from the recent past.

ANOMALIES BY REGIME

There are two objective signs of regimes: price action and overall investor sentiment. Thomson Reuters' Elijah DePalma documented the effects of sentiment regimes on the predictable returns of several market anomalies.[16] DePalma expanded on the work of academics such as Livnat and Petrovits (2009),[17] who found that post–earnings announcement stock price drift is significantly greater when market sentiment is opposite the direction of the earnings surprise. As DePalma puts it, "During periods of high (low) sentiment investors generally expect good (bad) news, and if a firm reports earnings contrary to these expectations, then investors' under-reaction to the earnings surprise may be magnified." When the baseline mood of investors is positive, disappointments weigh down prices over a longer period than good surprises lift them. Drawing inspiration from Tolstoy: Happy investors react quickly to good news but slowly to bad news (perhaps because they initially disbelieve it and thus underreact to it). Unhappy investors react quickly to bad news, but digest good news slowly, thus fueling price drift.

There is an assumption in traditional finance that higher-risk stocks generate higher returns. Yet when risk is measured as stock beta (stock price volatility), this relationship does not hold in every regime. DePalma identified that high-beta stocks (those that are more volatile relative to the overall stock market) do outperform low-beta stocks, but only following months of negative news sentiment. The opposite relationship is true after positive sentiment months, when high-beta stocks underperform. Figure 22.1 shows the significance of low- versus high-beta stock performance in each regime (positive versus negative).

On the left in Figure 22.1, when monthly sentiment is negative, low-beta stocks (the furthest left bar) significantly underperform over the following month. The opposite effect is true when a positive sentiment climate is present. To the far right, high-beta stocks underperform following a positive sentiment month.

During a negative sentiment month, investors may perceive greater risk in equities, and the prices of riskier stocks fall due to elevated risk perceptions. Yet this decline in price is likely an overreaction, and the following month, the prices rebound. Following positive sentiment months, investors perceive less risk and overreact in the positive direction, underpricing risk, and buying too many risky stocks.

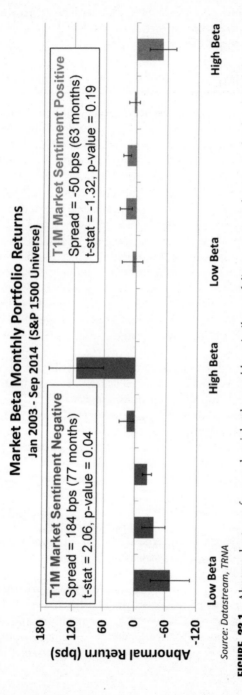

FIGURE 22.1 Abnormal returns for equal-weighted, monthly quintile portfolios constructed using market beta. High-beta stocks outperform after negative market sentiment months, but underperform after positive sentiment months.

Source: DePalma, E. (2014). "Sentiment & Investor Behavior." Thomson Reuters Elektron white paper.

Another well-known market price anomaly is called the post–earnings announcement drift (PEAD) anomaly. PEAD refers to the tendency of stock prices to continue moving in the direction of an earnings surprise after the event. For example, after a positive earnings surprise, most stocks will immediately jump higher. Over subsequent days, the price will continue to move in the positive direction, continuing the upwards momentum.

DePalma identified differences in the performance of the PEAD anomaly depending on the prevailing sentiment climate. He identified that PEAD following a positive earnings surprise is significantly greater following a month of overall negative sentiment. The opposite held true for PEAD following a negative earnings surprise. After a positive market sentiment month, negative earnings surprises were followed by greater price drift lower, as seen in Figure 22.2.

In order to avoid being out of step with the market's best strategies, Dr. DePalma proposed a dynamic methodology in which strategies are selected depending on the predominant sentiment environment. His dynamic model allocates investment capital to strategies, depending on how they are expected to perform in the current sentiment climate. The results of such a dynamic strategy earn an annualized return more than 7 percent above the S&P 500 from 2003 through mid-2014, in its most-sophisticated version.

EMOTION VERSUS FACT

In some ways, *sentiment* is a blanket term for emotion. When investors are emotional, they behave differently than when they are analytical. While creating version 2.0 of the TRMI, an index based on the overall level of emotionality in the media called emotionVsFact was added. This TRMI is calculated as a ratio between emotional tones in text (fear, anger, joy, etc.) versus purely factual (fundamental, accounting, earnings, etc.) commentary on each asset. During a market panic, this index would have a high value due to the higher levels of emotionality and opinion expressed in the media. During an unsurprising earnings season during a bull market, the emotionVsFact ratio would be a lower number, since the news would be more fact-based than dramatic.

In order to study this index, CJ Liu used his signature cross-sectional analysis technique. The top 100 U.S. companies with the highest buzz in the media over the past one week were identified and ranked by the average value of the emotionVsFact index over the past week. A portfolio that buys the top quartile of the most emotional companies and shorts the quartile of least emotional (the most factual) companies was performed from 1998 to 2015. The equity curve that results is visible in Figure 22.3.

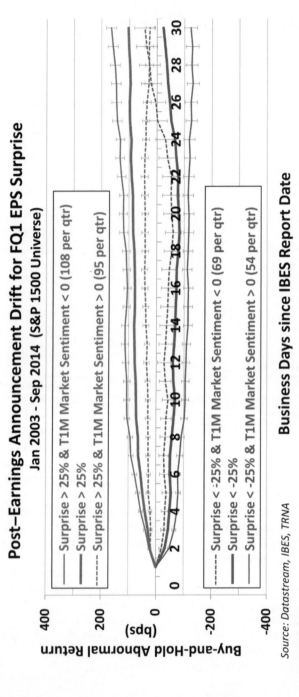

FIGURE 22.2 Post–earnings announcement drift in different sentiment conditions, where the thick lines represent the standard PEAD strategy results. Differentiating by sentiment environment leads to higher overall returns from the PEAD strategy.
Source: DePalma, E. (2014). "Sentiment & Investor Behavior." Thomson Reuters Elektron white paper.

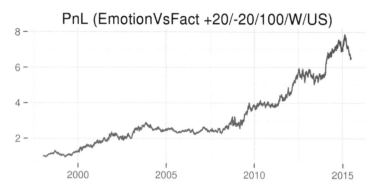

FIGURE 22.3   A weekly arbitrage of the top versus bottom quintile of U.S. stocks ranked on the EmotionVsFact TRMI out of the top 100 mentioned in the media each year.

Figure 22.3 demonstrates that buying the most emotional and shorting the most factual quintile of stocks produces a low-volatility absolute return equity curve. Importantly, this curve is relatively impervious to regimes.

Cross-sectional arbitrage of the Sentiment TRMI itself shows no predictive power for most assets and time periods over the period 1998–2015, with the only potential exception being the weekly social media sentiment result depicted in Figure 8.1. Despite unstable results from the bipolar sentiment index, arbitrage of emotionVsFact yields positive returns over several time horizons and asset classes, including monthly and yearly and on equities and currencies, although a concrete explanation for this indexes' broad applicability evades us.

None of the individual emotion indexes in the TRMI (fear, anger, joy, gloom) accounted for the stability and magnitude of the performance of emotionVsFact. When negative emotions dominate (as during a bear market), investors and media express relatively high levels of negative emotion about declining stocks, perhaps signaling investor overreaction. In bull markets media commentary pores over fundamentals, and complacent investors are more likely to underreact to positive but complex fundamental news. Perhaps the emotionVsFact index dynamically captures shifts in perceptions and self-corrects for sentiment regimes by capturing a unique (although still under investigation) asset price driver.

IN SEARCH OF CONSISTENCY

Man's mind, once stretched by a new idea, never regains its original dimensions.

—Oliver Wendell Holmes Sr.

Deep Mind's innovative learning algorithms suggest that in order to understand patterns in markets, investors ought to independently consider the big picture—the context—before diving into the details. The big picture is the regime. The regime of the market—bullish or bearish or even sideways—changes how market participants process information, their reactivity to events, and how they price risk. Elijah DePalma demonstrated that successful regime-switching models may be generated for several important anomalies by including the prior month's media sentiment. As George Soros's theory of reflexivity implies, the media may be changing investor perceptions with the content it publishes. Furthermore, the media also reflects a changing information flow. Both media processes reinforce each other in a positive feedback loop, and as a result, market regimes tend to have staying power. Active professional investors are best served by adapting their strategies to regimes and thus learning how to prosper in every market environment.

IN SUMMARY

- Deep learning is a statistical technique in which the overall context of a problem is first classified before more detailed learning occurs.
- The terms *bull market* and *bear market* describe sentiment regimes.
- Sentiment regimes are characterized not only by bullish or bearish information flow, but also by differing mindsets among investors.
- Academics have hypothesized that liquidity flows driven by sentiment cause the three- to five-year waxing and waning in alpha for traditional price anomalies that has been observed.
- Price responses to new information vary across regimes. Researchers find that negative news has a greater impact on prices in bearish regimes, and positive news has a larger effect during bullish regimes.
- According to research by Thomson Reuters' Elijah DePalma, the profitability of regime specific anomalies—such as the low-beta anomaly and post-earnings announcement drift—can be predicted by the prior month's news sentiment tone.
- DePalma also found there is greater price underreaction following positive news in a negative market environment and negative news in a positive environment (measured in the post–earnings announcement drift anomaly). This underreaction is perhaps due to the cognitive dissonance generated when new information conflicts with contextual beliefs and expectations.
- The emotionVsFact TRMI appears to capture regimes across stocks and currencies. Over various time horizons, this index generates an opportunity for emotional arbitrage across stocks and currencies.

NOTES

1. Leon C. Megginson, "Lessons from Europe for American Business," *Southwestern Social Science Quarterly* 44(1) (1963), pp. 3–13, at p. 4.
2. Antonio Regalado, "Is Google Cornering the Market on Deep Learning?" *MIT Technology Review* (January 29, 2014).
3. http://www.ted.com/talks/larry_page_where_s_google_going_next/transcript?language=en.
4. Tom Simonite, "Google's Intelligence Designer," *MIT Technology Review* (December 2, 2014). Retrieved May 20, 2015, from: http://www.technology review.com/news/532876/googles-intelligence-designer/.
5. Robert D. Hof, "10 Breakthrough Technologies 2013: Deep Learning," *MIT Technology Review* (April 23, 2013).
6. Simonite.
7. Diego Garcia, "Sentiment During Recessions," *Journal of Finance* 68(3) (2013), pp. 1267–1300.
8. G. Mujtaba Mian and Srinivasan Sankaraguruswamy, "Investor Sentiment and Stock Market Response to Earnings News," *The Accounting Review* 87(4) (July 2012), pp. 1357–1384.
9. Ibid.
10. J. Yumei, "Investor Sentiment and Stock Market Response to Earnings Announcement," *Proceedings of International Conference on Management and Service Science* (2011), pp. 1–5.
11. Ferhat Akbas, Will J. Armstrong, Sorin Sorescu, and Avanidhar Subrahmanyam, "Time Varying Market Efficiency in the Cross-Section of Expected Stock Returns," in AFA 2013 San Diego Meetings Paper (2013), http://subra.x10host.com/amproj6.pdf.
12. N. Barberis, A. Shleifer, and R. Vishny, "A Model of Investor Sentiment," *Journal of Financial Economics* 49 (1998), pp. 307–343.
13. B. L. Bernard and J. K. Thomas, "Evidence that Stock Prices Do Not Fully Reflect the Implications of Current Earnings for Future Earnings," *Journal of Accounting and Economics* 13 (1990), pp. 305–340.
14. W. F. M. De Bondt and R. Thaler, "Further Evidence on Investor Overreaction and Stock Market Seasonality," *Journal of Finance* 42 (1987), pp. 557–581.
15. Robert Bloomfield and Jeffrey Hales, "Predicting the Next Step of a Random Walk: Experimental Evidence of Regime-Shifting Beliefs," *Journal of Financial Economics* 65(3) (2002), pp. 397–414. Downloaded May 20, 2015, from: http://rmgsc.cr.usgs.gov/outgoing/threshold_articles/Bloomfield_Hales2002.pdf.
16. E. Depalma, "Sentiment and Investor Behavior," Thomson Reuters Machine Readable News, White Paper (2014). Retrieved May 10, 2015, via: https://forms.thomsonreuters.com/sentimentandinvestorbehavior/.
17. J. Livnat and C. Petrovits, "Investor Sentiment, Post-Earnings Announcement Drift, and Accruals." Unpublished Working Paper, New York University, 2009.

Managing the Mind

CHAPTER 23

Mental Hygiene

If you don't know who you are, the stock market is an expensive place to find out.

—Adam Smith (George Goodman)

In 2005 Playchess.com hosted a novel type of chess competition—one in which contestants could enlist the help of partners including other players or computers. The prize money was significant, and there were many notable entrants into the competition including several groups of grandmasters working with multiple chess-playing computers.

In general, the teams of humans working with the assistance of chess software dominated the tournament. Even a single human using a weak laptop could defeat the strongest chess-playing computers. As Garry Kasparov, widely considered to be the greatest chess player of all time, noted, "Human strategic guidance combined with the tactical acuity of a computer was overwhelming."[1]

But despite the early lead by grandmaster-plus-computer teams, the tournament's ultimate winner came as a shock. The winner was a pair of amateur chess players using three computers at the same time. These amateurs used the computers to deeply and logically investigate specific moves, an advantage that offset the superior strategic knowledge of the grandmasters and the better computational power of the computers. "Weak human + machine + better process was superior to a strong computer alone and, more remarkably, superior to a strong human + machine + inferior process."[2]

Most traders already work in human–machine teams, relying on charting software, newsfeeds, and screeners to enhance their judgment. Yet traders are at risk of becoming lost in the details of market information. Superior detailed knowledge must also be combined with an understanding of general relationships. It is finding the correct balance between detail and generalities, and understanding when to transition between the macro and the micro, that can be difficult for human traders. As Kasparov summarizes from chess competitions:

> [C]orrectly evaluating a small handful of moves is far more important in human chess, and human decision-making in general, than the systematically deeper and deeper search for better moves—the number of moves "seen ahead"—that computers rely on.[3]

Traders do not need to be deep experts in order to be successful. In fact, the contrary is likely true in financial markets. As Warren Buffett commented, "The difference between successful people and very successful people is that very successful people say 'no' to almost everything." In effect, successful investors pare the information flow down to its essence.

Also notable about the Playchess.com competition's outcome was that a team of human *amateurs*, with computer assistance, won the first competition. The psychology of amateurs is notably different from that of experts. Amateurs are more flexible in their thinking and are without fixed beliefs.

This chapter explores techniques for cultivating flexibility and openness with the intention of reducing underreaction to important but easily overlooked information. In its second half the chapter explains practices to decrease stress, thus preempting the most common cause of overreaction among investors.

TRAITS OF SUPER-FORECASTERS

> We will need to blend computer-based forecasting and subjective judgement in the future. So it's time to get serious about both.
> —Phillip Tetlock and Dan Gardner, Superforecasting, 2015.

Complex environments like financial markets have numerous interacting feedback loops between inputs, the internal environment, and the system's output. How investors process such disparate information is at the core of how humans forecast the future. Yet most professionals have tremendous difficulty forecasting markets and economies. As Alan Greenspan himself famously commented, "We really can't forecast all that well, and yet we pretend that we can, but we really can't."[4]

Psychology professor Philip Tetlock researched the ability of experts to forecast the future. Tetlock notes that for many years the intelligence community—an area where precision in forecasting is literally a life-and-death affair—used verbal probability estimates with no standard-ization. In assessing the probability of a Soviet invasion of Yugoslavia in 1951, the intelligence community concluded in a written report that a Soviet assault was "a serious possibility." The authors agreed on the statement to convey their confidence in this verbal forecast. Yet months later when asked separately to explain the numerical odds they intended to convey in this estimate, the various authors rated the probability of an invasion as ranging between 20 and 80 percent likelihood, meaning the language was subject to interpretation. In another example of the failure of verbal probability estimates, Tetlock notes that President John F. Kennedy was told the CIA estimated a "fair" chance that United States'-sponsored Bay of Pigs invasion would succeed. The author of that assessment later said he used "fair" to indicate a 3-to-1 chance of failure.[5]

Following the total failure of intelligence around Saddam Hussein's supposed Weapons of Mass Destruction (WMD)—the intelligence esti-mates asserted a 100 percent likelihood that Saddam Hussein was hiding such weapons—the U.S. intelligence community took steps to standardize evidence-based forecasting. In the process they funded Tetlock's research, a few of whose results I bullet-point below.

Tetlock found that experts' forecasting ability is near random, but a small group of what he calls *super-forecasters* consistently make better predictions. His super-forecasters were a group of regular people who were often in retirement or with routine jobs. Many of them participated in Tetlock's studies as a diversion. Yet these normal people outperformed government intelligence analysts and domain experts with superior access to information. Tetlock identified four of the broad cognitive traits of superforecasters (condensed from the book):

- Probabilistic thinking
- A growth mindset
- Numeracy
- Intelligence (averaging around the 80th percentile)

Tetlock identified these strengths in their forecasting habits:

- Breaking down problems into the most basic estimates using the Fermi method
- Frequent updating
- Humility and a willingness (and even eagerness) to admit mistakes
- Aggressively and impartially learning from mistakes

Super-forecasters keep their egos—the emotional investment in being proven right—out of their forecasting. They can change their minds rapidly when justified by the evidence, with little regret or remorse. Such a rapid change in outlook requires both humility and openness to new ideas. Per a BBC news report describing super-forecasters:

> *But they all shared one other trait too: open-mindedness. In every-day life, open-mindedness may be mistaken for having liberal political views, but in psychology it is thought to reflect how well you deal with uncertainty. Crucially, open-minded people tend to be able to see problems from all sides, which seems to help forecasters overcome their preconceptions in the light of new evidence. "You need to change your mind fast, and often," says Tetlock.*[6]

Intriguingly, super-forecasters also review their past behavior and emotional reactions. They study and learn from their own overreaction and underreaction in order to improve calibration to new information.

According to a *New York Times* review, the lessons of "Superforecasting" can be distilled into a few directives for those in the prediction business. Be curious about and work to reduce personal biases. Think in terms of probabilities and recognize that everything is uncertain. Base predictions on data and logic. Unpack a question into its component parts, distinguishing between what is known and unknown and scrutinizing your assumptions. Keep score of performance and accuracy, and review those past forecasts.[7]

Tetlock pointed out that some advantages of the superforecasters, like probabilistic thinking, are correlated with lower levels of well-being. A belief in fate leads to greater happiness than a cold-eyed appreciation of reality.

ADAPTABILITY

> *[A trader] who makes it his business to watch these things conscientiously, without blind passion or stubbornness, will hit upon the right thing innumerable times, though not always.*
> —Josef De La Vega, 1688[8]

Richard Dennis's experiment with the Turtles, described in Chapter 11, demonstrated that while trading rules and principles can be successfully taught, markets change. Fixed rules often stop working. Recent academic research shows that the best-performing investors change their strategies to take advantage of opportunities outside of their usual domain, and evidence is accumulating around the benefits of adaptation in markets.[9] Adapting to change is not easy, and as seen in Chapter 11, slow learning and adaptation are speculated to be one cause of underreaction in market prices.

In our own research, over 28,000 people have taken MarketPsych's free online financial tests since 2004. The Investment Personality Test has been the most popular test. It measures the Big 5 personality traits: extraversion vs. introversion, agreeableness vs. self-interest, neuroticism vs. emotional stability, openness to new experiences vs. traditionalism, and conscientiousness vs. spontaneity. The Big 5 personality traits are not strongly correlated with investing success (several subtraits are more interesting), but given the large sample size, we are able see statistically significant correlations between investing success and openness to new experiences. Openness embodies the psychological traits of mental flexibility and adaptability.

Openness has genetic components. Identical twins show similar scores on openness to experience, even when they have been adopted into different families and raised in different environments. While traders can learn techniques to become more adaptable, they may not have as much choice as desired in the matter. As a result, enforcing an external discipline to learn and explore new perspectives, even when it feels uncomfortable or unnecessary, is a crucial mental habit. Openness facilitates identification of high expected value opportunities.

Openness and adaptability are hallmarks of investing legends like Soros—himself founder of the Open Society Institute. Sir John Templeton was also remarkably open, being an early emerging markets value investor when others shunned the idea. Soros's former partner at the Quantum Fund, Jim Rogers, authored the books *Investment Biker* and *Adventure Capitalist* and holds world records for the longest motorcycle and automobile trips around the globe. Soros, Templeton, and Rogers are great investors not because they follow fixed rules, but because they adapt to events in the markets, policy, and economics. As George Soros describes below, being open is not just about trying new things; it's also about examining oneself—warts and all—and non-judgmentally working to improve oneself.

THE POWER OF NOT KNOWING

> *To others, being wrong is a source of shame. To me, recognizing my mistakes is a source of pride. Once we realize that imperfect understanding is the human condition, there's no shame in being wrong, only in failing to correct our mistakes.*
> —George Soros, *Soros on Soros*

Like George Soros, rather than emotionally overreacting, traders can learn from and adapt to failures. In order to do so, past losses should be approached like an objective investigator. In medicine there is a morbidity and mortality report in which everyone on the medical team involved in a medical mistake or poor outcome objectively examines the error to understand what—if anything—could have been done differently. Judgmentalism is not helpful during this exercise. It's impossible to learn while in an accusatory state of mind.

Adaptability has many flavors. Ray Dalio, founder of Bridgewater Associates, the world's largest hedge fund, practices transcendental meditation—a technique that itself increases self-awareness and adaptability. He asks employees to digest a list of 210 Principles.[10] (The list of Principles grows and changes somewhat over the years.) Bridgewater's investing style is predicated on the discovery of simple but fundamental rules that underlie economic activity (and over the long term, govern market pricing). These core rules are evolving as new policy and monetary mechanisms come into being. Simplicity and clarity facilitate the of emotional baggage and an experience of greater openness.

Ray Dalio was interviewed by *Institutional Investor* on the evolution of his unique style of analysis.[11] Dalio recounted an episode in 1982 when he was convinced that the United States would head into a depression. Back then he publicly—including in congressional testimony—announced a bet against the U.S. economy based on his beliefs about the likely outcome of the monetary tightening by Fed Chairman Volcker. He was completely wrong:

> *This episode taught me the importance of always fearing being wrong, no matter how confident I am that I'm right. As a result, I began seeking out the smartest people I could find who disagreed with me so that I could understand their reasoning. Only after I fully grasped their points of view could I decide to reject or accept them.*

Per Dalio, people who are able to process others' contrary points of view "possess the ability to calmly take in what other people are thinking rather than block it out, and to clearly lay out the reasons why they haven't reached the same conclusion. They are able to listen carefully and objectively to the reasoning behind differing opinions."

To free one's mind from unconscious biases during analysis of an investment, it helps to openly and critically understand the merits of all arguments. Only then can sharp reasoning be honed. Yet facing down imperfections in reasoning can be stressful, so an important aspect of such mental flexibility is stress management. Stress hormones themselves create mental rigidity.

The following tips are straightforward prerequisites for high-performance decision making, yet they can be difficult to execute. If you find yourself frozen, inflexible, or complacent, then consider the following tips to pull yourself back into a creative state of mind:

1. Play. Tell a joke. Playfulness is key to remaining flexible and creative, and it encourages out-of-the-box thinking.
2. If stuck on a challenging decision, role play as if from the perspective of an art graduate, or a diplomat, or another with whom you have little interaction. Practice curiosity about the many perspectives others may have. Turn the dilemma upside down, roll it around, stretch it out.
3. Take a walk in nature. Studies show that creativity increases following exposure to greenery and the complexity of natural environments.
4. Sleep well. Sleep aids the creative process, specifically in the REM stage. Avoid excessive alcohol intake, which impairs REM sleep.

The pervasive attitude driving open and adaptable investors is one of "How can I continually improve?" The improvements they make to their decision making often reduce stress. Stress often occurs in response to perceived threats, and if one feels out of control when confronting those threats, then stress leads to more overreaction in decision making.

STRESS MANAGEMENT IS RISK MANAGEMENT

> *I think I am the single most conservative trader on earth in the sense that I absolutely hate losing money.*
>
> —Paul Tudor Jones

Fear of loss is generally a useful trait. Yet if such fear is not applied systematically—to the risks that are *actually* dangerous, versus those that are simply *perceived* to be dangerous—then that fear is maladaptive. How can investors balance between rational and irrational fear? And how can investors optimally deal with the stress that such fear provokes? This section addresses these questions.

Chronic fear creates stress and impairs one's fluidity of thinking. Stress creates biases in cognition, including catastrophization (believing the worst case is more likely than it actually is), black-and-white thinking (all-or-none thinking), and overgeneralization (believing that all related issues are similar). A key feature of market sentiments like fear is that they infect all who come into contact.

Many of the world's best investors are exceptionally uncomfortable with losing. In fact, the discomfort of losses is often experienced as physical pain. Pain is stressful however, and stressed-out investors are susceptible to the physiological consequences of chronic stress, including premature aging (as they say, "traders age in dog-years"). Top investors learn strategies to manage the stress, and they go to great lengths to limit losses and prevent maladaptive stress from permeating their decision making. Top investors distinguish between losses as a part of doing business, such as when they were wrong despite following a sound process, and losses due to sloppiness or mistakes. Most stressful is when a loss is preventable due to poor decision making or a flaw in risk management.

Paul Tudor Jones is widely renowned as one of the greatest traders in history. In Jack Schwager's book, *Stock Market Wizards,* Jones comments on how his life and trading have changed since a large loss he suffered during one of his first years as a professional trader: "Now I spend my day trying to make myself as happy and relaxed as I can be. If I have positions going against me, I get right out; if they are going for me, I keep them." Jones optimizes his mental state during the trading day by reducing emotional interference, and one way of doing that is by cutting painful losing positions quickly.

Jones illustrates that how traders handle losing is more important to their long-term prosperity than how we approach winning. As Warren Buffett noted: "Rule No. 1: Never lose money. Rule No. 2: Never forget rule No.1." And the best way to not lose money is to identify and prepare for potential losses in advance.

The pain of stress can be a useful signal, indicating that something has gone wrong with an investment. If the stress is allowed to linger, and the pain festers, than a state of chronic stress may ensue. Chronic stress erodes homeostatic mechanisms, creating a state of hormonal imbalance and psychological hypervigilance and susceptibility to overreaction.

FACING YOUR FEARS

To manage the influence of unconscious emotions on judgment, it helps to approach the mind in a disciplined fashion. Staying grounded in the midst of chaos requires mental strength—strength which is built through mental exercise. Investing greats such as Ray Dalio, Paul Tudor Jones, and Bill Gross practice forms of meditation. Research shows that meditation decreases stress, increases mental flexibility, and boosts insight. Meditation is a key form of both stress prevention and stress treatment. The basic flow of insight meditation for immediate stress relief and long-term understanding is embodied in the acronym "GROUND":

Step 1: Manage Stress

1. Ground in the present. Become aware of the present moment and your immediately felt sensations, breathing, and environment.
2. Recognize the situation. Have you been in this state of being before?
3. Observe your thoughts. How are your thoughts and feelings influencing each other?
4. Understand the cycle. When you think of one topic, does that change how you feel? Does this happen often in similar situations?

Step 2: Take Action

5. Noodle on it. Analyze the context, patterns, and best prior outcomes.
6. Do something about it. Once you've identified the best approach based on past experiences and an understanding of the big picture, take positive action.

Stress too often fools investors into selling or buying at the wrong time—fueling the price patterns described throughout this book. A key goal of this book is to teach investors about such patterns so they can avoid falling into them. Stress will always be present for investors and traders; it's how they manage and channel stress that dictates their success in markets.

REVERSING STRESS

The essence of risk management lies in maximizing the areas where we have some control over the outcome while minimizing the areas where we have absolutely no control over the outcome and the linkage between effect and cause is hidden from us.
                                        —Peter L. Bernstein[12]

J. K. Rowling is the billionaire author of the *Harry Potter* series (the best-selling book series of all time). Before becoming a success, she lived in relative poverty on government benefits following a series of personal and career setbacks. She noted of failure:

You might never fail on the scale I did, but some failure in life is inevitable. It is impossible to live without failing at something, unless you live so cautiously that you might as well not have lived at all—in which case, you fail by default.

The fear of failure generates far more stress than it merits. Despite the fear of failure hanging over high-risk decisions, stress can actually be turned to one's advantage. Recent research demonstrates that humans often have more control over stressful events—and their responses to them—than typically realized. Professor Kelli McGonigal at Stanford University is an expert on the psychology of decision making. In an article in the *Wall Street Journal* she described how stressful situations can be reframed to both change one's outlook and improve performance.[13]

McGonigal described an experiment in which 140 people were invited to give a speech.[14] Public speaking is a nerve-wracking event for most people. Part of the group was told to relax and to calm their nerves before delivering the speech by saying to themselves, "I am calm." The others were told to embrace their anxiety and to tell themselves, "I am excited." Observers who rated the quality of the talks found the excited speakers more persuasive, confident, and competent than the participants who had tried to calm down. The anxious speakers had transformed their anxiety into energy (by calling it "excitement") and thus performed better under pressure.

In another study linking stress to performance, a group of researchers followed midcareer teachers and physicians for a year to see if perceptions of stress influenced well-being at work. At the beginning of the year, the teachers and doctors were asked if they saw anxiety as a helpful feeling, providing energy and motivation, or as harmful. At the end of the year, those who saw their anxiety as helpful were less likely to be burned out, frustrated, or drained by their work.

Traders have control over how they experience stress. The best way to handle stress is to embrace it rather than to minimize it. Welcoming stress can boost confidence and improve performance.[15] Especially during stressful times in markets, it is key to view stress as energizing rather than demoralizing. There is a fine line between tension and excitement, and traders do their best when they interpret stress as a positive, energizing force.

IN SUMMARY

- Traders can improve their decision making by understanding and managing unconscious reactions to new information.
- The personality trait of openness correlates with superior forecasting ability and investor performance.
- Practicing curiosity and honesty about losses and missed opportunities improves adaptability, a key performance trait.

- Fear is a natural human reaction to threat-related information, and prolonged fear generates a state of stress.
- Stress predisposes investors to overreact to threats.
- Investors can interpret stressful feelings either as dysfunctional or as a source of positive energy. Deliberately reframing stressful feelings as a positive leads to improved motivation and performance.
- Understanding both the normalcy of loss in markets and the continuous possibility of recovery reduces stress.

NOTES

1. Garry Kasparov, "The Chess Master and the Computer," *New York Review of Books* (February 11, 2010).
2. Ibid.
3. Ibid.
4. Steven Perlberg, "'You Just Learned This?!?' — Jon Stewart Struggles to Understand How Former Fed Head Greenspan Missed Wall Street 'Screwiness,'" *Business Insider*, October 22, 2013.
5. Tetlock, P. E., and Gardner, D. (2015), "Superforecasting: The Art and Science of Prediction," Signal Books: Oxford.
6. David Robson, "The Best Way to Predict the Future," BBC (June 12, 2014). Retrieved May 20, 2015, from: http://www.bbc.com/future/story/20140612-the-best-way-to-see-the-future.
7. Leonard Mlodinow, "'Mindware' and 'Superforecasting,'" *New York Times*, Oct. 15, 2015. Downloaded November 19, 2015, from: http://www.nytimes.com/2015/10/18/books/review/mindware-and-superforecasting.html.
8. Josef De La Vega, "1688," *Confusion de Confusiones*: Portions Descriptive of the Amsterdam Stock Exchange. (Translation by H. Kellenbenz, Harvard University, 1957.)
9. Russ Wermers, "Matter of Style: The Causes and Consequences of Style Drift in Institutional Portfolios." Available at SSRN 2024259 (2012). http://papers.ssrn.com/sol3/papers.cfm?abstract_id=2024259.
10. Ray Dalio, "Principles," © 2011. Retrieved July 20, 2015, from: http://www.bwater.com/Uploads/FileManager/Principles/Bridgewater-Associates-Ray-Dalio-Principles.pdf.
11. Ray Dalio, "Bridgewater's Ray Dalio Explains the Power of Not Knowing," *Institutional Investor* (March 6, 2015). http://www.institutionalinvestor.com/blogarticle/3433519/asset-management-hedge-funds-and-alternatives/bridgewaters-ray-dalio-explains-the-power-of-not-knowing.html#.VSFSqvnF9_o.
12. Peter L. Bernstein, *Against the Gods: The Remarkable Story of Risk* (New York: John Wiley & Sons, 1996).

13. Kelly McGonigal, "Use Stress to Your Advantage," *Wall Street Journal* (May 15, 2015). Retrieved May 20, 2015, from: http://www.wsj.com/articles/use-stress-to-your-advantage-1431700708.

14. Alison Wood Brooks, "Get Excited: Reappraising Pre-Performance Anxiety as Excitement," *Journal of Experimental Psychology: General* 143(3) (2014), p. 1144. Retrieved May 20, 2015, from: http://www.apa.org/pubs/journals/releases/xge-a0035325.pdf.

15. McGonigal.

Postscript

When I was 12 years old, I did not imagine that frustration with markets would drive my career. Fortunately, such feelings may either lead one astray or power the search for the optimal solution. We are far from finding a simple explanation for market behavior, yet some are making significant progress.

Researchers such as Brian Knutson at Stanford University are working toward a unified understanding of financial risk-taking behavior that will bridge the gap between information flow, demographic factors, psychological traits, beliefs, and investing behavior. This book scratched the surface of one step in that chain—information analytics.

Many of the greatest investors refer to the importance of collective investor psychology in driving repeating price patterns. This book sheds light on how feelings and collateral psychological states—including attention, uncertainty, and urgency, to name a few—are reflected in social media and news reports. As explained in this book, when such feelings arise collectively at unusually high or low levels, they may become leading indicators of price movement.

Investors can find opportunity in the gap where the perceptions of others—those who comprise "the market"—deviate from fundamental realities. At times perceptions overwhelm reality and prices become driven by collective emotions of fear, anger, mistrust, and uncertainty. Such investor overreaction typically precedes price mean reversion. Conversely, when information that is too complex, boring, or in disagreement with investors' prejudices occurs, trends form as investors underreact to it. As a result this book is ultimately—as are so many aspects of the markets—a journey into the human mind.

The findings in this book are in some cases supported by references as far back as classical Greece, De La Vega in 1688, Homma in 1755, Hamilton in 1789, and Rothschild in 1815. Yet only time will tell if the linkages made in this book will stand the test of time. Given that the patterns described arise from activity in the same human minds that attempt to decipher them, requiring multiple levels of understanding, it seems likely that they will persist.

Fundamentally, the message conveyed by this book is positive. By understanding the effects of information on human behavior, we can both manage and profit from it. We hope that you will experience a tangible improvement in your life (and investing) as a result of taking this journey with us.

Happy Investing!

Richard L. Peterson, M.D.

Understanding the Thomson Reuters MarketPsych Indices

Since 2004, MarketPsych has honed its unique methodology for extracting detailed, relevant concepts from a variety of business and investment text. The MarketPsych lexicon is an extensive, expert-curated repository of simple and complex English-language words and phrases of potential interest for traders, investors, and economists. Used in conjunction with the MarketPsych lexicon, MarketPsych's natural-language processing software employs grammatical templates customized to extract meanings from financial news, social media, earnings conference call transcripts, and executive interviews.

SOURCE TYPE CUSTOMIZATION

There is a vast difference in communication styles between social and news media. Compared to news, social media contains significant levels of sarcasm and irony, incomplete thoughts, misplaced or excessive punctuation, misspellings, nonstandard grammar, case insensitivity, and crude language. Additionally, in social media many common words are used with colloquial meanings. A statement such as "That trade was the bomb!" with reference to a successful trade is far different from a reference to warfare, as would be interpreted by a historically trained linguistic analysis engine.

Because new colloquial language enters social use periodically, including expressions such as "You killed it!" (as a compliment), MarketPsych's text analytics dictionaries and grammatical technology are updated every two to three years (we're on commercial version 2.2 currently). When new proper nouns or companies enter the lexicon, including countries such as "South Sudan" or companies such as "China Life," they are included during monthly entity updates.

New text sources are added to the data feed over time as they become active, such as Twitter content in 2009. Over the years, the media and its audience migrate; most notably Yahoo! Finance message board volume has dropped by 80 percent while social media–consuming investors migrated to alternative social media sites such as Twitter and SeekingAlpha. Eventually, these sources will fade in significance as well. Given the changing nature of communication over the past 17 years of social Internet data, MarketPsych's analysts look for universal themes in text topics and in source audiences, and the focus is domain-specific. For example, only business, investing, and political articles are accepted for text analytics. Sometimes entertainment articles are included, as when two movie studios are undergoing a corporate merger, but these are excluded if they are not related to corporate activity.

A significant difference between social and news media lies in how viewpoints are conveyed. In social media, there is typically less editorial oversight and more leeway for a passionate author to unreservedly express his or her opinion or emotional state. In contrast, journalists are trained to offer multiple perspectives on the underlying story. Rather than conveying their own emotions, journalists see their role as describing the emotional states of those they are reporting on. As a result, information obtained from social media is typically less inclusive of contrary viewpoints and more emotionally expressive from the first-person perspective than news information.

Direct expressions of emotion in news and social media also vary. In social media, authors may utilize a complex array of text or graphic emoticons (e.g., ">:-(") and acronyms (e.g., "LOL") that developed organically, with regional, industrial, and national differences. Furthermore, word context is much more important in social media than in news media for interpreting intended meaning.

As a result of all these differences between news and social media, sentiment scoring accuracy is improved by text analytic models calibrated to source type. MarketPsych currently uses differentiated models for news, social media forums, tweets, SEC filings, and earnings conference call transcripts.

LEXICAL ANALYSIS

There are a variety of approaches used in sentiment analysis. The most common technique is called lexical analysis, and this approach is used in many historical academic studies of sentiment and stock returns.[1] Lexical analysis identifies explicit words and phrases in a body of text. Relevant content is organized and scored according to a hard-coded ontology. The simplest example of a lexical approach is called "bag of words." In the "bag of words" technique, all words are counted according to their frequency, and no additional grammatical or relational post-processing is performed.

There are several known limitations to a purely lexical approach. The most significant one, for the purposes of producing TRMI, is that most lexical approaches are focused only on extracting one-dimensional sentiment. In cases where a variety of sentiment dimensions may be scored using lexical analysis, such as when using the *Harvard General Inquirer* dictionary, the word tokens representing specific sentiments are occasionally incongruent with meanings in contemporary business English.

Another weakness of using uncurated dictionaries is lexical ambiguity across domains. For example, financial terms such as *investor* and *financier* are classified as negative sentiment terms in some open-source sentiment dictionaries. MarketPsych has overcome lexical ambiguity with extensive business-specific customization and curation of lexicons.

Insensitivity to grammatical structures is perhaps the most significant weakness of the lexical approach. In order to address this weakness, MarketPsych engineers embedded a complex grammatical framework with traits specific to different text sources such as social media, earnings conference call transcripts, financial news, and regulatory filings. The result is that customized lexicons, superior disambiguation, and optimized grammatical structures stand behind MarketPsych's textual analytics. For space reasons, we will not describe the grammatical nuances of the natural language processing underlying the TRMI.

ENTITY IDENTIFICATION AND CORRELATE FILTERING

Consider that entities such as IBM may be referred to as "IBM," "Big Blue," and "International Business Machines" in the press. Additionally, international press may or may not use accent marks in common location names such as Düsseldorf. In order to identify entities such as IBM and Düsseldorf that have multiple spellings or reference names, MarketPsych prepared a list of over 60,000 entity names with aliases. This list has been improved by human review, and it is updated monthly with new and changed (acquired, merged, etc.) entities.

To improve entity name disambiguation, MarketPsych used supervised machine learning to identify correlate and anti-correlate words in proximity of ambiguous entity references. For example, gold and silver are commonly spoken of as both commodities and constituents of jewelry, but every two years they are frequently mentioned as Olympic medals. To prevent entity identification errors, anti-correlate filters are utilized to eliminate Olympic references such as "gold medal" and "won a silver." Another example is the South Korean won, which could be confused with a successful competition by a South Korean athlete who "won" an event. Anti-correlate filtering and case-sensitivity both improve precision of the scoring process and entity identification.

In addition to an anti-correlate filter to exclude irrelevant entities, for some entities MarketPsych software uses a correlate filter to ensure that only entities with the correct co-references are included in the entity identification. For example, when a Twitter user tweets that "I am enjoying my instant oats," MarketPsych's software will not count that reference as applicable to the commodity oats. References to oats are counted only if they also contain key identification correlates such as "prices" and "futures."

LINGUISTIC ANALYSIS FLOW

When applied to text, the confluence of the various text processing described above generates over 4,000 variables (Vars), each with the potential to be applied to a different entity. Alphabetically, a few Vars include:

AccountingBad

AccountingGood

Ambiguity

Anger

Each Var is then qualified by tense, such as the following:

AccountingBad_n: present-tense negative accounting news

AccountingGood_p: past-tense positive accounting news

Ambiguity_c: conditional-tense uncertainty

Anger_f: anger about anticipated events

SENTENCE-LEVEL EXAMPLE

Using the principles outlined above, let's now take a closer look at the MarketPsych software in action and see how it analyzes the following sentence:

"Analysts expect Mattel to report much higher earnings next quarter."

The language analyzer performs the following sequence:

1. Associates ticker symbol MAT with entity reference "Mattel."
2. Identifies "earnings" as an Earnings word in the lexicon.

3. Identifies "expect" as a future-oriented word and assigns future tense to the phrase.
4. Identifies "higher" as an Up-Word.
5. Multiplies "higher" by 2 due to presence of the modifier word "much."
6. Associates "higher" (Up-Word) with "earnings" (Earnings) due to proximity.

The analysis algorithm will report:

Date	Time	Ticker	Var	Score
20110804	15:00.123	MAT	*EarningsUp_f*	2

In the example above, 2 is the raw score produced for EarningsUp_f.

CREATING AN INDEX

The TRMI themselves derived from two groups of sources—news and social media—and the data feed itself consists of three feeds: a social media feed, a news media feed, and an aggregated feed of combined social and news media content. The TRMI are updated minutely. Over 2 million articles are processed daily and contribute to the TRMI feed within minutes of their publication. The following sections further describe the construction of the TRMI, from raw content to Vars to published TRMI.

SOURCE TEXT

The TRMI are derived from an unparalleled collection of premium news, global Internet news coverage, and a broad and credible range of social media. The TRMI social media feed consists of both MarketPsych and Moreover social media content. Moreover Technologies' aggregated social media feed is derived from tens of thousands of social media sites and is incorporated into the TRMI from 2009 to the present. MarketPsych social media content was downloaded from public social media sites from 1998 to the present.

The TRMI News indices are derived from live content delivered via Thomson Reuters News Feed Direct and two Thomson Reuters news archives: a Reuters-only one from 1998 to 2002 and one with Reuters and select third-party wires from 2003 to the present. In addition, we incorporate Moreover Technologies aggregated newsfeed, which is derived from 40,000 Internet news sites and spans 2005 to present. MarketPsych crawler content from hundreds of financial news sites is also included. MarketPsych-specific sources of text include *The New York Times, The Wall Street Journal, Financial Times, Seeking Alpha,* and dozens more sources widely read by professional investors.

Figure A.1 shows a graphic displaying the time course of each text feed within the TRMI. The TRMI thus cover the period 1998 through the present. Currently, all source text for the MarketPsych sentiment products is English-language.

INDEX CONSTRUCTION

Each TRMI is composed of a combination of variables (Vars). First, the absolute values of all TRMI-contributing Vars, for all asset constituents, over the past 24 hours are determined. These absolute values are then summed for all constituents. This sum is called the "Buzz," and it is published in conjunction with each asset's TRMIs. More specifically, where V is the set of all Vars underlying *any* TRMI of the asset class, where *a* denotes an asset, and where $C(a)$ is the set of all constituents* of *a*, we can define the Buzz of *a* as the following:

$$Buzz(a) = \sum_{c \in C(a),\ v \in V} |Var_{c,v}|$$

Each TRMI is then computed as a ratio of the sum of all relevant Vars to the Buzz. We define $V(t)$ as the set of all Vars relevant to a particular TRMI t. Next we define a function to determine whether a Var $v \in V(t)$ is additive or subtractive to a TRMI as the following:

$$I(t,v) = \begin{cases} +1 \ if\ additive \\ -1 \ if\ subtractive \end{cases}$$

Thus the TRMI t of asset a can be computed as the following:

$$TRMI_t(a) = \frac{\sum_{c \in C(A),\ v \in V(t)}(I(t,v) \times Psych\,Var_v(c))}{Buzz(Asset)}$$

---

*For example, Mattel is a constituent of MarketPsych's Nasdaq 100 index proxy asset (MPQQQ).

Historical Text Evolution

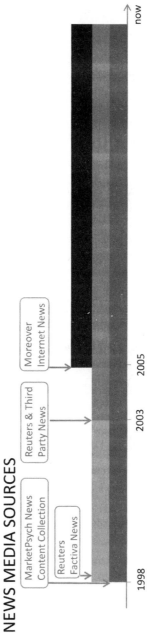

SOCIAL MEDIA SOURCES

NEWS MEDIA SOURCES

FIGURE A.1 Timeline of textual content analyzed for the social and news media TRMI.

Entities by Asset Class

12	22	132	8,000+	32
Agricultural Commodities	Materials and Energy	Countries	Global Equities	Currencies

Agricultural Commodities

Cattle
Cocoa
Coffee
Corn
Cotton
Hogs
Orange Juice
Palm Oil
Rice
Soybeans
Sugar
Wheat

Materials and Energy

Aluminum
Biofuels
Coal
Copper
Crude Oil
Ethanol
Gasoline
Gold
Heating Oil
Iron
Jet Fuel
Liquefied Natural Gas
Naphtha
Natural Gas
Nickel
North Sea Oil
Palladium
Platinum
Rare Earths
Silver
Steel
Uranium

Countries

Afghanistan
Algeria
Angola
Argentina
Armenia
Australia
Austria
Bahrain
Bangladesh
Belarus
. . .
. . .
. . .
United Arab Emirates
United Kingdom
United States
Uruguay
Uzbekistan
Venezuela
Vietnam
Yemen
Zimbabwe

Global Equities

17 Global Equity Indices:
Russell 2000
China Composite
Hang Seng
Nikkei 225
Straits Times ...

10 Sectors, e.g:
· Technology
· Energy
· Telecommunications

25 Industries

Global Stocks, ex:
· China
· Korea
· India
· Japan
· Hong Kong ...

Currencies

Australian Dollar
Brazilian Real
Canadian Dollar
Chinese Yuan Renminbi
Danish Krone
Egyptian Pound
Euro
Hong Kong Dollar
Indian Rupee
Israeli Shekel
Japanese Yen
Mexican Peso
New Zealand Dollar
Norwegian Krone
Russian Ruble
Singapore Dollar
South African Rand
South Korean Won
Swiss Franc
Taiwanese Dollar
Turkish Lira
U.S. Dollar
U.K. Pound Sterling

FIGURE A.2 Asset classes covered by the Thomson Reuters MarketPsych Indices.

It's worth noting that, particularly for Equities where the assets all correspond to indices and sectors, an individual constituent may contribute to multiple assets. For example, Mattel is a constituent of both the Consumer Goods sector and the Nasdaq 100 index proxies. As a result, Mattel's Var scores will be incorporated into the TRMI for both.

Similarly, a single Var can contribute to multiple TRMI. For example, the earningsUp_f Var noted in the "Sentence-level Example" section above is not only a constituent of earningsForecast but also of the Sentiment, Optimism, and fundamentalStrength TRMI.

ASSET CLASSES COVERED

The Thomson Reuters MarketPsych Indices cover tradable assets in five different asset classes. Please see an abbreviated list of coverage in Figure A.2.

TRMI DEFINITIONS

The Thomson Reuters MarketPsych Indices consist of several different sentiments, 14 of which are common to all five scored asset classes. Macroeconomic and topic TRMI vary by asset class. More documentation about the individual assets and indices covered is available in the online Thomson Reuters MarketPsych Indices User Guide.[2]

Company and Equity Index TRMI Indices

There are 31 TRMI indices for the companies and equity index asset classes. Each TRMI carries six significant digits past the decimal point. Negative numbers have a leading minus (–) sign. The table below summarizes these fields.

Index	Description: *Score of references in news and social media to ...*	Range
sentiment	overall positive references, net of negative references	−1 to 1
optimism	optimism, net of references to pessimism	−1 to 1
fear	fear and anxiety	0 to 1
joy	happiness and affection	0 to 1
trust	trustworthiness, net of references connoting corruption	−1 to 1

(continued)

Index	Description: *Score of references in news and social media to …*	Range
violence	violence and war	0 to 1
conflict	disagreement and swearing net of agreement and conciliation	−1 to 1
gloom	gloom and negative future outlook	0 to 1
stress	distress and danger	0 to 1
timeUrgency	urgency and timeliness, net of references to tardiness and delays	−1 to 1
uncertainty	uncertainty and confusion	0 to 1
emotionVsFact	all emotional sentiments, net of all factual and topical references	−1 to 1
longShort	buying, net of references to shorting or selling	−1 to 1
longShortForecast	forecasts of buying, net of references to forecasts of shorting or selling	−1 to 1
priceDirection	price increases, net of references to price decreases	−1 to 1
priceForecast	forecasts of asset price rises, net of references to forecasts of asset price drops	−1 to 1
volatility	volatility in market prices or business conditions	0 to 1
loveHate	love, net of references to hate	−1 to 1
anger	anger and disgust	0 to 1
debtDefault	debt defaults and bankruptcies	0 to 1
innovation	innovativeness	0 to 1
marketRisk	positive emotionality and positive expectations net of negative emotionality and negative expectations. Includes factors from social media found characteristic of speculative bubbles—higher values indicate greater bubble risk. Also known as the "bubbleometer."	−1 to 1
analystRating	upgrade activity, net of references to downgrade activity	−1 to 1
dividends	dividends rising, net of references to dividends falling	0 to 1

Index	Description: *Score of references in news and social media to ...*	Range
earningsForecast	expectations about improving earnings, less those of worsening earnings	−1 to 1
fundamentalStrength	positivity about accounting fundamentals, net of references to negativity about accounting fundamentals	−1 to 1
layoffs	staff reductions and layoffs	0 to 1
litigation	litigation and legal activity	0 to 1
managementChange	changes in a company's management team, net of references to stability in the management team	−1 to 1
managementTrust	trust expressed in a company's management team, net of references to reports of unethical behavior among the management team	−1 to 1
mergers	merger or acquisition activity	0 to 1

Currency TRMI Indices

There are 21 TRMI indices for the currency asset class.

Index	Description: *Score of references in news and social media to ...*	Range
sentiment	overall positive references, net of negative references	−1 to 1
optimism	optimism, net of references to pessimism	−1 to 1
fear	fear and anxiety	0 to 1
joy	happiness and affection	0 to 1
trust	trustworthiness, net of references connoting corruption	−1 to 1
violence	violence and war	0 to 1
conflict	disagreement and swearing net of agreement and conciliation	−1 to 1
gloom	gloom and negative future outlook	0 to 1
stress	distress and danger	0 to 1

(continued)

Index	Description: *Score of references in news and social media to ...*	Range
timeUrgency	urgency and timeliness, net of references to tardiness and delays	−1 to 1
uncertainty	uncertainty and confusion	0 to 1
emotionVsFact	all emotional sentiments, net of all factual and topical references	−1 to 1
longShort	buying, net of references to shorting or selling	−1 to 1
longShortForecast	forecasts of buying, net of references to forecasts of shorting or selling	−1 to 1
priceDirection	price increases, net of references to price decreases	−1 to 1
priceForecast	forecasts of asset price rises, net of references to forecasts of asset price drops	−1 to 1
volatility	volatility in market prices or business conditions	0 to 1
loveHate	love, net of references to hate	−1 to 1
carryTrade	carry trade	0 to 1
currencyPegInstability	the instability of a currency peg, net of references to the stability of a currency peg	−1 to 1
priceMomentum	currency price trend strength, net of references to trend weakness	−1 to 1

Agricultural Commodity TRMI Indices

There are 27 TRMI indices for the agricultural commodity asset class.

Index	Description: *24-hour rolling average score of references in news and social media to ...*	Range
sentiment	overall positive references, net of negative references	−1 to 1
optimism	optimism, net of references to pessimism	−1 to 1
fear	fear and anxiety	0 to 1
joy	happiness and affection	0 to 1

Index	Description: *24-hour rolling average score of references in news and social media to …*	Range
trust	trustworthiness, net of references connoting corruption	−1 to 1
violence	violence and war	0 to 1
conflict	disagreement and swearing, net of agreement and conciliation	−1 to 1
gloom	gloom and negative future outlook	0 to 1
stress	distress and danger	0 to 1
timeUrgency	urgency and timeliness, net of references to tardiness and delays	−1 to 1
uncertainty	uncertainty and confusion	0 to 1
emotionVsFact	all emotional sentiments, net of all factual and topical references	−1 to 1
longShort	buying, net of references to shorting or selling	−1 to 1
longShortForecast	forecasts of buying, net of references to forecasts of shorting or selling	−1 to 1
priceDirection	price increases, net of references to price decreases	−1 to 1
priceForecast	forecasts of asset price rises, net of references to forecasts of asset price drops	−1 to 1
volatility	volatility in market prices or business conditions	0 to 1
consumptionVolume	factors leading to increased consumption, net of references to factors leading to decreased consumption	−1 to 1
productionVolume	increased production, net of references to factors leading to decreased production	−1 to 1
regulatoryIssues	regulatory issues	0 to 1
supplyVsDemand	surplus supply and lack of demand, net of references to supply shortage and high demand	−1 to 1
supplyVsDemand Forecast	expectations of supply outstripping demand, net of references to expectations of demand outstripping supply	−1 to 1

(*continued*)

Index	Description: *24-hour rolling average score of references in news and social media to ...*	Range
acreageCultivated	increases in acreage and crop cultivation, net or references to decreases in acreage and crop cultivation	−1 to 1
agDisease	commodity disease	0 to 1
subsidies	subsidies affecting commodity prices	0 to 1
subsidiesSentiment	increases in subsidies, net of references to decreases in subsidies	−1 to 1
weatherDamage	commodity weather damage	0 to 1

Energy and Material Commodity TRMI Indices

The 24 TRMI indices for the energy and material commodity asset class.

Index	Description: *24-hour rolling average score of references in news and social media to ...*	Range
sentiment	overall positive references, net of negative references	−1 to 1
optimism	optimism, net of references to pessimism	−1 to 1
fear	fear and anxiety	0 to 1
joy	happiness and affection	0 to 1
trust	trustworthiness, net of references connoting corruption	−1 to 1
violence	violence and war	0 to 1
conflict	disagreement and swearing net of agreement and conciliation	−1 to 1
gloom	gloom and negative future outlook	0 to 1
stress	distress and danger	0 to 1
timeUrgency	urgency and timeliness, net of references to tardiness and delays	−1 to 1
uncertainty	uncertainty and confusion	0 to 1
emotionVsFact	all emotional sentiments, net of all factual and topical references	−1 to 1
longShort	buying, net of references to shorting or selling	−1 to 1
longShortForecast	forecasts of buying, net of references to forecasts of shorting or selling	−1 to 1

Index	Description: *24-hour rolling average score of references in news and social media to ...*	Range
priceDirection	price increases, net of references to price decreases	−1 to 1
priceForecast	forecasts of asset price rises, net of references to forecasts of asset price drops	−1 to 1
volatility	volatility in market prices or business conditions	0 to 1
consumptionVolume	factors leading to increased consumption, net of references to factors leading to decreased consumption	−1 to 1
productionVolume	increased production, net of references to factors leading to decreased production	−1 to 1
regulatoryIssues	regulatory issues	0 to 1
supplyVsDemand	surplus supply and lack of demand, net of references to supply shortage and high demand	−1 to 1
supplyVsDemand Forecast	expectations of supply outstripping demand, net of references to expectations of demand outstripping supply	−1 to 1
newExploration	new ventures/exploration	0 to 1
safetyAccident	safety accidents	0 to 1

Country TRMI Indices

The 48 TRMI indices for the country asset class.

Index	Description: *24-hour rolling average score of references in news and social media to ...*	Range
sentiment	overall positive references, net of negative references	−1 to 1
optimism	optimism, net of references to pessimism	−1 to 1
fear	fear and anxiety	0 to 1

(continued)

Index	Description: *24-hour rolling average score of references in news and social media to ...*	Range
joy	happiness and affection	0 to 1
trust	trustworthiness, net of references connoting corruption	−1 to 1
violence	violence and war	0 to 1
conflict	disagreement and swearing net of agreement and conciliation	−1 to 1
gloom	gloom and negative future outlook	0 to 1
stress	distress and danger	0 to 1
timeUrgency	urgency and timeliness, net of references to tardiness and delays	−1 to 1
uncertainty	uncertainty and confusion	0 to 1
emotionVsFact	all emotional sentiments, net of all factual and topical references	−1 to 1
loveHate	love, net of references to hate	−1 to 1
anger	anger and disgust	0 to 1
debtDefault	debt defaults and bankruptcies	0 to 1
innovation	innovativeness	0 to 1
marketRisk	positive emotionality and positive expectations net of negative emotionality and negative expectations. Includes factors from social media found characteristic of speculative bubbles—higher values indicate greater bubble risk. Also known as the "bubbleometer."	−1 to 1
budgetDeficit	a budget deficit, net of references to a surplus	−1 to 1
businessExpansion	businesses expanding, net of references to contraction	−1 to 1
centralBank	the central bank of a country	0 to 1
commercialReal EstateSentiment	positive references to commercial real estate, net of negative references	−1 to 1
consumerSentiment	positive consumer sentiment, net of references to negative consumer sentiment	−1 to 1

Index	Description: *24-hour rolling average score of references in news and social media to ...*	Range
creditEasyVsTight	credit conditions being easy, net of references to credit conditions being tight	−1 to 1
economicGrowth	increased business activity, net of references to decreased business activity	−1 to 1
economicUncertainty	uncertainty about business climate, net of confidence and certainty	−1 to 1
economicVolatility	increasing economic volatility, net of economic stability	−1 to 1
financialSystem Instability	financial system instability, net of references to financial system stability	−1 to 1
fiscalPolicyLooseVs Tight	fiscal policy being loose, net of references to fiscal policy being tight	−1 to 1
governmentAnger	anger and disgust about government officials and departments	0 to 1
government Corruption	fraud and corruption in government, net of references to trust in government	−1 to 1
governmentInstability	governmental instability, net of references to governmental stability	−1 to 1
inflation	consumer price increases, net of references to consumer price decreases	−1 to 1
inflationForecast	forecasts of consumer price increases, net of forecasts of consumer price decreases (deflation)	−1 to 1
interestRates	interest rates rising, net of references to rates falling	−1 to 1
interestRatesForecast	forecasts of interest rates rising, net of forecasts of rates falling	−1 to 1
investmentFlows	investment inflows, net of references to investment outflows	−1 to 1
monetaryPolicyLoose VsTight	monetary policy being loose, net of references to monetary policy being tight	−1 to 1
naturalDisasters	natural disasters	0 to 1

(*continued*)

Index	Description: *24-hour rolling average score of references in news and social media to ...*	Range
regimeChange	regime change	0 to 1
residentialRealEstate Growth	residential real estate expansion, net of references to contraction	−1 to 1
residentialRealEstate Sales	residential real estate sales rising, net of references to sales decreasing	−1 to 1
residentialRealEstate Sentiment	positive references to residential real estate, net of negative references	−1 to 1
residentialRealEstate Values	residential real estate values rising, net of references to declining values	−1 to 1
sanctions	sanctions or embargoes emanating from or against a country	0 to 1
socialInequality	social inequality	0 to 1
socialUnrest	social unrest and calls for political change	0 to 1
tradeBalance	exports, net of references to imports	−1 to 1
Unemployment	unemployment rising, net of references to unemployment falling	−1 to 1

VISUAL VALIDATION

One simple technique for validating that the TRMI data reflect their intended output is to visualize actual events. Social unrest is one event with high psychological impact that has been in the news following the Arab Spring and other revolutions against totalitarianism. The SocialUnrest TRMI can be seen in Figure A.3, which demonstrates the general accuracy of the TRMI in tracking important global events where darker shading indicates higher levels of socialUnrest. TRMI for many Sub-Saharan African nations are not published in version 2.2, and their shading is light gray in the figure.

NOTES

1. P. Tetlock, "Giving Content to Investor Sentiment: The Role of Media in the Stock Market," *Journal of Finance* 62(3) (2007).
2. Available to Thomson Reuters customers at: https://customers.reuters.com/a/support/paz/Default.aspx?pId=2381.

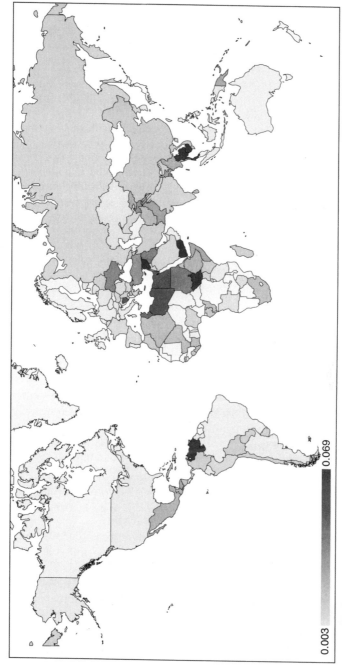

0.003

0.069

FIGURE A.3 An image of average SocialUnrest TRMI values for countries in the year 2014.

Methods for Modeling Economic Activity

For the purpose of the research and modeling of economic activity, 48 country-level TRMI indexes were tested as potential economic indicators. See Appendix A in this book for a more detailed description of the TRMI data, including the country-specific TRMI. In this Appendix testing of the available indexes and the selection of appropriate statistical methods is described.

PROFESSIONAL ECONOMIC NEWS VS. SOCIAL MEDIA

The TRMI data for social media and news media are qualitatively different, both in terms of sources analyzed and in terms of content. Social media sources include unstructured and ad-hoc articles generated by anyone with a computer and an opinion, including finance-relevant tweets, comments, blog posts, and forum postings. News media content is third-party edited and is derived from professional news sources. When news reporters express libelous statements, they are often disciplined. When social media authors post defamatory content, they may gain more readers. As a result, the information present in the separate news and social media TRMI is of significantly different credibility.

Sentiment data derived from professional news is generally superior for our purposes to that based on social media sources, and is less susceptible to external manipulation. However, national propaganda may play a role in distorting both news and social media sources. In 2014, the MarketRisk TRMI for Russia showed a significant disparity between the values quantified in news and social media (Figure B.1). As a result of such a disparity, the optimal techniques for handling such dissimilarities were explored.

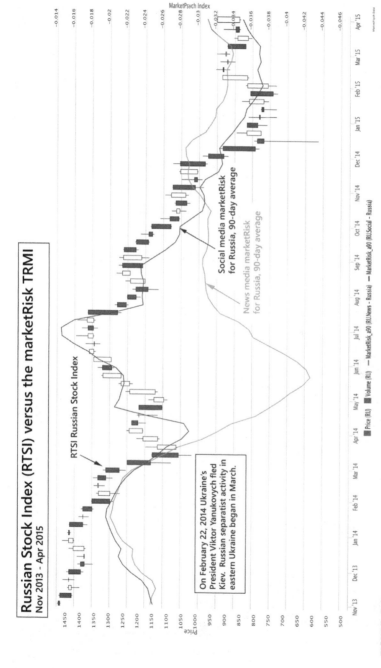

FIGURE B.1 Divergence between news and social media–based marketRisk TRMI for Russia. In this case, news was more accurate in assessing a higher risk to investors.

The greater accuracy of news versus social media in Figure B.1 may represent institutionalized English-language trolling. For example, the Russian state is reported to support social media propaganda efforts with the aim of promoting Russian markets and policies.[1,2] Beyond the effect of trolls on social media tone, there are many other relevant differences between country-level social media and professional newsfeeds. Some topics are less frequently discussed in national news outlets versus social media, and some expressions—such as cursing and emoticons—are utilized by social media authors with regional variations but are entirely absent from news media. Fortunately, weighting algorithms can detect data nuances and adapt to data variability. In the model of economic activity presented in Chapter 21, inputs from both news and social media are utilized, and in some cases the differences between the two types of media provide advantages.

ANALYSIS OF SINGLE TRMI

A correlogram presenting strength of individual United States TRMI correlations with PMI is presented in Figure B.2.

TESTING METHODOLOGY

The data analysis procedures in MPMI modeling were identical for all countries. For the purpose of generating predictive learning models, the dependent variable was selected as the Manufacturing PMI from Markit. Twelve countries with large economies and developed markets were selected for modeling. In each model, the longest possible data range was used for learning and testing of the models.

A daily model of MPMI appeared ideal, and in order to create a daily model using a monthly dependent variable—to merge interpolated daily PMI observations with daily TRMI data—a spline interpolation of PMI data points was performed. Various methods of interpolation were performed for testing, and based on initial results, the monotone Hermite spline (according to the method of Fritsch and Carlson[3]) was chosen.

A daily PMI data series was available for each country. A group of moving averages using each TRMI for each country was assembled. Based on prior experience, such smoothing decreases data variability and dampens the impact of sudden index changes. As a result of the averaging, a short-term surge in discussion about unemployment or national debt should have a moderated impact on the overall average. Based on testing of fit, Aleksander Fafula determined which indexes should have greater short-term responsiveness due to their more immediate effects on economic activity.

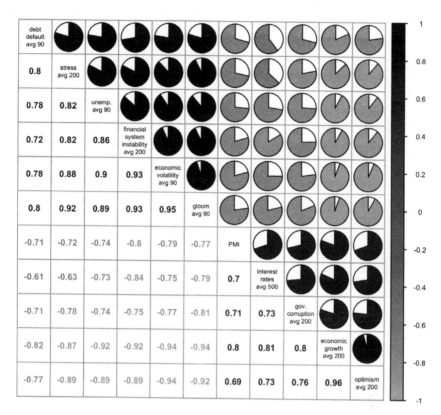

FIGURE B.2 A correlogram comparing various United States TRMI to monthly PMI values.

SELECTED MODELS AND ALGORITHMS TUNING

It was initially unclear which statistical methods applied to TRMI would show superior results in order to model the PMI values. Four statistical techniques were tested to determine best fit: generalized linear model (GLM),[4] supported vector machines (SVM),[5] the lasso technique (LASSO),[6] and linear regression with stepwise selection (REGSEQ).[7] Numerous algorithms were tested, and the best results are presented. These techniques have proven to be most accurate, while their predictions have a stable error rate.

Model learning was performed with the rolling forecasting technique described by Kuhn and Johnson (2013).[8] For each model, an initial window of 10 percent of the dataset was selected for in-sample testing. This process was repeated 10 times with 30 observations within each

TABLE B.1 MPMI vs. Market's PMI—Out-of-Sample Results in Which the MPMI Value on the Final Day of the Month Is Compared to the Beginning of Month Published PMI Value

Date	PMI	MPMI	Country
31/12/14	53.9	53.94482	US
31/01/15	53.7	54.98985	US
28/02/15	55.1	55.18179	US
31/12/14	50.6	50.70074	EZ
31/01/15	51.0	50.52083	EZ
28/02/15	51.0	50.51830	EZ
31/12/14	50.2	50.17626	BR
31/01/15	50.7	50.49850	BR
28/02/15	49.6	50.38711	BR
31/12/14	46.9	46.89270	AU
31/01/15	49.0	46.73971	AU
28/02/15	45.4	46.02761	AU
31/12/14	49.6	50.08564	CN
31/01/15	49.7	50.11660	CN
28/02/15	50.7	50.20819	CN
31/12/14	54.5	54.42573	IN
31/01/15	52.9	53.77388	IN
28/02/15	51.2	53.52643	IN
31/12/14	52.7	52.81274	GB
31/01/15	53.1	54.05255	GB
28/02/15	54.1	54.79723	GB
31/12/14	48.9	48.92096	RU
31/01/15	47.6	49.68465	RU
28/02/15	49.7	49.90198	RU
31/12/14	52.0	51.96607	JP
31/01/15	52.2	52.27547	JP
28/02/15	51.6	52.12585	JP
31/12/14	48.4	48.58531	IT
31/01/15	49.9	48.84462	IT
28/02/15	51.9	48.94019	IT
31/12/14	51.2	50.46392	DE
31/01/15	50.9	50.82493	DE
28/02/15	51.1	50.71927	DE
31/12/14	47.5	47.88387	FR
31/01/15	49.2	46.80170	FR
28/02/15	47.6	48.21623	FR

window (10-fold). Based on average prediction quality in each fold, final modeling techniques were selected. The learning window was not fixed, which meant that the models were adaptive and expanded their window length with every 30 observations.

The algorithms were modelled on a sliding window using TRMI moving averages. The set of variables can change over time as the model selects the TRMI which provide the best fit. This adaptation allows the model to change with the times. For example, TRMI with poor fit are underweighted. They won't affect the model and are eliminated. The MPMI models choose their features automatically, as a feature of the adaptive algorithm. They choose sets similar to the one presented in Figure B.2. There is a significant risk of overfitting, but since the first MPMI model was developed in 2012, advances in technique seem to have overcome that issue. Based on the above extensive testing, an elastic net model was selected as the optimal technique for modeling PMI activity using the TRMI data.

RESULTS TABLE

For all countries studied in the out-of-sample period, the final results were collected in Table B.1. The overall accuracy of the models in predicting directional PMI changes from the prior month to the current month's values was 69 percent for all 12 countries. The average difference between prediction and the actual PMI was 0.68. In the results presented below the model was not adaptive—it was not retrained monthly on the latest PMI release—however, that is a feature of the model that may improve accuracy further. In the present case, it operates for three months without feedback. The model was subsequently updated through July 2015, with U.S. results visible in Figure 21.4. Overall, the quality of the predictions is stable.

NOTES

1. Daisy Sindelar, "The Kremlin's Troll Army," *The Atlantic* (August 12, 2014). Retrieved July 20, 2105, from: http://www.theatlantic.com/international/archive/2014/08/the-kremlins-troll-army/375932/.
2. Adrian Chen, "The Agency," *New York Times* (June 2, 2015). Retrieved July 20, 2015, from: http://www.nytimes.com/2015/06/07/magazine/the-agency.html?_r=0.
3. F. N. Fritsch and R. E. Carlson, "Monotone Piecewise Cubic Interpolation," *SIAM Journal on Numerical Analysis* 17 (1980), pp. 238–246.
4. A. J. Dobson, *An Introduction to Generalized Linear Models* (London: Chapman and Hall, 1990).

5. J. Platt, "Probabilistic Outputs for Support Vector Machines and Comparison to Regularized Likelihood Methods," in *Advances in Large Margin Classifiers*, A. Smola, P. Bartlett, B. Schoelkopf and D. Schuurmans, eds. (Cambridge, MA: MIT Press, 2000).

6. B. Efron, T. Hastie, I. Johnstone, and R. Tibshirani, "Least Angle Regression," *Ann. Statist* 32(2) (2004), pp. 407–499.

7. A. Miller, *Subset Selection in Regression* (Boca Raton, FL: Chapman and Hall/CRC, 2002).

8. M. Kuhn and K. Johnson, *Applied Predictive Modeling* (New York: Springer, 2013).

Glossary

Note: Please refer to Appendix A for individual Thomson Reuters Mar-ketPsych Indices (TRMI) definitions.

Absolute return. The measure of the gain or loss on an investment portfolio designed to achieve returns regardless of the price movements of asset markets. Unlike traditional asset managers, who try to track and outperform a benchmark (a reference index such as the S&P 500), absolute return managers employ strategies intended to produce a positive return in any market regime.

Affect. Feeling or emotion, especially as manifested by facial expression or body language. Affect can refer to the entire range of emotion-related mental experience. Attitudes, preferences, emotions, feelings, and moods are all affective processes.

Alpha. A measure of the excess performance of a portfolio of investments or an investment strategy above a passive benchmark index. Alpha is also referred to as a market-beating return.

Alpha capture. In a classic alpha capture system, researchers and analysts submit trading ideas to a central location in electronic format. Observers of the trade idea flow generate trading signals based on the submitted ideas. First used in 2001 by Marshall Wace.

Anomaly (market). A market price pattern. The exploitation of market anomalies using investment strategies generates alpha (excess returns above a similar but passive benchmark).

Anterior insula. A region of the brain's loss avoidance system whose activation is promoted by physical pain, monetary loss, and other unpleasant sensations. Its activation predicts risk aversion among subjects partaking in investment experiments.

Anticipation. Foreknowledge, intuition, and presentiment. Anticipation is a state of expectancy in which a known outcome is understood to be forthcoming.

Anxiety. A mental state of worry, concern, or dread. Anticipation of negative events, creating feelings of unease and discomfort.

Arbitrage. The simultaneous buying and selling of securities, currency, or commodities in different markets or based on differing criteria in order to take advantage of predicted price movements. Arbitrage reduces overall market risk, while taking advantage of differences in pricing between two groups of assets.

Arousal. Physiological activation, often characterized by somatic signs including sweating, tremulousness, hypervigilance, pupil dilation, and excitability.

Attribution bias. The tendency to attribute outcomes to another cause.

Bear market. A multi-year period of declining stock prices.

Bearish. A pessimistic attitude toward asset prices characterized by an expectation of future price declines.

Beauty contest (Keynesian). A Keynesian beauty contest is a concept developed by John Maynard Keynes to explain how investors ought to think strategically about others' intentions in equity markets. Keynes used an analogy based on a fictional newspaper contest, in which entrants are asked to choose the six most attractive faces from a hundred photographs. Those who picked the most popular faces are then eligible for a prize. In order to win, players ought to think not only about their own preferences, but also about the likely choices of others.

Belief. Any thought held as logically true.

Beta. In finance beta refers to stock price volatility relative to the overall stock market. Prices of high beta stocks will move more than the overall market on a given day.

Book value. The monetary amount by which an asset is valued in business records, a figure not necessarily identical to the amount the asset could bring on the open market.

Bubble. An economic bubble occurs when speculation in an asset causes the price to increase, producing more speculation, in a positive feedback effect. The price reaches an unsustainable level, and the bubble is followed by a sudden drop in prices, known as a crash.

Buffett, Warren. Born August 30, 1930; a wealthy American investor and business-man. As of 2015, he was the third wealthiest private citizen in the world, worth over $72 billion.

Bull market. A multi-year period of climbing stock prices.

Bullish. An optimistic attitude toward asset prices characterized by an expectation of future price increases.

Carry trade. A strategy in which an investor sells short a currency with a low interest rate and buys a currency with a higher interest rate. The interest rate differential between the currencies produces profits. The strategy is vulnerable to losses if the value of the high-yielding currency declines relative to that of the low-yielding currency.

Clemens, Samuel. Pen name "Mark Twain"; an American writer and humorist.

Comparator. The brain circuits used to compare expectations of goal progress versus reality. Feelings arise as a result of the comparison, where elation accompanies faster-than-expected progress toward a goal, while disappointment accompanies slower-then-expected progress.

Confidence. Assurance, freedom from doubt, belief in one's abilities.

Contrarian. A contrarian investor seeks opportunities to buy or sell specific investments when the majority of investors appear to be doing the opposite, to the point where that investment has become mispriced. Contrarian investing occurs in opposition to the prevailing sentiment.

Crash (market). A sudden large decline of business or the prices of assets. Crashes often occur after the peaking of a speculative bubble or mania.

Dalio, Ray. American founder of the investment firm Bridgewater Associates, which currently has more assets under management than any other private global hedge fund. In 2012, Dalio appeared on the annual Time 100 list of the

100 most influential people in the world. Net worth approximately $15 billion as of October 2014.

Decision making. The cognitive process of selecting a course of action from among multiple alternatives.

Dopamine. A monoamine neurotransmitter essential to the normal functioning of the central nervous system. Dopamine is predominantly found in five major neuronal tracts or pathways. In the reward system, dopamine is found in the meso-limbic tract.

Earnings-to-price (E/P) ratio. The earnings-to-price ratio is often inverted and used as the price-to-earnings ratio (P/E). The E/P measures the ratio of a company's earnings to its stock price. High ratios reflect greater intrinsic value at a company, which is termed a value stock.

Earnings surprise. The positive or negative difference between the actual reported earnings and the expected (such as consensus estimate) earnings of a company.

Emotion. In psychology and common use, emotion is the language of a person's mental state of being, normally based in or tied to the person's internal (physical) and external (social) sensory feeling. Feelings such as happiness, sadness, anger, elation, irritation, and joy are emotions.

Emotional arbitrage. Investment strategies designed to profit from the price differentials between two groups of assets based on strikingly divergent feelings about or perceptions of each group.

Equity. A stock.

Equity risk premium. The equity risk premium is the amount by which stocks are expected to outperform bonds based on the increased risk perceptions (and thus price discounting) associated with stocks.

Equity premium puzzle. The phenomenon that observed returns on stocks over the past century are higher, by approximately 5 percent, than returns on government bonds. Economists expect arbitrage opportunities would reduce the difference in returns on these two investment opportunities to reflect the risk premium investors demand to invest in relatively more risky stocks.

Excitement. Exhilaration; the feeling of lively and cheerful joy.

Expected value. In probability (and especially gambling), the expected value of a risk is the sum of the probability of each possible outcome multiplied by its payoff (value). Thus, it represents the average amount one "expects" to win per bet if bets with identical odds are repeated many times.

Fear. Defined as an unpleasant, often strong emotion caused by anticipation or awareness of danger.

Feelings. Conscious experiences that help in the identification of emotions. When one feels afraid, one can identify the emotion of fear. Not all feelings are emotions, but all (conscious) emotional experiences are feelings.

Frontal cortex. The portion of the brain involved with reasoning, planning, abstract thought and other complex cognitive functions in addition to motor function.

Functional magnetic resonance imaging (fMRI). Allows researchers to measure changes in brain activity over short time intervals (two seconds) in small regions of the brain (two cubic millimeters). Changes in brain activity are indicated by alterations in regional metabolism, tissue oxygen usage, and blood flow (blood-oxygen level dependent signal—BOLD).

Fundament alanalysis. The use of corporate statistics—including management efficacy, earnings, asset value, and debt—to forecast future stock returns.

Futures contract. A derivative that gives the owner the right to purchase a commodity or equity at a future date at a predetermined price.

Game theory. The analysis of strategies for dealing with competitive situations where the outcome of a participant's choice of action depends critically on the actions of other participants. Participants may be classified recursively as Level 0, Level 1, Level 2, and higher.

Glamour (stock). A stock that is well-regarded and popular among investors. Glamour stocks are usually expected to have strong growth potential. Glamour stocks are more expensive than other stocks when measured with the earnings-to-price (E/P) ratio, having lower values on this metric because their anticipated growth is in part already priced in.

Goal. The purpose toward which an endeavor is directed; an objective.

Going long. The act of buying an asset in order to profit from price appreciation, whether a stock, call option, or future contract.

Going short. The act of selling an asset one does not already own in order to profit from a price decline.

Graham, Benjamin (1894–1976). A British-born American economist and professional investor. Graham is considered the father of value investing.

Greed. Excessive desire to acquire or possess significantly more material wealth than one needs for prolonged sustenance of daily routines and maintenance of security.

Herding. When many investors make the same choice based on the observations of others, independent of their own knowledge.

Hope. The general feeling that some desire will be fulfilled.

Hubris. The lack of preparedness and attentiveness to risks that follows success in a venture. Hubris often precedes losses.

Impulse-control (impulsivity). The ability to manage one's urges, caprices, and sudden desires.

Information. The communication or reception of knowledge or intelligence (Merriam-Webster).

Initial public offering (IPO). The first sale of shares of stock by a private company to the public.

Investor. One who owns shares of a company or asset, typically with the expectation that the profits of the business or the value of the asset will increase over time.

Investment. The use of money for the purpose of making more money, to gain income or increase capital, or both, usually through the purchase of a security or asset.

Judgment. The cognitive process of reaching a decision or drawing conclusions.

Kahneman, Daniel. Born 1934 in Tel Aviv, Israel; a key pioneer and theorist of behavioral finance, which integrates economics and cognitive science to explain seemingly irrational risk management behavior in humans.

Keynes, John Maynard (1883–1946). An English economist whose ideas about the value of stimulative fiscal policies fundamentally changed the theory and practice of modern macroeconomics and the economic policies of governments.

Limbic system. A deep, evolutionarily older system of brain circuits and structures involved in emotion. Major subsections include the reward system (nucleus accumbens), the loss-avoidance system (amygdala), hormonal control (the hypothalamus), and memory centers (the hippocampus).

Long. Holding an asset in order to profit from an appreciation in its price.

Loss aversion. In prospect theory, loss aversion refers to the tendency for people to strongly prefer avoiding losses than acquiring gains. Some studies suggest that losses are as much as twice as psychologically powerful as gains. Loss aversion was first theorized by Amos Tversky and Daniel Kahneman (winner of the 2002 Nobel Prize in economics).

Loss-avoidance system. A fundamental motivation system in the brain, geared toward the avoidance of harm and potential danger. Consists of several subcortical structures related to negative emotion processing and response, including the amygdala, hippocampus, hypothalamus. Cortical structures include the insula and the anterior cingulate gyrus.

MACD (see Moving Average Crossover).

Mean-reversion. The assumption that an asset's price will tend to move toward its long-run average price over time. Large price movement away from the average typically precedes mean-reversion (reversal) of the price.

Momentum (investing). A style of investing in which equities that have recently appreciated in price are purchased, with the presumption that they will continue to outperform over time. Academic research has identified the momentum effect in stocks that appreciate over the prior 6 months. These stocks are likely to have market-beating returns over the subsequent 6 to 18 months.

Moving Average Crossover. Called MACD in this book, and based on the technical analysis tool of the moving average convergence divergence indicator, the moving average crossover is a simple binary tool used to generate either a long or a short signal depending on the relative positions of two simple moving averages of data. In this book, MACDs are always assumed to have either a long or a short position at any given time.

Neuroeconomics. A field of study examining the brain bases of economic decision making.

Neurofinance. The study and application of neuroscience to investment activity.

Nowcasting. Using sources of real-time data as proxies for currently occurring phenomenon, such as measures of economic activity.

Nucleus accumbens (NACC). A nucleus forming the floor of the caudal part of the anterior prolongation of the lateral ventricle of the brain. Is activated by anticipation of reward and reward pursuit and produces positive affect when activated.

Optimism. A feeling or expectation that positive events will happen in the future. The Optimism TRMI is defined as the net difference between all future-tense positive expressions and all future-tense negative expressions divided by the total of all relevant references (buzz), where all expressions refer to a specific asset, group of assets, or associated geographical locations. The resulting value for a given time period represents the Optimism TRMI.

Option. A contract whereby the contract buyer has a right to exercise a feature of the contract (the option) on or before a future date (the exercise date). The writer (seller) has the obligation to honor the specified feature of the contract. Since the option gives the buyer a right and the seller an obligation, the buyer has received something of value.

Option premium. The amount the buyer pays the seller for an option above its current tangible value.

Panic. A sudden terror that dominates thinking and often affects groups of people. An overwhelming feeling of fear and anxiety.

Predict. The act of foretelling on the basis of observation, experience, or scientific reason.

Prefrontal cortex. A recently evolved region of the brain that plays a central role in executive cognitive function, decision making, gratification postponement, attention-shifting, and regulation (often inhibition) of limbic system impulses.

Price-to-earnings (P/E). (See Earnings-to-price ratio).

Rally. A rapid increase in an asset's price.

Regime (market). Markets often move through stages such as sideways, bull, and bear market phases. When these phases persist, lasting longer than would be expected by chance, they are referred to as regimes. Asset price behavior, price patterns, and investor behavior vary significantly across market regimes.

Reversion (price). (See Mean-reversion).

Reward system. The neural circuitry directing desire and motivation. Extends from dopamine nuclei in the ventral tegmental area through the nucleus accumbens (NACC) to the medial prefrontal cortex (MPFC) in the meso-limbic dopamine pathway.

Risk (actual). The mathematically determined likelihood and magnitude of a threat to an asset's price, typically based on historical patterns in data. For example, the actual risk of a hurricane is based on mathematical models of climate, ocean surface temperatures, and other data gathered over a historical period of time.

Risk (perceived). The likelihood and magnitude of downside believed to exist in an asset's price. Perceptions and beliefs are affected by emotions, and fear is one measure of risk perception, where high fear is directly correlated with high risk perceptions.

Risk premium. The risk premium of an asset is the amount by which it is expected to outperform a "safe" asset over time. Risk perceptions of investors lead them to demand a higher return (premium) in exchange for the excess perceived risk.

Rumor. A piece of unverified information of uncertain origin usually spread by word of mouth.

Security. An equity, derivative, or commodity share or contract.

Sentiment. A feeling, emotion, attitude, or outlook.

Shiller, Robert. Born March 29, 1946, he is an American Nobel Laureate (2013), economist, academic, and best-selling author of *Irrational Exuberance*. He currently serves as a professor of economics at Yale University. He is also the co-founder and chief economist of the investment management firm MacroMarkets LLC.

Short. Holding a position that profits from the decline in the value of an asset. Short selling may be executed by borrowing shares of a stock, owning a put option, or selling a futures contract.

Soros, George. Born August 12, 1930, in Budapest, Hungary, as Soros György, widely known as an American hedge fund manager and a philanthropist. Currently, he is the chairman of Soros Fund Management and the Open Society Institute and is a former member of the board of directors of the Council on Foreign Relations. Despite his extensive spending on philanthropy, his 2015 net worth is estimated at $23 billion, which was earned through trading and fund management activities.

Speculation. Investment in assets in the hope of further price gain. Speculation is investment with the expectation of capital gain without consideration for long-term earnings, dividends, or other value-supporting revenue sources.

Stock market. A general term used to refer to the organized trading of securities through various physical exchanges, electronic platforms, and the over-the counter market. A stock exchange is a specific form of a stock market, a physical location where stocks and bonds are bought and sold, such as the New York Stock Exchange, Nasdaq, or the American Stock Exchange.

Stress. A state of mental or emotional strain or suspense.

Technical analysis. Also known as charting; utilizes quantitative and visual interpretations of financial data to generate forecasts.

Thomson Reuters MarketPsych Indices (TRMI). Numerical time-series indexes of sentiments and macroeconomic factors derived from media references to individual assets. The TRMI are derived through the real-time automated text-analysis of news and social media articles.

Trader. Individual who buys and sells for personal accounts for short-term profit. Also, an employee of a broker/dealer or financial institution who specializes in handling purchases and sales of securities for the firm and/or its clients.

Trend. The general movement of asset prices in one direction over time.

Trust. The trait of believing in the honesty and reliability of others.

Uncertainty. The state of being unsettled or in doubt. Conditions where outcomes, odds, and preexisting information are unknown.

Valence (emotional). A bipolar conception of emotion, in which feelings lie on a spectrum from positive to negative.

Value (stocks). Stocks whose shares are priced cheaply relative to the value of their underlying assets or earnings potential are value stocks. Three widely used financial ratios used to measure value (though there are many others) are: (1) the price-to-book ratio, (2) the earnings-to-price ratio, and (3) the price-to-cash-flow ratio.

Volatility. The degree of variation in an asset price over time; the standard deviation of price changes.

V-bottom. A pattern in which an asset price steeply declines and then sharply recovers, similar to the shape of the letter V.

Index

Note: Page references followed by "f" and "t" indicate an illustrated figure and table, respectively.